THE

PLAYS

OF

PHILIP MASSINGER,

IN FOUR VOLUMES.

WITH NOTES CRITICAL AND EXPLANATORY,

BY W. GIFFORD, ESQ.

HAUD TAMEN INVIDEAS VATI QUEM PULPITA PASCUNT.

THE SECOND EDITION.

VOLUME THE SECOND.

CONTAINING

THE BONDMAN.
THE RENEGADO.
THE PARLIAMENT OF LOVE.
THE ROMAN ACTOR.
THE GREAT DUKE OF FLORENCE.

LONDON:

PRINTED FOR G. AND W. NICOL; F. C. AND J. RIVINGTON; CADELL
AND DAVIES; LONGMAN AND CO.; LACKINGTON AND CO.;
J. BARKER; WHITE AND COCHRANE; R. H. EVANS; J. MURRAY;
J. MAWMAN; J. FAULDER, AND R. BALDWIN;
By W. Bulmer and Co. Cleveland-Row, St. James's.

1813.

AMS PRESS, INC.
NEW YORK
1966

AMS PRESS, INC.
New York, N.Y. 10003
1966

Manufactured in the United States of America

THE

BONDMAN.

THE BONDMAN.] Hitherto we have had no clue to guide us in ascertaining the true date of these dramas. The fortunate discovery of Sir Henry Herbert's Office-book enables us, from this period, to proceed with every degree of certainty.

The Bondman was allowed by the Master of the Revels, and performed at the Cockpit in Drury Lane, on the third of December, 1623. It was printed in the following year, and again in 1638. This last edition is full of errors, which I have been enabled to remove by the assistance of the first copy, for which I am indebted to the kindness of Mr. Malone.

This ancient story (for so it is called by Massinger) is founded on the life of Timoleon the Corinthian, as recorded by Plutarch. The revolt and subsequent reduction of the slaves to their duty, is taken from Herodotus, or, more probably, from Justin,* who repeats the tale. The tale, however, more especially the catastrophe, is trifling enough, and does little honour to those who invented, or those who adopted it; but the beautiful episode here founded upon it, and which is entirely Massinger's own, is an inimitable piece of art.

This is one of the few plays of Massinger that have been revived since the Restoration. In 1660 it was brought on the stage by Betterton, then a young man, who played, as Downes the prompter informs us, the part of Pisander, for which nature had eminently qualified him. It was again performed at Drury Lane in 1719, and given to the press with a second title of *Love and Liberty*, and a few insignificant alterations; and in 1779 a modification of it was produced by Mr. Cumberland, and played for a few nights at Covent Garden, but, as it appears, with no extraordinary encouragement. It was not printed.

---

* It may, indeed, be taken from an account of Russia in *Purchas's Pilgrims*, a book that formed the delight of our ancestors. There it is said, that the Boiards of Noviorogod reduced their slaves, who had seized the town, by the whip, just as the Scythians are said to have done theirs.

TO

The Right Honourable, my singular good Lord,

PHILIP EARL OF MONTGOMERY,

KNIGHT OF THE MOST NOBLE ORDER OF THE GARTER, &c.

RIGHT HONOURABLE,

*H*OWEVER *I could never arrive at the happiness to be made known to your lordship, yet a desire, born with me, to make a tender of all duties and service to the noble family of the Herberts, descended to me as an inheritance from my dead father, Arthur Massinger.* Many years he happily spent in the service of your honourable house, and died a servant to it; leaving his† to be ever most glad and ready, to be at the command of all such as derive themselves from his most honoured master, your lordship's most noble father. The consideration of this encouraged me (having no other means to present my humblest service to your honour) to shroud this trifle under the wings of your noble protection; and I hope, out of the clemency of your heroic disposition, it will find, though perhaps not a welcome entertainment, yet, at the worst, a gracious pardon. When it was first acted, your lordship's liberal suffrage taught others to allow it for current, it having received the undoubted stamp of your lordship's allowance: and if in the perusal of any vacant hour, when your honour's more serious occasions shall give you leave to read it, it answer, in your lordship's judgment, the report and opinion it had upon the stage, I shall esteem my labours not ill employed, and, while I live, continue*

the humeblst of those that

truly honour your lordship,

PHILIP MASSINGER.

* *My dead father,* Arthur Massinger.] So reads the first edition. The modern editors follow the second, which has *Philip Massinger.* See the Introduction.

† *Leaving* his *to be ever most glad,* &c.] So it stands in both the old quartos, and in Coxeter. Mr. M. Mason, without authority, and indeed without reason, inserts *son* after *his:* but the dedication, as given by him, and his predecessor after the second quarto, is full of errors.

* B 2

DRAMATIS PERSONÆ.

Timoleon, *the general, of* Corinth.
Archidamus, *prætor of* Syracusa.
Diphilus, *a senator of* Syracusa.
Cleon, *a fat impotent lord.*
Marullo, *the* BONDMAN (*i. e.* Pisander, *a gentle-man of* Thebes ; *disguised as a slave.*)
Poliphron, *friend to* Marullo ; *also disguised as a slave.*
Leosthenes, *a gentleman of* Syracusa, *enamoured of* Cleora.
Asotus, *a foolish lover, and the son of* Cleon.
Timagoras, *the son of* Archidamus.
Gracculo, ⎱ *slaves.*
Cimbrio, ⎰
A Gaoler.

Cleora, *daughter of* Archidamus.
Corisca, *a proud wanton lady, wife to* Cleon.
Olympia, *a rich widow.*
Timandra, *slave to* Cleora (*i. e.* Statilia *sister to* Pisander.)
Zanthia, *slave to* Corisca.

Other Slaves, Soldiers, Officers, Senators.

SCENE, Syracuse, *and the adjacent country.*

THE

B O N D M A N.

ACT I. SCENE I.

The Camp of Timoleon, *near* Syracuse.

Enter Timagoras *and* Leosthenes.

Timag. Why should you droop, Leosthenes, or
    despair
My sister's favour? What, before, you purchased
By courtship and fair language, in these wars
(For from her soul you know she loves a soldier)
You may deserve by action.
    Leost. Good Timagoras,
When I have said my friend, think all is spoken
That may assure me yours; and pray you believe,
The dreadful voice of war that shakes the city,
The thundering threats of Carthage, nor their
    army
Raised to make good those threats, affright not
    me.—
If fair Cleora were confirm'd his prize,
That has the strongest arm and sharpest sword,
I'd court Bellona in her horrid trim,
As if she were a mistress; and bless fortune,
That offers my young valour to the proof,
How much I dare do for your sister's love.
But, when that I consider how averse
Your noble father, great Archidamus,

Is, and hath ever been, to my desires,
Reason may warrant me to doubt and fear,
What seeds soever I sow in these wars
Of noble courage, his determinate will
May blast, and give my harvest to another,
That never toil'd for it.

    Timag. Prithee, do not nourish
These jealous thoughts; I am thine, (and pardon
      me,
Though I repeat it,) thy Timagoras,[1]
That, for thy sake, when the bold Theban sued,
Far-famed Pisander, for my sister's love,
Sent him disgraced and discontented home.
I wrought my father then; and I, that stopp'd not
In the career of my affection to thee,
When that renowned worthy, that, brought with
      him[2]
High birth, wealth, courage, as fee'd advocates
To mediate for him ; never will consent
A fool, that only has the shape of man,
Asotus, though he be rich Cleon's heir,
Shall bear her from thee.

    Leost. In that trust I love.[3]

---

[1] ——————— (*and pardon me,*
Though I repeat it,) thy Timagoras,] So the old copies. What
induced the modern editors to make nonsense of the passage,
and print *my Leosthenes*, I cannot even guess.

[2] *When that renowned worthy,* that, *brought with him*] In this
line Mr. M. Mason omits the second *that,* which, he says,
" destroys both sense and metre." The reduplication is entirely in Massinger's manner, and assuredly destroys neither.
With respect to the sense, that is enforced by it; and no very
exquisite ear is required, to perceive that the metre is improved.—How often will it be necessary to observe, that our
old dramatists never counted their syllables on their fingers?

[3] Leost. *In that trust I* love.] *Love* is the reading of both
the quartos. In the modern editions it is unnecessarily altered
to *live.*

Timag. Which never shall deceive you.

Enter MARULLO.

Mar. Sir, the general,
Timoleon, by his trumpets hath given warning
For a remove.
    Timag. 'Tis well; provide my horse.
    Mar. I shall, sir.   [*Exit.*
    Leost. This slave has a strange aspect.
    Timag. Fit for his fortune; 'tis a strong-limb'd
        knave:
My father bought him for my sister's litter.
O pride of women! Coaches are too common—
They surfeit in the happiness of peace,
And ladies think they keep not state enough,
If, for their pomp and ease,[4] they are not born
In triumph on men's shoulders.
    Leost. Who commands
The Carthaginian fleet?
    Timag. Gisco's their admiral,
And 'tis our happiness; a raw young fellow,
One never train'd in arms, but rather fashion'd
To tilt with ladies' lips, than crack a lance;
Ravish a feather from a mistress' fan,
And wear it as a favour. A steel helmet,
Made horrid with a glorious plume, will crack
His woman's neck.

---

4 *If, for their pomp and ease,* &c.] Mr. Gilchrist thinks (and
I believe, rightly) that Massinger, who evidently regarded the
duke of Buckingham with no favourable eye, here reflects on
the use of sedan-chairs, which he first introduced, from Spain,
about this period. They were carried, as Massinger says, " on
mens' shoulders," and the novelty provoked no small displeasure against the favourite, who in thus employing his servants,
was charged, by the writers of those times, with " degrading
Englishmen into slaves and beasts of burden, to gratify his in-
ordinate vanity."

Leost. No more of him.—The motives,
That Corinth gives us aid?
    Timag. The common danger;
For Sicily being afire, she is not safe:
It being apparent that ambitious Carthage,
That, to enlarge her empire, strives to fasten
An unjust gripe on us that live free lords
Of Syracusa, will not end, till Greece
Acknowledge her their sovereign.
    Leost. I am satisfied.
What think you of our general?
    Timag. He's a man   [*Trumpets within.*
Of strange and reserved parts; but a great soldier.[5]
His trumpets call us, I'll forbear his character:
To morrow, in the senate-house, at large
He will express himself.
    Leost. I'll follow you.   [*Exeunt.*

SCENE II.

Syracuse.   *A Room in* Cleon's *House.*

Enter CLEON, CORISCA, *and* GRACCULO.

    Coris. Nay, good chuck.
    Cleon. I've said it; stay at home:
I cannot brook your gadding; you're a fair one,
Beauty invites temptations, and short heels
Are soon tripp'd up.
    Coris. Deny me! by my honour,

---

   [5] Timag. *He's a man*
  Of strange *and reserved parts, but a great soldier.*] *Strange*
signifies here *distant.* M. MASON.

    I do not pretend to know the meaning of *distant* parts,
unless it be *remote*, or *foreign* parts. Massinger, however, is
clear enough: strange *and reserved*, in his language, means,
strangely (i. e. singularly) *reserved*.

You take no pity on me. I shall swoon
As soon as you are absent; ask my man else,
You know he dares not tell a lie.

Grac. Indeed,
You are no sooner out of sight, but she
Does feel strange qualms; then sends for her young doctor,
Who ministers physic to her on her back,
Her ladyship lying as she were entranced:
(I've peep'd in at the keyhole, and observed them:)
And sure his potions never fail to work,
For she's so pleasant in the taking them,
She tickles again.

Coris. And all's to make you merry,
When you come home.

Cleon. You flatter me; I am old,
And wisdom cries, Beware!

Coris. Old! duck. To me
You are a young Adonis.

Grac. Well said, Venus!
I am sure she Vulcans him.   [*Aside.*

Coris. I will not change thee
For twenty boisterous young things without beards.
These bristles give the gentlest titillations,
And such a sweet dew flows on them, it cures
My lips without pomatum. Here's a round belly!
'Tis a down pillow to my back; I sleep
So quietly by it: and this tunable nose,
Faith, when you hear it not, affords such music,
That I curse all night-fiddlers.

Grae. This is gross.
Not finds she flouts him!   [*Aside.*

Coris. As I live, I am jealous.

Cleon. Jealous of me, wife?

Coris. Yes; and I have reason;
Knowing how lusty and active a man you are.
Cleon. Hum, hum!
Grac. This is no cunning quean!⁶ 'slight, she
    will make him
To think that, like a stag, he has cast his horns,
And is grown young again.   [*Aside.*
    Coris. You have forgot
What you did in your sleep, and, when you waked,
Call'd for a caudle.
Grac. It was in his sleep;
For, waking, I durst trust my mother with him.
                                   [*Aside.*
    Coris. I long to see the man of war: Cleora,
Archidamus' daughter, goes, and rich Olympia;
I will not miss the show.
    Cleon. There's no contending:
For this time I am pleased, but I'll no more on't.
                                   [*Exeunt.*

---

⁶ Grac. *This is* no *cunning quean!*] In our author's time, as
is justly observed by Warburton, " the negative, in common
speech, was used ironically to express the excess of a thing."
Thus, in *the Roman Actor:*

        " This is *no* flattery!"

And again, in *the City Madam:*

        " Here's *no* gross flattery! Will she swallow this?"

and in a thousand other places.

SCENE III.

The Same.   The Senate-house.

Enter ARCHIDAMUS, CLEON, DIPHILUS, OLYM-
PIA, CORISCA, CLEORA, *and* ZANTHIA.

Archid. So careless we have been, my noble
      lords,
In the disposing of our own affairs,
And ignorant in the art of government,
That now we need a stranger to instruct us.
Yet we are happy that our neighbour Corinth,
Pitying the unjust gripe Carthage would lay
On Syracusa, hath vouchsafed to lend us
Her man of men, Timoleon, to defend
Our country and our liberties.
      Diph. 'Tis a favour
We are unworthy of, and we may blush
Necessity compels us to receive it.
      Archid. O shame! that we, that are a populous
      nation,
Engaged to liberal nature, for all blessings
An island can bring forth; we, that have limbs,
And able bodies; shipping, arms, and treasure,
The sinews of the war, now we are call'd
To stand upon our guard, cannot produce
One fit to be our general.
      Cleon. I am old and fat;
I could say something, else.
      Archid. We must obey
The time and our occasions; ruinous buildings,
Whose bases and foundations are infirm,
Must use supporters: we are circled round

With danger; o'er our heads, with sail-stretch'd
  wings,
Destruction hovers,[7] and a cloud of mischief
Ready to break upon us; no hope left us
That may divert it, but our sleeping virtue,
Roused up by brave Timoleon.
 Cleon. When arrives he?
 Diph. He is expected every hour.
 Archid. The braveries
Of Syracusa, among whom my son,
Timagoras, Leosthenes, and Asotus,
Your hopeful heir, lord Cleon, two days since
Rode forth to meet him, and attend him to
The city; every minute we expect
To be bless'd with his presence.
  [*Shouts within; then a flourish of trumpets.*
 Cleon. What shout's this?
 Diph. 'Tis seconded with loud music.
 Archid. Which confirms
His wish'd-for entrance. Let us entertain him
With all respect, solemnity, and pomp,
A man may merit, that comes to redeem us
From slavery and oppression.
 Cleon. I'll lock up
My doors, and guard my gold: these lads of
  Corinth
Have nimble fingers, and I fear them more,
Being within our walls, than those of Carthage;
They are far off.

<hr>

[7] ———— *o'er our heads, with* sail-stretch'd wings,
Destruction hovers, &c.] See Vol. I. p. 141.
[8] Archid. *The* braveries
Of Syracusa, &c.] i. e. the young nobility, the gay and
fashionable gallants of the city. Thus Clerimont, in his description of Sir Amorous La-Foole, observes that "he is one
of the *braveries,* though he be none of the wits." *The Silent
Woman.*

Archid. And, ladies, be it your care
To welcome him and his followers with all duty:
For rest resolved, their hands and swords must
    keep you
In that full height of happiness you live;
A dreadful change else follows.
      [*Exeunt Archidamus, Cleon, and Diphilus.*
Olymp. We are instructed.
Coris. I'll kiss him for the honour of my
    country,
With any she in Corinth.⁹
  Olymp. Were he a courtier,
I've sweatmeat in my closet shall content him,
Be his palate ne'er so curious.
  Coris. And, if need be,
I have a couch and a banqueting-house in my
    orchard,
Where many a man of honour¹ has not scorn'd
Te spend an afternoon.
  Olymp. These men of war,

  ⁹ Coris. *I'll kiss him for the honour of my country,*
With any she in Corinth.] The reputation of the Corinthian
ladies stood high among the ancients for gallantry; and to this
Corisca alludes.

  ¹ Coris. *And if need be,*
I have a couch and a banqueting-house *in my orchard,*
Where many a man of honour &c.] Our old plays are full of
allusions to these garden-houses, which appear to have been
often abused to the purposes of debauchery. A very homely passage from Stubbes's *Anatomie of Abuses,* 1599, will make all this
plain: " In the suberbes of the citie, they (the women) have
gardens either paled or walled round about very high, with their
harbers and bowers fit for the purpose; and lest they might be
espied in these open places, they have their *banqueting-houses,*
with galleries, turrets, and what not, therein sumptuously
erected; wherein they may, and doubtless do, many of them,
play the filthy persons." See too, *the City Madam.* I need not
observe that the poet, like his contemporaries, gives the customs, &c. of his native land to his foreign scene. He speaks,
indeed, of Syracuse; but he thinks only of London, See p. 34.

As I have heard, know not to court a lady.
They cannot praise our dressings, kiss our hands,
Usher us to our litters, tell love-stories,
Commend our feet and legs, and so search up-
      wards;
A sweet becoming boldness! they are rough,
Boisterous, and saucy, and at the first sight
Ruffle and touze us, and, as they find their
      stomachs,
Fall roundly to it.
      Coris. 'Troth, I like them the better:
I can't endure to have a perfumed sir
Stand cringing in the hams, licking his lips
Like a spaniel over a furmenty-pot, and yet
Has not the boldness to come on, or offer
What they know we expect.
      Olymp. We may commend
A gentleman's modesty, manners, and fine lan-
      guage,
His singing, dancing, riding of great horses,
The wearing of his clothes, his fair complexion;
Take presents from him, and extol his bounty:
Yet, though he observe, and waste his estate
      upon us,[2]
If he be staunch,[3] and bid not for the stock

—————— *and waste his* state *upon us,*] Every where
the modern editors print this word with the mark of elision, as
if it were contracted from *estate:* but it is not so: *state* is the
genuine word, and is used by all our old poets, and by Massinger
himself, in many hundred places, where we should now write
and print *estate.* I may incidentally observe here, that many
terms which are now used with a mark of elision, and supposed
to have suffered an aphæresis, are really and substantially perfect. In some cases, the Saxon prefix has been corrupted into a
component part of the word, and in others, prepositions have
been added in the progress of refinement, for the sake of eu-
phony, or metre; but, generally speaking, the simple term is
the complete one.
      [3] *If he be* staunch, &c.] I don't think that *staunch* can be

That we were born to traffic with; the truth is,
We care not for his company.
Coris. Musing, Cleora?

sense in this passage; we should probably read *starch'd,* that is *precise, formal.* M. MASON.

This is a singular conjecture. Let the reader peruse again Olympia's description, which is that of a complete gentleman; and then say what there is of starched, formal, or precise, in it. *Staunch* is as good a word as she could have chosen, and is here used in its proper sense for steady, firm, full of integrity: and her meaning is, " if, with all the accomplishments of a fine gentleman, he possesses the fixed principles of a man of honour, and does not attempt to debauch us, he is not for our purpose."

When I wrote this, I had not seen the appendix which is subjoined to some copies of the last edition. Mr. M. Mason has there revised his note, and given his more mature thoughts on the subject: " On the first consideration of this passage, I did not apprehend that the word *staunch* could import any meaning that would render it intelligible, and I therefore amended the passage by reading *starch'd* instead of *staunch;* but I have since found a similar acceptation of that word in Jonson's *Silent Woman,* where Truewit says: ' If your mistress love valour, talk of your sword, and be frequent in the mention of quarrels, though you be *staunch* in fighting.' This is one of the many instances that may be produced to prove how necessary it is for the editor of any ancient dramatic writer, to read with attention the other dramatic productions of the time."

I participate in Mr. M. Mason's self-congratulations on this important discovery, and will venture to suggest another, still more important, which appears to have eluded his researches: it is simply—" the necessity for the editor of any ancient dramatic writer to read with attention that dramatic writer himself."

But what, after all, does Mr. M. Mason imagine that he has found out? and what is the sense which he would finally affix to *staunch?* these are trifles which he has omitted to mention. I can discover nothing from his long note, but that he misunderstands Jonson now, as he misunderstood Massinger before. Each of these great poets uses the word in its proper and ordinary sense: " Though you be *staunch* in fighting," says Truewit, (i. e. really brave, and consequently not prone to boasting,) " yet, to please your mistress, you must talk of your sword," &c.

Olymp. She's studying how to entertain these
    strangers,
And to engross them to herself.
  Cleo. No, surely ;
I will not cheapen any of their wares,
Till you have made your market; you will buy,
I know, at any rate.
  Coris. She has given it you.
  Olymp. No more; they come: the first kiss
    for this jewel.

Flourish of trumpets. Enter TIMAGORAS, LEOS-
THENES, ASOTUS, TIMOLEON *in black, led in by*
ARCHIDAMUS, DIPHILUS, *and* CLEON; *followed
by* MARULLO, GRACCULO, CIMBRIO, *and other
Slaves.*

  Archid. It is your seat : which, with a general
    suffrage,   [*Offering Timoleon the state.*[4]
As to the supreme magistrate, Sicily tenders,[5]
And prays Timoleon to accept.
  Timol. Such honours
To one ambitious of rule[6] or titles,

[4] *Offering Timoleon the state.*] *The state* was a raised platform,
on which was placed a chair with a canopy over it. The word
occurs perpetually in our old writers. It is used by Dryden,
but seems to have been growing obsolete while he was writing:
in the first edition of Mac Fleckno, the monarch is placed on a
state; in the subsequent ones, he is seated like his fellow kings,
on a throne: it occurs also, and I believe for the last time, in
Swift: " As she affected not the grandeur of a *state* with a
canopy, she thought there was no offence in an elbow chair."
Hist. of John Bull, c. i.
[5] *As to the supreme magistrate,* Sicily *tenders,*] For *Sicily,* the
old copies have *surely.* The emendation, which is a very happy
one, was made by Coxeter.
[6] ——————— *such honours*
To one ambitious of rule, &c.] Massinger has here finely drawn

Whose heaven on earth is placed in his command,
And absolute power o'er others, would with joy,
And veins swollen high with pride, be entertain'd.
They take not me ; for I have ever loved
An equal freedom, and proclaim'd all such
As would usurp on others' liberties,[7]
Rebels to nature, to whose bounteous blessings
All men lay claim as true legitimate sons :
But such as have made forfeit of themselves
By vicious courses, and their birthright lost,
'Tis not injustice they are mark'd for slaves,
To serve the virtuous. For myself, I know
Honours and great employments are great bur-
   thens,
And must require an Atlas to support them.
He that would govern others, first should be
The master of himself, richly endued
With depth of understanding, height of courage,
And those remarkable graces which I dare not
Ascribe unto myself.
  Archid. Sir, empty men
Are trumpets of their own deserts ; but you,
That are not in opinion, but in proof,
Really good, and full of glorious parts,
Leave the report of what you are to fame ;
Which, from the ready tongues of all good men,
Aloud proclaims you.

the character of Timoleon, and been very true to history. He
was descended from one of the noblest families in Corinth, loved
his country passionately, and discovered upon all occasions a
singular humanity of temper, except against tyrants and bad men.
He was an excellent captain ; and as in his youth he had all the
maturity of age, in age he had all the fire and courage of the
most ardent youth. COXETER.
 7 *As would usurp* on others' *liberties*,] So the first quarto ;
the second, which the modern editors follow, has, *another's*
liberties. In the preceding line, for *proclaim'd*, Mr. M. Mason
arbitrarily reads, *proclaim:* an injudicious alteration.

Diph. Besides, you stand bound,
Having so large a field to exercise
Your active virtues offer'd you, to impart
Your strength to such as need it.

    Timol. 'Tis confess'd :
And, since you'il have it so, such as I am,
For you, and for the liberty of Greece,
I am most ready to lay down my life :
But yet consider, men of Syracusa,
Before that you deliver up the power,
Which yet is yours, to me,—to whom 'tis given ;
To an impartial man, with whom nor threats,
Nor prayers, shall prevail ; for I must steer
An even course.

    Archid. Which is desired of all.

    Timol. Timophanes, my brother, for whose
        death
I am tainted in the world, * and foully tainted ;

---

    * *Timol.* Timophanes, *my brother, for whose death*
I am tainted in the world, &c.] Timoleon had an elder brother,
called Timophanes, whom he tenderly loved, as he had demon-
strated in a battle, in which he covered him with his body, and
saved his life at the great danger of his own ; but his country
was still dearer to him. That brother having made himself
tyrant of it, so black a crime gave him the sharpest affliction.
He made use of all possible means to bring him back to his duty:
kindness, friendship, affection, remonstrances, and even menaces.
But, finding all his endeavours ineffectual, and that nothing
could prevail upon an heart abandoned to ambition, he caused
his brother to be assassinated in his presence [no ; *not in his
presence*] by two of his friends and intimates, and thought,
that upon such an occasion, the laws of nature ought to give
place to those of his country. Coxeter.

    Coxeter has copied with sufficient accuracy, the leading traits
of Timoleon's character, from the old translation of *Plutarch's
Lives.* With Plutarch, indeed, Timoleon appears to be a favourite, and not undeservedly. In an age of great men, he was
eminently conspicuous : his greatest praise, however, is, that
he profited by experience, and suffered the wild and savage
enthusiasm of his youth to mellow into a steady and rational

In whose remembrance I have ever worn,
In peace and war, this livery of sorrow,
Can witness for me how much I detest
Tyrannous usurpation. With grief,
I must remember it; for, when no persuasion
Could win him to desist from his bad practice,
To change the aristocracy of Corinth
Into an absolute monarchy, I chose rather
To prove a pious and obedient son
To my country, my best mother,⁹ than to lend
Assistance to Timophanes, though my brother,
That, like a tyrant, strove to set his foot
Upon the city's freedom.
        Timag. 'Twas a deed
Deserving rather trophies than reproof.
        Leost. And will be still remember'd to your
            honour,
If you forsake not us.

---

love of liberty. The assassination of his brother, which *sat heavy on his soul,* taught him " that an action should not only" (it is Plutarch who speaks) " be just and laudable in itself, but the principle from which it proceeds, firm and immoveable; in order that our conduct may have the sanction of our own approbation."

It is impossible to read a page of his latter history, without seeing that prudence was the virtue on which he chiefly relied for fame : prodigies and portents forerun all his achievements ; part of which he undoubtedly fabricated, and all of which he had the dexterity to turn to his account: but he was not only indebted to prudence for fame, but for tranquillity also; since, when he had given victory and peace to the Syracusans, he wisely declined returning to Greece, where proscription or death probably awaited him ; and chose to spend the remainder of his days at Syracuse. Those days were long and happy ; and when he died he was honoured with a public funeral, and the tears of a people whom he had saved.

9 *To my country,* my best mother,] In this expression, Timoleon alludes to the conduct of his natural mother, who would never see him after the assassination of his brother, and always, as Corn. Nepos informs us, called him *fratricidam, impiumque.*

Diph. If you free Sicily
From barbarous Carthage' yoke,[1] it will be said,
In him you slew a tyrant.

Archid. But, giving way
To her invasion, not vouchsafing us
That fly to your protection, aid and comfort,
'Twill be believed, that, for your private ends,
You kill'd a brother.

Timol. As I then proceed,
To all posterity may that act be crown'd
With a deserved applause, or branded with
The mark of infamy !-- Stay yet ; ere I take
This seat of justice, or engage myself
To fight for you abroad, or to reform
Your state at home, swear all upon my sword,
And call the gods of Sicily to witness
The oath you take, that whatsoe'er I shall
Propound for safety of your commonwealth,
Not circumscribed or bound in, shall by you
Be willingly obey'd.

Archid. Diph. Cleon. So may we prosper,
As we obey in all things !

Timag. Leost. Asot. And observe
All your commands as oracles !

Timol. Do not repent it.   [*Takes the state.*

Olymp. He ask'd not our consent.

Coris. He's a clown, I warrant him.

Olymp. I offer'd myself twice, and yet the churl
Would not salute me.

---

[1] Diph. *If you free Sicily,*
From barbarous Carthage' yoke, &c.] This speech and the next
are literally from Plutarch. Massinger has in this instance
adhered more closely to his story than usual ; for, to confess
the truth, it cannot be said of him, that his historical plays are
" more authentic than the chronicles"!

Coris. Let him kiss his drum!
I'll save my lips, I rest on it.[2]
   Olymp. He thinks women
No part of the republic.
   Coris. He shall find
We are a commonwealth.
   Cleo. The less your honour.
   Timol. First, then, a word or two, but without
      bitterness,
(And yet mistake me not, I am no flatterer,)
Concerning your ill government of the state;
In which the greatest, noblest, and most rich,
Stand, in the first file, guilty.
   Cleon. Ha! how's this?
   Timol. You have not, as good patriots should
      do, studied
The public good, but your particular ends;
Factious among yourselves, preferring such
To offices and honours, as ne'er read
The elements of saving policy;
But deeply skill'd in all the principles
That usher to destruction.
   Leost. Sharp!
   Timag. The better.
   Timol. Your senate-house, which used not to
      admit
A man, however popular, to stand
At the helm of government, whose youth was not
Made glorious by action; whose experience,
Crown'd with gray hairs, gave warrant to his
      counsels,

---

[2] *I'll save my lips,* I rest on it,] I am fixed, determined, on it; a metaphor taken from play, where the highest stake the parties were disposed to venture, was called *the rest.* To appropriate this term to any particular game, as is sometimes done, is extremely incorrect; since it was anciently applied to cards, to dice, to bowls, in short to any amusement, of chance, where money was wagered, or, to use a phrase of the times, set up.

Heard and received with reverence, is now fill'd
With green heads, that determine of the state
Over their cups, or when their sated lusts
Afford them leisure; or supplied by those
Who, rising from base arts and sordid thrift,
Are eminent for their[3] wealth, not for their
    wisdom:
Which is the reason that to hold a place
In council, which was once esteem'd an honour,
And a reward for virtue, hath quite lost
Lustre and reputation, and is made
A mercenary purchase.
   Timag. He speaks home.
   Leost. And to the purpose.
   Timol. From whence it proceeds,
That the treasure of the city is engross'd
By a few private men, the public coffers
Hollow with want; and they, that will not spare
One talent for the common good, to feed
The pride and bravery of their wives, consume,
In plate, in jewels, and superfluous slaves,
What would maintain an army.
   Coris. Have at us!
   Olymp. We thought we were forgot.
   Cleo. But it appears,
You will be treated of.
   Timol. Yet, in this plenty,
And fat of peace, your young men ne'er were
    train'd
In martial discipline; and your ships unrigg'd,
Rot in the harbour: no defence prepared,
But thought unuseful; as if that the gods,
Indulgent to your sloth, had granted you
A perpetuity of pride and pleasure,

   [3] *Are eminent for* their *wealth, not for their* wisdom :] I have
inserted *their* from the invaluable first quarto: it strengthens
and completes the verse.

No change fear'd or expected. Now you find
That Carthage, looking on your stupid sleeps,
And dull security, was invited to
Invade your territories.
  Archid. You have made us see, sir,
To our shame, the country's sickness : now, from
   you,
As from a careful and a wise physician,
We do expect the cure.
  Timol. Old fester'd sores
Must be lanced to the quick, and cauterized ;
Which born with patience, after I'll apply
Soft unguents. For the maintenance of the
   war,
It is decreed all monies in the hand
Of private men, shall instantly be brought
To the public treasury.
  Timag. This bites sore.
  Cleon. The cure
Is worse than the disease ; I'll never yield to't :
What could the enemy, though victorious,
Inflict more on us ? All that my youth hath toil'd
   for,
Purchased with industry, and preserved with care,
Forced from me in a moment !
  Diph. This rough course
Will never be allow'd of.
  Timol. O blind men !
If you refuse the first means that is offer'd
To give you health, no hope's left to recover
Your desperate sickness. Do you prize your
   muck
Above your liberties ; and rather choose
To be made bondmen, than to part with that
To which already you are slaves ? Or can it
Be probable in your flattering apprehensions,
You can capitulate with the conquerors,

And keep that yours which they come to possess,
And, while you kneel in vain, will ravish from
        you?
—But take your own ways; brood upon your gold.
Sacrifice to your idol, and preserve
The prey entire, and merit the report
Of careful stewards : yield a just account
To your proud masters, who, with whips of iron,
Will force you to give up what you conceal,
Or tear it from your throats : adorn your walls
With Persian hangings wrought of gold and pearl;
Cover the floors, on which they are to tread,
With costly Median silks? perfume the rooms
With cassia and amber, where they are
To feast and revel; while, like servile grooms,
You wait upon their trenchers : feed their eyes
With massy plate, until your cupboards crack
With the weight that they sustain; set forth your
        wives
And daughters in as many varied shapes
As there are nations, to provoke their lusts,
And let them be embraced before your eyes,
The object may content you! and, to perfect
Their entertainment, offer up your sons,
And able men, for slaves; while you, that are
Unfit for labour, are spurn'd out to starve,
Unpitied, in some desert, no friend by,
Whose sorrow may spare one compassionate tear,
In the remembrance of what once you were.
    Leost. The blood turns.
    Timag. Observe how old Cleon shakes,
As if in picture he had shown him what
He was to suffer.
    Coris. I am sick; the man
Speaks poniards and diseases.
    Olymp. O my doctor!
I never shall recover.

Cleo. [*coming forward.*] If a virgin,
Whose speech was ever yet usher'd with fear;
One knowing modesty and humble silence
To be the choicest ornaments of our sex,
In the presence of so many reverend men
Struck dumb with terror and astonishment,
Presume to clothe her thought in vocal sounds,
Let her find pardon. First to you, great sir,
A bashful maid's thanks, and her zealous prayers
Wing'd with pure innocence, bearing them to
    heaven,
For all prosperity that the gods can give
To one whose piety must exact their care,
Thus low I offer.
    Timol. 'Tis a happy omen.
Rise, blest one, and speak boldly. On my virtue,
I am thy warrant, from so clear a spring
Sweet rivers ever flow.
    Cleo. Then, thus to you,
My noble father, and these lords, to whom
I next owe duty: no respect forgotten
To you, my brother, and these bold young men,
(Such I would have them,) that are, or should
    be,
The city's sword and target of defence.
To all of you I speak; and, if a blush
Steal on my cheeks, it is shown to reprove
Your paleness, willingly I would not say,
Your cowardice or fear: Think you all treasure
Hid in the bowels of the earth, or shipwreck'd
In Neptune's wat'ry kingdom, can hold weight,
When liberty and honour fill one scale,
Triumphant Justice sitting on the beam?
Or dare you but imagine that your gold is
Too dear a salary for such as hazard
Their blood and lives in your defence? For me,
An ignorant girl, bear witness, heaven! so far

I prize a soldier, that, to give him pay,
With such devotion as our flamens offer
Their sacrifices at the holy altar,
I do lay down these jewels, will make sale
Of my superfluous wardrobe, to supply
The meanest of their wants.

> [*Lays down her jewels, &c.; the rest follow her*
> *example.*

 Timol. Brave masculine spirit !
 Diph. We are shown, to our shame, what we
  in honour
Should have taught others.
 Archid. Such a fair example
Must needs be follow'd.
 Timag. Ever my dear sister,
But now our family's glory !
 Leost. Were she deform'd,
The virtues of her mind would force a stoic
To sue to be her servant.
 Cleon. I must yield ;
And, though my heart-blood part with it, I will
Deliver in my wealth.
 Asot. I would say something ;
But, the truth is, I know not what.
 Timol. We have money ;
And men must now be though on.
 Archid. We can press
Of labourers in the country, men inured
To cold and heat, ten thousand.
 Diph. Or, if need be,
Enrol our slaves, lusty and able varlets,
And fit for service.
 Cleon. They shall go for me ;
I will not pay and fight too.
 Cleo. How ! your slaves ?
O stain of honour !——Once more, sir, your
  pardon ;

And, to their shames, let me deliver what
I know in justice you may speak.
 Timol. Most gladly :
I could not wish my thoughts a better organ
Than your tongue, to express them
 Cleo. Are you men !
(For age may qualify, though not excuse,
The backwardness of these,) able young men !
Yet, now your country's liberty's at the stake,
Honour and glorious triumph made the garland[4]
For such as dare deserve them ; a rich feast
Prepared by Victory, of immortal viands,
Not for base men, but such as with their swords
Dare force admittance, and will be her guests :
And can you coldly suffer such rewards
To be proposed to labourers and slaves?
While you, that are born noble, to whom these,
Valued at their best rate, are next to horses,
Or other beasts of carriage, cry aim ![5]

 [4] *Yet, now your country's liberty's at* the *stake,*
Honour and glorious triumph made the *garland*] Mr. M. Mason
has improved these lines, in his opinion, by omitting the article
in the first, and changing *the* in the second, into *a.* These are
very strange liberties to take with an author, upon caprice, or
blind conjecture.

 [5] *While you——cry aim!*
 Like idle lookers on,] Coxeter, who seems not to have understood the expression, gave the incorrect reading of the second
quarto, *cry, Ay me !* which, after all, was nothing more than an
accidental disjunction of the last word *(ayme)* at the press.
Mr. M. Mason follows him in the text, but observes, in a note,
that we should read *cry aim.* There is no doubt of it; and so
it is distinctly given in the first and best copy. The expression is
so common in the writers of Massinger's time, and, indeed, in
Massinger himself, that it is difficult to say how it could ever
be misunderstood. The phrase, as Warburton observes, *Merry
Wives of Windsor,* Act II. sc. iii. was taken from archery :
" When any one had challenged another to shoot at the butts,
the standers-by used to say one to the other, *Cry aim,* i. e accept the challenge." Steevens rejects this explanation, which,
in fact, has neither truth nor probability to recommed it ; and

Like idle lookers on, till their proud worth
Make them become your masters!
    Timol. By my hopes,
There's fire and spirit enough in this to make
Thersites valiant.
    Cleo. No; far, far be it from you:
Let these of meaner quality contend

adds: " It seems to have been the office of the *aim-cryer*, to give notice to the *archer* when he was within a proper distance of his mark," &c. Here this acute critic has fallen, with the rest of the commentators, into an error. *Aim!* for so it should be printed, and not *cry aim*, was always addressed to the person about to shoot: it was an hortatory exclamation of the by-standers, or, as Massinger has it, of the *idle lookers on*, intended for his encouragement. But the mistake of Steevens arises from his confounding cry *aim!* with *give aim*. To cry *aim!* as I have already observed, was to ENCOURAGE ; to *give aim*, was to DIRECT, and in these distinct and appropriate senses the words perpetually occur. There was no such office as *aim-cryer*, as asserted above; the business of encouragement being abandoned to such of the spectators as chose to interfere: to that of *direction*, indeed, there was a special person appointed. Those who cried *aim!* stood by the archers; he who *gave it*, was stationed near the butts, and pointed out, after every discharge, how wide, or how short, the arrow fell of the mark. A few examples will make all this clear :
    " It ill becomes this presence to cry *aim!*
    " To these ill tuned repetitions."   *King John.*
i. e. to encourage.
    " Before his face plotting his own abuse,
    " To which himself *gives aim* :
    " While the broad arrow with the forked head,
    " Misses his brows but narrowly." *A Mad World my Masters.*
i. e. directs.
    " Now to be patient——were to play the pander
    " To the viceroy's base embraces, and cry *aim!*
    " While he by force," &c.   *The Renegado.*
i. e. encourage them.
    " This way I toil in vain, and *give* but *aim*
    " To infamy and ruin ; he will fall,
    " My blessing cannot stay him."   *The Roaring Girl.*
i. e. direct them.
    " —Standyng rather in his window to—crye *aime!* than help-

Who can endure most labour; plough the earth,
And think they are rewarded when their sweat
Brings home a fruitful harvest to their lords;
Let them prove good artificers, and serve you
For use and ornament, but not presume
To touch at what is noble. If you think them
Unworthy to taste of those cates you feed on,
Or wear such costly garments, will you grant them
The privilege and prerogative of great minds,
Which you were born to? Honour won in war,
And to be styled preservers of their country,
Are titles fit for free and generous spirits,
And not for bondmen: had I been born a man,
And such ne'er-dying glories made the prize
To bold heroic courage, by Diana,
I would not to my brother, nay, my father,
Be bribed to part with the least piece of honour
I should gain in this action!
   Timol. She's inspired,
Or in her speaks the genius of your country,
To fire your blood in her defence: I am rapt

---

yng any waye to part the fraye." Fenton's *Tragical Discourses.*
i. e. to encourage.
   " I myself *gave aim* thus,—Wide, four bows! short, three and
a half." Middleton's *Spanish Gypsie.*
i. e. directed.
   Again:
        ———." I would bid
   " The rest weep on, while I *give aim* to tears,
   " And *mark* who grieve most deep at my foul actions."

And, still more explicitly,

   " I am the mark, sir; I'll *give aim* to you,
   " And tell how near you shoot."   *White Devil.*

   I should apologize for the length of this note, and the number
of quotations (so contrary to my usual practice) were it not that
I flatter myself the distinct and appropriate meaning of these two
phrases is ascertained by them, and fully and finally established.

With the imagination. Noble maid,
Timoleon is your soldier, and will sweat
Drops of his best blood, but he will bring home
Triumphant conquest to you. Let me wear
Your colours, lady ; and though youthful heats,⁶
That look no further than your outward form,
Are long since buried in me; while I live,
I am a constant lover of your mind,
That does transcend all precedents.

    Cleo. 'Tis an honour,   [*Gives her scarf.*
And so I do receive it.

    ⁶   ——————————— *Let me wear*
Your colours, lady ; and though youthful heats,
That look no further than your outward form,
Are long since buried in me : *while I live,*
I am, &c.] This is evidently copied from that much contested
speech of Othello, Act I. sc. iii. : " I therefore beg it not," &c.
as is the following passage, in *the Fair Maid of the Inn :*

    " Shall we take our fortune ? and while our cold fathers,
    " In whom long since their *youthful heats were dead,*
    " Talk much of Mars, serve under Venus' ensigns,
    " And seek a mistress ?"

And as this shows how Shakspeare's contemporaries understood
the lines, it should, I think, with us, be decisive of their meaning. The old reading, with the alteration of one letter by
Johnson, stands thus :

    " ——————————— I therefore beg it not
    " To please the palate of my appetite ;
    " Nor to comply with heat, the young affects
    " In me defunct, and proper satisfaction," &c.

    The admirers of Shakspeare cannot but recollect with dismay,
the prodigious mass of conjectural criticism which Steevens has
accumulated on this simple passage, as well as the melancholy
presage with which it terminates; that, after all, " it will probably prove a lasting source of doubt and controversy." I
confess I see little or rather no occasion for either ; nor can I
possibly conceive why, after the rational and unforced explanation of Johnson, the worthless reveries of Theobald, Tollet, &c.
were admitted.—*Affects* occur incessantly in the sense of passions,
affections : *young affects* are therefore perfectly synonymous
with *youthful heats:* Othello, like Timoleon, was not an old

Coris. Plague upon it!
She has got the start of us : I could even burst
With envy at her fortune.
   Olymp. A raw young thing!
We have too much tongue sometimes, our hus-
     bands say, —
And she outstrip us!
   Leost. I am for the journey.
   Timag. May all diseases sloth and letchery
     bring,
Fall upon him that stays at home!
   Archid. Though old,
I will be there in person.

---

man, though he had lost the fire of youth ; the critics might therefore have dismissed that concern for the lady, which they have so delicately communicated for the edification of the rising generation.

I have said thus much on the subject, because I observe, that the numerous editions of Shakspeare now preparing, lay claim to patronage on the score of religiously following the text of Steevens. I am not prepared to deny that this is the best which has hitherto appeared ; though I have no difficulty in affirming that those will deserve well of the public, who shall bring back some readings which he has discarded, and reject others which he has adopted. In the present instance, for example, his text, besides being unwarranted, and totally foreign from the meaning of his author, can scarcely be reconciled either to grammar or sense.

I would wish the future editors of Shakspeare to consider, whether he might not have given *affect* in the singular, (this also is used for passion,*) to correspond with *heat ;* and then the lines may be thus regulated :

    " Nor to comply with heat, (the young affect's
    " In me defunct,) and proper satisfaction."

---

* See an elegy on the death of sir Thomas Wyatt, by lord Surrey :

    " An eye whose judgment no *affect* could blinde
    " Friends to allure, and foes to reconcile, &c."

Diph. So will I :
Methinks I am not what I was ; her words
Have made me younger, by a score of years,
Than I was when I came hither.
        Cleon. I am still
Old Cleon, fat and unwieldy ; I shall never
Make a good soldier, and therefore desire
To be excused at home.
        Asot. 'Tis my suit too :
I am a gristle, and these spider fingers
Will never hold a sword.   Let us alone
To rule the slaves at home : I can so yerk them—
But in my conscience I shall never prove
Good justice in the war.
        Timol. Have your desires ;
You would be burthens to us, no way aids.—
Lead, fairest, to the temple ; first we'll pay
A sacrifice to the gods for good success :
For all great actions the wish'd course do run,
That are, with their allowance, well begun.
                [*Exeunt all but Mar. Grac. and Cimb.*
        Mar. Stay, Cimbrio and Gracculo.
        Cimb. The business ?
        Mar. Meet me to morrow night near to the
                grove,
Neighbouring the east part of the city.
        Grac. Well.
        Mar. And bring the rest of our condition
                with you :
I've something to impart may break our fetters,
If you dare second me.
        Cimb. We'll not fail.
        Grac. A cart-rope
Shall not bind me at home.
        Mar. Think on't, and prosper.   [*Exeunt.*

ACT II. SCENE I.

The Same. A Room in Archidamus's *House.*

Enter ARCHIDAMUS, TIMAGORAS, LEOSTHENES,
with gorgets; and MARULLO.

Archid. So, so, 'tis well: how do I look?
Mar. Most sprightfully.
Archid. I shrink not in the shoulders; though
    I'm old
I'm tough, steel to the back; I have not wasted
My stock of strength in featherbeds: here's an
    arm too;
There's stuff in't, and I hope will use a sword
As well as any beardless boy of you all.
   Timag. I'm glad to see you, sir, so well prepared
To endure the travail of the war.
   Archid. Go to, sirrah!
I shall endure, when some of you keep your cabins,
For all your flaunting feathers; nay, Leosthenes,
You are welcome too,[7] all friends and fellows now.
   Leost. Your servant, sir.
   Archid. Pish! leave these compliments,
They stink in a soldier's mouth; I could be merry,
For, now my gown's off, farewell gravity![8]

---

[7] —————— *nay, Leosthenes,*
You are welcome too, &c.] It should be remembered that Archidamus is, with great judgment, represented in the first scene, as averse to the marriage of Leosthenes with his daughter.

[8] *For, now my gown's off, farewell gravity!*] This is said to have been a frequent expression with the great but playful sir Thomas More, who was never so happy as when he shook off the pomp of office. Fuller tells a similar story of lord Burleigh.

And must be bold to put a question to you,
Without offence, I hope.
    Leost. Sir, what you please.
    Archid. And you will answer truly?
    Timag. On our words, sir.
    Archid. Go to, then: I presume you will confess
That you are two notorious whoremasters—
Nay, spare your blushing, I've been wild myself,
A smack or so for physic does no harm;
Nay, it is physic, if used moderately:
But to lie at rack and manger——
    Leost. Say we grant this,
For if we should deny't, you'll not believe us,
What will you infer upon it?
    Archid. What you'll groan for,
I fear, when you come to the test.   Old stories
        tell us,
There's a month call'd October,* which brings in
Cold weather; there are trenches too, 'tis rumour'd,
In which to stand all night to the knees in water,
In gallants breeds the toothach; there's a sport
        too,
Named *lying perdue,* do you mark me? 'tis a game
Which you must learn to play at: now in these
        seasons,

   ———————— Old stories tell us,
  There's a month called October, *&c.*] This pleasant old man
forgets that he is talking of Sicily, where October is the most
delightful month of the year.   All our old poets loved and
thought only of their country.   Whatever region was the subject, England was the real theme: their habits, customs, pecu-
liarities were all derived from thence.   This, though it must
condemn them as historians, may save them as patriots: and,
indeed, it is not much to be regretted that they should overlook
manners, with which they were very imperfectly acquainted, in
favour of those with which they were hourly conversant—at
least it would be ungrateful in us, who profit so much by their
minute descriptions, to be offended at their disregard of " the
proper *costumi.*"

And choice variety of exercises,
(Nay, I come to you,) and fasts, not for devotion,
Your rambling hunt-smock feels strange alte-
    rations;
And, in a frosty morning, looks as if
He could with ease creep in a pottle-pot,
Instead of his mistress' placket. Then he curses
The time he spent in midnight visitations;
And finds what he superfluously parted with,
To be reported good at length, and well breath'd,[9]
If but retrieved into his back again,[1]
Would keep him warmer than a scarlet waistcoat,

Enter DIPHILUS *and* CLEORA.

Or an armour lined with fur — O welcome!
    welcome!
You have cut off my discourse; but I will perfect
My lecture in the camp.
    Diph. Come, we are stay'd for;
The general's afire for a remove,
And longs to be in action.
    Archid. 'Tis my wish too.
We must part—nay, no tears, my best Cleora;
I shall melt too, and that were ominous.
Millions of blessings on thee! All that's mine
I give up to thy charge; and, sirrah, look
                                [To Marullo.
You with that care and reverence observe her,
Which you would pay to me.—A kiss; farewell,
    girl!

[9] *To be reported good*, at length, *and well breath'd,*] *at length*,
which completes the verse, is carelessly dropt by both the editors.
[1] *If but* retrieved into his back *again*,] This (with the ex-
ception of *But if*, for *If but*, which I am accountable for) is the
reading of the second quarto; the first reads:
    " *But if* retain'd into his lack *again*."

Diph. Peace wait upon you, fair one !
          [*Exeunt Archidamus, Diphilus, and Marullo.*
Timag. 'Twere impertinence
To wish you to be careful of your honour,
That ever keep in pay a guard about you
Of faithful virtues: farewell!—Friend, I leave you
To wipe our kisses off; I know that lovers
Part with more circumstance and ceremony:
Which I give way to.   [*Exit.*
      Leost. 'Tis a noble favour,
For which I ever owe you. We are alone;
But how I should begin, or in what language
Speak the unwilling word of parting from you,
I am yet to learn.
      Cleo. And still continue ignorant;
For I must be most cruel to myself,
If I should teach you.
      Leost. Yet it must be spoken,
Or you will chide my slackness. You have fired
          me
With the heat of noble action to deserve you ;
And the least spark of honour that took life
From your sweet breath, still fann'd by it and
          cherish'd,
Must mount up in a glorious flame, or I
Am much unworthy.
      Cleo. May it not burn here,²
And, as a seamark, serve to guide true lovers,
Toss'd on the ocean of luxurious wishes,
Safe from the rocks of lust into the harbour
Of pure affection? rising up an example

---

² *May it not burn here,*] In the former edition, Coxeter's
reading (*yet*) was adopted. I am now persuaded, with Mr.
Waldron, that the old copies are right. *Here* means, in Syracuse, and not, as I supposed, in the breast of Leosthenes: the
object of Cleora's transient wish is to detain her lover from the
war.

Which aftertimes shall witness, to our glory,
First took from us beginning.

Leost. 'Tis a happiness
My duty to my country, and mine honour
Cannot consent to; besides, add to these,
It was your pleasure, fortified by persuasion,
And strength of reason, for the general good,
That I should go.

Cleo. Alas! I then was witty
To plead against myself; and mine eye, fix'd
Upon the hill of honour, ne'er descended
To look into the vale of certain dangers,
Through which you were to cut your passage to it.

Leost. I'll stay at home, then.

Cleo. No, that must not be;
For so, to serve my own ends, and to gain
A petty wreath myself, I rob you of
A certain triumph, which must fall upon you,
Or Virtue's turn'd a handmaid to blind Fortune.
How is my soul divided! to confirm you
In the opinion of the world, most worthy
To be beloved, (with me you're at the height,
And can advance no further,) I must send you
To court the goddess of stern war, who, if
She see you with my eyes, will ne'er return you.
But grow enamour'd of you.

Leost. Sweet, take comfort!
And what I offer you, you must vouchsafe me
Or I am wretched. All the dangers that
I can encounter in the war, are trifles;
My enemies abroad to be contemn'd:
The dreadful foes, that have the power to hurt me,
I leave at home with you.

Cleo. With me!

Leost. Nay, in you,
In every part about you, they are arm'd
To fight against me.

Cleo. Where?

Leost. There's no perfection
That you are mistress of, but musters up
A legion against me, and all sworn
To my destruction.

Cleo. This is strange!

Leost. But true, sweet;
Excess of love can work such miracles!
Upon this ivory forehead are intrench'd
Ten thousand rivals, and these suns command
Supplies from all the world, on pain to forfeit
Their comfortable beams; these ruby lips,
A rich exchequer to assure their pay:
This hand, Sibylla's golden bough to guard them
Through hell, and horror, to the Elysian springs:
Which who'll not venture for? and, should I name
Such as the virtues of your mind invite,
Their numbers would be infinite.

Cleo. Can you think
I may be tempted?

Leost. You were never proved.*
For me, I have conversed with you no further
Than would become a brother. I ne'er tuned
Loose notes to your chaste ears; or brought rich presents
For my artillery, to batter down
The fortress of your honour; nor endeavour'd
To make your blood run high at solemn feasts,
With viands that provoke; the speeding philtres:
I work'd no bawds to tempt you; never practised
The cunning and corrupting arts they study,
That wander in the wild maze of desire;

---

* Leost. *You were never proved.*] The whole of this scene is eminently beautiful; yet I cannot avoid recommending to the reader's particular notice the speech which follows. Its rhythm is so perfect, that it drops on the ear like the sweetest melody.

Honest simplicity and truth were all
The agents I employ'd ; and when I came
To see you, it was with that reverence
As I beheld the altars of the gods :
And Love, that came along with me, was taught
To leave his arrows and his torch behind,
Quench'd in my fear to give offence.

    Cleo. And 'twas
That modesty that took me, and preserves me,
Like a fresh rose, in mine own natural sweetness ;
Which, sullied with the touch of impure hands,
Loses both scent and beauty.

    Leost. But, Cleora,
When I am absent, as I must go from you,
(Such is the cruelty of my fate,) and leave you,
Unguarded, to the violent assaults
Of loose temptations ; when the memory
Of my so many years of love and service
Is lost in other objects ; when you are courted
By such as keep a catalogue of their conquests,
Won upon credulous virgins ; when nor father
Is here to owe you, brother to advise you,[3]
Nor your poor servant by, to keep such off,
By lust instructed how to undermine,
And blow your chastity up ; when your weak
      senses,
At once assaulted, shall conspire against you,
And play the traitors to your soul, your virtue ;
How can you stand ? 'Faith, though you fall,
    and I

---

[3] ————————— *when nor father*
Is here to owe *you, brother to* advise *you,*] *Owe* (i. e. own)
is the reading of both the quartos ; and is evidently right. The
property of Cleora was in the father : this is distinguished from
the only right the brother had ;—*to advise.* The modern editors,
not comprehending this, sophisticate the text, and print—*here
to* awe *you !*

    * E 2

The judge, before whom you then stood accused,
I should acquit you.

   Cleo. Will you then confirm
That love and jealousy, though of different natures,
Must of necessity be twins; the younger
Created only to defeat the elder,
And spoil him of his birthright ?[4] 'tis not well.
But being to part, I will not chide, I will not;
Nor with one syllable or tear, express
How deeply I am wounded with the arrows
Of your distrust: but when that you shall hear,
At your return, how I have born myself,
And what an austere penance I take on me,
To satisfy your doubts; when, like a Vestal,
I shew you, to your shame, the fire still burning,
Committed to my charge by true affection,
The people joining with you in the wonder ;
When, by the glorious splendour of my sufferings,
The prying eyes of jealousy are struck blind,
The monster too that feeds on fears, e'en starv'd
For want of seeming matter to accuse me;
Expect, Leosthenes, a sharp reproof
From my just anger.

   Leost. What will you do?

   Cleo. Obey me,
Or from this minute you are a stranger to me;
And do't without reply. All-seeing sun,
Thou witness of my innocence, thus I close
Mine eyes against thy comfortable light,
'Till the return of this distrustful man !
Now bind them sure ;—nay, do't: [*He binds her
    eyes with her scarf.*] If, uncompell'd,
I loose this knot, until the hands that made it

---

   4 *And spoil him of his birthright ?*] This is a happy allusion
to the history of Jacob and Esau. It is the more so, for being
void of all profaneness; to which, indeed, Massinger had no
tendency.

Be pleased to untie it, may consuming plagues
Fall heavy on me! pray you guide me to your lips·
This kiss, when you come back, shall be a virgin
To bid you welcome; nay, I have not done yet:
I will continue dumb, and, you once gone,
No accent shall come from me. Now to my
    chamber,
My tomb, if you miscarry: there I'll spend
My hours in silent mourning, and thus much
Shall be reported of me to my glory,
And you confess it, whether I live or die,
My chastity triumphs o'er your jealousy. [*Exeunt.*

SCENE II.

The same. A Room in Cleon's *House.*

Enter Asotus, *driving in* Gracculo.

Asot. You slave! you dog! down, cur.
  Grac. Hold, good young master,
For pity's sake!
  Asot. Now am I in my kingdom :—
Who says I am not valiant? I begin
To frown again: quake, villain!
  Grac. So I do, sir;
Your looks are agues to me.
  Asot. Are they so, sir!
'Slight, if I had them at this bay that flout me,
And say I look like a sheep and an ass, I'd make
    them
Feel that I am a lion.
  Grac. Do not roar, sir,
As you are a valiant beast: but do you know
Why you use me thus?
  Asot. I'll beat thee a little more

Then study for a reason. O! I have it:
One brake a jest on me, and then I swore,
(Because I durst not strike him,) when I came
        home,
That I would break thy head.
    Grac. Plague on his mirth!⁵
I am sure I mourn for't.
    Asot. Remember too, I charge you,
To teach my horse good manners yet; this
        morning,
As I rode to take the air, the untutor'd jade
Threw me, and kick'd me.   [*Aside.*
    Grac. I thank him for't.   [*Aside,*
    Asot. What's that?
    Grac. I say, sir, I will teach him to hold his
        heels,
If you will rule your fingers.
    Asot. I'll think upon't.
    Grac. I am bruised to jelly: better be a dog,
Than slave to a fool or coward.   [*Aside.*
    Asot. Here's my mother,

Enter CORISCA *and* ZANTHIA.

She is chastising too: how brave we live,
That have our slaves to beat, to keep us in breath
When we want exercise!
    Coris. Careless harlotry,   [*Striking her.*
Look to't; if a curl fall, or wind or sun
Take my complexion off, I will not leave
One hair upon thine head.

---

⁵ *Grac.* Plague *on his mirth.*] This is marked as a side speech
by the modern editors; it is spoken, however, to Asotus:
and alludes to what he calls a *jest* in the preceding line. It is
worth observing that the editor of the second quarto frequently
varies the exclamations of the first, and always for the worse:
thus *Plague!* is uniformly turned into *P—x!* Coxeter and Mr.
M. Mason follow him.

Grac. Here's a second show
Of the family of pride !   [*Aside.*
 Coris. Fie on these wars !
I'm starv'd for want of action; not a gamester left
To keep a woman play. If this world last
A little longer with us, ladies must study
Some new-found mystery to cool one another,
We shall burn to cinders else. I have heard there
  have been
Such arts in a long vacation; would they were
Reveal'd to me ! they have made my doctor, too,
Physician to the army : he was used
To serve the turn at a pinch ; but I am now
Quite unprovided.
 Asot. My mother-in-law is, sure,
At her devotion.
 Coris. There are none but our slaves left,
Nor are they to be trusted. Some great women,
Which I could name, in a dearth of visitants,
Rather than be idle, have been glad to play
At small game ; but I am so queasy-stomach'd,
And from my youth have been so used to dainties,
I cannot taste such gross meat. Some that are
  hungry
Draw on their shoemakers, and take a fall
From such as mend mats in their galleries ;
Or when a tailor settles a petticoat on,
Take measure of his bodkin ; fie upon't !
'Tis base; for my part, I could rather lie with
A gallant's breeches, and conceive upon them,
Than stoop so low.
 Asot. Fair madam, and my mother.
 Coris. Leave the last out, it smells rank of the
  country,
And shews coarse breeding ; your true courtier
  knows not
His niece, or sister, from another woman,

If she be apt and cunning.—I could tempt now
This fool, but he will be so long a working !
Then he's my husband's son :—the fitter to
Supply his wants ; I have the way already,
I'll try if it will take.—When were you with
Your mistress, fair Cleora ?

   Asot. Two days sithence ;
But she's so coy, forsooth, that ere I can
Speak a penn'd speech I have bought and studied
      for her,
Her woman calls her away.

   Coris. Here's a dull thing !
But better taught, I hope.—Send off your man.

   Asot. Sirrah, begone.

   Grac. This is the first good turn
She ever did me.   [*Aside, and exit.*

   Coris. We'll have a scene of mirth ;
I must not have you shamed for want of practice.
I stand here for Cleora, and, do you hear, minion,
That you may tell her what her woman should do,
Repeat the lesson over that I taught you,
When my young lord came to visit me : if you
      miss
In a syllable or posture——

   Zant. I am perfect.

   Asot. Would I were so ! I fear I shall be out.

   Coris. If you are, I'll help you in. Thus I walk
      musing :
You are to enter, and, as you pass by,
Salute my woman ;—be but bold enough,
You'll speed, I warrant you.   Begin.

   Asot. Have at it——
Save thee, sweet heart ! a kiss.

   Zant. Venus forbid, sir,
I should presume to taste your honour's lips
Before my lady.

   Coris. This is well on both parts.

Asot. How does thy lady?

Zant. Happy in your lordship,
As oft as she thinks on you.

Coris. Very good;
This wench will learn in time.

Asot. Does she think of me?

Zant. O, sir! and speaks the best of you;
      admires
Your wit, your clothes, discourse; and swears,
      but that
You are not forward enough for a lord, you were
The most complete and absolute man,—I'll show
Your lordship a secret.

Asot. Not of thine own?

Zant. O! no, sir,
'Tis of my lady: but, upon your honour,
You must conceal it.

Asot. By all means.

Zant. Sometimes
I lie with my lady, as the last night I did;
She could not say her prayers for thinking of you:
Nay, she talk'd of you in her sleep, and sigh'd out,
O sweet Asotus, sure thou art so backward,
That I must ravish thee! and in that fervour
She took me in her arms, threw me upon her,
Kiss'd me, and hugg'd me, and then waked, and
      wept,
Because 'twas but a dream.

Coris. This will bring him on,
Or he's a block.—A good girl!

Asot. I am mad,
Till I am at it.

Zant. Be not put off, sir,
With, *Away, I dare not;—fie, you are immodest;—*
My brother's up;—My father will hear.—Shoot
      home, sir,
You cannot miss the mark.

Asot. There's for thy counsel.
This is the fairest interlude—if it prove earnest,
I shall wish I were a player.
    Coris. Now my turn comes.—
I am exceeding sick, pray you send my page
For young Asotus, I cannot live without him;
Pray him to visit me; yet, when he's present,
I must be strange to him.
    Asot. Not so, you are caught:
Lo, whom you wish; behold Asotus here!
    Coris. You wait well, minion; shortly I shall
    not speak
My thoughts in my private chamber, but they
    must
Lie open to discovery.
    Asot. 'Slid, she's angry.
    Zant. No, no, sir, she but seems so. To her again.
    Asot. Lady, I would descend to kiss your hand,
But that 'tis gloved, and civet makes me sick;
And to presume to taste your lip 's not safe,
Your woman by.
    Coris. I hope she's no observer
Of whom I grace.   [*Zanthia looks on a book.*
    Asot. She's at her book, O rare! [*Kisses her.*
    Coris. A kiss for entertainment is sufficient;
Too much of one dish cloys me.
    Asot. I would serve in
The second course; but still I fear your woman.
    Coris. You are very cautelous.[6]
    [*Zanthia seems to sleep.*

---

[6] *Coris. You are very* cautelous.] This word occurs continually
in the sense of wary, suspicious, over-circumspect, &c.
    " This cannot be Brisac, that worthy gentleman,
    " He is too prudent, and too *cautelous:*" *The Elder Brother.*
yet Mr. M. Mason chooses to displace it for *cautious,* which,
besides being a feebler expression, has the further recommenda-
tion of spoiling the metre. I cannot avoid subjoining, that this

Asot. 'Slight, she's asleep !
'Tis pity these instructions are not printed ;
They would sell well to chambermaids. 'Tis no
    time now
To play with my good fortune, and your fa-
    vour ;
Yet to be taken, as they say :—a scout,
To give the signal when the enemy comes,
                       [*Exit Zanthia.*
Were now worth gold.—She's gone to watch.
A waiter so train'd up were worth a million
To a wanton city madam.
   Coris. You are grown conceited.[7]
   Asot. You teach me. Lady, now your cabinet—
   Coris. You speak as it were yours.
   Asot. When we are there,
I'll shew you my best evidence.   [*Seizing her.*
   Coris. Hold ! you forget,
I only play Cleora's part.
   Asot. No matter,
Now we've begun, let's end the act.
   Coris. Forbear, sir ;
Your father's wife !——
   Asot. Why, being his heir, I am bound,
Since he can make no satisfaction to you,
To see his debts paid.

and the preceding scene are most negligently given by both the
editors; scarcely a single speech being without a misprint or
an omission.
   7 Coris. *You are grown* conceited.] i. e. facetious, witty : so
in *Ram Alley* or *Merry Tricks.*
   Throate. What brought you hither ?
   Boat. Why, these small legs.
   Throate. You are *conceited*, sir.

Re-enter ZANTHIA *running.*

Zant. Madam, my lord!
Coris. Fall off:
I must trifle with the time too, hell confound it!
Asot. Plague on his toothless chaps! he can-
    not do't
Himself, yet hinders such as have good stomachs.

Enter CLEON.

Cleon. Where are you, wife? I fain would go
    abroad,
But cannot find my slaves that bear my litter;
I am tired. Your shoulder, son;—nay, sweet,
    thy hand too:
A turn or two in the garden, and then to supper,
And so to bed.
Asot. Never to rise, I hope, more.   [*Aside.*
                                        [*Exeunt.*

SCENE III.

A Grove near the Walls of Syracuse.

Enter MARULLO *and* POLIPHRON. *A Table set
    out with wine, &c.*

Mar. 'Twill take, I warrant thee.
Poliph. You may do your pleasure;
But, in my judgment, better to make use of
The present opportunity.
Mar. No more.
Poliph. I am silenced.
Mar. More wine; prithee drink hard, friend,
And when we're hot, whatever I propound,

Enter CIMBRIO, GRACCULO, *and other Slaves.*

Second with vehemence.—Men of your words, all
    welcome!
Slaves use no ceremony; sit down, here's a
    health.
  Poliph. Let it run round, fill every man his
    glass.
  Grac. We look for no waiters;—this is wine!
  Mar. The better,
Strong, lusty wine: drink deep, this juice will
    make us
As free as our lords.   [*Drinks.*
  Grac. But if they find we taste it,
We are all damn'd to the quarry during life,
Without hope of redemption.
  Mar. Pish! for that
We'll talk anon: another rouse![8] we lose time;
                      [*Drinks.*
When our low blood's wound up a little higher,
I'll offer my design; nay, we are cold yet;
These glasses contain nothing:—do me right,
                [*Takes the bottle.*
As e'er you hope for liberty. 'Tis done bravely;
How do you feel yourselves now?
  Cimb. I begin
To have strange conundrums in my head.
  Grac. And I
To loath base water: I would be hang'd in peace
    now,
For one month of such holidays.
  Mar. An age, boys,
And yet defy the whip; if you are men,
Or dare believe you have souls.

---

[8] ———— *another* rouse!] Another full glass,
another bumper. See *the Duke of Milan,* Vol. I. p. 239.

Cimb. We are no brokers.

Grac. Nor whores, whose marks are out of
    their mouths, they have none ;[9]
They hardly can get salt enough to keep them
From stinking above ground.

Mar. Our lords are no gods—

Grac. They are devils to us, I am sure.

Mar. But subject to
Cold, hunger, and diseases.

Grac. In abundance.
Your lord that feels no ach in his chine at
    twenty,
Forfeits his privilege ; how should their surgeons
    build else,
Or ride on their footcloths ?

Mar. Equal Nature fashion'd us
All in one mould. The bear serves not the bear,
Nor the wolf the wolf; 'twas odds of strength in
    tyrants,
That pluck'd the first link from the golden chain
With which that THING OF THINGS[1] bound in
    the world.
Why then, since we are taught, by their examples,
To love our liberty, if not command,
Should the strong serve the weak, the fair,
    deform'd ones ?
Or such as know the cause of things, pay tribute
To ignorant fools? All's but the outward gloss,
And politic form, that does distinguish us.—
Cimbrio, thou art a strong man ; if, in place

[9] Grac. *Nor whores, whose marks are out of their mouths,* they
    have none;] *They have none ;* is omitted both by Coxeter
and M. Mason.

[1] *That* THING OF THINGS] A literal translation, as Mr. M.
Mason observes, of ENS ENTIUM. I know not where Pisander
acquired his revolutionary philosophy : his golden chain, perhaps, he found in Homer.

Of carrying burthens, thou hadst been train'd up
In martial discipline, thou might'st have proved
A general, fit to lead and fight for Sicily,
As fortunate as Timoleon.

    Cimb. A little fighting
Will serve a general's turn.

    Mar. Thou, Gracculo,
Hast fluency of language, quick conceit;
And, I think, cover'd with a senator's robe,
Formally set on the bench, thou wouldst appear
As brave a senator.

    Grac. Would I had lands,
Or money to buy a place! and if I did not
Sleep on the bench with the drowsiest of them,
    play with my chain,
Look on my watch, when my guts chimed twelve,
    and wear
A state beard, with my barber's help, rank with
    them
In their most choice peculiar gifts; degrade me,
And put me to drink water again, which, now
I have tasted wine, were poison!

    Mar. 'Tis spoke nobly,
And like a gownman: none of these, I think too,
But would prove good burghers.

    Grac. Hum! the fools are modest;
I know their insides: here's an ill-faced fellow,
(But that will not be seen in a dark shop,)
If he did not in a month learn to outswear,
In the selling of his wares, the cunning'st trades-
    man
In Syracuse, I have no skill. Here's another,
Observe but what a cozening look he has!—
Hold up thy head, man; if, for drawing gallants
Into mortgages for commodities,[2] cheating heirs

[2] —————— *if, for drawing gallants*
Into mortgages for commodities, &c.] i. e. for wares, of which

With your new counterfeit gold thread,[3] and
    gumm'd velvets,
He does not transcend all that went before him,
Call in his patent: pass the rest; they'll all make
Sufficient beccos, and, with their brow-antlers,
Bear up the cap of maintenance.
    Mar. Is't not pity, then,
Men of such eminent virtues should be slaves?
    Cimb. Our fortune.
    Mar. 'Tis your folly; daring men
Command and make their fates. Say, at this
    instant,
I mark'd you out a way to liberty;
Possess'd you of those blessings, our proud lords
So long have surfeited in; and, what is sweetest,
Arm you with power, by strong hand to revenge
Your stripes, your unregarded toil, the pride
The insolence of such as tread upon
Your patient sufferings; fill your famish'd mouths
With the fat and plenty of the land; redeem you

the needy borrower made what he could: " First, here's young
master Rash; he's in for a *commodity* of brown paper and old
ginger, ninescore and seventeen pounds; of which he made five
marks ready money :"! *Measure for Measure.* This is ridiculous
enough; and, indeed, our old writers are extremely pleasant
on the heterogeneous articles, which the usurers of their days
forced on the necessity of the thoughtless spendthrift, in lieu of
the money for which he had rashly signed. Fielding has imi-
tated them in his *Miser,* without adding much to their humour;
and Foote, in *the Minor,* has servilely followed his example.
The spectators of those scenes probably thought that the writers had gone beyond real life, and drawn on imagination for
their amusement : but transactions (not altogether proper, perhaps, to be specified here) have actually taken place in our own
times, which leave their boldest conceptions at an humble distance; and prove beyond a doubt, that, in the arts of raising
money, the invention of the most fertile poet must yield to that
of the meanest scrivener.
  [3] *With your counterfeit gold thread, &c.*] See the *New Way
to Pay Old Debts,* Vol. IV.

From the dark vale of servitude, and seat you
Upon a hill of happiness; what would you do
To purchase this, and more?
   Grac. Do! any thing:
To burn a church or two, and dance by the light
     on't,
Were but a May-game.
   Poliph. I have a father living;
But, if the cutting of his throat could work this,
He should excuse me.
   Cimb. 'Slight! I would cut mine own,
Rather than miss it; so I might but have
A taste on't, ere I die.
   Mar. Be resolute men;
You shall run no such hazard, nor groan under
The burthen of such crying sins.
   Cimb. The means?
   Grac. I feel a woman's longing.
   Poliph. Do not torment us
With expectation.
   Mar. Thus, then: Our proud masters,
And all the able freemen of the city,
Are gone unto the wars——
   Poliph. Observe but that.
   Mar. Old men, and such as can make no re-
     sistance,
Are only left at home——
   Grac. And the proud young fool,
My master—if this take, I'll hamper him.
   Mar. Their arsenal, their treasure, 's in our
     power,
If we have hearts to seize them. If our lords fall
In the present action, the whole country's ours:
Say they return victorious, we have means
To keep the town against them; at the worst,
To make our own conditions. Now, if you dare
Fall on their daughters and their wives, break up

Their iron chests, banquet on their rich beds,
And carve yourselves of all delights and pleasures
You have been barr'd from, with one voice cry
    with me,
Liberty ! liberty !
   All. Liberty ! liberty !
   Mar. Go then, and take possession : use all
    freedom ;
But shed no blood. [*Exeunt Slaves.*]—So, this is
    well begun ;
But not to be commended, till't be done. [*Exit.*

ACT III. SCENE I.

The same. A Gallery in Archidamus's *House.*

Enter MARULLO *and* TIMANDRA.

   Mar. Why, think you that I plot against
    myself ?*
Fear nothing, you are safe : these thick-skinn'd
    slaves,
I use as instruments to serve my ends,
Pierce not my deep designs ; nor shall they dare
To lift an arm against you.
   Timand. With your will.
But turbulent spirits, raised beyond themselves
With ease, are not so soon laid ; they oft prove
Dangerous to him that call'd them up.
   Mar. 'Tis true,
In what is rashly undertook. Long since

   * Mar. *Why, think you that I plot aginst myself ?*] The plot
opens here with wonderful address, and the succeeding conference, or rather scene, betwen Pisander and Cleora, is inimitably
beautiful.

I have consider'd seriously their natures,
Proceeded with mature advice, and know
I hold their will and faculties in more awe
Than I can do my own. Now, for their license,
And riot in the city, I can make
A just defence and use : it may appear too
A politic prevention of such ills
As might, with greater violence and danger,
Hereafter be attempted; though some smart for't,
It matters not :—however, I'm resolved ;
And sleep you with security. Holds Cleora
Constant to her rash vow?

   Timand. Beyond belief ;
To me, that see her hourly, it seems a fable.
By signs I guess at her commands, and serve them
With silence ; such her pleasure is, made known
By holding her fair hand thus. She eats little,
Sleeps less, as I imagine ; once a day
I lead her to this gallery, where she walks
Some half a dozen turns, and, having offer'd
To her absent saint a sacrifice of sighs,
She points back to her prison.

   Mar. Guide her hither,
And make her understand the slaves' revolt ;
And, with your utmost eloquence, enlarge
Their insolence, and rapes done in the city
Forget not too, I am their chief, and tell her
You strongly think my extreme dotage on her,
As I'm Marullo, caused this sudden uproar,
To make way to enjoy her.

   Timand. Punctually
I will discharge my part.   *[Exit.*

Enter POLIPHRON.

Poliph. O, sir, I sought you:
You've miss'd the best⁵ sport! Hell, I think's
      broke loose;
There's such variety of all disorders,
As leaping, shouting, drinking, dancing, whoring,
Among the slaves; answer'd with crying, howling,
By the citizens and their wives; such a confu-
      sion,
In a word, not to tire you, as I think,
The like was never read of.
      Mar. I share in
The pleasure, though I'm absent.   This is some
Revenge for my disgrace.
      Poliph. But, sir, I fear,
If your authority restrain them not,
They'll fire the city, or kill one another,
They are so apt to outrage; neither know I
Whether you wish it, and came therefore to
Acquaint you with so much.
      Mar. I will among them;
But must not long be absent.
      Poliph. At your pleasure.   [*Exeunt.*

SCENE II.

The same.   A Room in the same.

Shouts within. Enter CLEORA *and* TIMANDRA.

      Timand. They are at our gates: my heart!
      affrights and horrors

      ⁵ *You've miss'd the* best *sport !*] *Best,* which is not in Coxeter
or M. Mason, is only found in the first edition; it seems necessary to the metre.

Increase each minute. No way left to save us,
No flattering hope to comfort us, or means,
But miracle, to redeem us from base lust
And lawless rapine! Are there gods, yet suffer
Such innocent sweetness to be made the spoil
Of brutish appetite? or, since they decree
To ruin nature's masterpiece, of which
They have not left one pattern, must they choose,
To set their tyranny off, slaves to pollute
The spring of chastity, and poison it
With their most loath'd embraces? and, of those,
He that should offer up his life to guard it,
Marullo, curs'd Marullo, your own bondman,
Purchased to serve you, and fed by your fa-
  vours?—
Nay, start not: it is he; he, the grand captain
Of these libidinous beasts, that have not left
One cruel act undone, that barbarous conquest
Yet ever practised in a captive city,
He, doating on your beauty, and to have fellows
In his foul sin, hath raised these mutinous slaves,
Who have begun the game by violent rapes
Upon the wives and daughters of their lords:
And he, to quench the fire of his base lust,
By force, comes to enjoy you—do not wring
Your innocent hands, 'tis bootless; use the means
That may preserve you. 'Tis no crime to break
A vow when you are forced to it; shew your face,
And with the majesty of commanding beauty,
Strike dead his loose affections: if that fail,
Give liberty to your tongue, and use entreaties;
There cannot be a breast of flesh and blood,
Or heart so made of flint, but must receive
Impression from your words; or eyes so stern,
But, from the clear reflection of your tears,
Must melt, and bear them company. Will you
  not

Do these good offices to yourself? poor I, then,
Can only weep your fortune : here he comes.

Enter MARULLO, *speaking at the door.*

Mar. He that advances
A foot beyond this, comes upon my sword :
You have had your ways, disturb not mine.
Timand. Speak gently,
Her fears may kill her else.
Mar. Now Love inspire me !
Still shall this canopy of envious night
Obscure my suns of comfort? and those dainties
Of purest white and red, which I take in at
My greedy eyes, denied my famish'd senses?—
The organs of your hearing yet are open ;
And you infringe no vow, though you vouchsafe
To give them warrant to convey unto
Your understanding parts, the story of
A tortured and despairing lover, whom
Not fortune but affection marks your slave :—
Shake not, best lady ! for believ't, you are
As far from danger as I am from force :
All violence I shall offer, tends no further
Than to relate my sufferings, which I dare not
Presume to do, till, by some gracious sign,
You shew you are pleased to hear me.
Timand. If you are,
Hold forth your right hand.
      [*Cleora holds forth her right hand.*
Mar. So, 'tis done; and I
With my glad lips seal humbly on your foot,
My soul's thanks for the favour : I forbear
To tell you who I am, what wealth, what honours
I made exchange of, to become your servant :
And, though I knew worthy Leosthenes
(For sure he must be worthy, for whose love

You have endured so much) to be my rival;
When rage and jealousy counsell'd me to kill him,
Which then I could have done with much more
    ease,
Than now, in fear to grieve you, I dare speak it,
Love, seconded with duty, boldly told me
The man I hated, fair Cleora favour'd:
And that was his protection.   [*Cleora bows.*
    Timand. See, she bows
Her head in sign of thankfulness.
    Mar. He removed by
The occasion of the war, (my fires increasing
By being closed and stopp'd up,) frantic affection
Prompted me to do something in his absence,
That might deliver you into my power,
Which you see is effected: and, even now,
When my rebellious passions chide my dulness,
And tell me how much I abuse my fortunes,
Now it is in my power to bear you hence,
                         [*Cleora starts.*
Or take my wishes here, (nay, fear not, madam,
True love's a servant, brutish lust a tyrant,)
I dare not touch those viands that ne'er taste well,
But when they're freely offer'd: only thus much,
Be pleased I may speak in my own dear cause,
And think it worthy your consideration,
(I have loved truly, cannot say deserved,
Since duty must not take the name of merit,)
That I so far prize your content, before
All blessings that my hope can fashion to me,
That willingly I entertain despair,
And, for your sake, embrace it: for I know,
This opportunity lost, by no endeavour
The like can be recover'd. To conclude,
Forget not, that I lose myself to save you:
For what can I expect but death and torture,
The war being ended? and, what is a task

Would trouble Hercules to undertake,
I do deny you to myself, to give you,
A pure unspotted present, to my rival.
I have said: If it distase not, best of virgins,
Reward my temperance with some lawful favour,
Though you contemn my person.

> [*Cleora kneels, then pulls off her glove, and*
> *offers her hand to Marullo.*

   Timand. See, she kneels;
And seems to call upon the gods to pay
The debt she owes your virtue: to perform which,
As a sure pledge of friendship, she vouchsafes you
Her fair[6] right hand.

   Mar. I am paid for all my sufferings.
Now, when you please, pass to your private
    chamber:
My love and duty, faithful guards, shall keep you
From all disturbance; and when you are sated
With thinking of Leosthenes, as a fee
Due to my service, spare one sigh for me.

> [*Exeunt. Cleora makes a low courtesy as she*
> *goes off.*

SCENE III.

The same.   A Room in Cleon's *House.*

Enter GRACCULO, *leading* ASOTUS *in an ape's*
habit, with a chain about his neck; ZANTHIA *in*
CORISCA's *clothes, she bearing up her train.*

   Grac. Come on, sir.
   Asot. Oh!
   Grac. Do you grumble? you were ever

---

   [6] *Her* fair *right hand.*] I have inserted *fair* from the first
quarto: the subsequent editions dropt it.

A brainless ass; but if this hold, I'll teach you
To come aloft and do tricks like an ape.
Your morning's lesson: if you miss—
   Asot. O no, sir.
   Grac. What for the Carthaginians? [*Asotus
   makes moppes.*] A good beast.[7]
What for ourself, your lord? [*Dances.*] Exceeding
   well.[8]
There's your reward. [*Gives him an apple.*]—Not
   kiss your paw! So, so, so.
   Zant. Was ever lady, the first day of her honour,
So waited on by a wrinkled crone? She looks now,

[7] Grac. *What for the Carthaginians?* [Asotus makes *moppes*.]
For this word, which signifies that quick and grinning motion
of the teeth and lips which apes make when thay are irritated,
and which is found in both the copies, the modern editors, in
kindness to their readers, I suppose, have *mouths*: indeed they
do not seem to have understood the humour of this scene,
which, in both, especially in Mr. M. Mason, is most negligently
printed.

[8] *What for ourself, your lord?*] Here Asotus must be supposed to *come aloft,* i. e. to leap, or rather tumble, in token of
obedience. Our ancestors certainly excelled us in the education which they bestowed on their animals. Banks's horse far
surpassed all that have been brought up in the academy of Mr.
Astley; and the apes of these days are mere clowns to their
progenitors. The apes of Massinger's time were gifted with a
pretty smattering of politics, and philosophy. The widow Wild
had one of them: " He would *come over* for all my friends,
but was the dogged'st thing to my enemies! he would sit upon
his tail before them, and frown like John-a-napes when the pope
is named." *The Parson's Wedding.* Another may be found in
Ram Alley:

  " Men say you've tricks; remember, noble captain,
  " You skip when I shall shake my whip. Now, sir,
  " What can you do for the great Turk?
  " What can you do for the pope of Rome?
  " Lo!
  " He stirreth not, he moveth not, he waggeth not.
  " What can you do for the town of Geneva, sirrah?
      [" *Captain holds up his hand,*" &c.

Without her painting, curling, and perfumes,
Like the last day of January ; and stinks worse
Than a hot brache in the dogdays. Further
  off!
So—stand there like an image ; if you stir,
Till, with a quarter of a look, I call you,
You know what follows.
  Coris. O, what am I fallen to!
But 'tis a punishment for my lust and pride,
Justly return'd upon me.
  Grac. How dost thou like
Thy ladyship, Zanthia?
  Zant. Very well ; and bear it
With as much state as your lordship.
  Grac. Give me thy hand :
Let us, like conquering Romans, walk in triumph,'
Our captives following ; then mount our tri-
  bunals,
And make the slaves our footstools.
  Zant. Fine, by Jove!
Are your hands clean, minion?
  Coris. Yes, forsooth.
  Zant. Fall off then.
So! now come on ; and, having made your three
  duties ——
Down, I say—are you stiff in the hams?—now
  kneel,
And tie our shoe : now kiss it, and be happy.
  Grac. This is state, indeed!
  Zant. It is such as she taught me ;
A tickling itch of greatness, your proud ladies

---

⁹ Grac. *Give me thy hand :*
Let us, like conquering Romans, *walk in triumph,*] Gracculo
speaks in the spirit of prophecy ; for the *conquering Romans* were
at this time struggling with their neighbours for a few miserable huts to hide their heads in ; and if any *captives followed,* or
rather preceded, their *triumphs,* it was a herd of stolen beeves.

Expect from their poor waiters: we have changed
    parts;
She does what she forced me to do in her reign,
And I must practise it in mine.
    Grac. 'Tis justice:
O! here come more.

Enter CIMBRIO, CLEON, POLIPHRON, *and*
    OLYMPIA.

    Cimb. Discover to a drachma,
Or I will famish thee.
    Cleon. O! I am pined already.
    Cimb. Hunger shall force thee to cut off the
    brawns
From thy arms and thighs, then broil them on
    the coals
For carbonadoes.
    Poliph. Spare the old jade, he's founder'd.
    Grac. Cut his throat then,
And hang him out for a scarecrow.
    Poliph. You have all your wishes
In your revenge, and I have mine. You see
I use no tyranny: when I was her slave,
She kept me as a sinner, to lie at her back
In frosty nights, and fed me high with dainties,
Which still she had in her belly again ere
    morning;
And in requital of those courtesies,
Having made one another free, we are married:
And, if you wish us joy, join with us in
A dance at our wedding.
    Grac. Agreed; for I have thought of
A most triumphant one, which shall express
We are lords, and these our slaves.
    Poliph. But we shall want
A woman.

Grac. No, here's Jane-of-apes shall serve;[1]
Carry your body swimming.—Where's the music?
Poliph. I have placed it in yon window.
Grac. Begin then sprightly.
> [*Music, and then a dance.*

Enter MARULLO *behind.*

Poliph. Well done on all sides! I have prepared
    a banquet;
Let's drink and cool us.
Grac. A good motion.
Cimb. Wait here;
You have been tired with feasting, learn to fast
    now.
Grac. I'll have an apple for jack, and may be
    some scraps
May fall to your share.
> [*Exeunt Grac. Zant. Cimb. Poliph. and Olymp.*
Coris. Whom can we accuse
But ourselves, for what we suffer? Thou art just,
Thou all creating Power! and misery
Instructs me now, that yesterday acknowledged
No deity beyond my lust and pride,
There is a heaven above us, that looks down
With the eyes of justice, upon such as number
Those blessings freely given, in the accompt
Of their poor merits: else it could not be,
Now miserable I, to please whose palate
The elements were ransack'd, yet complain'd
Of nature, as not liberal enough
In her provision of rarities
To sooth my taste, and pamper my proud flesh,
Should wish in vain for bread.

---

[1] *Grac. No, here's* Jane-of-apes *shall serve;*] Meaning Corisca: he plays upon *Jack-an-apes,* the name he had given to Asotus.

Cleon. Yes, I do wish too,
For what I fed my dogs with.
    Coris. I, that forgot
I was made of flesh and blood, and thought the silk
Spun by the diligent worm out of their entrails,
Too coarse to clothe me, and the softest down
Too hard to sleep on; that disdain'd to look
On virtue being in rags, that stopp'd my nose
At those that did not use adulterate arts
To better nature; that from those that served me
Expected adoration, am made justly
The scorn of my own bondwoman
    Asot. I am punish'd,
For seeking to cuckold mine own natural father:
Had I been gelded then, or used myself
Like a man, I had not been transform'd, and forced
To play an overgrown ape.
    Cleon. I know I cannot
Last long, that's all my comfort. Come, I forgive both:
'Tis in vain to be angry; let us, therefore,
Lament together like friends.
    Mar. What a true mirror
Were this sad spectacle for secure greatness!
Here they, that never see themselves, but in
The glass of servile flattery, might behold
The weak foundation upon which they build
Their trust in human frailty. Happy are those,
That knowing, in their births, they are subject to
Uncertain change, are still prepared, and arm'd
For either fortune: a rare principle,
And with much labour, learn'd in wisdom's school!
For, as these bondmen, by their actions, shew
That their prosperity, like too large a sail
For their small bark of judgment, sinks them with

A fore-right gale of liberty, ere they reach
The port they long to touch at: so these wretches,
Swollen with the false opinion of their worth,
And proud of blessings left them, not acquired;
That did believe they could with giant arms
Fathom the earth, and were above their fates,
Those borrow'd helps, that did support them,
　　　vanish'd,
Fall of themselves, and by unmanly suffering,
Betray their proper weakness, and make known
Their boasted greatness was lent, not their own.
　　Cleon. O for some meat! they sit long.
　　Coris. We forgot,
When we drew out intemperate feasts till
　　midnight;
Their hunger was not thought on, nor their
　　watchings;
Nor did we hold ourselves served to the height,
But when we did exact and force their duties
Beyond their strength and power.
　　Asot. We pay for't now:
I now could be content to have my head
Broke with a rib of beef, or, for a coffin,
Be buried in the dripping-pan.

Re-enter POLIPHRON, CIMBRIO, GRACCULO,
ZANTHIA, *and* OLYMPIA, *drunk and quarrelling.*

　　Cimb. Do not hold me:
Not kiss the bride!
　　Poliph. No, sir.
　　Cimb. She's common good,
And so we'll use her.
　　Grac. We'll have nothing private.
　　Mar. [*coming forward.*] Hold!
　　Zant. Here's Marullo.
　　Olymp. He's your chief.

Cimb. We are equals;
I will know no obedience.
   Grac. Nor superior—
Nay, if you are lion drunk, I will make one;
For lightly ever he that parts the fray,
Goes away with the blows.[2]
   Mar. Art thou mad too?
No more, as you respect me.
   Poliph. I obey, sir.
   Mar. Quarrel among yourselves!
   Cimb Yes, in our wine, sir,
And for our wenches.
   Grac. How could we be lords else?
   Mar. Take heed; I've news will cool this
      heat, and make you
Remember what you were.
   Cimb. How!
   Mar. Send off these,
And then I'll tell you.   [*Zanthia beats Corisca.*
   Olymp. This is tyranny,
Now she offends not.
   Zant. 'Tis for exercise,
And to help digestion. What is she good for
      else?
To me, it was her language.
   Mar. Lead her off.
And take heed, madam minx, the wheel may
      turn.

---

[2] *For* lightly *ever* he that *parts the* fray
  Goes away with the blows.] *Lightly* is commonly, usually; s
in *the New Inn :*
   Beau. What insolent half-witted things, these are
   Lat. So are all smatterers, insolent and impudent;
  They *lightly* go together.
Again, in *the Fox :*
   " ————— I knew 'twould take;
   " For *lightly*, they that use themselves most license,
   " Are still most jealous."

Go to your meat, and rest; and from this hour
Remember, he that is a lord to day,
May be a slave to morrow.
   Cleon. Good morality!
   [*Exeunt Cleon, Asot. Zant. Olymp. and Coris.*
   Cimb. But what would you impart?
   Mar. What must invite you
To stand upon your guard, and leave your feast-
     ing;
Or but imagine what it is to be
Most miserable, and rest assured you are so.
Our masters are victorious.
   All. How!
   Mar. Within
A day's march of the city, flesh'd with spoil,
And proud of conquest; the armado sunk,
The Carthaginian admiral, hand to hand,
Slain by Leosthenes.
   Cimb. I feel the whip
Upon my back already.
   Grac. Every man
Seek a convenient tree, and hang himself.
   Poliph. Better die once, than live an age
     to suffer
New tortures every hour.
   Cimb. Say, we submit,
And yield us to their mercy?—
   Mar. Can you flatter
Yourselves with such false hopes? Or dare you
     think
That your imperious lords, that never fail'd
To punish with severity petty slips
In your neglect of labour, may be won
To pardon those licentious outrages
Which noble enemies forbear to practise
Upon the conquer'd? What have you omitted,
That may call on their just revenge with horror,

And studied cruelty? we have gone too far
To think now of retiring; in our courage,
And daring,[3] lies our safety: if you are not
Slaves in your abject minds, as in your fortunes,
Since to die is the worst, better expose
Our naked breasts to their keen swords, and sell
Our lives with the most advantage, than to trust
In a forestall'd remission, or yield up
Our bodies to the furnace of their fury,
Thrice heated with revenge.
    Grac. You led us on.
    Cimb. And 'tis but justice you should bring
      us off.
    Grac. And we expect it.
    Mar. Hear then, and obey me;
And I will either save you, or fall with you.
Man the walls strongly, and make good the ports;
Boldly deny their entrance, and rip up
Your grievances, and what compell'd you to
This desperate course: if they disdain to hear
Of composition, we have in our powers
Their aged fathers, children, and their wives,
Who, to preserve themselves, must willingly
Make intercession for us. 'Tis not time now
To talk, but do: a glorious end, or freedom,
Is now proposed us; stand resolved for either,
And, like good fellows, live or die together.
                     [*Exeunt.*

---

[3] ——————— *in our courage,*
    And **daring,** *lies our safety :*] The old copies read *during :*
but it is an evident misprint.

SCENE IV.

The Country near Syracuse. *The Camp of* Timoleon.

Enter LEOSTHENES *and* TIMAGORAS.

Timag. I am so far from envy, I am proud
You have outstripp'd me in the race of honour.
O 'twas a glorious day, and bravely won!
Your bold performance gave such lustre to
Timoleon's wise directions, as the army
Rests doubtful, to whom they stand most engaged
For their so great success.
  Leost. The gods first honour'd,
The glory be the general's; 'tis far from me
To be his rival.
  Timag. You abuse your fortune,
To entertain her choice and gracious favours
With a contracted brow; plumed Victory
Is truly painted with a cheerful look,
Equally distant from proud insolence,
And base dejection.
  Leost. O, Timagoras,
You only are acquainted with the cause
That loads my sad heart with a hill of lead;
Whose ponderous weight, neither my new-got
    honour,
Assisted by the general applause
The soldier crowns it with,[4] nor all war's glories,
Can lessen or remove: and, would you please,
With fit consideration, to remember

---

[4] *The* soldier crowns *it with,*] This is a much better reading than the sophistication of the modern editors, the *soldiers crown,* &c.

How much I wrong'd Cleora's innocence
With my rash doubts; and what a grievous
        penance
She did impose upon her tender sweetness,
To pluck away the vulture, jealousy,
That fed upon my liver; you cannot blame me,
But call it a fit justice on myself,
Though I resolve to be a stranger to
The thought of mirth or pleasure.
        Timag. You have redeem'd
The forfeit of your fault with such a ransom
Of honourable action, as my sister
Must of necessity confess her sufferings,
Weigh'd down by your fair merits; and, when
        she views you,
Like a triumphant conqueror, carried through
The streets of Syracusa, the glad people
Pressing to meet you, and the senators
Contending who shall heap most honours on you;
The oxen, crown'd with garlands, led before you,
Appointed for the sacrifice; and the altars
Smoking with thankful incense to the gods:
The soldiers chanting loud hymns to your praise,
The windows fill'd with matrons and with virgins,
Throwing upon your head, as you pass by,
The choicest flowers, and silently invoking
The queen of love, with their particular vows,
To be thought worthy of you; can Cleora
(Though, in the glass of self-love, she behold
Her best deserts) but with all joy acknowledge,
What she endured was but a noble trial
You made of her affection? and her anger,
Rising from your too amorous cares,⁵ soon drench'd
In Lethe, and forgotten.

---

⁵ *Rising from your too amorous* cares,] The old copies read
cares, an error of the press, for cares. Coxeter, however,

Leost. If those glories
You so set forth were mine, they might plead for
          me;
But I can lay no claim to the least honour
Which you, with foul injustice, ravish from her.
Her beauty in me wrought a miracle,
Taught me to aim at things beyond my power,
Which her perfections purchased, and gave to me
From her free bounties; she inspired me with
That valour which I dare not call mine own;
And, from the fair reflexion of her mind,
My soul received the sparkling beams of courage.
She, from the magazine of her proper goodness,
Stock'd me with virtuous purposes; sent me forth
To trade for honour; and, she being the owner
Of the bark of my adventures, I must yield her
A just account of all, as fits a factor.
And, howsoever others think me happy,
And cry aloud, I have made a prosperous voyage;
One frown of her dislike at my return,
Which, as a punishment for my fault, I look for,
Strikes dead all comfort.
     Timag. Tush! these fears are needless;
She cannot, must not, shall not, be so cruel.
A free confession of a fault wins pardon,
But, being seconded by desert, commands ît.
The general is your own, and, sure, my father
Repents his harshness; for myself, I am
Ever your creature.—One day shall be happy
In your triumph, and your marriage.
     Leost. May it prove so,
With her consent and pardon.
     Timag. Ever touching

printed it *ears*, which, being without any meaning, was corrected at random by Mr. M. Mason into *fears*. The correction
was not amiss; but the genuine word is undoubtedly that which
I have given.

On that harsh string! She is your own, and you
Without disturbance seize on what's your due.

[Exeunt.

ACT IV. SCENE I.

Syracuse. *A Room in* Archidamus's *House.*

Enter MARULLO *and* TIMANDRA.

Mar. She has her health, then?
Timand. Yes, sir; and as often
As I speak of you, lends attentive ear
To all that I deliver; nor seems tired,
Though I dwell long on the relation of
Your sufferings for her, heaping praise on praise
On your unequall'd temperance, and command
You hold o'er your affections.
Mar. To my wish:
Have you acquainted her with the defeature[6]
Of the Carthaginians, and with what honours
Leosthenes comes crown'd home with?
Timand. With all care.

---

[6] *Have you acquainted her with the* defeature] The modern
editors removed this word in favour of *defeat*, and, doubtless,
applauded their labour; it happens, however, as in most cases
where they have interposed, that they might have spared it altogether; for the words are the same, and used indiscriminately
by our old writers: " *Desfaicte,*" says Cotgrave, " a *defeat,* or
defeature;" and, in the second part of his Dictionary, he verbally
repeats the explanation. There is much strange conjecture on
this word, in the last act of *the Comedy of Errors:* I wonder that
none of the commentators should light upon its meaning;—but
it was too simple for their apprehension. It occurs more than
once in Daniel, in the same sense as in the text.

Mar. And how does she receive it?

Timand. As I guess,
With a seeming kind of joy; but yet appears not
Transported, or proud of his happy fortune.
But when I tell her of the certain ruin
You must encounter with at their arrival
In Syracusa, and that death, with torments,
Must fall upon you, which you yet repent not,
Esteeming it a glorious martyrdom,
And a reward of pure unspotted love,
Preserved in the white robe of innocence,
Though she were in your power; and, still
    spurr'd on
By insolent lust, you rather chose to suffer
The fruit untasted, for whose glad possession
You have call'd on the fury of your lord,
Than that she should be grieved, or tainted in
Her reputation——

Mar. Doth it work compunction?
Pities she my misfortune?

Timand. She express'd
All signs of sorrow which, her vow observed,
Could witness a grieved heart. At the first hearing,
She fell upon her face, rent her fair hair,
Her hands held up to heaven, and vented sighs,
In which she silently seem'd to complain
Of heaven's injustice.

Mar. 'Tis enough: wait carefully,
And, on all watch'd occasions, continue
Speech and discourse of me: 'tis time must work
    her.

Timand. I'll not be wanting, but still strive to
    serve you.   [*Exit.*

Enter POLIPHRON.

Mar. Now, Poliphron, the news?
Poliph. The conquering army
Is within ken.
Mar. How brook the slaves the object?
Poliph. Cheerfully yet; they do refuse no
    labour,
And seem to scoff at danger; 'tis your presence
That must confirm them: with a full consent
You are chosen to relate the tyranny
Of our proud masters; and what you subscribe to,
They gladly will allow of, or hold out
To the last man.
Mar. I'll instantly among them.
If we prove constant to ourselves, good fortune
Will not, I hope, forsake us.
Poliph. 'Tis our best refuge. [*Exeunt.*

SCENE II.

Before the Walls of Syracuse.

Enter TIMOLEON, ARCHIDAMUS, DIPHILUS,
    LEOSTHENES, TIMAGORAS, *and Soldiers.*

Timol. Thus far we are return'd victorious;
    crown'd
With wreaths triumphant, (famine, blood, and
    death,
Banish'd your peaceful confines,) and bring home
Security and peace. 'Tis therefore fit
That such as boldly stood the shock of war,
And with the dear expense of sweat and blood
Have purchased honour, should with pleasure reap

The harvest of their toil: and we stand bound,
Out of the first file of the best deservers,
(Though all must be consider'd to their merits,)
To think of you, Leosthenes, that stand,
And worthily, most dear in our esteem,
For your heroic valour.
    Archid. When I look on
The labour of so many men and ages,
This well-built city, not long since design'd
To spoil and rapine, by the favour of
The gods, and you, their ministers, preserved,
I cannot, in my height of joy, but offer
These tears for a glad sacrifice.
    Diph. Sleep the citizens?
Or are they overwhelm'd with the excess
Of comfort that flows to them?
    Leost. We receive
A silent entertainment.
    Timag. I long since
Expected that the virgins and the matrons,
The old men striving with their age, the priests,
Carrying the images of their gods before them,
Should have met us with procession.—Ha! the
      gates
Are shut against us!
    Archid. And, upon the walls,
Arm'd men seem to defy us!

Enter above, on the Walls, MARULLO, POLIPHRON,
    CIMBRIO, GRACCULO, *and other Slaves.*

    Diph. I should know
These faces: they are our slaves.
    Timag. The mystery, rascals!
Open the ports, and play not with an anger
That will consume you.
    Timol. This is above wonder.

Archid. Our bondmen stand against us!

Grac. Some such things
We were in man's remembrance. The slaves are turn'd
Lords of the town, or so—nay, be not angry:
Perhaps, upon good terms, giving security
You will be quiet men, we may allow you
Some lodgings in our garrets or outhouses:
Your great looks cannot carry it.

Cimb. The truth is,
We've been bold with your wives, toy'd with your daughters——

Leost. O my prophetic soul!

Grac. Rifled your chests,
Been busy with your wardrobes.

Timag. Can we endure this?

Leost O my Cleora!

Grac. A caudle for the gentleman;
He'll die o' the pip else.

Timag. Scorn'd too! are you turn'd stone?
Hold parley with our bondmen! force our entrance,
Then, villains, expect——

Timol. Hold! You wear men's shapes,
And if, like men, you have reason, shew a cause
That leads you to this desperate course, which must end
In your destruction.

Grac. That, as please the Fates;
But we vouchsafe——Speak, captain.

Timag. Hell and furies!

Archid. Bay'd by our own curs!

Cimb. Take heed you be not worried.

Poliph. We are sharp set.

Cimb. And sudden.

Mar. Briefly thus, then,
Since I must speak for all—Your tyranny

Drew us from our obedience. Happy those times
When lords were styled fathers of families,
And not imperious masters! when they number'd
Their servants almost equal with their sons,
Or one degree beneath them! when their labours
Were cherish'd and rewarded, and a period
Set to their sufferings; when they did not press
Their duties or their wills, beyond the power
And strength of their performance! all things order'd
With such decorum, as [7] wise lawmakers,
From each well-govern'd private house derived
The perfect model of a commonwealth.
Humanity then lodged in the hearts of men,
And thankful masters carefully provided
For creatures wanting reason. The noble horse,
That, in his fiery youth, from his wide nostrils
Neigh'd courage to his rider, and brake through
Groves of opposed pikes, bearing his lord
Safe to triumphant victory; old or wounded,
Was set at liberty, and freed from service.
The Athenian mules, that from the quarry drew
Marble, hew'd for the temples of the gods,
The great work ended, were dismiss'd, and fed
At the public cost; nay, faithful dogs have found
Their sepulchres; but man, to man more cruel,
Appoints no end to the sufferings of his slave;
Since pride stepp'd in and riot, and o'erturn'd
This goodly frame of concord, teaching masters
To glory in the abuse of such as are

---

[7] *With such decorum* as *wise lawmakers*,] *As*, in this passage,
has the force of *that*. M. MASON.

Or rather, there is an ellipsis of *that*, as usual. Some of the
incidents mentioned in this speech, Massinger derived from
Plutarch.

Brought under their command; who, grown unuseful,
Are less esteem'd than beasts.—This you have practised,
Practised on us with rigour; this hath forced us
To shake our heavy yokes off; and, if redress
Of these just grievances be not granted us,
We'll right ourselves, and by strong hand defend
What we are now possess'd of.

Grac. And not leave
One house unfired.

Cimb Or throat uncut of those
We have in our power.

Poliph. Nor will we fall alone;
You shall buy us dearly.

Timag. O the gods!
Unheard-of insolence!

Timol. What are your demands?

Mar. A general pardon[8] first, for all offences
Committed in your absence. Liberty
To all such as desire to make return
Into their countries; and, to those that stay,
A competence of land freely allotted
To each man's proper use, no lord acknowledged:
Lastly, with your consent, to choose them wives
Out of your families.

Timag. Let the city sink first.

Leost. And ruin seize on all, ere we subscribe
To such conditions.

Archid. Carthage, though victorious,
Could not have forced more from us.

---

[8] *Mar. A general pardon,* &c.] It is evident, from the unreasonable nature of these demands, that Pisander does not wish them to be accepted. The last article, indeed, has a reference to himself, but he seems desirous of previously trying the fortune of arms. See, however, the next scene, and his defence, in the last act.

Leost. Scale the walls;
Capitulate after.
  Timol. He that wins the top first,
Shall wear a mural wreath.   [*Exeunt.*
  Mar. Each to his place. [*Flourish and alarms.*
Or death or victory! Charge them home, and
        fear not.   [*Exeunt Marullo and Slaves.*

Re-enter TIMOLEON, ARCHIDAMUS, *and Senators.*

  Timol. We wrong ourselves, and we are justly
        punish'd,
To deal with bondmen, as if we encounter'd
An equal enemy.
  Archid. They fight like devils;
And run upon our swords, as if their breasts
Were proof beyond their armour.

Re-enter LEOSTHENES *and* TIMAGORAS.

  Timag. Make a firm stand.
The slaves, not satisfied they have beat us off,
Prepare to sally forth.
  Timol. They are wild beasts,
And to be tamed by policy. Each man take
A tough whip in his hand, such as you used
To punish them with, as masters: in your looks
Carry severity and awe; 'twill fright them
More than your weapons. Savage lions fly from
The sight of fire; and these, that have forgot
That duty you ne'er taught them with your
        swords,
When, unexpected, they behold those terrors

----

9 [*Flourish and* alarms.] Flourish and *arms*, says Mr. M.
Mason, after Coxeter. No degree of nonsense could tempt him
to consult the old copies.

Advanced aloft, that they were made to shake at,
'Twill force them to remember what they are,
And stoop to due obedience.
Archid. Here they come.

Enter, from the City, CIMBRIO, GRACCULO, *and
other Slaves.*

Cimb. Leave not a man alive; a wound's but
    a flea-biting,
To what we suffer'd, being slaves.
Grac. O, my heart!
Cimbrio, what do we see? the whip! our masters![1]
Timag. Dare you rebel, slaves!
    [*The Senators shake their whips, the Slaves
      throw away their weapons, and run off.*
Cimb. Mercy! mercy! where
Shall we hide us from their fury?
Grac. Fly, they follow.
O, we shall be tormented!
Timol. Enter with them,
But yet forbear to kill them: still remember
They are part of your wealth; and being disarm'd,
There is no danger.
Archid. Let us first deliver
Such as they have in fetters, and at leisure
Determine of their punishment.
Leost. Friend, to you
I leave the disposition of what's mine:

   [1] *Cimbrio, what do we see? the whip! our masters!*] "O most
lame and impotent conclusion!" Surely Massinger was not so
strictly bound to the literal relation of this foolish adventure,
but that he might have given it a little probability, if it were
only to maintain the decorum of his action, and the interest of
his under-plot. He sometimes deviates from his authorities with
fewer prospects of advantage than were here opened to him.

I cannot think I am safe without your sister,
She is only worth my thought; and, till I see
What she has suffer'd, I am on the rack,
And Furies my tormentors.   [*Exeunt.*

SCENE III.

Syracuse.   *A Room in* Archidamus's *House.*

Enter MARULLO *and* TIMANDRA.

Mar. I know I am pursued; nor would I fly,
Although the ports were open, and a convoy
Ready to bring me off: the baseness of
These villains, from the pride of all my hopes,
Hath thrown me to the bottomless abyss
Of horror and despair: had they stood firm,
I could have bought Cleora's free consent
With the safety of her father's life, and brother's;
And forced Leosthenes to quit his claim,
And kneel a suitor for me [2]
    Timand You must not think
What might have been, but what must now be
        practised,
And suddenly resolve.

[2] *And kneel a suitor* for *me.*] This is the reading of all the
old copies, and is undoubtedly genuine; yet the modern editors,
by an obliquity of reasoning into which I cannot enter, choose
to vary the expression, and print,

        ——*kneel a suitor to me!*

Is it not evident " to any formal capacity," that Pisander means
——If my designs had succeeded, I would not only have compelled Leosthenes to renounce his pretensions to Cleora, but
even to entreat her father and brother to give her to me; what
is there in this that requires alteration, especially into nonsense?
for Leosthenes could have nothing to ask of Pisander.

Mar. All my poor fortunes
Are at the stake, and I must run the hazard.
Unseen, convey me to Cleora's chamber;
For in her sight, if it were possible,
I would be apprehended: do not enquire
The reason why, but help me. [*Knocking within.*
Timand. Make haste,—one knocks.
[*Exit Marullo.*
Jove turn all to the best!

Enter LEOSTHENES.

You are welcome, sir.
Leost. Thou giv'st it in a heavy tone.
Timand. Alas! sir,
We have so long fed on the bread of sorrow,
Drinking the bitter water of afflictions,
Made loathsome too by our continued fears,
Comfort's a stranger to us.
Leost. Fears! your sufferings:—[2]
For which I am so overgone with grief,
I dare not ask, without compassionate tears,
The villain's name that robb'd thee of thy honour:
For being train'd up in chastity's cold school,
And taught by such a mistress as Cleora,
'Twere impious in me to think Timandra
Fell with her own consent.
Timand. How mean you, fell, sir?
I understand you not.
Leost. I would thou did'st not,
Or that I could not read upon thy face,
In blushing characters, the story of
Libidinous rape: confess it, for you stand not

---

[2] *Leost. Fears! your sufferings:*—] The character of Leosthenes is everywhere preserved with great nicety. His jealous disposition breaks out in this scene with peculiar beauty.

Accountable for a sin, against whose strength
Your o'ermatch'd innocence could make no re-
 sistance ;
Under which odds, I know, Cleora fell too,
Heaven's help in vain invoked ; the amazed sun
Hiding his face behind a mask of clouds,
Nor daring to look on it ! In her sufferings
All sorrow's comprehended : what Timandra,
Or the city, has endured, her loss consider'd,
Deserves not to be named.

 Timand. Pray you, do not bring, sir,
In the chimeras of your jealous fears,
New monsters to affright us.

 Leost. O, Timandra,
That I had faith enough but to believe thee !
I should receive it with a joy beyond
Assurance of Elysian shades hereafter,
Or all the blessings, in this life, a mother
Could wish her children crown'd with — but I
 must not
Credit impossibilities ; yet I strive
To find out that whose knowledge is a curse,
And ignorance a blessing. Come, discover
What kind of look he had that forced thy lady,
(Thy ravisher I will enquire at leisure,)
That when, hereafter, I behold a stranger
But near him in aspéct, I may conclude,
Though men and angels should proclaim him
 honest,
He is a hell bred villain.

 Timand. You are unworthy
To know she is preserved, preserved untainted :
Sorrow, but ill bestow'd, hath only made
A rape upon her comforts in your absence.
Come forth, dear madam. [*Leads in Cleora.*

 Leost. Ha !   [*Kneels.*

 Timand. Nay, she deserves

The bending of your heart; that, to content you,
Has kept a vow, the breach of which a Vestal,
Though the infringing it had call'd upon her
A living funeral,[4] must of force have shrunk at.
No danger could compel her to dispense with
Her cruel penance, though hot lust came arm'd
To seize upon her ; when one look or accent
Might have redeem'd her.

    Leost. Might! O do not shew me
A beam of comfort, and straight take it from me.
The means by which she was freed? speak, O speak quickly ;
Each minute of delay's an age of torment;
O speak, Timandra.

    Timand. Free her from her oath ;
Herself can best deliver it.

    Leost. O blest office !   [*Unbinds her eyes.*
Never did galley-slave shake off his chains,
Or look'd on his redemption from the oar,
With such true feeling of delight, as now
I find myself possess'd of.—Now I behold
True light indeed ; for, since these fairest stars,
Cover'd with clouds of your determinate will,
Denied their influence to my optic sense,
The splendour of the sun appear'd to me
But as some little glimpse of his bright beams

---

[4] *Though the infringing it had call'd upon her*
A living funeral, &c.] The poet alludes to the manner in
which the Vestals, who had broken their vow of chastity, were
punished. They had literally a *living funeral*, being plunged
alive into a subterraneous cavern, of which the opening was immediately closed upon them, and walled up. The confusion of
countries and customs may possibly strike the critical reader ;
but of this, as I have already observed, our old dramatists were
either not aware or not solicitous.

Convey'd into a dungeon, to remember
The dark inhabitants there, how much they
    wanted.[5]
Open these long shut lips, and strike mine ears
With music more harmonious than the spheres
Yield in their heavenly motions: and if ever
A true submission for a crime acknowledged,
May find a gracious hearing, teach your tongue,
In the first sweet articulate sounds it utters,
To sign my wish'd-for pardon.
    Cleo. I forgive you.
    Leost. How greedily I receive this! Stay, best
    lady,
And let me by degrees ascend the height
Of human happiness! all at once deliver'd,
The torrent of my joys will overwhelm me:—
So! now a little more; and pray excuse me,
If, like a wanton epicure, I desire
The pleasant taste these cates of comfort yield
    me,
Should not too soon be swallow'd. Have you not,
By your unspotted truth I do conjure you
To answer truly, suffer'd in your honour,
By force, I mean, for in your will I free you,
Since I left Syracusa?
    Cleo. I restore
This kiss, so help me goodness! which I borrow'd,
When I last saw you.[6]

---

[5] ——————————— to remember
The dark inhabitants there, how much they wanted.] In this
beautiful passage, *remember* is used for *cause* to remember, in
which sense it frequently occurs in our old writers. So Beaumont and Fletcher:

    " *Croc.* Do you *remember*
    " Her to come after you, that she may behold
    " Her daughter's charity."   *The Sea Voyage.*
[6] Cleo. *I restore*
This kiss, so help me goodness! which I borrow'd,

Leost. Miracle of virtue!
One pause more, I beseech you : I am like
A man whose vital spirits consumed and wasted
With a long and tedious fever, unto whom
Too much of a strong cordial, at once taken,
Brings death, and not restores him. Yet I cannot
Fix here ; but must enquire the man to whom
I stand indebted for a benefit,
Which to requite at full, though in this hand
I grasp all sceptres the world's empire bows to,
Would leave me a poor bankrupt. Name him,
        lady ;
If of a mean estate, I'll gladly part with
My utmost fortunes to him ; but if noble,
In thankful duty study how to serve him ;
Or if of higher rank, erect him altars,
And as a god adore him.
    Cleo. If that goodness,
And noble temperance, the queen of virtues,
Bridling rebellious passions, to whose sway,
Such as have conquer'd nations have lived slaves,
Did ever wing great minds to fly to heaven,
He, that preserved mine honour, may hope boldly
To fill a seat among the gods, and shake off
Our frail corruption.
    Leost. Forward.

When I last saw you.] This is a modest imitation of Shakspeare :
      " Now by the jealous queen of heaven, that kiss
      " I carried from thee, dear ; and my true lip
      " Hath virgin'd it e'er since."   *Coriolanus.*
There is a pretty contrast to the jealousy of Leosthenes, in the *Coronation.*
        Arcadius. " Thou art jealous now :
      Come, let me take the kiss I gave thee last :
      I am so confident of thee, no lip
      Hath ravished it from thine !"

Cleo. Or if ever
The Powers above did mask in human shapes,
To teach mortality, not by cold precepts
Forgot as soon as told, but by examples,
To imitate their pureness, and draw near
To their celestial natures, I believe
He's more than man.
    Leost. You do describe a wonder.
    Cleo. Which will encrease, when you shall un-
      derstand
He was a lover.
    Leost. Not yours, lady?
    Cleo. Yes;
Loved me, Leosthenes; nay, more, so doted,
(If e'er affections scorning gross desires
May without wrong be styled so,) that he durst
      not,
With an immodest syllable or look,
In fear it might take from me, whom he made
The object of his better part, discover
I was the saint he sued to.
    Leost. A rare temper!⁷
    Cleo. I cannot speak it to the worth: all
      praise
I can bestow upon it will appear
Envious detraction. Not to rack you further,
Yet make the miracle full, though, of all men,
He hated you, Leosthenes, as his rival,
So high yet he prized my content, that, knowing
You were a man I favour'd, he disdain'd not,
Against himself, to serve you.
    Leost. You conceal still
The owner of these excellencies.

---

⁷ *A rare* temper!] The old copies read *tempter:* corrected
by Mr. M. Mason.

Cleo. 'Tis Marullo,
My father's bondman.
   Leost. Ha, ha, ha!
   Cleo. Why do you laugh?
   Leost. To hear the labouring mountain of your
      praise
Deliver'd of a mouse.
   Cleo. The man deserves not
This scorn, I can assure you.
   Leost. Do you call
What was his duty, merit?
   Cleo. Yes, and place it
As high in my esteem, as all the honours
Descended from your ancestors, or the glory,
Which you may call your own, got in this action,
In which, I must confess, you have done nobly;
And I could add, as I desired, but that
I fear 'twould make you proud.
   Leost. Why, lady, can you
Be won to give allowance, that your slave
Should dare to love you?
   Cleo. The immortal gods
Accept the meanest altars,[8] that are raised

---

[8] *Cleo. The immortal gods,*
Accept the meanest altars, &c.] Milton's invocation on the
opening of Paradise Lost is not unlike this.
      " And chiefly thou, O spirit," &c.   COXETER.
   I cannot discover much *likeness* in the two quotations; the
author had Horace in his thoughts:

> *Immunis aram si tetigit manus,*
> *Non sumptuoso blandior hostia*
> *Mollirit aversos penates*
> *Farre pio, saliente mica.*

A beautiful passage, which the critics, with Dacier and Sanadon
at their head, strangely maintain to be ironical. I believe that
Horace was perfectly sincere. The lessons of piety are so consonant to human feelings, that very frequently those who do
not experience their full influence themselves, earnestly and
honestly labour to impress them upon others.

By pure devotions; and sometimes prefer
An ounce of frankincense, honey or milk,
Before whole hecatombs, or Sabæan gums,
Offer'd in ostentation.—Are you sick
Of your old disease? I'll fit you.   [*Aside.*
    Leost. You seem moved.
    Cleo. Zealous, I grant, in the defence of
    virtue.
Why, good Leosthenes, though I endured
A penance for your sake, above example;
I have not so far sold myself, I take it,
To be at your devotion, but I may
Cherish desert in others, where I find it.
How would you tyrannize, if you stood possess'd
    of
That which is only yours in expectation,
That now prescribe such hard conditions to me?
    Leost. One kiss, and I am silenced.
    Cleo. I vouchsafe it;
Yet, I must tell you 'tis a favour that
Marullo, when I was his, not mine own,
Durst not presume to ask: no; when the city
Bow'd humbly to licentious rapes and lust,
And when I was, of men and gods forsaken,
Deliver'd to his power, he did not press me
To grace him with one look or syllable,
Or urged the dispensation of an oath
Made for your satisfaction:—the poor wretch,
Having related only his own sufferings,
And kiss'd my hand, which I could not deny
    him,
Defending me from others, never since
Solicited my favours.
    Leost. Pray you, end:
The story does not please me.
    Cleo. Well, take heed
Of doubts and fears;—for know, Leosthenes,

A greater injury cannot be offer'd
To innocent chastity, than unjust suspicion.
I love Marullo's fair mind, not his person ;
Let that secure you.   And I here command you,
If I have any power in you, to stand
Between him and all punishment, and oppose
His temperance to his folly ; if you fail——
No more ; I will not threaten.   [*Exit.*

  Leost. What a bridge
Of glass I walk upon, over a river
Of certain ruin, mine own weighty fears
Cracking what should support me ! and those
        helps,
Which confidence lends to others, are from me
Ravish'd by doubts, and wilful jealousy. [*Exit.*

SCENE IV.

Another Room in the same.

Enter TIMAGORAS, CLEON, ASOTUS, CORISCA,
        and OLYMPIA.

  Cleon. But are you sure we are safe ?
  Timag. You need not fear ;
They are all under guard, their fangs pared off :
The wounds their insolence gave you, to be cured
With the balm of your revenge.
  Asot. And shall I be
The thing I was born, my lord ?
  Timag. The same wise thing.
'Slight, what a beast they have made thee !
        Africk never
Produced the like.
  Asot. I think so :—nor the land

Where apes and monkeys grow, like crabs and
            walnuts,
On the same tree.   Not all the catalogue
Of conjurers or wise women bound together
Could have so soon transform'd me, as my rascal
Did with his whip; for not in outside only,
But in my own belief, I thought myself
As perfect a baboon——
    Timag. An ass thou wert ever.
    Asot. And would have given one leg, with all
        my heart,
For good security to have been a man
After three lives, or one and twenty years,
Though I had died on crutches.
    Cleon. Never varlets
So triumph'd o'er an old fat man : I was famish'd.
    Timag. Indeed you are fallen away.
    Asot. Three years of feeding
On cullises and jelly, though his cooks
Lard all he eats with marrow, or his doctors
Pour in his mouth restoratives as he sleeps,
Will not recover him.
    Timag. But your ladyship looks
Sad on the matter, as if you had miss'd
Your ten-crown amber possets, good to smooth
The cutis, as you call it, and prepare you
Active, and high, for an afternoon's encounter
With a rough gamester, on your couch. Fie on't !
You are grown thrifty, smell like other women ;
The college of physicians have not sat,
As they were used, in counsel, how to fill
The crannies in your cheeks, or raise a rampire
With mummy, ceruses, or infants' fat,
To keep off age and time.
    Coris. Pray you, forbear ;
I am an alter'd woman.
    Timag. So it seems ;

A part of your honour's ruff stands out of rank
    too.
  Coris. No matter, I have other thoughts.
  Timag. O strange!
Not ten days since it would have vex'd you more
Than the loss of your good name: pity, this cure
For your proud itch came no sooner! Marry,
    Olympia
Seems to bear up still.
  Olymp. I complain not, sir;
I have borne my fortune patiently.
  Timag. Thou wert ever
An excellent bearer; so is all your tribe,
If you may choose your carriage.

Enter LEOSTHENES *and* DIPHILUS *with a Guard.*

                How now, friend:
Looks our Cleora lovely?
  Leost. In my thoughts, sir.
  Timag. But why this guard?
  Diph. It is Timoleon's pleasure:
The slaves have been examin'd, and confess
Their riot took beginning from your house;
And the first mover of them to rebellion,
Your slave Marullo.   [*Exeunt Diph. and Guard.*
  Leost. Ha! I more than fear.
  Timag. They may search boldly.

Enter TIMANDRA, *speaking to the Guard within.*

  Timand. You are unmanner'd grooms,
To pry into my lady's private lodgings;
There's no Marullos there.

Re-enter DIPHILUS, *and Guard with* MARULLO.

Timag. Now I suspect too.
Where found you him?
  Diph. Close hid in your sister's chamber.
  Timag. Is that the villain's sanctuary?
  Leost. This confirms
All she deliver'd, false.
  Timag. But that I scorn
To rust my good sword[9] in thy slavish blood,
Thou now wert dead.
  Mar. He's more a slave than fortune
Or misery can make me, that insults
Upon unweapon'd innocence.
  Timag. Prate you, dog!
  Mar. Curs snap at lions in the toil, whose
    looks
Frighted them, being free.
  Timag. As a wild beast,
Drive him before you.
  Mar. O divine Cleora!
  Leost. Dar'st thou presume to name her?
  Mar. Yes, and love her;
And may say, have deserved her.
  Timag. Stop his mouth,
Load him with irons too.
                    [*Exit Guard with Marullo.*
  Cleon. I am deadly sick
To look on him.
  Asot. If he get loose, I know it,
I caper like an ape again: I feel
The whip already.

---

[9] *To rust my* good *sword* &c.] *Good,* which completes the
metre, is only found in the first quarto: the modern editors
follow the second, which abounds in similar omissions, almost
beyond credibility.

Timand. This goes to my lady.   [*Exit.*

Timag. Come, cheer you, sir; we'll urge his
    punishment
To the full satisfaction of your anger.

    Leost. He is not worth my thoughts.   No
    corner left
In all the spacious rooms of my vex'd heart,
But is fill'd with Cleora: and the rape
She has done upon her honour, with my wrong,
The heavy burthen of my sorrow's song. [*Exeunt.*

ACT V. SCENE I.

The same.   *A Room in* Archidamus's *House.*

Enter ARCHIDAMUS *and* CLEORA.

    Archid. Thou art thine own disposer.   Were
    his honours
And glories centupled, as I must confess,
Leosthenes is most worthy, yet I will not,
However I may counsel, force affection.

    Cleo. It needs not, sir; I prize him to his worth,
Nay, love him truly; yet would not live slaved
To his jealous humours: since, by the hopes of
    heaven,
As I am free from violence, in a thought
I am not guilty.

    Archid. 'Tis believed, Cleora;
And much the rather, our great gods be praised
    for't!
In that I find, beyond my hopes, no sign
Of riot in my house, but all things order'd,
As if I had been present.

Cleo. May that move you
To pity poor Marullo!
    Archid. 'Tis my purpose
To do him all the good I can, Cleora;
But this offence, being against the state,
Must have a public trial. In the mean time,
Be careful of yourself, and stand engaged
No further to Leosthenes, than you may
Come off with honour; for, being once his wife,
You are no more your own, nor mine, but must
Resolve to serve, and suffer his commands,
And not dispute them:—ere it be too late,
Consider it duly. I must to the senate. [*Exit.*

    Cleo. I am much distracted: in Leosthenes,
I can find nothing justly to accuse,
But his excess of love, which I have studied
To cure with more than common means; yet still
It grows upon him. And, if I may call
My sufferings merit,[1] I stand bound to think on
Marullo's dangers—though I save his life,
His love is unrewarded:—I confess,
Both have deserved me; yet, of force, must be
Unjust to one; such is my destiny.—

Enter TIMANDRA.

How now! whence flow these tears?
    Timand. I have met, madam,

---

[1] My *sufferings merit*] So it stood in every edition previous to
that of Mr. M. Mason, who reads, his *sufferings merit*. It is evident that he mistook the sense of the passage. Three lines
below, he reads, after Coxeter, indeed, *yet of force* I *must be*—
the pronoun, which injures both the measure and the rhyme, is
not in the old copies: but these are not the only errors in this
short speech, which disgrace the modern editions. This conference with Cleora is managed with singular art, and effect, on
the part of Timandra.

An object of such cruelty, as would force
A savage to compassion.

    Cleo. Speak, what is it?

    Timand. Men pity beasts of rapine, if o'er-
        match'd,
Though baited for their pleasure; but these
        monsters,
Upon a man that can make no resistance,
Are senseless in their tyranny. Let it be granted,
Marullo is a slave, he's still a man;
A capital offender, yet in justice
Not to be tortured, till the judge pronounce
His punishment.

    Cleo. Where is he?

    Timand. Dragg'd to prison
With more than barbarous violence; spurn'd and
        spit on
By the insulting officers, his hands
Pinion'd behind his back; loaden with fetters:
Yet, with a saint-like patience, he still offers
His face to their rude buffets.

    Cleo. O my grieved soul!—
By whose command?

    Timand. It seems, my lord your brother's,
For he's a looker-on: and it takes from
Honour'd Leosthenes, to suffer it,
For his respect to you, whose name in vain
The grieved wretch loudly calls on.

    Cleo. By Diana,
'Tis base in both; and to their teeth I'll tell them
That I am wrong'd in't.   [*Going forth.*

    Timand. What will you do?

    Cleo. In person
Visit and comfort him.

    Timand. That will bring fuel
To the jealous fires which burn too hot already
In lord Leosthenes.

Cleo. Let them consume him!
I am mistress of myself. Where cruelty reigns,
There dwells nor love, nor honour.   [*Exit.*
    Timand. So! it works.
Though hitherto I have run a desperate course
To serve my brother's purposes, now 'tis fit

Enter LEOSTHENES *and* TIMAGORAS.

I study mine own ends.   They come :—assist
        me
In these my undertakings, Love's great patron,
As my intents are honest!
    Leost. 'Tis my fault :[2]

---

[2]   Leost. *'Tis my* fault:
    Distrust of others springs, Timagoras,
    From diffidence in ourselves :] My *fault,* i. e. my misfortune.
That the word anciently had this meaning, I could prove by
many examples ; one, however, will be thought sufficiently decisive :
    " *Bawd.* You are lit into my hands, where you are like to
live.
    Marina. The more my *fault,*
To scape his hands, where I was like to die."
                                    Pericles, Act. IV. sc. iii.
This too will ascertain, beyond a doubt, the meaning of Shallow, which Steevens evidently mistook, and Mr. Malone delivered with some degree of hesitation :
    " *Slen.* How does your fallow greyhound, sir ? I heard say,
he was out-run on Cotsale.
    Page. It could not be judg'd, sir.
    Slen. You'll not confess, you'll not confess.
    Shal. That he will not ;—'tis your *fault,* 'tis your *fault :*—
'Tis a good dog."
    Poor Slender is one of Job's comforters, as they say ; he
persists in reminding Page, who evidently dislikes the subject,
of his defeat: hence the good-natured consolation of Shallow :
    " He needs not confess it, cousin ;—you were unfortunate, sir ;
your loss must be attributed to accident, for your dog is a good
dog."

Distrust of other springs, Timagoras,
From diffidence in ourselves : but I will strive,
With the assurance of my worth and merits,
To kill this monster, jealousy.

   Timag. 'Tis a guest,
In wisdom, never to be entertain'd
On trivial probabilities ; but, when
He does appear in pregnant proofs, not fashion'd
By idle doubts and fears, to be received :
They make their own horns that are too secure,
As well as such as give them growth and being
From mere imagination. Though I prize
Cleora's honour equal with mine own,
And know what large additions of power
This match brings to our family, I prefer
Our friendship, and your peace of mind so far
Above my own respects, or hers, that if
She hold not her true value in the test,
'Tis far from my ambition, for her cure
That you should wound yourself.

   Timand. This argues for me.   [*Aside.*

   Timag. Why she should be so passionate for a
     bondman,
Falls not in compass of my understanding,
But for some nearer interest : or he raise
This mutiny, if he loved her, as, you say,
She does confess he did, but to enjoy,
By fair or foul play, what he ventured for,
To me's a riddle.

   Leost. Pray you, no more ; already
I have answered that objection, in my strong
Assurance of her virtue.

   Timag. 'Tis unfit then,
That I should press it further.

   Timand. Now I must
Make in, or all is lost.
     [*Rushes forward distractedly.*

Timag. What would Timandra?

Leost. How wild she looks! How is it with thy
    lady?

Timag. Collect thyself, and speak.

Timand. As you are noble,
Have pity, or love piety.[3]—Oh!

Leost. Take breath.

Timag. Out with it boldly.

Timand. O, the best of ladies,
I fear, is gone for ever.

Leost. Who, Cleora?

Timag. Deliver, how? 'Sdeath, be a man, sir!—
    Speak.

Timand. Take it then in as many sighs as words,
My lady——

Timag. What of her?

Timand. No sooner heard
Marullo was imprison'd, but she fell
Into a deadly swoon.

Timag. But she recover'd:
Say so, or he will sink too; hold, sir; fie!
This is unmanly.

Timand. Brought again to life,
But with much labour, she awhile stood silent,
Yet in that interim vented sighs, as if
They labour'd, from the prison of her flesh,
To give her grieved soul freedom. On the sudden,
Transported on the wings of rage and sorrow,
She flew out of the house, and, unattended,
Enter'd the common prison.

Leost. This confirms
What but before I fear'd.

Timand. There you may find her;
And, if you love her as a sister——

---

   3 *Have pity, or love* piety.—] So the old copies: the modern
editors here, as almost everywhere else, corrupt this last word,
and feebly read, *Have pity, or love* pity.

Timag. Damn her!

Timand. Or you respect her safety as a lover,
Procure Marullo's liberty.

Timag. Impudence
Beyond expression!

Leost. Shall I be a bawd
To her lust, and my dishonour?

Timand. She'll run mad, else,
Or do some violent act upon herself:
My lord, her father, sensible of her sufferings,
Labours to gain his freedom.

Leost. O, the devil!
Has she bewitch'd him too?

Timag. I'll hear no more.
Come, sir, we'll follow her; and if no persuasion
Can make her take again her natural form,
Which by lust's powerful spell she has cast off,
This sword shall disenchant her.

Leost. O my heart-strings!
                    [*Exeunt Leosthenes and Timagoras.*

Timand. I knew 'twould take. Pardon me, fair
        Cleora,
Though I appear a traitress; which thou wilt do,
In pity of my woes, when I make known
My lawful claim, and only seek mine own. [*Exit.*

SCENE II.

A Prison.   MARULLO *discovered in chains.*

Enter CLEORA *and* Gaoler.

Cleo. There's for your privacy. Stay, unbind
        his hands.

Gaol. I dare not, madam.

Cleo. I will buy thy danger ·

Take more gold;—do not trouble me with thanks,
I do suppose it done.   [*Exit Gaoler.*

   Mar. My better angel
Assumes this shape to comfort me, and wisely;
Since, from the choice of all celestial figures,
He could not take a visible form so full
Of glorious sweetness.   [*Kneels.*

   Cleo. Rise. I am flesh and blood,
And do partake thy tortures.

   Mar. Can it be,
That charity should persuade you to descend
So far from your own height, as to vouchsafe
To look upon my sufferings? How I bless
My fetters now, and stand engaged to fortune
For my captivity—no, my freedom, rather!
For who dare think that place a prison, which
You sanctify with your presence? or believe,
Sorrow has power to use her sting on him,
That is in your compassion arm'd, and made
Impregnable, though tyranny raise at once
All engines to assault him?

   Cleo. Indeed virtue,
With which you have made evident proofs that
      you
Are strongly fortified, cannot fall, though shaken
With the shock of fierce temptations; but still
      triumphs
In spite of opposition. For myself,
I may endeavour to confirm your goodness,
(A sure retreat, which never will deceive you,)
And with unfeigned tears express my sorrow
For what I cannot help.

   Mar. Do you weep for me!
O, save that precious balm for nobler uses:
I am unworthy of the smallest drop,
Which, in your prodigality of pity,
You throw away on me. Ten of these pearls

Were a large ransom to redeem a kingdom
From a consuming plague, or stop heaven's ven-
    geance,
Call'd down by crying sins, though, at that instant,
In dreadful flashes falling on the roofs
Of bold blasphemers. I am justly punish'd
For my intent of violence to such pureness;
And all the torments flesh is sensible of,
A soft and gentle penance.
    Cleo. Which is ended
In this your free confession.

    Enter LEOSTHENES *and* TIMAGORAS *behind.*

    Leost. What an object
Have I encountered!
    Timag. I am blasted too:
Yet hear a little further.
    Mar. Could I expire now,
These white and innocent hands closing my eyes
    thus,
'Twere not to die, but in a heavenly dream
To be transported, without the help of Charon,
To the Elysian shades. You make me bold;
And, but to wish such happiness, I fear,
May give offence.
    Cleo. No; for believe't, Marullo,
You've won so much upon me, that I know not
That happiness in my gift, but you may chal-
    lenge.
    Leost. Are you yet satisfied?
    Cleo. Nor can you wish
But what my vows will second, though it were
Your freedom first, and then in me full power
To make a second tender of myself,
And you receive the present. By this kiss,

From me a virgin bounty,[4] I will practise
All arts for your deliverance; and that purchased,
In what concerns your further aims, I speak it,
Do not despair, but hope——

    [*Timagoras and Leosthenes come forward.*

 Timag. To have the hangman,
When he is married to the cross, in scorn
To say, *Gods give you joy !*

  Leost. But look on me,
And be not too indulgent to your folly ;
And then, but that grief stops my speech, imagine
What language I should use.

  Cleo. Against thyself:
Thy malice cannot reach me.

  Timag. How?

  Cleo. No, brother,
Though you join in the dialogue to accuse me:
What I have done, I'll justify ; and these favours,
Which, you presume, will taint me in my honour,
Though jealousy use all her eyes to spy out
One stain in my behaviour, or envy
As many tongues to wound it, shall appear
My best perfections. For, to the world,
I can in my defence allege such reasons,
As my accusers shall stand dumb to hear them ;
When in his fetters this man's worth and virtues,
But truly told, shall shame your boasted glories,
Which fortune claims a share in.

  Timag. The base villain
Shall never live to hear it.   [*Draws his sword.*

  Cleo. Murder ! help !
Through me, you shall pass to him.

---

 4   ——*By this kiss,*
From me a virgin bounty,] i. e. to Pisander, for she had
given one to Leosthenes before. See p. 41. Both, indeed,
were *virgin* kisses.

Enter ARCDHIDAMUS, DIPHILUS, *and* Officers.

Archid. What's the matter?
On whom is your sword drawn? are you a judge?
Or else ambitious of the hangman's office,
Before it be design'd you?—You are bold, too;
Unhand my daughter.
    Leost. She's my valour's prize.
    Archid. With her consent, not otherwise. You
        may urge
Your title in the court; if it prove good,
Possess her freely.—Guard him safely off too.
    Timag. You'll hear me, sir?
    Archid. If you have aught to say,
Deliver it in public; all shall find
A just judge of Timoleon.
    Diph. You must
Of force now use your patience.
        [*Exeunt all but Timagoras and Leosthenes.*
    Timag. Vengeance rather!
Whirlwinds of rage possess me: you are wrong'd
Beyond a Stoic sufferance; yet you stand
As you were rooted.
    Leost. I feel something here,
That boldly tells me, all the love and service
I pay Cleora is another's due,
And therefore cannot prosper.
    Timag. Melancholy;
Which now you must not yield to.
    Leost. 'Tis apparent:
In fact your sister's innocent, however
Changed by her violent will.
    Timag. If you believe so,
Follow the chase still; and in open court
Plead your own interest: we shall find the judge
Our friend, I fear not.

Leost. Something I shall say,
But what——
    Timag. Collect yourself as we walk thither.
                                        [*Exeunt.*

SCENE III.

The Court of Justice.

Enter TIMOLEON, ARCHIDAMUS, CLEORA, *and*
        Officers.

    Timol. 'Tis wonderous strange! nor can it fall
        within
The reach of my belief, a slave should be
The owner of a temperance which this age
Can hardly parallel in freeborn lords,
Or kings proud of their purple.
    Archid 'Tis most true;
And, though at first it did appear a fable,
All circumstances meet to give it credit;
Which works so on me, that I am compell'd
To be a suitor, not to be denied,
He may have equal hearing.
    Cleo. Sir, you graced me
With the title of your mistress;[5] but my fortune
Is so far distant from command, that I
Lay by the power you gave me, and plead humbly
For the preserver of my fame and honour.
And pray you, sir, in charity believe,

---

    [5] Cleo. *Sir, you graced me*
    With the title of your mistress;] This alludes to the request in
the first act, that he might be permitted *to wear her colours.* In
those days of gallantry, I mean those of Massinger, not, of
Timoleon, to wear a lady's colours, that is, a scarf, or a riband,
taken from her person was to become her authorized champion
and servant. See p. 30.

That, since I had ability of speech,
My tongue has been so much inured to truth,
I know not how to lie.
    Timol. I'll rather doubt
The oracles of the gods, than question what
Your innocence delivers; and, as far
As justice and mine honour can give way,
He shall have favour. Bring him in unbound:
                       [Exeunt Officers.
And though Leosthenes may challenge from
    me,
For his late worthy service, credit to
All things he can allege in his own cause,
Marullo, so, I think, you call his name,
Shall find I do reserve one ear for him,

Enter CLEON, ASOTUS, DIPHILUS, OLYMPIA,
    and CORISCA.

To let in mercy. Sit, and take your places;
The right of this fair virgin first determined,
Your bondmen shall be censured.[6]
    Cleon. With all rigour,
We do expect.
    Coris. Temper'd, I say, with mercy.

Enter at one door LEOSTHENES *and* TIMAGORAS;
    at the other, Officers *with* MARULLO, *and*
    TIMANDRA.

    Timol. Your hand, Leosthenes: I cannot doubt,

---

[6] *Your bondmen shall be* censured.] i. e. judged. To prevent
the necessity of recurring to this word, about which more than
sufficient has been written, it may be proper to observe, that
our ancestors used *censure* precisely as we now do judgment:
sometimes for a quality of the mind, and, sometimes for a judi-
cial determination.

You, that have been victorious in the war,
Should, in a combat fought with words, come off
But with assured triumph.

    Leost. My deserts, sir,
If, without arrogance, I may style them such,
Arm me from doubt and fear.

    Timol. 'Tis nobly spoken.
Nor be thou daunted (howsoe'er thy fortune
Has mark'd thee out a slave) to speak thy merits:
For virtue, though in rags, may challenge more
Than vice, set off with all the trim of greatness.

    Mar. I had rather fall under so just a judge,
Than be acquitted by a man corrupt,
And partial, in his censure.

    Archid. Note his language;
It relishes of better breeding than
His present state dares promise.

    Timol. I observe it.
Place the fair lady in the midst, that both,
Looking with covetous eyes upon the prize
They are to plead for, may, from the fair object,
Teach Hermes eloquence.

    Leost. Am I fallen so low?[7]
My birth, my honour, and, what's dearest to
    me,
My love, and, witness of my love, my service,
So undervalued, that I must contend
With one, where my excess of glory must
Make his o'erthrow a conquest? Shall my fulness
Supply defects in such a thing, that never

---

    [7] *Am I fallen so low, &c.*] From Ovid, as Mr. Gilchrist observes:

        ——*Demit honorem*
Æmulus Ajaci, non est tenuisse superbum
Si licet hoc ingens, quidquid speravit Ulysses,
Iste tulit pretium jam nunc certaminis hujus
Quo cum victus erit mecum certasse feretur.

                        Met. Lib. xiii.

Knew any thing but want and emptiness,
Give him a name, and keep it such, from this
Unequal competition? If my pride,
Or any bold assurance of my worth,
Has pluck'd this mountain of disgrace upon me,
I am justly punish'd, and submit; but if
I have been modest, and esteem'd myself
More injured in the tribute of the praise,
Which no desert of mine, prized by self-love,
Ever exacted, may this cause and minute
For ever be forgotten! I dwell long
Upon mine anger, and now turn to you,
Ungrateful fair one; and, since you are such,
'Tis lawful for me to proclaim myself,
And what I have deserved.

    Cleo. Neglect and scorn
From me, for this proud vaunt.

    Leost. You nourish, lady,
Your own dishonour in this harsh reply,
And almost prove what some hold of your sex,
You are all made up of passion: for, if reason
Or judgment could find entertainment with you,
Or that you would distinguish of the objects
You look on, in a true glass, not seduced
By the false light of your too violent will,
I should not need to plead for that which you,
With joy, should offer. Is my high birth a
    blemish?
Or does my wealth, which all the vain expense
Of women cannot waste, breed loathing in you?
The honours I can call mine own, thought
    scandals?
Am I deform'd, or, for my father's sins,
Mulcted by nature? If you interpret these
As crimes, 'tis fit I should yield up myself
Most miserably guilty. But, perhaps,
(Which yet I would not credit,) you have seen

q

This gallant pitch the bar, or bear a burthen
Would crack the shoulders of a weaker bondman:
Or any other boisterous exercise,
Assuring a strong back to satisfy
Your loose desires, insatiate as the grave.
    Cleo. You are foul-mouth'd.
    Archid. Ill-manner'd too.
    Leost. I speak
In the way of supposition, and entreat you,
With all the fervour of a constant lover,
That you would free yourself from these asper-
    sions,
Or any imputation black-tongued slander
Could throw on your unspotted virgin whiteness:
To which there is no easier way, than by
Vouchsafing him your favour; him, to whom,
Next to the general, and the gods and fautors,[8]
The country owes her safety.
    Timag. Are you stupid?
'Slight, leap into his arms, and there ask pardon—
Oh! you expect your slave's reply; no doubt
We shall have a fine oration: I will teach
My spaniel to howl in sweeter language,
And keep a better method.
    Archid. You forget
The dignity of the place.
    Diph. Silence!
    Timol. [*to Marullo.*] Speak boldly.
    Mar. 'Tis your authority gives me a tongue,
I should be dumb else; and I am secure,

[8] *Next to the general, and the gods and* fautors,] So read both the quartos: the modern editors not knowing what to make of *the gods and fautors,* (which, in the language of the author, means the *favouring* gods,) accommodate the line to their own conceptions with wonderous facility, and read:
    Next to the general, and to the gods.
Alas, for Massinger!

I cannot clothe my thoughts, and just defence,
In such an abject phrase, but 'twill appear
Equal, if not above my low condition.
I need no bombast language stolen from such
As make nobility from prodigious terms
The hearers understand not; I bring with me
No wealth to boast of, neither can I number
Uncertain fortune's favours with my merits;
I dare not force affection, or presume
To censure her discretion, that looks on me
As a weak man, and not her fancy's idol.
How I have loved, and how much I have suffer'd,
And with what pleasure undergone the burthen
Of my ambitious hopes, (in aiming at
The glad possession of a happiness,
The abstract of all goodness in mankind
Can at no part deserve,) with my confession
Of mine own wants, is all that can plead for me.
But if that pure desires, not blended with
Foul thoughts, that, like a river, keeps his course,
Retaining still the clearness of the spring
From whence it took beginning, may be thought
Worthy acceptance; then I dare rise up,
And tell this gay man to his teeth, I never
Durst doubt her constancy, that, like a rock,
Beats off temptations, as that mocks the fury
Of the proud waves; nor, from my jealous fears,
Question that goodness to which, as an altar
Of all perfection, he that truly loved
Should rather bring a sacrifice of service,
Than raze it with the engines of suspicion:
Of which, when he can wash an Æthiop white,
Leosthenes may hope to free himself;
But, till then, never.
    Timag. Bold, presumptuous villain!
    Mar. I will go further, and make good upon
      him,

I' the pride of all his honours, birth, and fortunes,
He's more unworthy than myself.

    Leost. Thou liest.

    Timag. Confute him with a whip, and, the
        doubt decided,
Punish him with a halter.

    Mar. O the gods!
My ribs, though made of brass, cannot contain
My heart, swollen big with rage. The lie!—a
    whip!—
Let fury then disperse these clouds, in which
I long have march'd disguised;[9] [*Throws off his
      disguise.*] that, when they know
Whom they have injured, they may faint with
    horror
Of my revenge, which, wretched men! expect,
As sure as fate, to suffer.

    Leost. Ha! Pisander!

    Timag. 'Tis the bold Theban!

    Asot. There's no hope for me then:
I thought I should have put in for a share,
And born Cleora from them both; but now,
This stranger looks so terrible, that I dare not
So much as look on her.

    Pisan. Now as myself,
Thy equal at thy best, Leosthenes.
For you, Timagoras, praise heaven you were born
Cleora's brother, 'tis your safest armour.
But I lose time,—The base lie cast upon me,
I thus return: Thou art a perjured man,
False, and perfidious, and hast made a tender
Of love and service to this lady, when

   9 *Let fury then disperse the clouds in which*
   I long have march'd *disguised;*] The old copies read *mask'd;*
but this seems so unworthy of the author, that I have not
scrupled to place the other word (march'd) in the text. I believe
that Massinger had the first Æneid in his thoughts.

Thy soul, if thou hast any, can bear witness,
That thou wert not thine own: for proof of this,
Look better on this virgin, and consider,
This Persian shape laid by,[1] and she appearing
In a Greekish dress, such as when first you saw her,
If she resemble not Pisander's sister,
One call'd Statilia?

Leost. 'Tis the same! My guilt
So chokes my spirits, I cannot deny
My falsehood, nor excuse it.

Pisan. This is she,
To whom thou wert contracted: this the lady,
That, when thou wert my prisoner, fairly taken
In the Spartan war, that, begg'd thy liberty,
And with it gave herself to thee, ungrateful!

Statil. No more, sir, I entreat you: I perceive
True sorrow in his looks, and a consent
To make me reparation in mine honour;
And then I am most happy.

Pisan. The wrong done her,
Drew me from Thebes, with a full intent to kill
thee:
But this fair object met me in my fury,
And quite disarm'd me. Being denied to have her,
By you, my lord Archidamus, and not able
To live far from her; love, the mistress of
All quaint devices, prompted me to treat
With a friend of mine, who, as a pirate, sold me
For a slave to you, my lord, and gave my sister,
As a present, to Cleora.

Timol. Strange meanders!

---

[1] *This Persian* shape *laid by,*] i. e. the *dress* of a Persian
slave, which Statilia had assumed, with the name of Timandra.
Shape is a term borrowed from the tiring-room of the theatres.
In the list of dramatis personæ prefixed to *the Virgin Martyr*,
Harpax is said to be, " an evil spirit following Theophilus in
the *shape* (habit) of a secretary."

Pisan. There how I bare myself, needs no
  relation :
But, if so far descending from the height
Of my then flourishing fortunes, to the lowest
Condition of a man, to have means only
To feed my eye with the sight of what I honour'd;
The dangers too I underwent, the sufferings;
The clearness of my interest, may deserve
A noble recompense in your lawful favour;
Now 'tis apparent that Leosthenes
Can claim no interest in you, you may please
To think upon my service.
  Cleo. Sir, my want
Of power to satisfy so great a debt,
Makes me accuse my fortune; but if that,
Out of the bounty of your mind, you think
A free surrender of myself full payment,
I gladly tender it.
  Archid. With my consent too,
All injuries forgotten.
  Timag. I will study,
In my future service, to deserve your favour,
And good opinion.
  Leost. Thus I gladly fee.
This advocate to plead for me.   [*Kissing Statilia.*
  Pisan. You will find me
An easy judge. When I have yielded reasons
Of your bondmen's falling off from their obe-
  dience,
Then after, as you please, determine of me.
I found their natures apt to mutiny
From your too cruel usage, and made trial
How far they might be wrought on; to instruct
  you
To look with more prevention and care
To what they may hereafter undertake
Upon the like occasions. The hurt's little

They have committed; nor was ever cure,
But with some pain, effected. I confess,
In hope to force a grant of fair Cleora,
I urged them to defend the town against you;
Nor had the terror of your whips, but that
I was preparing for defence elsewhere,
So soon got entrance :[2] In this I am guilty;
Now, as you please, your censure.
    Timol. Bring them in;
And, though you've given me power, I do
      entreat
Such as have undergone their insolence,
It may not be offensive, though I study
Pity, more than revenge.
    Coris. 'Twill best become you.
    Cleon. I must consent.
    Asot. For me, I'll find a time
To be revenged hereafter.

Enter GRACCULO, CIMBRIO, POLIPHRON, ZAN-
    THIA, *and the other Slaves, with halters about
    their necks.*

    Grac. Give me leave;
I'll speak for all.
    Timol. What canst thou say, to hinder
The course of justice?
    Grac. Nothing.—You may see
We are prepared for hanging, and confess
We have deserved it : our most humble suit is,
We may not twice be executed.

    [2] *Nor had the terror of your whips, but that
      I was preparing for defence elsewhere,
       So soon got entrance :*] I am pleased with this, because it
looks as if the author was sensible of the improbability of the
circumstance. It is, indeed, the only defective part of this
beautiful story. See p. 81.

Timol. Twice!
How mean'st thou?

Grac. At the gallows first, and after in a ballad
Sung to some villainous tune. There are ten-
      groat rhymers
About the town, grown fat on these occasions.
Let but a chapel fall, or a street be fired,[3]
A foolish lover hang himself for pure love,

[3] *Let but a* chapel fall, *or a* street be fired, &c.] There is
much good humour, as well as truth, in these remarks. They
are, it must be confessed, strangely out of time, and still more
strangely out of place; but the readers of our old dramatists
must be prepared, as they have more than once been reminded,
to overlook such anomalies.

Much of the wit, and more perhaps of the interest, of our old
dramas, is irretrievably lost through our ignorance of collateral
circumstances. A thousand temporary allusions are received
with indifference, or perhaps escape us altogether, which excited
the strongest sensations of pleasure and pain in the bosoms of
our ancestors. This play was performed for the first time
December 3d, 1623; and on the 24th of October, in the same
year, a *chapel*, or, as the continuator of Stow calls it, a *chamber,
fell down* " in Hunsdon House, in the Black Fryars, where was
assembled above three hundred men, women, and youths, to
hear a Romane Catholique priest preach, in which *fall* was
slaine the preacher, and almost one hundred of his auditory, and
well nigh as many more hurt." Immediately after this, follows
an article of *firing a street*: " Wednesday the 12th of November,
1623, one of the warehouses of sir W. Cockayne," (a name
familiar to Massinger,) " knight, alderman of London, in
Broad Street, took *fire* in the evening, and ceased not till two
o' the clock the next morning, in which space it burnt his whole
house, and three of his neighbours' houses, to the great danger
and damage of many neere inhabitants," &c. *Annales,* p. 1035,
ed. 1631.

These apposite references, for which I am indebted to Mr.
Gilchrist, prove, I think, that the tragicel events in Gracculo's
speech were not the suggestions of fancy. The *foolish lover,* who
hung himself *for pure love,* was perhaps beneath the notice of the
Chronicler; but I suspect that, if we could have recourse to the
d——d *ditties* of the day, we should find his melancholy story
to be no less real than the other unfortunate occurrences.

Or any such like accident, and, before
They are cold in their graves, some damn'd ditty's
    made,
Which makes their ghosts walk.—Let the state
    take order
For the redress of this abuse, recording
'Twas done by my advice, and, for my part,
I'll cut as clean a caper from the ladder,
As ever merry Greek did.
    Timol. Yet I think
You would shew more activity to delight
Your master for a pardon.
    Grac. O! I would dance,
As I were all air and fire.   *[Capers.*
    Timol. And ever be
Obedient and humble?
    Grac. As his spaniel,
Though he kick'd me for exercise; and the like
I promise for all the rest.
    Timol. Rise then, you have it.
    All the Slaves. Timoleon! Timoleon!
    Timol. Cease these clamours.
And now, the war being ended to our wishes,
And such as went the pilgrimage of love,
Happy in full fruition of their hopes,
'Tis lawful, thanks paid to the Powers divine,
To drown our cares in honest mirth and wine.
        [Exeunt. *

* Massinger never writes with more effect, than when he combines his own fancy with somewhat of real history. In this case, the reader will not expect that the history should proceed in a regular order, or without the admission of foreign incidents, or that it should maintain to the end, the commanding interest with which it begins. It is enough for Massinger if he can secure attention at the outset, through the remembrance of some important event, and if, under cover of this, he can prepare the part which imagination is to supply. It is on these principles he has proceeded in *the Bondman,* and produced a piece which,

with a few exceptions, is at once stately and playful, impressive
and tender. He matures the love under cover of the history;
till at length the interest changes, and the history becomes subordinate to the love.

The characters are drawn with much variety and interest;
the modest gravity and self-command of Timoleon well agree
with the ancient descriptions of the man, from whose mouth
nihil unquam insolens, neque gloriosum exiit; and our admiration
of the heroic Pisander, who cannot appear in his proper character till towards the conclusion, is skilfully excited by early
notices apparently incidental, of his great powers of body, his
language, sentiments, &c. far above his supposed condition.
His signal temperance, the charm which wins the pure Cleora,
is well contrasted with the unreasonable distrust and jealousy
of Leosthenes, who, however, observes, with much self-com-
placency, while he mars his own happiness by his impatience,
that women have but little judgment, and are mostly made up
of passion! It may be remarked here, that Massinger seems
fond of punishing his men for undue suspicions and alarms in
matters of love; and that this is one of the methods which he
takes to exalt the character of his females, and to exhibit, as in
Cleora, the complete ascendence of chastity over jealousy. Other
marks of his accustomed management appear in this play. He
is fond of fulfilling expressions in a sense not intended by the
speakers. Timagoras unconsciously says that Pisander was
" bought for his sister's service ;" and Archidamus bids him treat
her with particular " care and reverence," the very circumstance
which gains her affections. In *the Duke of Milan* too, Sforza
and Marcelia, wish that, after a life of unvaried happiness, " one
grave may receive them ;" and they are buried together, after
she has fallen by his hand. He is fond of reserving some injured
person, whose late appearance may justify what has been done,
and hasten the conclusion of the plot. He reserves Statilia for
the sake of vindicating Pisander, and reminds us of Eugenia,
whose wrongs explain the vengeance of Francisco. He is also
fond of throwing his lovers into difficulties, by confessing their
attachment, while those who are interested in opposing it, listen
from behind. Cleora precipitates her expressions of kindness
for Pisander, that her family may be enraged at the discovery.
And a similar contrivance will by and by strike the reader, in the
plot of *the Renegado,* where Donusa and Vitelli are overheard
by Asambeg and Mustapha.

The comic characters are not without their merit, always
excepting the licentiousness which stains them; licentiousness,
however, which, fortunately, is neither spirited nor attractive.
The slaves turned masters, " fret their hour" in their new dig-

nity, with becoming insolence. It is a fine stroke of nature which Plautus has given to one of his slaves: suddenly growing rich, and laying the plan of his future enjoyments, he determines to have slaves of his own :

———*domum instruam, agram, ædis,* mancipia,

Rudens, Act. IV. sc. ii.

If Massinger is to be suspected of political allusions, this play betrays him. The character of Gisco the admiral does not suit him, but agrees very well with the duke of Buckingham :

" ——— a raw young fellow,
" One never train'd in arms, but rather fashion'd
" To tilt with ladies' lips, than crack a lance," &c.

The " green heads that determine of the state over their cups," &c. were now in possession of all power, and playing their wildest schemes. And towards the end of the reign of James, (the date of this play,) it might well be said, by the friends to the safety of their country :

" ——— in this plenty
" And fat of peace, your young men ne'er were train'd
" In martial discipline ; and your ships unrigg'd,
" Rot in the harbour."———

One of those friends of his country was Massinger; and it is hardly possible to point out, in any writer ancient or modern, a finer strain of patriotism amidst the public danger, than that which animates the last scene of the first act.

THE

RENEGADO.

THE RENEGADO.] This Tragi-Comedy, for so Massinger terms it, appears, from the Office-book of the Master of the Revels, to have been first produced on the stage, April 17th, 1624: it was not given to the public till several years after; the entry, in the Stationer's Register, bearing date March 6th, 1629-30.

The story, though wild and extravagant, is not all, perhaps, invention; the pirates of Tunis and Algiers ravaged the northern coasts of the Mediterranean at pleasure; and the Spanish and Italian writers of those days are full of adventures similar to this before us; some of which were undoubtedly founded in fact.

The language and ideas of this play are strictly Catholic; notwithstanding which, it seems to have been a favourite with the public; and even the modest author speaks of its merits with some degree of complacency. It was not, however, re-printed.

It is said, in the title-page, to have been "often acted by the Queen's Majesties Servants, at the private Play-house in Drury Lane." After the death of queen Anne, in 1618, (as Mr. Malone informs me,) the players at this house were called, the *Lady Elizabeth's Servants,* (i. e. James's daughter, then married to the Palsgrave,) although she was not in England: but after the marriage of Charles, they took the name of the *Queen's Servants;* i. e. of Henrietta Maria. The denomination, therefore, in the title-page of the old play, alludes to the time of its publication, and not to that of its "allowance;" when, as it appears from the first edition of *the Bondman,* 1624, the players were still in possession of the former appellation.

TO

The Right Honourable

GEORGE HARDING,

BARON BERKELEY, OF BERKELEY CASTLE, AND KNIGHT OF THE HONOURABLE ORDER OF THE BATH.*

MY GOOD LORD,

T O be honoured for old nobility, or hereditary titles, is not alone proper to yourself, but to some few of your rank, who may challenge the like privilege with you: but in our age to vouchsafe (as you have often done) a ready hand to raise the dejected spirits of the contemned sons of the Muses; such as would not suffer the glorious fire of poesy to be wholly extinguished, is so remarkable and peculiar to your lordship, that with a full vote and suffrage, it is acknowledged that the patronage and protection of the dramatic poem, is yours, and almost without a rival. I despair not therefore, but that my ambition to present my service in this kind, may in your clemency meet with a gentle interpretation, Confirm it, my good lord, in your gracious acceptance of this trifle; in which, if I were not confident there are some pieces worthy the perusal, it should have been taught an humbler flight; and the writer, your countryman, never yet made happy in your notice and favour, had not made this an advocate to plead for his admission among such as are wholly and sincerely devoted to your service. I may live to tender my humble thankfulness in some higher strain; and till then, comfort myself with hope, that you descend from your height to receive

Your honour's commanded servant,

PHILIP MASSINGER.

* He was made a knight of the Bath at the creation of Charles Prince of Wales, November 4th, 1616: three years after he succeeded his grandfather, Henry, eleventh lord Berkeley.

DRAMATIS PERSONÆ. ACTORS' NAMES.

Asambeg, *viceroy of* Tunis,	John Blanye
Mustapha, *basha of* Aleppo,	John Sumner.
Vitelli, *a Venetian gentleman, disguised as a merchant,*	Mich. Bowyer.
Francisco, *a Jesuit,*	Wm. Reignalds.
Antonio Grimaldi, the RENEGADO,	Wm. Allen.
Carazie, *an eunuch,*	Wm. Robins.
Gazet, *servant to* Vitelli,	Ed. Shakerley.
Aga.	
Capiaga.	
Janizaries.	
Master.	
Boatswain.	
Sailors.	
A Gaoler. Turks.	

Donusa, *niece to* Amurath,	Ed. Rogers.
Paulina, *sister to* Vitelli,	Theo. Bourne.
Manto, *servant to* Donusa,	

SCENE, Tunis.

THE

RENEGADO.

ACT I. SCENE I.

A Street near the Bazar.

Enter VITELLI *and* GAZET.

Vitel. You have hired a shop, then?
Gaz. Yes, sir; and our wares,
Though brittle as a maidenhead at sixteen,
Are safe unladen; not a crystal crack'd,
Or China dish needs soldering; our choice pic-
 tures,
As they came from the workman, without blemish:
And I have studied speeches for each piece,
And, in a thrifty tone, to sell them off,
Will swear by Mahomet and Termagant,[1]

---

[1] *Will swear by Mahomet and* Termagant,] Dr. Percy, in his
remarks on the ancient ballad of *King Estmere,* says, that
Termagant is the name given by the authors of the old romances
to the god of the Saracens: and as he was generally represented
as a very furious being, the word Termagant was applied to any
person of a turbulent outrageous disposition, though at present
it is appropriated to the female sex. M. MASON.
  I have retained a part of this note, though there is little in it.
Our zealous ancestors, who were somewhat of sir Andrew's way
of thinking, and cordially disposed to beat the Turks like dogs,
for being Mahomedans, innocently charged them with deities
whom they never acknowledged. Termagant, whether derived
from the Saxon, or (which, in this case, is nearly the same)
from the Latin, cannot possibly be a Saracenic divinity; the

That this is mistress to the great duke of Florence,
That, niece to old king Pepin, and a third,
An Austrian princess by her Roman nose,
Howe'er my conscience tells me they are figures
Of bawds and common courtezans in Venice.

    Vitel. You make no scruple of an oath, then?

    Gaz. Fie, sir!
'Tis out of my indentures; I am bound there,
To swear for my master's profit, as securely
As your intelligencer[2] must for his prince,
That sends him forth an honourable spy,
To serve his purposes. And, if it be lawful
In a Christian shopkeeper to cheat his father,
I cannot find but to abuse a Turk
In the sale of our commodities, must be thought
A meritorious work.

    Vitel. I wonder, sirrah,
What's your religion?

    Gaz. Troth, to answer truly,
I would not be of one that should command me
To feed upon poor John,[3] when I see pheasants

---

word was originally used, I suppose, as an attribute of the
Supreme Being of the Saxons, a people little less odious to our
romance writers, than the Saracens, and sometimes confounded
with them.

    2   ——— *I am bound there,*
To swear for my master's profit, as securely
As your intelligencer, &c.] Here is, probably, an allusion to
the celebrated definition of an ambassador, by sir Henry
Wotton: "An honest man appointed to *lye* abroad for the good
of his country." A definition, by the bye, which cost him dear,
for sir Henry, not satisfied with entertaining his countrymen,
would needs translate his wit into Latin, for the amusement of
foreigners. *Lye*, which was then the term for lodge or dwell,
made a tolerable pun; but *mentiendum*, into which it was turned,
had neither humour nor ambiguity in it, and sorely scandalized
the corps diplomatic.

    2 *To feed upon* poor John,] *Poor John*, Mr. Malone says, is
hake, dried and salted.

And partridges on the table : nor do I like
The other, that allows us to eat flesh
In Lent, though it be rotten, rather than be
Thought superstitious ; as your zealous cobler,
And learned botcher, preach at Amsterdam,
Over a hotchpotch.[4] I would not be confined
In my belief : when all your sects and sec-
          taries
Are grown of one opinion, if I like it,
I will profess myself,—in the mean time,
Live I in England, Spain, France, Rome, Geneva,
I'm of that country's faith.
    Vitel. And what in Tunis ?
Will you turn Turk here ?
    Gaz. No : so I should lose
A collop of that part my Doll enjoin'd me
To bring home as she left it : 'tis her venture,
Nor dare I barter that commodity,
Without her special warrant.
    Vitel. You are a knave, sir :
Leaving your roguery, think upon my business,
It is no time to fool now.
Remember where you are too : though this mart-
          time

---

[4]   ——— *as your zealous cobler,*
And learned botcher, preach at Amsterdam,
Over a hotchpotch.] The religious troubles of Holland, in the
16th century, arose principally from the Anabaptists. There
was an insurrection at Amsterdam, headed by a tailor, a disciple
of John of Leyden, (the Munster king,) himself a tailor : but,
indeed, the toleration allowed to religious sects of all denomi-
nations, had, about this time, filled Amsterdam with fanatics
from every country in Europe. To this aggregation of zealots,
there are perpetual allusions in our old writers. Thus Shirley :
" Well, if I live, I will to *Amsterdam,* and add another
schism to the two hundred four score and odd." *Gentleman of
Venice.* And Beaumont and Fletcher : " I am a schoolmaster,
sir, and would fain confer with you about erecting four new sects
of religion at *Amsterdam.*" *The Fair Maid of the Inn.*

We are allow'd free trading, and with safety,
Temper your tongue, and meddle not with the
     Turks,
Their manners, nor religion.
   Gaz. Take you heed, sir,
What colours you wear. Not two hours since,
     there landed
An English pirate's whore, with a green apron,[5]
And, as she walked the streets, one of their
     muftis,
We call them priests at Venice, with a razor
Cuts it off, petticoat, smock and all, and leaves
     her
As naked as my nail; the young fry wondering
What strange beast it should be. I scaped a
     scouring——
My mistress's busk point, of that forbidden co-
     lour,
Then tied my codpiece; had it been discover'd,
I had been capon'd.
   Vitel. And had been well served.
Haste to the shop, and set my wares in order,
I will not long be absent.
   Gaz. Though I strive, sir,
To put off melancholy, to which you are ever
Too much inclined, it shall not hinder me,
With my best care, to serve you.   [*Exit.*

Enter FRANCISCO.

   Vitel. I believe thee.——
O welcome, sir! stay of my steps in this life,

---

5 ——————*with a* green *apron*,] It should be observed,
that this colour is appropriated solely to the descendants of
Mahomet. To " land at Tunis," or any other town professing
the Mahometan religion, in a green dress, at this day, would
perhaps cost the unwary stranger his life.

And guide to all my blessed hopes hereafter.
What comforts, sir? Have your endeavours pros-
    per'd?
Have we tired Fortune's malice with our suffer-
    ings?
Is she at length, after so many frowns,
Pleased to vouchsafe one cheerful look upon us?
    Fran. You give too much to fortune and your
    passions,
O'er which a wise man, if religious, triumphs.
That name fools worship; and those tyrants,
    which
We arm against our better part, our reason,
May add, but never take from our afflictions.
    Vitel. Sir, as I am a sinful man, I cannot
But like one suffer.
    Fran. I exact not from you
A fortitude insensible of calamity,
To which the saints themselves have bow'd and
    shown[6]
They are made of flesh and blood; all that I
    challenge,
Is manly patience. Will you, that were train'd up
In a religious school, where divine maxims,
Scorning comparison with moral precepts,
Were daily taught you, bear your constancy's trial,
Not like Vitelli, but a village nurse,
With curses in your mouth, tears in your eyes?—
How poorly it shows in you.
    Vitel. I am school'd, sir,
And will hereafter, to my utmost strength,
Study to be myself.
    Fran. So shall you find me
Most ready to assist you; neither have I
Slept in your great occasions: since I left you,

---

[6] ———— *and* shown] So the old copy: the modern
editors read, *and* shew.

I have been at the viceroy's court, and press'd,
As far as they allow, a Christian entrance ;
And something I have learn'd, that may concern
The purpose of this journey.
   Vitel. Dear sir, what is it ?
   Fran. By the command of Asambeg, the
      viceroy,
The city swells with barbarous pomp and pride,
For the entertainment of stout Mustapha,
The basha of Aleppo, who in person
Comes to receive the niece of Amurath,
The fair Donusa, for his bride.
   Vitel. I find not
How this may profit us.
   Fran. Pray you give me leave.
Among the rest that wait upon the viceroy,
Such as have, under him, command in Tunis,
Who, as you've often heard, are all false pirates,
I saw the shame of Venice, and the scorn
Of all good men, the perjured RENEGADO,
Antonio Grimaldi.
   Vitel. Ha! his name
Is poison to me.
   Fran. Yet again?
   Vitel. I have done, sir.
   Fran. This debauch'd villain, whom we ever
      thought
(After his impious scorn done, in St Mark's,
To me, as I stood at the holy altar)
The thief that ravish'd your fair sister from you.
The virtuous Paulina, not long since,
As I am truly given to understand,
Sold to the viceroy a fair Christian virgin
On whom, maugre his fierce and cruel nature,
Asambeg dotes extremely,
   Vitel. 'Tis my sister:
It must be she, my better angel tells me

'Tis poor Paulina.   Farewell all disguises!
I'll show, in my revenge, that I am noble.
  Fran. You are not mad?
  Vitel. No, sir; my virtuous anger
Makes every vein an artery; I feel in me
The strength of twenty men; and, being arm'd
With my good cause, to wreak' wrong'd inno-
    cence,
I dare alone run to the viceroy's court,
And with this poniard, before his face,
Dig out Grimaldi's heart.
  Fran. Is this religious?
  Vitel. Would you have me tame now? Can I
    know my sister
Mew'd up in his seraglio, and in danger
Not alone to lose her honour, but her soul;
The hell-bred villain by too, that has sold both
To black destruction, and not haste to send him
To the devil, his tutor? To be patient now,
Were, in another name, to play the pander
To the viceroy's loose embraces, and cry aim!'
While he, by force or flattery, compels her
To yield her fair name up to his foul lust,
And, after, turn apostata to the faith
That she was bred in.
  Fran. Do but give me hearing,
And you shall soon grant how ridiculous
This childish fury is. A wise man never
Attempts impossibilities; 'tis as easy
For any single arm to quell an army,
As to effect your wishes. We come hither

---

⁷ ——————· *to* wreak *wrong'd innocence,*] i. e. **to revenge**;
so in *the Fatal Dowry*, Vol. III.
   " But there's a heaven above, from whose just *wreak*
   " No mists of policy can hide offenders."
⁸ ——————— *and cry* aim!] Sanction or encourage. See *the
Bondman*, p. 27.

To learn Paulina's fate,[9] and to redeem her:
Leave your revenge to heaven.   I oft have told
     you
Of a relic[1] that I gave her, which has power,
If we may credit holy men's traditions,
To keep the owner free from violence:
This on her breast she wears, and does preserve
The virtue of it, by her daily prayers.
So, if she fall not by her own consent,
Which it were sin to think, I fear no force.
Be, therefore, patient; keep this borrow'd shape,
Till time and opportunity present us
With some fit means to see her; which perform'd,
I'll join with you in any desperate course
For her delivery.
     Vitel. You have charm'd me, sir,
And I obey in all things : pray you, pardon
The weakness of my passion.
     Faan. And excuse it.
Be cheerful, man, for know that good intents
Are, in the end, crown'd with as fair events.
                              [*Exeunt.*

9 *To learn Paulina's* fate,] The old copy reads *faith ;* the alteration, which seems judicious, was made by Mr. M. Mason.
     1 ———————— *I oft have told you*
Of a relic that I gave her, &c.] I have already observed, that
the language of this play is Catholic : the idea, however, of the
power of relics, in the preservation of chastity, may be found
in many old romances and books of knight-errantry, which were
undoubtedly familiar to Massinger.

SCENE II.

A Room in Donusa's *Palace.*

Enter Donusa, Manto, *and* Carazie.

Don. Have you seen the Christian captive,
The great basha is so enamour'd of?
Mant. Yes, an it please your excellency,
I took a full view of her, when she was
Presented to him.
Don. And is she such a wonder,
As 'tis reported?
Mant. She was drown'd in tears then,
Which took much from her beauty; yet, in spite
Of sorrow, she appear'd the mistress of
Most rare perfections; and, though low of stature,
Her well-proportion'd limbs invite affection:
And, when she speaks, each syllable is music
That does enchant the hearers: but your high-
ness,[3]
That are not to be parallell'd, I yet never
Beheld her equal.
Don. Come, you flatter me;
But I forgive it. We, that are born great,
Seldom distaste[3] our servants, though they give us

---

2   ——————— but *your highness,*] i. e. *except* your
highness, &c. In the next line the modern editors had so trans-
posed the words, as to make it downright prose: it is now re-
formed.

3   ———————*We, that are born great,*
Seldom distaste *our servants, though they give us*
More than we can pretend to.] i. e. *dislike;* in which sense the

More than we can pretend to. I have heard
That Christian ladies live with much more freedom
Than such as are born here. Our jealous Turks,
Never permit their fair wives to be seen,
But at the public bagnios, or the mosques,
And, even then, veil'd and guarded. Thou, Ca-
       razie,
Wert born in England; what's the custom there,
Among your women? Come, be free and merry :
I am no severe mistress; nor hast thou met with
A heavy bondage.
    Car. Heavy ! I was made lighter
By two stone weight, at least, to be fit to serve
       you.
But to your question, madam; women in England,
For the most part, live like queens. Your coun-
       try ladies
Have liberty to hawk, to hunt, to feast,
To give free entertainment to all comers,
To talk, to kiss; there's no such thing known
       there
As an Italian girdle. Your city dame,
Without leave, wears the breeches, has her hus-
       band
At as much command as her prentice; and, if
       need be,
Can make him cuckold by her father's copy.
    Don. But your court lady?
    Car. She, I assure you, madam,
Knows nothing but her will; must be allow'd

word frequently occurs. Thus Shirley, in the Epilogue to *Love
in a Maze* :
       "   ————————— he desires that you
       " Should not *distaste* his muse, because of late
       " Transplanted," &c.

Her footmen, her caroch,[4] her ushers, pages,
Her doctor, chaplains; and, as I have heard,
They're grown of late so learn'd, that they main-
    tain
A strange position, which their lords, with all
Their wit, cannot confute.
    Don. What's that, I prithee?
    Car. Marry, that it is not only fit, but lawful,
Your madam there, her much rest and high
    feeding
Duly consider'd, should, to ease her husband,
Be allow'd a private friend : they have drawn a
    bill
To this good purpose, and, the next assembly,
Doubt not to pass it.
    Don. We enjoy no more,
That are o' the Othoman race, though our religion
Allows all pleasure.   I am dull : some music.
Take my chapines [5] off.   So, a lusty strain.
             [*A galliard. Knocking within.*
Who knocks there?
          [*Manto goes to the door, and returns.*
    Mant. 'Tis the basha of Aleppo,
Who humbly makes request he may present
His service to you.
    Don. Reach a chair.   We must

----

[4] *Her footmen, her caroch, her ushers, pages,*] If the reader
would have a promising specimen of what can be done by a nice
ear in editing an ancient poet, let him cast an eye on this line,
as it stands in Coxeter and Mr. M. Mason :
    Her footmen, her coach, her ushers, her pages,
tum-ti-ti, tum-ti-ti, &c. Dactylics, a little lame.

[5] *Take my* chapines *off.*] *Chapines* (Spanish, and not Italian,
as the commentators on Shakspeare assert) are a kind of clogs
with thick cork soles, which the ladies wear on their shoes
when they go abroad.   They are mentioned by most of our old
dramatists.

             * L 2

Receive him like ourself, and not depart[6] with
One piece of ceremony, state, and greatness,
That may beget respect and reverence
In one that's born our vassal. Now admit him.

Enter Mustapha ; *he puts off his yellow pantofles.*

   Musta. The place is sacred ; and I am to enter
The room where she abides, with such devotion
As pilgrims pay at Mecca, when they visit
The tomb of our great prophet.   [*Kneels.*
   Don. Rise ; the sign
            [*Carazie takes up the pantofles.*
That we vouchsafe your presence.
   Musta. May those Powers
That raised the Othoman empire, and still guard it,
Reward your highness for this gracious favour
You throw upon your servant ! It hath pleased
The most invincible, mightiest Amurath,
(To speak his other titles would take from him
That in himself does comprehend all greatness,)
To make me the unworthy instrument
Of his command. Receive, divinest lady,
           [*Delivers a letter.*
This letter, sign'd by his victorious hand,
And made authentic by the imperial seal.
There, when you find me mention'd, far be it from
    you
To think it my ambition to presume
At such a happiness, which his powerful will,
From his great mind's magnificence, not my merit,

---

  [6]   ——— —— *and not* depart *with* &c.] **To** *depart*
and *part* were anciently synonymous. Thus Jonson :
    " He that *departs* with his own honesty
    " For vulgar praise, doth it too dearly buy." *Epig.* ii.

Hath shower'd upon me.   But, if your consent
Join with his good opinion and allowance,
To perfect what his favours have begun,
I shall, in my obsequiousness and duty,
Endeavour [7] to prevent all just complaints,
Which want of will to serve you may call on me.
  Don. His sacred majesty writes here, that your
        valour
Against the Persian hath so won upon him,
That there's no grace or honour in his gift,
Of which he can imagine you unworthy;
And, what's the greatest you can hope, or aim at,
It is his pleasure you should be received
Into his royal family—provided,
For so far I am unconfined, that I
Affect and like your person.   I expect not
The ceremony which he uses in
Bestowing of his daughters and his nieces:
As that he should present you for my slave,
To love you, if you pleased me; or deliver
A poniard, on my least dislike, to kill you.
Such tyranny and pride agree not with
My softer disposition.   Let it suffice,
For my first answer, that thus far I grace you:
                    [*Gives him her hand to kiss.*
Hereafter, some time spent to make enquiry
Of the good parts and faculties of your mind,
You shall hear further from me.
  Musta. Though all torments
Really suffer'd, or in hell imagined

7 *I shall in my obsequiousness and duty*
    Endeavour &c.] This, and what follows, are pretty correct
specimens of the manner in which the great officers of the state
are still said to pay their addresses to the princesses of the imperial family.   The age of Massinger produced many good his-
tories of the Turks: he follows them, however, by starts only,
for in none of his plays are the manners of different countries
so mingled and confounded as in this.

By curious fiction, in one hour's delay
Are wholly comprehended; I confess
That I stand bound in duty, not to check at
Whatever you command, or please to impose,
For trial of my patience.

    Don. Let us find
Some other subject; too much of one theme cloys
      me:
Is't a full mart?

    Musta. A confluence of all nations
Are met together: there's variety, too,
Of all that merchants traffic for.

    Don. I know not—
I feel a virgin's longing to descend
So far from my own greatness, as to be,
Though not a buyer, yet a looker on
Their strange commodities.

    Musta. If without a train
You dare be seen abroad, I'll dismiss mine,
And wait upon you as a common man,
And satisfy your wishes.

    Don. I embrace it.
Provide my veil; and, at the postern gate,
Convey us out unseen. I trouble you.

    Musta. It is my happiness you deign to com-
      mand me.   [*Exeunt.*

SCENE III.

The Bazar.

Gazet *in his Shop;* Francisco *and* Vitelli
walking before it.

    Gaz. What do you lack?[8] Your choice China

  [8] *What do you lack?* &c.] Gazet adopts the identical language

dishes, your pure Venetian crystal of all sorts, of all neat and new fashions, from the mirror of the madam, to the private utensil of her chambermaid ; and curious pictures of the rarest beauties of Europe : What do you lack, gentlemen?

Fran. Take heed, I say ; howe'er it may appear
Impertinent, I must express my love,
My advice, and counsel. You are young, Vitelli,⁹
And may be tempted ; and these Turkish dames,
(Like English mastiffs, that increase their fierceness
By being chain'd up,) from the restraint of freedom,
If lust once fire their blood from a fair object,
Will run a course the fiends themselves would shake at,
To enjoy their wanton ends.

Vitel. Sir, you mistake me :
I am too full of woe, to entertain
One thought of pleasure, though all Europe's queens
Kneel'd at my feet, and courted me ; much less
To mix with such, whose difference of faith
Must, of necessity, (or I must grant
Myself neglectful of all you have taught me,)
Strangle such base desires.

Fran. Be constant in
That resolution ; I'll abroad again,
And learn, as far as it is possible.

---

which Massinger heard every day in passing the streets of London. The expression was so common, that our old dramatists characterize the citizens by it. Thus in *Philaster*, the Captain frequently exclaims to the shop-keepers who had taken arms, " Come, my dear *what-do-you-lacks !* &c.

⁹ —————— *You are young*, Vitelli,] I have added the name, which seems to have dropt out at the press, to complete the verse.

What may concern Paulina.   Some two hours
Shall bring me back.   [*Exit.*

 Vitel. All blessings wait upon you!

 Gaz. Cold doings, sir? a mart do you call
  this? 'slight!
A pudding-wife, or a witch with a thrum cap,
That sells ale underground to such as come
To know their fortunes in a dead vacation,
Have, ten to one, more stirring.

 Vitel. We must be patient.

 Gaz. Your seller by retail ought to be angry,
But when he's fingering money.

Enter GRIMALDI, Master, Boatswain, Sailors, *and*
    Turks.

 Vitel. Here are company——
Defend me, my good angel, [*seeing Grimaldi.*] I
  behold
A basilisk!

 Gaz. What do you lack? what do you lack?
pure China dishes, clear crystal glasses, a dumb
mistress to make love to?   What do you lack,
gentlemen?

 Grim. Thy mother for a bawd; or, if thou hast
A handsome one, thy sister for a whore;
Without these, do not tell me of your trash,
Or I shall spoil your market.

 Vitel. —Old Grimaldi!

 Grim. 'Zounds, wherefore do we put to sea, or
  stand
The raging winds, aloft, or p—— upon
The foamy waves, when they rage most; deride
The thunder of the enemy's shot, board boldly
A merchant's ship for prize, though we behold
The desperate gunner ready to give fire,
And blow the deck up? wherefore shake we off

Those scrupulous rags of charity and conscience,
Invented only to keep churchmen warm,
Or feed the hungry mouths of famish'd beggars;
But, when we touch the shore, to wallow in
All sensual pleasures?

Mast. Ay, but, noble captain,
To spare a little for an after-clap,
Were not improvidence.

Grim. Hang consideration!
When this is spent, is not our ship the same,
Our courage too the same, to fetch in more?
The earth, where it is fertilest, returns not
More than three harvests, while the glorious sun
Posts through the zodiac, and makes up the year:
But the sea, which is our mother, (that embraces
Both the rich Indies in her outstretch'd arms,)
Yields every day a crop, if we dare reap it.
No, no, my mates, let tradesmen think of thrift,
And usurers hoard up; let our expense
Be, as our comings in are, without bounds.
We are the Neptunes of the ocean,
And such as traffic shall pay sacrifice
Of their best lading; I will have this canvass
Your boy wears, lined with tissue, and the cates
You taste, serv'd up in gold:—Though we carouse
The tears of orphans in our Greekish wines,
The sighs of undone widows paying for
The music bought to cheer us, ravish'd virgins
To slavery sold, for coin to feed our riots,
We will have no compunction.

Gaz. Do you hear, sir?
We have paid for our ground.

Grim. Hum!

Gaz. And hum, too!
For all your big words, get you further off,
And hinder not the prospect of our shop,
Or ————

Grim. What will you do?

Gaz. Nothing, sir—but pray
Your worship to give me handsel.

Grim. [*Seizing him.*] By the ears,
Thus, sir, by the ears.

Mast. Hold, hold!

Vitel. You'll still be prating.

Grim. Come, let's be drunk; then each man to
    his whore.
'Slight, how do you look? you had best go find
    a corner
To pray in, and repent: do, do, and cry;
It will shew fine in pirates.   [*Exit.*

Mast. We must follow,
Or he will spend our shares.

Boatsw. I fought for mine.

Mast. Nor am I so precise but I can drab too:
We will not sit out for our parts.

Boatsw. Agreed. [*Exeunt Mast. Boatsw. Sailors.*

Gaz. The devil gnaw off his fingers! If he
    were
In London, among the clubs, up went his heels,
For striking of a prentice.[1]—What do you lack?
What do you lack, gentlemen?

---

¹ —————————— *If he were*
In London, among the clubs, *up went his heels,*
For striking of a prentice.] The police of the city seems to
have been wretchedly conducted at this time, when private injuries were left to private redress, and public brawls composed
by the interference of a giddy rabble. Every house, at least
every shop, was furnished with bludgeons, with which, on the
slightest appearance of a fray, the inhabitants armed themselves,
and rushed in swarms to the scene of action. From the petu-
lance of the young citizens, who then mixed little with the gentry, and the real or affected contempt in which the latter pro-
fessed to hold them, subjects of contention were perpetually
arising: the city signal for reinforcements, was a cry of
" clubs, clubs!" and the streets were instantly filled with armed

1 *Turk.* I wonder how the viceroy can endure
The insolence of this fellow.
2 *Turk.* He receives profit
From the prizes he brings in; and that excuses
Whatever he commits.   Ha! what are these?

Enter Mustapha *with* Donusa *veiled.*

1 *Turk.* They seem of rank and quality: observe them.
Gaz. What do you lack? see what you please to buy;
Wares of all sorts, most honourable madona.
Vitel. Peace, sirrah, make no noise; these are not people
To be jested with.
Don. Is this the Christians' custom,
In the venting their commodities?
Musta. Yes, best madam.
But you may please to keep your way, here's nothing
But toys and trifles, not worth your observing.
Don. Yes, for variety's sake: pray you, shew us, friend.
The chiefest of your wares.
Vitel. Your ladyship's servant;
And if, in worth, or title you are more,
My ignorance plead my pardon!

apprentices. To this curious system of preserving the peace,
our old dramatists have frequent allusions.   Thus, in Decker's
Honest Whore, where a mercer is struck, his servant exclaims:
" 'Sfoot, *clubs! clubs!* prentices, down with them! ah you
rogues, strike a *citizen* in his shop!"   Again, in Green's *Tu
Quoque,* Staines says;
 " Sirrah! by your outside you seem a *citizen,*
 " Whose coxcomb I were apt enough to break,
 " But for the law. Go, you're a prating Jack;
 " Nor is't your hopes of crying out for *clubs,*
 " Can save you from my chastisement."

Don. He speaks well.

Vitel. Take down the looking-glass.   Here is
a mirror
Steel'd so exactly, neither taking from
Nor flattering the object it returns
To the beholder, that Narcissus might
(And never grow enamour'd of himself)
View his fair feature in't.

Don. Poetical, too!

Vitel. Here China dishes to serve in a banquet,
Though the voluptuous Persian sat a guest.
Here crystal glasses, such as Ganymede
Did fill with nectar to the Thunderer,
When he drank to Alcides, and received him
In the fellowship of the gods; true to the owners:[2]
Corinthian plate, studded with diamonds,
Conceal'd oft deadly poison; this pure metal
So innocent is, and faithful to the mistress
Or master that possesses it, that, rather
Than hold one drop that's venomous, of itself
It flies in pieces, and deludes the traitor.

Don. How movingly could this fellow treat
upon

---

[2] *Here crystal glasses* ———— true to the owners: &c.] This,
and what follows, is a correct account of the notion once entertained, respecting the effect of poison on Venice glasses; a
circumstance which wonderfully increased their value. It may
be added, that the chief manufactory for glass was at this time,
in the vicinity of that city. Mr. Gilchrist adds from Stow, that
" the first making of *Venice* glasses in England, began at the
Crotched Fryars in London, about the beginning of the raigne
of Queen Elizabeth, by one Jacob Venaline, an Italian."
These, I suspect, were not, like the genuine ones, *true to the
owners.* There is an allusion in this speech to a beautiful passage in Juvenal:

——————— *nulla aconita bibuntur*
Fictilibus; tunc illa time, cum pocula sumes
Gemmata, et lato Setinum ardebit in auro.   Sat. x.

A worthy subject, that finds such discourse
To grace a trifle!

Vitel. Here's a picture, madam;
The masterpiece of Michael Angelo,
Our great Italian workman; here's another,
So perfect at all parts, that had Pygmalion
Seen this, his prayers had been made to Venus
To have given it life, and his carved ivory image
By poets ne'er remember'd. They are, indeed,
The rarest beauties of the Christian world,
And no where to be equall'd.

Don. You are partial
In the cause of those you favour; I believe
I instantly could shew you one, to theirs
Not much inferior.

Vitel. With your pardon, madam,
I am incredulous.

Don. Can you match me this?
          [Lifts her veil hastily.
Vitel. What wonder look I on! I'll search above,
And suddenly attend you.   *[Exit.*

Don. Are you amazed?
I'll bring you to yourself. *[Throws down the glasses.*
Musta. Ha! what's the matter?
Gaz. My master's ware!—We are undone!—O
  strange!
A lady to turn roarer, and break glasses![3]
'Tis time to shut up shop then.

Musta. You seem moved:
If any language of these Christian dogs
Have call'd your anger on, in a frown shew it,
And they are dead already.

Don. The offence

[3] *A lady to turn roarer, and break glasses!*] A *roarer* was the
cant term for what we now call a blusterer, or bully. Thus
Gazet, in the third act, says to Grimaldi in his state of reformation:

  Now, you do not roar, sir.

Looks not so far. The foolish, paltry fellow,
Shew'd me some trifles, and demanded of me,
For what I valued at so many aspers,
A thousand ducats.   I confess he moved me;
Yet I should wrong myself, should such a beggar
Receive least loss from me.

    Musta. Is it no more?

    Don. No, I assure you. Bid him bring his bill
To morrow to the palace, and enquire
For one Donusa; that word gives him passage
Through all the guard: say, there he shall receive
Full satisfaction. Now, when you please.

    Musta. I wait you. [*Exeunt Musta. and Don.*[4]

    1 *Turk.* We must not know them.—Let's shift
        off, and vanish.   [*Exeunt Turks.*

    Gaz. The swine's-pox overtake you! there's a
        curse
For a Turk, that eats no hog's flesh.

Re-enter VITELLI.

    Vitel. Is she gone?

    Gaz. Yes: You may see her handywork.

    Vitel. No matter.
Said she aught else?

    Gaz. That you should wait upon her,
And there receive court payment; and, to pass
The guards, she bids you only say you come
To one Donusa.

    Vitel. How! Remove the wares;
Do it without reply. The sultan's niece!
I have heard, among the Turks, for any lady

    [4] [*Exeunt Musta. and Don.*] Nothing can exceed the negli-
gence with which the exits and entrances are marked by Mr. M.
Mason: in this place he gives a speech to the Turks, after sending them off the stage!

To shew her face bare, argues love, or speaks
Her deadly hatred. What should I fear? my fortune
Is sunk so low, there cannot fall upon me
Aught worth my shunning. I will run the hazard:
She may be a means to free distress'd Paulina—
Or, if offended, at the worst, to die
Is a full period to calamity.   [*Exeunt.*

ACT II. SCENE I.

A Room in Donusa's *Palace.*

Enter CARAZIE *and* MANTO.

    Car. In the name of wonder, Manto, what hath
        my lady
Done with herself, since yesterday ?
    Mant. I know not.
Malicious men report we are all guided
In our affections by a wandering planet:
But such a sudden change in such a person,
May stand for an example, to confirm
Their false assertion.
    Car. She's now pettish, froward *;*
Music, discourse, observance, tedious to her.
    Mant. She slept not the last night; and yet
        prevented
The rising sun,[5] in being up before him :
Call'd for a costly bath, then will'd the rooms
Should be perfumed ; ransack'd her cabinets

---

   [5] Mant. *She slept not the last night ; and yet* prevented
The rising sun,] Massinger explains himself: but the expression is from the Psalms; " Mine eyes *prevent* the night-watches."

For her choice and richest jewels,[6] and appears now
Like Cynthia in full glory, waited on
By the fairest of the stars.
 Car. Can you guess the reason,
Why the aga of the janizaries, and he
That guards the entrance of the inmost port,
Were call'd before her?
 Mant. They are both her creatures,
And by her grace preferr'd : but I am ignorant
To what purpose they were sent for.

Enter DONUSA.

 Car. Her she comes,
Full of sad thoughts : we must stand further off.
What a frown was that!
 Mant. Forbear.
 Car. I pity her.
 Don What magic hath transform'd me from
  myself?
Where is my virgin pride? how have I lost
My boasted freedom? what new fire burns up
My scorched entrails; what unknown desires
Invade, and take possession of my soul,
All virtuous objects vanish'd? I, that have stood[7]
The shock of fierce temptations, stopp'd mine ears
Against all Syren notes lust ever sung,
To draw my bark of chastity (that with wonder
Hath kept a constant and an honour'd course)

<hr>

 [6] *For her* choice and richest *jewels*,] This is modernized by
Coxeter and Mr. M.Mason, into *choicest, richest* jewels : althogh
the frequent recurrence of the expression might have taught them
caution on the subject ; it is found again in this very play :
 " Adorned in her *choice and richest* jewels." Act V. sc. iii.
 [7] *I, that have stood* &c.] This fine speech, as it has been
hitherto given in all the editions, is absolute nonsense. I have
ventured to reform the pointing altogether, and to insert *that*
before *have*, which is the greatest liberty I have yet taken with
the old copy.

Into the gulf of a deserved ill-fame,
Now fall unpited; and, in a moment,
With mine own hands, dig up a grave to bury
The monumental heap of all my years,
Employ'd in noble actions. O my fate!
—But there is no resisting. I obey thee,
Imperious god of love, and willingly
Put mine own fetters on, to grace thy triumph:
'Twere therefore more than cruelty in thee,
To use me like a tyrant. What poor means
Must I make use of now! and flatter such,
To whom, till I betray'd my liberty,
One gracious look of mine would have erected
An altar to my service! How now, Manto!—
My ever careful woman; and Carazie,
Thou hast been faithful too.

    Car. I dare not call
My life mine own, since it is yours, but gladly
Will part with it, whene'er you shall command me;
And think I fall a martyr, so my death
May give life to your pleasures.

    Mant. But vouchsafe
To let me understand what you desire
Should be effected; I will undertake it,
And curse myself for cowardice, if I paused
To ask a reason why.

    Don. I am comforted
In the tender of your service, but shall be
Confirm'd in my full joys, in the performance.
Yet, trust me, I will not impose upon you
But what you stand engaged for to a mistress,
Such as I have been to you. All I ask,
Is faith and secrecy.

    Car. Say but you doubt me,
And, to secure you, I'll cut out my tongue;
I am libb'd in the breech already.

Mant. Do not hinder
Yourself, by these delays.
    Don. Thus then I whisper
Mine own shame to you.—O that I should blush
To speak what I so much desire to do!
And, further—[*Whispers, and uses vehement action.*
    Mant. Is this all?
    Don. Think it not base;
Although I know the office undergoes
A coarse construction.
    Car. Coarse! 'tis but procuring;
A smock employment, which has made more knights,
In a country I could name, than twenty years
Of service in the field.
    Don. You have my ends.
    Mant. Which say you have arrived at: be not wanting
To yourself, and fear not us.
    Car. I know my burthen;
I'll bear it with delight.
    Mant. Talk not, but do. [*Exeunt Car. and Mant.*
    Don. O love, what poor shifts thou dost force
        us to!   [*Exit.*

SCENE II.

A Court in the Same.

Enter Aga, Capiaga, *and* Janizaries.

Aga. She was ever our good mistress, and our maker,
And should we check at a little hazard for her,
We were unthankful.
    Cap. I dare pawn my head,

'Tis some disguised minion of the court,
Sent from great Amurath, to learn from her
The viceroy's actions.
 Aga. That concerns not us;
His fall may be our rise : whate'er he be,
He passes through my guards.
 Cap. And mine—provided
He give the word.

Enter VITELLI.

 Vitel. To faint now, being thus far,
Would argue me of cowardice.
 Aga. Stand: the word;
Or, being a Christian, to press thus far,
Forfeits thy life.
 Vitel. Donusa.
 Aga. Pass in peace. [*Exeunt Aga and Janizaries.*
 Vitel. What a privilege her name bears !
'Tis wondrous strange ! If the great officer,
The guardian of the inner port, deny not—
 Cap. Thy warrant : Speak, or thou art dead.
 Vitel. Donusa.
 Cap. That protects thee;
Without fear enter. So :—discharge the watch.
[*Exeunt Vitelli and Capiaga.*

SCENE III.

An outer Room in the same.

Enter CARAZIE *and* MANTO.

 Car. Though he hath past the aga and chief
   porter,
This cannot be the man.
* M 2

Mant. By her description,
I am sure it is.
Car. O women, women,
What are you ? A great lady dote upon
A haberdasher of small wares !
Mant. Pish ! thou hast none.
Car. No ; if I had, I might have served the
turn :
This 'tis to want munition, when a man
Should make a breach, and enter.

Enter VITELLI.

Mant. Sir, you are welcome :
Think what 'tis to be happy, and possess it.
Car. Perfume the rooms there, and make way.
Let music
With choice notes entertain the man the princess
Now purposes to honour.*
Vitel. I am ravish'd.   [*Exeunt.*

SCENE IV.

*A Room of State in the same.   A table set forth,
with jewels and bags of money upon it.*

Loud music.   Enter DONUSA, *(followed by*
CARAZIE,*) and takes her seat.*

Don. Sing o'er the ditty that I last composed
Upon my love-sick passion : suit your voice

---

³ Car. *Perfume the rooms there, and make way. Let music*
With *choice notes entertain the man the princess*
Now purposes to honour.] These lines are thus arranged by
Coxeter and Mr. M. Mason:
        Car. *Perfume the rooms there, and make way.*

To the music that's placed yonder, we shall
    hear you
With more delight and pleasure.
    Car. I obey you.   [*Song.*

During the song, enter MANTO *and* VITELLI.

    Vitel. Is not this Tempe, or the blessed shades,
Where innocent spirits reside? or do I dream,
And this a heavenly vision? Howsoever,
It is a sight too glorious to behold,
For such a wretch as I am.
    Car. He is daunted.
    Mant. Speak to him, madam; cheer him up, or
    you
Destroy what you have built.
    Car. Would I were furnish'd
With his artillery, and if I stood
Gaping as he does, hang me.   [*Aside.*
                [*Exeunt Carazie and Manto.*
    Vitel. That I might
Ever dream thus!   [*Kneels.*
    Don. Banish amazement:
You wake; your debtor tells you so, your debtor.
And, to assure you that I am a substance,[9]
And no aërial figure, thus I raise you.
Why do you shake? my soft touch brings no ague;
No biting frost is in this palm; nor are

> *Let music's choice notes entertain the man,*
> *The princess now purposes to honour.*

The reader may consider whether it was worth while to sophisticate the old copy, for the sake of producing three lines of
barbarous prose.

    9 *And to assure you that I am a substance,*] The omission of
the article by Coxeter and Mr. M. Mason utterly destroys
the metre.

My looks like to the Gorgon's head, that turn[1]
Men into statues; rather they have power,
Or I have been abused, where they bestow
Their influence, (let me prove it truth in you,)
To give to dead men motion.
    Vitel. Can this be?
May I believe my senses? Dare I think
I have a memory, or that you are
That excellent creature that of late disdain'd not
To look on my poor trifles?
    Don. I am she.
    Vitel. The owner of that blessed name, Donusa,
Which, like a potent charm, although pronounced
By my profane, but much unworthier, tongue,
Hath brought me safe to this forbidden place,
Where Christian yet ne'er trod?
    Don. I am the same.
    Vitel. And to what end, great lady—pardon me,
That I presume to ask, did your command
Command me hither? Or what am I, to whom
You should vouchsafe you favours; nay, your
       angers?
If any wild or uncollected speech,
Offensively deliver'd, or my doubt
Of your unknown perfections, have displeased
      you,
You wrong your indignation to pronounce,
Yourself, my sentence: to have seen you only,
And to have touch'd that fortune-making hand,

---

[1]   ——————— *that* turn] Mr. M. Mason
reads, that *turns:* but he mistakes the government of the verb,
which is not *Gorgon's head*, but *looks*, as is sufficiently clear from
what follows. I must observe here, (what has probably already
occurred to the reader,) that Massinger is too apt, in the words
of honest Dogberry, to let *his writing and reading appear when
there is no need of such vanity.* Not only Vitelli, but Donusa and
all her court appear as familiar with the heathen mythology, as
Ovid himself.

Will with delight weigh down all tortures, that
A flinty hangman's rage could execute,
Or rigid tyranny command with pleasure.
    Don. How the abundance of good flowing to
        thee,
Is wrong'd in this simplicity ! and these bounties,
Which all our Eastern kings have kneel'd in vain
    for,
Do, by thy ignorance, or wilful fear,
Meet with a false construction ! Christian, know
(For till thou art mine by a nearer name,
That title, though abhorr'd here, takes not from
Thy entertainment) that 'tis not the fashion
Among the greatest and the fairest dames
This Turkish empire gladly owes² and bows to,
To punish where there's no offence, or nourish
Displeasures against those, without whose mercy
They part with all felicity. Prithee, be wise,
And gently understand me ; do not force her,
That ne'er knew aught but to command, nor e'er
    read
The elements of affection, but from such
As gladly sued to her, in the infancy
Of her new-born desires, to be at once
Importunate and immodest.
    Vitel. Did I know,
Great lady, your commands ; or, to what pur-
    pose
This personated passion tends, (since 'twere
A crime in me deserving death, to think
It is your own,) I should, to make you sport,

---

   ² *This Turkish empire gladly* owes *and bows to,*] Though nothing
is more common in our old writers, than the use of this word
(owe) in the sense of possess, yet Coxeter and Mr. M. Mason
invariably corrupt it into *own* I have already noticed this ;
and, for the future, shall content myself with silently restoring
the genuine reading.

Take any shape you please t'impose upon me;
And with joy strive to serve you.
 Don. Sport! Thou art cruel,
If that thou canst interpret my descent
From my high birth and greatness, but to be
A part,[3] in which I truly act myself:
And I must hold thee for a dull spectator,
If it stir not affection, and invite
Compassion for my sufferings. Be thou taught
By my example, to make satisfaction
For wrongs unjustly offer'd. Willingly
I do confess my fault; I injured thee
In some poor petty trifles: thus I pay for
The trespass I did to thee. Here—receive
These bags, stuff'd full of our imperial coin;
Or, if this payment be too light, take here
These gems, for which the slavish Indian dives
To the bottom of the main: or, if thou scorn
These as base dross, which take but common minds,
But fancy any honour in my gift,
Which is unbounded as the sultan's power,
And be possest of it.
 Vitel. I am overwhelm'd
With the weight of happiness you throw upon me:
Nor can it fall in my imagination,
What wrong you e'er have done me;[4] and much less
How, like a royal[4] merchant, to return
Your great magnificence.

    [3]   ————— *but to be*
A part, &c.] i. e. *to be nothing more than* a fictitious character;
alluding to his terming her passion *personated,* or played.

 [4] *What wrong you e'er have done* me;] The old copy reads,
What wrong I e'er have done you. This transposition of pronouns,
for which I am answerable, seems absolutely necessary to make
sense of the passage.

 [5] *How, like a* royal *merchant, to return*
 Your great magnificence.] We are not to imagine the word
royal to be only a ranting epithet.—In the thirteenth century,

Don. They are degrees,
Not ends, of my intended favours to thee.
These seeds of bounty I yet scatter on
A glebe I have not tried :—but, be thou thankful;
The harvest is to come.
    Vitel. What can be added
To that which I already have received,
I cannot comprehend.
    Don. The tender of
Myself. Why dost thou start? and in that gift,
Full restitution of that virgin freedom
Which thou hast robb'd me of. Yet, I profess,
I so far prize the lovely thief that stole it,
That, were it possible thou couldst restore
What thou unwittingly hast ravish'd from me,
I should refuse the present.
    Vitel. How I shake
In my constant resolution! and my flesh,
Rebellious to my better part, now tells me,
As if it were a strong defence of frailty,
A hermit in a desert, trench'd with prayers,
Could not resist this battery.
    Don. Thou an Italian,
Nay more, I know't, a natural Venetian,
Such as are courtiers born to please fair ladies,
Yet come thus slowly on !
    Vitel. Excuse me, madam :
What imputation soe'er the world
Is pleased to lay upon us, in myself
I am so innocent, that I know not what 'tis
That I should offer.

---

the Venetians were masters of the sea; the Sanudos, the Jus-
tiniani, the Grimaldi, &c. all *merchants*, erected principalities in
several places of the Archipelago, (which their descendants en-
joyed for many generations,) and thereby became truly and
properly *royal merchants:* which, indeed, was the title generally
given them all over Europe. WARBURTON.

Don. By instínct I'll teach thee,
And with such ease as love makes me to ask it.
When a young lady wrings you by the hand, thus,
Or with an amorous touch presses your foot,
Looks babies in your eyes, plays with your locks,
Do not you find, without a tutor's help,
What 'tis she looks for ?
  Vitel. I am grown already
Skilful in the mystery.
  Don. Or, if thus she kiss you,
Then tastes your lips again—— [*Kisses him.*
  Vitel. That latter blow
Has beat all chaste thoughts from me.
  Don. Say, she points to
Some private room the sunbeams never enter,
Provoking dishes passing by, to heighten
Declined appetite, active music ushering
Your fainting steps, the waiters too, as born dumb,
Not daring to look on you.
     [*Exit, inviting him to follow.*
  Vitel. Though the devil
Stood by, and roar'd, I follow : Now I find
That virtue's but a word, and no sure guard,
If set upon by beauty and reward. [*Exit.*

SCENE V.

A Hall in Asambeg's *Palace.*

Enter Aga, Capiaga, GRIMALDI, Master,
  Boatswain, *and Sailors.*

Aga. The devil's in him, I think.
Grim. Let him be damn'd too.
I'll look on him, though he stared as wild as hell ;

Nay, I'll go near* to tell him to his teeth,
If he mends not suddenly, and proves more
　　thankful,
We do him too much service.　Were't not for
　　shame now,
I could turn honest, and forswear my trade ;
Which, next to being truss'd up at the mainyard
By some low country butterbox, I hate
As deadly as I do fasting, or long grace
When meat cools on the table.
　　Cap. But take heed ;
You know his violent nature.
　　Grim. Let his whores
And catamites know't ! I understand myself,
And how unmanly 'tis to sit at home,
And rail at us, that run abroad all hazards,
If every week we bring not home new pillage,
For the fatting his seraglio.

　　Enter ASAMBEG, MUSTAPHA, *and Attendants.*

　　Aga. Here he comes.
　　Cap. How terrible he looks !
　　Grim. To such as fear him.
The viceroy, Asambeg! were he the sultan's self
He'll let us know a reason for his fury ;
Or we must take leave, without his allowance,
To be merry with our ignorance.
　　Asam. Mahomet's hell
Light on you all ! You crouch and cringe now:—
　　Where

* *Nay,* I'll go near *to tell him to his teeth,*] This is a collo-
quial phrase, and means, *I am not unlikely, I will not scruple
much,* to tell him to his teeth ;—the modern editors, comprehending neither the sense, nor the measure of the line, read,
　　Nay, I'll go nearer *to tell him to his teeth !*

Was the terror of my just frowns, when you
          suffer'd
Those thieves of Malta, almost in our harbour,
To board a ship, and bear her safely off,
While you stood idle lookers on?
    Aga. The odds
In the men and shipping, and the suddenness
Of their departure, yielding us no leisure
To send forth others to relieve our own,
Deterr'd us, mighty sir.
    Asam. Deterr'd you, cowards !
How durst you only entertain the knowledge
Of what fear was, but in the not performance
Of our command? In me great Amurath spake;
My voice did echo to your ears his thunder,
And will'd you, like so many sea-born tritons,
Arm'd only with the trumpets of your courage,
To swim up to her, and, like remoras
Hanging upon her keel, to stay her flight,
Till rescue, sent from us, had fetch'd you off.
You think you're safe now. Who durst but dis-
          pute it,
Or make it questionable, if, this moment,
I charged you, from yon hanging cliff, that glasses
His rugged forehead in the neighbouring lake,
To throw yourselves down headlong? or, like
          faggots,
To fill the ditches of defended forts,
While on your backs we march'd up to the breach?
    Grim. That would not I.
    Asam. Ha !
    Grim. Yet I dare as much
As any of the sultan's boldest sons,
Whose heaven and hell hang on his frown or
          smile,
His warlike janizaries.
    Asam. Add one syllable more,

Thou dost pronounce upon thyself a sentence
That, earthquake-like, will swallow thee.
   Grim. Let it open,
I'll stand the hazard: those contemned thieves,
Your fellow-pirates, sir, the bold Maltese,
Whom with your looks you think to quell, at
     Rhodes
Laugh'd at great Solyman's anger: and, if treason
Had not delivered them into his power,
He had grown old in glory as in years,
At that so fatal siege; or risen with shame,
His hopes and threats deluded.
   Asam. Our great prophet!
How have I lost my anger and my power!
   Grim. Find it, and use it on thy flatterers,
And not upon thy friends, that dare speak
     truth.
These knights of Malta, but a handful to
Your armies, that drink[7] rivers up, have stood
Your fury at the height, and with their crosses
Struck pale your horned moons;[8] these men of
     Malta,
Since I took pay from you, I've met and fought
     with
Upon advantage too; yet, to speak truth,
By the soul of honour, I have ever found them
As provident to direct, and bold to do,
As any train'd up in your discipline,
Ravish'd from other nations.

[7] *Your armies that* drink *rivers up,*] Injudiciously altered by
Mr. M. Mason, to *drank* rivers up.
  [8] —————————— *and with their* crosses
Struck pale your horned moons;] This elegant allusion to the
impress of the Maltese and Turkish standards, is beautifully va-
ried in *the Knight of Malta,* by Fletcher:
  " And all their silver *crescents* then I saw,
  " Like falling meteors spent, and set for ever
  " Under the *cross* of Malta.

Musta. I perceive
The lightning in his fiery looks; the cloud
Is broke already.   [*Aside.*
  Grim. Think not, therefore, sir,
That you alone are giants, and such pigmies
You war upon.
  Asam. Villain! I'll make thee know
Thou has blasphemed the Othoman power, and
      safer,
At noonday, might'st have given fire to St.
      Mark's,
Your proud Venetian temple.—Seize upon him:
I am not so near reconciled to him,
To bid him die; that were a benefit
The dog's unworthy of. To our use confiscate
All that he stands possess'd of; let him taste
The misery of want, and his vain riots,
Like to so many walking ghosts, affright him,
Where'er he sets his desperate foot. Who is't
That does command you?
  Grim. Is this the reward
For all my service, and the rape I made
On fair Paulina?
  Asam. Drag him hence:—he dies,
That dallies but a minute.
          [*Grimaldi is dragg'd off, his head covered.*
  Boatsw. What's become of
Our shares now, master?
  Mast. Would he had been born dumb!
The beggar's cure, patience, is all that's left us.
          [*Exeunt Master, Boatswain, and Sailors.*
  Musta. 'Twas but intemperance of speech,
      excuse him;
Let me prevail so far. Fame gives him out
For a deserving fellow.
  Asam. At Aleppo,
I durst not press you so far: give me leave

To use my own will, and command in Tunis;
And, if you please, my privacy.
   Musta. I will see you,
When this high wind's blown o'er.   [*Exit.*
   Asam. So shall you find me
Ready to do you service. Rage, now leave me;
Stern looks, and all the ceremonious forms
Attending on dread majesty, fly from
Transformed Asambeg. Why should I hug
           [*Pulls out a key.*
So near my heart, what leads me to my prison;
Where she that is inthrall'd, commands her
    keeper,
And robs me of the fierceness I was born with?
Stout men quake at my frowns, and, in return,
I tremble at her softness. Base Grimaldi
But only named Paulina, and the charm
Had almost choak'd my fury, ere I could
Pronounce his sentence. Would, when first I saw
    her,
Mine eyes had met with lightning, and, in place
Of hearing her enchanting tongue, the shrieks
Of mandrakes had made music to my slumbers!
For now I only walk a loving dream,
And, but to my dishonour, never wake;
And yet am blind, but when I see the object,
And madly dote on it. Appear, bright spark
      [*Opens a door; Paulina comes forth.*
Of all perfection! any simile
Borrow'd from diamonds, or the fairest stars,
To help me to express how dear I prize
Thy unmatch'd graces, will rise up, and chide me
For poor detraction.
   Paul. I despise thy flatteries:
Thus spit at them, and scorn them; and being
    arm'd
In the assurance of my innocent virtue,

I stamp upon all doubts, all fears, all tortures,
Thy barbarous cruelty, or, what's worse, thy
   dotage,
The worthy parent of thy jealousy,
Can shower upon me.

 Asam. If these bitter taunts
Ravish me from myself, and make me think
My greedy ears receive angelical sounds;
How would this tongue, tuned to a loving note,
Invade, and take possession of my soul,
Which then I durst not call mine own!

 Paul. Thou art false,
Falser than thy religion. Do but think me
Something above a beast, nay more, a monster
Would fright the sun to look on, and then tell me,
If this base usage can invite affection?
If to be mewed up, and excluded from
Human society; the use of pleasures;
The necessary, not superfluous duties
Of servants, to discharge those offices
I blush to name—

 Asam. Of servants! Can you think
That I, that dare not trust the eye of heaven
To look upon your beauties; that deny
Myself the happiness to touch your pureness,
Will e'er consent an eunuch, or bought handmaid,
Shall once approach you?—There is something
   in you
That can work miracles, or I am cozen'd;
Dispose and alter sexes, to my wrong,
In spite of nature. I will be your nurse,
Your woman, your physician, and your fool;
Till, with your free consent, which I have vow'd
Never to force, you grace me with a name
That shall supply all these.

 Paul. What is it?

 Asam. Your husband.

Paul. My hangman, when thou pleasest.
Asam. Thus I guard me
Against your further angers. [*Leads her to the door.*
Paul. Which shall reach thee,
Though I were in the centre.
  [*Asambeg closes the door upon her, and locks it.*
Asam. Such a spirit,
In such a small proportion, I ne'er read of,
Which time must alter: Ravish her I dare not;
The magic that she wears about her neck,
I think, defends her :—this devotion paid
To this sweet saint, mistress of my sour pain,
'Tis fit I take mine own rough shape again. [*Exit.*

SCENE VI.

A Street near Donusa's *Palace.*

Enter FRANCISCO *and* GAZET.

Fran. I think he's lost.
Gaz. 'Tis ten to one of that;
I ne'er knew citizen turn courtier yet,
But he lost his credit though he saved himself.
Why, look you, sir, there are so many lobbies,
Out-offices, and dispartations here,[9]

---

9 *Out-offices, and* dispartations *here,*] I have already observed
that there is but one edition of this play, which reads in this
place, *dispute actions :* the error was detected at the press, and
exchanged unfortunately for another, *disputations ;* which is the
reading of Coxeter and Mr. M. Mason. I have examined several
copies, but can find no further correction : *dispartation,* which is
here adopted, is the conjectural amendment of Mr. Davies, who
says, that it signifies " separate apartments ;" if it be so, it is
well ; at any rate it is better than the old reading, which signifies nothing. A friend, to whom I shewed the passage, is inclined to think that the genuine word was *disparations,* from the

Behind these Turkish hangings, that a Christian
Hardly gets off but circumcised.

Enter VITELLI *richly habited,* CARAZIE, *and*
MANTO.

Fran. I am troubled,
Troubled exceedingly.   Ha ! what are these ?
    Gaz. One, by his rich suit, should be some
        French embassador :
For his train, I think they are Turks.
    Fran. Peace ! be not seen.
    Car. You are now past all the guards, and,
        undiscover'd,
You may return.
    Vitel. There's for your pains ; forget not
My humblest service to the best of ladies.
    Mant. Deserve her favour, sir, in making haste
For a second entertainment.
                [*Exeunt Carazie and Manto.*
    Vitel. Do not doubt me ;
I shall not live till then.
    Gaz. The train is vanish'd :
They have done him some good office, he's so free
And liberal of his gold.—Ha ! do I dream,
Or is this mine own natural master ?
    Fran. 'Tis he :
But strangely metamorphosed.—You have made,
       sir,
A prosperous voyage ; heaven grant it be honest,
I shall rejoice then, too.
    Gaz. You make him blush,
To talk of honesty :—you were but now
In the giving vein, and may think of Gazet,
Your worship's prentice.

Latin *disparata.*—I leave the whole to the reader ; observing
only, that *disparates* (distinctions, differences) often occurs in
our old law books.

Vitel. There's gold : be thou free too,
And master of my shop, and all the wares
We brought from Venice.

 Gaz. Rivo ! then.[1]

 Vitel. Dear sir,
This place affords not privacy for discourse ;
But I can tell you wonders : my rich habit
Deserves least admiration ; there is nothing
That can fall in the compass of your wishes,
Though it were to redeem a thousand slaves
From the Turkish gallies, or, at home, to erect
Some pious work, to shame all hospitals,
But I am master of the means.

 Fran. 'Tis strange.

 Vitel. As I walk, I'll tell you more.

 Gaz. Pray you, a word, sir ;
And then I will put on : I have one boon more.

 Vitel. What is't ? speak freely.

 Gaz. Thus then :[2] As I am master
Of your shop and wares, pray you help me to
  some trucking
With your last she-customer ; though she crack
  my best piece,
I will endure it with patience.

 Vitel. Leave your prating.

 Gaz. I may: you have been doing ; we will
  do too.

---

[1] *Gaz. Rivo !*] This interjection (corrupted, perhaps, from the Spanish *rio !* which is figuratively used for a large quantity of liquor) is frequently introduced by our old poets, and generally as an incitement to boisterous mirth and revelry.

[2] *Gaz. Thus then: As I am master &c.*] This poor ribaldry is introduced to " set on some quantity of barren spectators to laugh," and 'tis to be regretted ; for the rest of the act has a vein of genuine poetry running through it, which would not debase the noblest compositions of the times. I suppose that Massinger's excuse must be that of a much greater man, *sic vivitur.*

Fran. I am amazed, yet will not blame nor
    chide you,
Till you inform me further: yet must say,
They steer not the right course, nor traffic well,
That seek a passage to reach heaven through hell.
                      [Exeunt.

ACT III. SCENE I.

A Room in Donusa's *Palace.*

Enter Donusa *and* Manto.

Don. When said he he would come again?
Mant. He swore,
Short minutes should be tedious ages to him,
Until the tender of his second service;
So much he seem'd transported with the first.
   Don. I am sure I was. I charge thee, Manto,
    tell me,
By all my favours, and my bounties, truly,
Whether thou art a virgin, or, like me,
Hast forfeited that name?
   Mant. A virgin, madam,[3]
At my years! being a waiting-woman, and in
    court too!
That were miraculous. I so long since lost

---

[3] *A virgin, madam,* &c] Manto had been studying modesty
in *the Maid's Tragedy,* from which too much of this dialogue
is borrowed. In the conclusion of her speech, as Davies remarks, there is an allusion to Quartilla: *Junonem meam iratam
habeam, si unquam me meminerim virginem fuisse.*

That barren burthen, I almost forget
That ever I was one.

   Don. And could thy friends
Read in thy face, thy maidenhead gone, that thou
Hadst parted with it?

   Mant. No, indeed: I past
For current many years after, till, by fortune,
Long and continued practice in the sport
Blew up my deck; a husband then was found out
By my indulgent father, and to the world
All was made whole again. What need you fear,
     then,
That, at your pleasure, may repair your honour,
Durst any envious or malicious tongue
Presume to taint it?

         Enter CARAZIE.

   Don. How now?
   Car. Madam, the basha
Humbly desires access.

   Don. If it had been
My neat Italian, thou hadst met my wishes.
Tell him we would be private.

   Car. So I did,
But he is much importunate.

   Mant. Best dispatch him:
His lingering here else will deter the other
From making his approach.

   Don. His entertainment
Shall not invite a second visit. Go;
Say we are pleased.

        Enter MUSTAPHA.

   Must. All happiness——
   Don. Be sudden.

'Twas saucy rudeness in you, sir, to press
On my retirements; but ridiculous folly
To waste the time, that might be better spent,
In complimental wishes.
   Car. There's a cooling
For his hot encounter!   [*Aside.*
   Don. Come you here to stare?
If you have lost your tongue, and use of speech,
Resign your government; there's a mute's place
    void
In my uncle's court, I hear; and you may work me,
To write for your preferment.
   Musta. This is strange!
I know not, madam, what neglect of mine
Has call'd this scorn upon me.
   Don. To the purpose——
My will's a reason, and we stand not bound
To yield account to you.
   Musta. Not of your angers:
But with erected ears I should hear from you
The story of your good opinion of me,
Confirm'd by love and favours.
   Don. How deserved?
I have considered you from head to foot,
And can find nothing in that wainscot face,
That can teach me to dote; nor am I taken
With your grim aspéct, or tad-pole-like com-
    plexion.
Those scars you glory in, I fear to look on;
And had much rather hear a merry tale,
Than all your battles won with blood and sweat,
Though you belch forth the stink too in the
    service,
And swear by your mustachios all is true.
You are yet too rough for me: purge and take
    physic,
Purchase perfumers, get me some French tailor

To new-create you; the first shape you were
    made with
Is quite worn out: let your barber wash your
    face too,
You look yet like a bugbear to fright children;
Till when I take my leave—Wait me Carazie.
                [Exeunt Donusa and Carazie.
    Musta. Stay you, my lady's cabinet-key.
                     [Seizes Manto.
    Mant. How's this, sir?
    Musta. Stay, and stand quietly, or you shall
    fall else,
Not to firk your belly up, flounder-like, but never
To rise again.　Offer but to unlock
These doors that stop your fugitive tongue, (ob-
    serve me,)
And, by my fury, I'll fix there this bolt
                  [Draws his scimitar.
To bar thy speech for ever.　So! be safe now;
And but resolve me, not of what I doubt,
But bring assurance to a thing believed,
Thou makest thyself a fortune; not depending
On the uncertain favours of a mistress,
But art thyself one.　I'll not so far question
My judgment and observance, as to ask
Why I am slighted and contemn'd; but in
Whose favour it is done? I, that have read
The copious volumes of all women's falsehood,
Commented on by the heart-breaking groans
Of abused lovers; all the doubts wash'd off
With fruitless tears, the spider's cobweb veil
Of arguments alleged in their defence,
Blown off with sighs of desperate men, and they
Appearing in their full deformity;
Know that some other hath displanted me,
With her dishonour.　Has she given it up?
Confirm it in two syllables.
    Mant. She has.

Musta. I cherish thy confession thus, and thus;
                              [*Gives her jewels.*
Be mine. Again I court thee thus, and thus:
Now prove but constant to my ends.
    Mant. By all——
    Musta. Enough; I dare not doubt thee.—O
        land crocodiles,
Made of Egyptian slime, accursed women!
But 'tis no time to rail—come, my best Manto.
                              [*Exeunt.*

SCENE II.

A Street.

Enter VITELLI *and* FRANCISCO.

    Vitel. Sir, as you are my confessor, you stand
        bound
Not to reveal whatever I discover
In that religious way: nor dare I doubt you.
Let it suffice you have made me see my follies,
And wrought, perhaps, compunction; for I would
        not
Appear an hypocrite. But, when you impose
A penance on me beyond flesh and blood
To undergo, you must instruct me how
To put off the condition of a man:
Or, if not pardon, at the least, excuse
My disobedience. Yet, despair not, sir;
For, though I take mine own way, I shall do
Something that may hereafter, to my glory,
Speak me your scholar.
    Fran. I enjoin you not
To go, but send.
    Vitel. That were a petty trial;
Not worth one, so long taught, and exercised,

Under so grave a master. Reverend Francisco,
My friend, my father, in that word, my all!
Rest confident you shall hear something of me,
That will redeem me in your good opinion;
Or judge me lost for ever. Send Gazet
(She shall give order that he may have entrance)
To acquaint you with my fortunes.   [*Exit.*
   Fran. Go, and prosper.
Holy saints guide and strengthen thee! however,
As thy endeavours are, so may they find
Gracious acceptance.

Enter GAZET, *and* GRIMALDI *in rags.*[4]

   Gaz. Now, you do not roar, sir;
You speak not tempests, nor take ear-rent from
A poor shop-keeper. Do you remember that, sir?
I wear your marks here still.
   Fran. Can this be possible?
All wonders are not ceased then.
   Grim. Do, abuse me,
Spit on me, spurn me, pull me by the nose,
Thrust out these fiery eyes, that yesterday
Would have look'd thee dead.
   Gaz. O save me, sir!
   Grim. Fear nothing.
I am tame and quiet; there's no wrong can force
    me
To remember what I was. I have forgot
I e'er had ireful fierceness, a steel'd heart,
Insensible of compassion to others;
Nor is it fit that I should think myself
Worth mine own pity. Oh!

   [4] *Enter* GAZET, *and* GRIMALDI *in rags.*] Mr. M. Mason reads,
Enter Gazet and Grimaldi, in rags. But Gazet had just been enriched by his master, and, as he says himself, was in prosperous
circumstances. It must be as it is here given from the old copy.

Fran. Grows this dejection
From his disgrace, do you say?
  Gaz. Why, he's cashier'd, sir;
His ships, his goods, his livery-punks, confis-
    cate:
And there is such a punishment laid upon him!—
The miserable rogue must steal no more,
Nor drink, nor drab.
  Fran. Does that torment him?
  Gaz. O, sir,
Should the state take order to bar men of acres
From these two laudable recreations,
Drinking and whoring, how should panders
    purchase,
Or thrifty whores build hospitals? 'Slid! if I,
That, since I am made free, may write myself
A city gallant, should forfeit two such charters,
I should be stoned to death, and ne'er be pitied
By the liveries of those companies.
  Fran. You'll be whipt, sir,
If you bridle not your tongue. Haste to the
    palace,
Your master looks for you.
  Gaz. My quondam master.
Rich sons forget they ever had poor fathers;
In servants 'tis more pardonable: as a companion,
Or so, I may consent: but, is there hope, sir,
He has got me a good chapwoman? pray you,
    write
A word or two in my behalf.
  Fran. Out, rascal!
  Gaz. I feel some insurrections.
  Fran. Hence!
  Gaz. I vanish.   [*Exit.*
  Grim. Why should I study a defence or com-
    fort,
In whom black guilt and misery, if balanced,

I know not which would turn the scale? look
    upward
I dare not; for, should it but be believed
That I, died deep in hell's most horrid colours,
Should dare to hope for mercy, it would leave
No check or feeling in men innocent,
To catch at sins the devil ne'er taught mankind
    yet.
No! I must downward, downward; though re-
    pentance
Could borrow all the glorious wings of grace,
My mountainous weight of sins would crack their
    pinions,
And sink them to hell with me.
   Fran. Dreadful! Hear me,
Thou miserable man.
   Grim. Good sir, deny not
But that there is no punishment beyond
Damnation.

     Enter Master *and* Boatswain.

   Master. Yonder he is; I pity him.
   Boatsw. Take comfort, captain; we live still
    to serve you.
   Grim. Serve me! I am a devil already: leave
    me—
Stand further off, you are blasted else! I have
    heard
Schoolmen affirm[6] man's body is composed

[6]   ——— *I have heard*
Schoolmen affirm man's body is composed
Of the four elements;] Grimaldi and sir Toby had evidently
studied under the same masters: the latter introduces his philosophy *more naturally,* but the grave application of it by the
former, is an improvement. Seriously, the conclusion of this
speech is very noble.

Of the four elements ; and, as in league together
They nourish life, so each of them affords
Liberty to the soul, when it grows weary
Of this fleshy prison. Which shall I make choice
    of?
The fire? no ;[6] I shall feel that hereafter,
The earth will not receive me. Should some
    whirlwind
Snatch me into the air, and I hang there,
Perpetual plagues would dwell upon the earth;
And those superior bodies, that pour down
Their cheerful influence, deny to pass it,
Through those vast regions I have infected.
The sea? ay, that is justice : there I plough'd up
Mischief as deep as hell : there, there, I'll hide
This cursed lump of clay. May it turn rocks,
Where plummet's weight could never reach the
    sands,
And grind the ribs of all such barks as press
The ocean's breast in my unlawful course !
I haste then to thee; let thy ravenous womb,
Whom all things else deny, be now my tomb !
                          [*Exit.*

   Master. Follow him, and restrain him.
                    [*Exit Boatswain.*
   Fran. Let this stand
For an example to you. I'll provide
A lodging for him, and apply such cures
To his wounded conscience, as heaven hath lent
    me.
He's now my second care; and my profession
Binds me to teach the desperate to repent,
As far as to confirm the innocent.   [*Exeunt.*

---

   6 *The* fire? *no ;*] *Fire* must be read as a dissyllable ; I suspect, however, that there was originally an interjection before
no, which was dropt at the press.

SCENE III.

A Room in Asambeg's *Palace.*

Enter ASAMBEG, MUSTAPHA, Aga, *and*
Capiaga.

Asam. Your pleasure ?
Musta. 'Twill exact your private ear;
And, when you have received it, you will think
Too many know it.
Asam. Leave the room; but be
Within our call.—   [*Exeunt Aga, and Capiaga.*
            Now, sir, what burning secret
(With which, it seems, you are turn'd cinders)
        bring you,
To quench in my advice or power?
Musta. The fire
Will rather reach you.
Asam. Me!
Musta. And consume both;
For 'tis impossible to be put out,
But with the blood of those that kindle it:
And yet one vial of it is so precious,
In being borrow'd from the Othoman spring,
That better 'tis, I think, both we should perish,
Than prove the desperate means that must re-
        strain it
From spreading further.
Asam. To the point, and quickly:
These winding circumstances in relations,
Seldom environ truth.
Musta. Truth, Asambeg!
Asam. Truth, Mustapha. I said it, and add
    more,

You touch upon a string that, to my ear,
Does sound Donusa.
   Musta. You then understand
Who 'tis I aim at.
   Asam. Take heed, Mustapha;
Remember what she is, and whose we are:
'Tis her neglect, perhaps, that you complain of;
And, should you practise to revenge her scorn,
With any plot to taint her in her honour,——
   Must. Hear me.
   Asam. I will be heard first,—there's no tongue
A subject owes, that shall out-thunder mine.
   Musta. Well, take your way.
   Asam. I then again repeat it;
If Mustapha dares with malicious breath,
On jealous suppositions, presume
To blast the blossom of Donusa's fame,
Because he is denied a happiness
Which men of equal, nay, of more desert,
Have sued in vain for——
   Musta. More!
   Asam. More. 'Twas I spake it.
The basha of Natolia and myself
Were rivals for her; either of us brought
More victories, more trophies, to plead for us
To our great master, than you dare lay claim
     to;
Yet still, by his allowance, she was left
To her election: each of us owed nature
As much for outward form and inward worth,
To make way for us to her grace and favour,
As you brought with you. We were heard, re-
     pulsed;
Yet thought it no dishonour to sit down
With the disgrace, if not to force affection
May merit such a name.
   Musta. Have you done yet?

Asam. Be, therefore, more than sure the ground
    on which
You raise your accusation, may admit
No undermining of defence in her :
For if, with pregnant and apparent proofs,
Such as may force a judge, more than inclined,
Or partial in her cause, to swear her guilty,
You win not me to set off your belief ;
Neither our ancient friendship, nor the rites
Of sacred hospitality, to which
I would not offer violence, shall protect you :
—Now, when you please.
    Musta. I will not dwell upon
Much circumstance ; yet cannot but profess,
With the assurance of a loyalty
Equal to yours, the reverence I owe
The sultan, and all such his blood makes sacred ;
That there is not a vein of mine, which yet is
Unemptied in his service, but this moment
Should freely open, so it might wash off
The stains of her dishonour. Could you think,
Or, though you saw it, credit your own eyes,
That she, the wonder and amazement of
Her sex, the pride and glory of the empire,
That hath disdain'd you, slighted me, and boasted
A frozen coldness, which no appetite
Or height of blood could thaw ; should now so far
Be hurried with the violence of her lust,
As, in it burying her high birth, and fame,
Basely descend to fill a Christian's arms ;
And to him yield her virgin honour up,
Nay, sue to him to take it ?
    Asam. A Christian !
    Musta. Temper
Your admiration :—and what Christian, think
    you ?
No prince disguised, no man of mark, nor honour ;

No daring undertaker in our service,
But one, whose lips her foot should scorn to touch;
A poor mechanic pedlar.
 Asam. He!
 Musta. Nay, more;
Whom do you think she made her scout, nay bawd,
To find him out, but me? What place make choice
  of
To wallow in her foul and loathsome pleasures,
But in the palace? Who the instruments
Of close conveyance, but the captain of
Your guard, the aga, and that man of trust,
The warden of the inmost port?—I'll prove this:
And, though I fail to shew her in the act,
Glued like a neighing gennet to her stallion,
Your incredulity shall be convinced
With proofs I blush to think on.
 Asam. Never yet
This flesh felt such a fever. By the life
And fortune of great Amurath, should our prophet
(Whose name I bow to) in a vision speak this,
'Twould make me doubtful of my faith!—Lead on;
And, when my eyes and ears are, like yours, guilty,
My rage shall then appear; for I will do
Something—but what, I am not yet determin'd.
         [*Exeunt.*

SCENE IV.

An outer Room in Donusa's *Palace.*

Enter CARAZIE, MANTO, *and* GAZET *gaily
dressed.*

 Car. They are private to their wishes?
 Mant. Doubt it not.
 Gaz. A pretty structure this! a court do you
  call it?

Vaulted and arch'd! O, here has been old
    jumbling
Behind this arras.

    Car. Prithee let's have some sport
With this fresh codshead.

    Mant. I am out of tune,
But do as you please.—My conscience!—tush!
    the hope
Of liberty throws[7] that burthen off; I must
Go watch, and make discovery. [*Aside, and exit.*

    Car. He is musing,
And will talk to himself; he cannot hold:
The poor fool's ravish'd.

    Gaz. I am in my master's clothes,
They fit me to a hair too; let but any
Indifferent gamester measure us inch by inch,
Or weigh us by the standard, I may pass:
I have been proved and proved again true metal.

    Car. How he surveys himself!

    Gaz. I have heard, that some
Havefooledthemselvesatcourtintogoodfortunes,
That never hoped to thrive by wit in the city,
Or honesty in the country. If I do not
Make the best laugh at me, I'll weep for myself,
If they give me hearing: 'tis resolved—I'll try
What may be done. By your favour, sir, I pray
    you,
Were you born a courtier?

    Car. No, sir; why do you ask?

    Gaz. Because I thought that none could be
    preferr'd,
But such as were begot there.

    Car. O, sir! many;
And, howsoe'er you are a citizen born,

---

    7 *Of liberty* throws, &c.] So the old copy. The modern editors
read, *does throw,* which destroys the metre, not only of this but
of the two subsequent lines.

Yet if your mother were a handsome woman,
And ever long'd to see a masque at court,[8]
It is an even lay, but that you had
A courtier to your father ; and I think so,
You bear yourself so sprightly.
   Gaz. It may be ;
Bur pray you, sir, had I such an itch upon me
To change my copy, is there hope a place
May be had here for money ?
   Car. Not without it,
That I dare warrant you.
   Gaz. I have a pretty stock,
And would not have my good parts undiscover'd ;
What places of credit are there ?
   Car. There's your beglerbeg.[9]
   Gaz. By no means that ; it comes too near the
     beggar,
And most prove so, that come there.
   Car. Or your sanzacke.[1]
   Gaz. Sauce-jack ! fie, none of that.[2]
   Car. Your chiaus.[3]

[8] *if your mother were a handsome woman,*
And ever long'd to see a masque at court,] It should be remembered that Carazie was born in England, and that he addresses a Venetian ; the consequences of masques, &c. were
therefore as intelligible to the one, as familiar to the other. It
is not always that so good a plea can be offered for the author's
allusions ; for, to confess the truth, the habits and manners of
different countries are, in some of these scenes, as I have said
before, most cruelly confounded.

[9] Car. *There's your* beglerbeg.] i. e. chief governor of a
province.

[1] Car. *Or your* sanzacke.] Governor of a city.

[2] *Gaz.* Sauce-jack ! *fie, none of that.*] The pleasantry of Gazet
is not very conspicuous for its humour ; the modern editors however have contrived to cloud it : they read, *Saucy* Jack !

[3] Car. *Your* chiaus.] An officer in the Turkish court, who
performs the duty of an usher ; also an ambassador to foreign
princes and states. COXETER.

Gaz. Nor that.

Car. Chief gardener.

Gaz. Out upon't!

'Twill put me in mind my mother was an herb-
woman.

What is your place, I pray you?

Car. Sir, an eunuch.

Gaz. An eunuch! very fine, i'faith; an eunuch!

And what are your employments?

Car.⁺ Neat and easy:

In the day, I wait on my lady when she eats,

Carry her pantofles, bear up her train;

Sing her asleep at night, and, when she pleases,

I am her bedfellow.

Gaz. How! her bedfellow?

And lie with her?

Car. Yes, and lie with her.

Gaz. O rare!

I'll be an eunuch, though I sell my shop for't,

And all my wares.

Car. It is but parting with

A precious stone or two: I know the price on't.

Gaz. I'll part with all my stones; and, when I
am

An eunuch, I'll so toss and touse the ladies——

Pray you help me to a chapman.

Car. The court surgeon

Shall do you that favour.

Gaz. I am made! an eunuch!

⁺ Car. *Neat and easy:*] I have taken this from Gazet, to
whom it has hitherto been allotted, and given it to Carazie.
The old copy has no mark of interrogation after *easy*, which
seems to prove that the words originally belonged to him.

Enter MANTO.

Mant. Carazie, quit the room.
Car. Come, sir; we'll treat of
Your business further.
Gaz. Excellent! an eunuch!   [*Exeunt.*

SCENE V.

An inner Room in the same.

Enter DONUSA *and* VITELLI.

Vitel. Leave me, or I am lost again : no prayers,
No penitence, can redeem me.
Don. Am I grown
Old or deform'd since yesterday ?
Vitel. You are still,
(Although the sating of your lust hath sullied
The immaculate whiteness of your virgin beauties,)
Too fair for me to look on: and, though pureness,
The sword with which you ever fought and con-
        quer'd,
Is ravish'd from you by unchaste desires,
You are too strong for flesh and blood to treat
        with,
Though iron grates were interposed between us,
To warrant me from treason.
Don. Whom do you fear?
Vitel. That human frailty I took from my
        mother,
That, as my youth increased, grew stronger on me;
That still pursues me, and, though once recover'd,
In scorn of reason, and, what's more, religion,
Again seeks to betray me.

Don. If you mean, sir,
To my embraces, you turn rebel to
The laws of nature, the great queen and mother
Of all productions, and deny allegiance,
Where you stand bound to pay it.

Vitel. I will stop
Mine ears against these charms, which, if Ulysses
Could live again, and hear this second Syren,
Though bound with cables to his mast, his ship too
Fasten'd with all her anchors, this enchantment
Would force him, in despite of all resistance,
To leap into the sea, and follow her;
Although destruction, with outstretch'd arms,
Stood ready to receive him.

Don. Gentle sir,
Though you deny to hear me, yet vouchsafe
To look upon me: though I use no language,
The grief for this unkind repulse will print
Such a dumb eloquence upon my face,
As will not only plead but prevail for me.

Vitel. I am a coward. I will see and hear you,
The trial, else, is nothing; nor the conquest,
My temperance shall crown me with hereafter,
Worthy to be remember'd. Up, my virtue!
And holy thoughts and resolutions arm me
Against this fierce temptation! give me voice
Tuned to a zealous anger, to express
At what an over-value I have purchased
The wanton treasure of your virgin bounties;
That, in their false fruition, heap upon me
Despair and horror.—That I could with that ease
Redeem my forfeit innocence, or cast up
The poison I received into my entrails,
From the alluring cup of your enticements,
As now I do deliver back the price
                                   [*Returns the jewels.*
And salary of your lust! or thus unclothe me

Of sin's gay trappings, the proud livery
            [Throws off his cloak and doublet.
Of wicked pleasure, which but worn and heated
With the fire of entertainment and consent,
Like to Alcides' fatal shirt, tears off
Our flesh and reputation both together,
Leaving our ulcerous follies bare and open
To all malicious censure !
    Don. You must grant,
If you hold that a loss to you, mine equals,
If not transcends it.   If you then first tasted
That poison, as you call it, I brought with me
A palate unacquainted with the relish
Of those delights, which most, as I have heard,
Greedily swallow; and then the offence,
If my opinion may be believed,
Is not so great: howe'er, the wrong no more,
Than if Hippolitus and the virgin huntress
Should meet and kiss together.
    Vitel. What defences
Can lust raise to maintain a precipice

       Enter ASAMBEG *and* MUSTAPHA, *above.*

To the abyss of looseness !—but affords not
The least stair, or the fastening of one foot,
To reascend that glorious height we fell from.
    Musta. By Mahomet, she courts him !
                    [Donusa kneels.
    Asam. Nay, kneels to him !
Observe, the scornful villain turns away too,
As glorying in his conquest.
    Don. Are you marble?
If Christians have mothers, sure they share in
The tigress' fierceness; for, if you were owner
Of human pity, you could not endure
A princess to kneel to you, or look on

These falling tears which hardest rocks would
    soften,
And yet remain unmoved. Did you but give
    me
A taste of happiness in your embraces,
That the remembrance of the sweetness of it
Might leave perpetual bitterness behind it?
Or shew'd me what it was to be a wife,
To live a widow ever?
    Asam. She has confest it!——
Seize on him, villains.

        Enter Capiaga *and* Aga, *with* Janizaries.

            O the Furies!
        [*Exeunt Asambeg and Mustapha above.*
    Don. How!
Are we betray'd?
    Vitel. The better; I expected
A Turkish faith.
    Don. Who am I, that you dare this?
'Tis I that do command you to forbear
A touch of violence.
    Aga. We, already, madam,
Have satisfied your pleasure further than
We know to answer it.
    Cap. Would we were well off!
We stand too far engaged, I fear.
    Don. For us?
We'll bring you safe off: who dares contradict
What is our pleasure?

        Re-enter ASAMBEG *and* MUSTAPHA, *below.*

    Asam. Spurn the dog to prison.
I'll answer you anon.

Vitel. What punishment
Soe'er I undergo, I am still a Christian.
              [Exit Guard with Vitelli.
  Don. What bold presumption's this? Under
    what law
Am I to fall, that set my foot upon
Your statutes and decrees?
  Musta. The crime committed,
Our Alcoran calls death.
  Don. Tush! who is here,
That is not Amurath's slave, and so, unfit
To sit a judge upon his blood?
  Asam. You have lost,
And shamed the privilege of it; robb'd me too
Of my soul, my understanding, to behold
Your base unworthy fall from your high virtue.
  Don. I do appeal to Amurath.
  Asam. We will offer
No violence to your person, till we know
His sacred pleasure; till when, under guard
You shall continue here.
  Don. Shall!
  Asam. I have said it.
  Don. We shall remember this.
  Asam. It ill becomes
Such as are guilty, to deliver threats
Against the innocent. [*The Guard leads off Do-*
    nusa.]—I could tear this flesh now,
But 'tis in vain; nor must I talk, but do.
Provide a well-mann'd galley for Constantinople:
Such sad news never came to our great master.
As he directs, we must proceed, and know
No will but his, to whom what's ours we owe.
              [Exeunt.

ACT IV. SCENE I.

A Room in Grimaldi's *House.*

Enter Master *and* Boatswain.

Mast. He does begin to eat?

Boatsw. A little, master;
But our best hope for his recovery is, that
His raving leaves him; and those dreadful words,
Damnation and despair, with which he ever
Ended all his discourses, are forgotten.

Mast. This stranger is a most religious man sure;
And I am doubtful, whether his charity
In the relieving of our wants, or care
To cure the wounded conscience of Grimaldi,
Deserves more admiration.

Boatsw. Can you guess
What the reason should be, that we never mention
The church, or the high altar, but his melancholy
Grows and increases on him?

Mast. I have heard him,
When he gloried to profess himself an atheist,
Talk often, and with much delight and boasting,
Of a rude prank he did ere he turn'd pirate;
The memory of which, as it appears,
Lies heavy on him.

Boatsw. Pray you, let me understand it.

Mast. Upon a solemn day, when the whole city
Join'd in devotion, and with barefoot steps
Pass'd to St. Mark's, the duke, and the whole
  signiory,
Helping to perfect the religious pomp
With which they were received; when all men else

Were full of tears, and groan'd beneath the weight
Of past offences, of whose heavy burthen
They came to be absolved and freed; our captain,
Whether in scorn of those so pious rites
He had no feeling of, or else drawn to it
Out of a wanton, irreligious madness,
(I know not which,) ran to the holy man,
As he was doing of the work of grace,[5]
And snatching from his hands the sanctified
    means,
Dash'd it upon the pavement.

  Boatsw. How escaped he,
It being a deed deserving death with torture?

  Mast. The general amazement of the people
Gave him leave to quit the temple, and a gondola,
Prepared, it seems, before, brought him aboard;
Since which he ne'er saw Venice. The remem-
    brance
Of this, it seems, torments him; aggravated
With a strong belief he cannot receive pardon
For this foul fact, but from his hands, against
    whom
It was committed.

  Boatsw. And what course intends
His heavenly physician, reverend Francisco,
To beat down this opinion?

  Mast. He promised
To use some holy and religious fineness,[6]

---

  [5] *As he was doing of the work of grace,* &c.] This is a reve-
rential description of the elevation of the host; and could only
be written by a man on whom that awful act of pious daring
had made a deep and lasting impression.

  [6] *To use some holy and religious* fineness,] i. e. subtile and
ingenious device. Coxeter, whose ideas of harmony were never
parallelled, unless by those of Mr. M. Mason, corrupted this
into *finesse,* though the line was reduced to absolute prose by
it. Massinger knew no such word; the introduction of which

To this good end; and, in the mean time, charged me
To keep him dark, and to admit no visitants:
But on no terms to cross him. Here he comes.

Enter GRIMALDI, *with a book.*[7]

Grim. For theft, he that restores treble the value,
Makes satisfaction; and, for want of means
To do so, as a slave must serve it out,
Till he hath made full payment. There's hope left here.
Oh! with what willingness would I give up
My liberty to those that I have pillaged;
And wish the numbers of my years, though wasted
In the most sordid slavery, might equal
The rapines I have made; till, with one voice,
My patient sufferings might exact, from my
Most cruel creditors, a full remission,
An eye's loss with an eye, limb's with a limb:
A sad account!—yet, to find peace within here,
Though all such as I have maim'd and dismember'd
In drunken quarrels, or o'ercome with rage,

is justly reprobated by Johnson, as wholly unnecessary. But, indeed, in all times, our language has been over-run and debased by fantastic terms,

"Which sweet Philisides fetch'd of late from France."

The word occurs, in its natural sense, in *the Devil's an Ass:*

"—— you'll mar all with your *fineness!*

Here, too, Mr. Sympson proposes to read *finesse!* while Whalley, who properly rejects his amendment, explains the original word, by "shyness, or coyness;" to which it bears not the slightest affinity.

7 —————— *with a* book.] The book was a very proper one for Grimaldi: from his references, it appears to be the Bible.

When they were given up to my power, stood
    here now,
And cried for restitution; to appease them,
I would do a bloody justice on myself:
Pull out these eyes, that guided me to ravish
Their sight from others; lop these legs, that bore
    me
To barbarous violence; with this hand cut off
This instrument of wrong, till nought were left
    me
But this poor bleeding limbless trunk, which gladly
I would divide among them.—Ha! what think I

Enter FRANCISCO *in a cope, like a Bishop.*

Of petty forfeitures! In this reverend habit,
All that I am turn'd into eyes, I look on
A deed of mine so fiend-like, that repentance,
Though with my tears I taught the sea new tides,
Can never wash off: all my thefts, my rapes,
Are venial trespasses, compared to what
I offer'd to that shape, and in a place too,
Where I stood bound to kneel to't.　　[*Kneels.*
    Fran. 'Tis forgiven:
I with his tongue, whom, in these sacred vestments,
With impure hands thou didst offend, pronounce
    it.
I bring peace to thee; see that thou deserve it
In thy fair life hereafter.
    Grim. Can it be!
Dare I believe this vision, or hope
A pardon e'er may find me?
    Fran. Purchase it
By zealous undertakings, and no more
'Twill be remembered.
    Grim. What celestial balm　　[*Rises.*
I feel now pour'd into my wounded conscience!

What penance is there I'll not undergo,
Though ne'er so sharp and rugged, with more
    pleasure
Than flesh and blood e'er tasted ! shew me true
    Sorrow,
Arm'd with an iron whip, and I will meet
The stripes she brings along with her, as if
They were the gentle touches of a hand
That comes to cure me. Can good deeds re-
    deem me?
I will rise up a wonder to the world,
When I have given strong proofs how I am alter'd.
I, that have sold such as profess'd the faith
That I was born in, to captivity,
Will make their number equal, that I shall
Deliver from the oar ; and win as many
By the clearness of my actions, to look on
Their misbelief, and loath it.   I will be
A convoy for all merchants ; and thought worthy
To be reported to the world, hereafter,
The child of your devotion; nurs'd up,
And made strong by your charity, to break
    through
All dangers hell can bring forth to oppose me.
Nor am I, though my fortunes were thought
    desperate,
Now you have reconciled me to myself,
So void of worldly means, but, in despite
Of the proud viceroy's wrongs, I can do some-
    thing
To witness of my change : when you please, try
    me,[8]

8   ——— *I can do something*
To witness of my change : when you please, **try me**, &c.] The
reader must be convinced, long ere this, that the modern editions of Massinger offer a very inadequate representation of his
works. Numerous as the errors pointed out are, a still greater

And I will perfect what you shall enjoin me,
Or fall a joyful martyr.
 Fran. You will reap
The comfort of it; live yet undiscover'd,
And with your holy meditations strengthen
Your Christian resolution : ere long,
You shall hear further from me.   [*Exit.*
 Grim. I'll attend
All your commands with patience;—come, my
  mates,
I hitherto have lived an ill example,
And, as your captain, led you on to mischief;
But now will truly labour, that good men
May say hereafter of me, to my glory,
(Let but my power and means hand with my
  will,⁹)
His good endeavours did weigh down his ill.
         [*Exeunt.*

  Re-enter FRANCISCO, *in his usual habit.*

 Fran. This penitence is not counterfeit: how-
  soever,
Good actions are in themselves rewarded.
My travail's to meet with a double crown.
If that Vitelli come off safe, and prove
Himself the master of his wild affections—

number have been corrected in silence : of these the source is
generally obvious ; here, however, is one for which no motive
can be assigned ; it is a gratuitous and wanton deviation from
the original, that no degree of folly can justify, no excess of
negligence account for :—In Coxeter and Mr. M. Mason the
passage stands thus—

    I can do something
  To prove that I have power, *when you please try me!*

 ⁹ (*Let but my power and means* hand with my will,)] i. e. **go**
hand *in hand, co-operate* with my will.

Enter GAZET.

O, I shall have intelligence ; how now, Gazet,
Why these sad looks and tears ?
   Gaz. Tears, sir ! I have lost
My worthy master. Your rich heir seems to
     mourn for
A miserable father, your young widow,
Following a bedrid husband to his grave,
Would have her neighbours think she cries and
     roars,
That she must part with such a goodman Do-
     nothing ;
When 'tis, because he stays so long above ground,
And hinders a rich suitor.—All's come out, sir.
We are smoak'd for being coney-catchers : my
     master
Is put in prison; his she-customer
Is under guard too; these are things to weep for:—
But mine own loss consider'd, and what a fortune
I have had, as they say, snatch'd out of my chops,
Would make a man run mad.
   Fran. I scarce have leisure,
I am so wholly taken up with sorrow
For my loved pupil, to enquire thy fate;
Yet I will hear it.
   Gaz. Why, sir, I had bought a place,
A place of credit too, an I had gone through
     with it ;
I should have been made an eunuch : there was
     honour
For a late poor prentice ! when, upon the sudden,
There was such a hurlyburly in the court,
That I was glad to run away, and carry
The price of my office with me.
   Fran. Is that all ?

You have made a saving voyage: we must think
    now,
Though not to free, to comfort sad Vitelli;
My grieved soul suffers for him.
    Gaz. I am sad too;
But had I been an eunuch——
    Fran. Think not on it.   [*Exeunt.*

SCENE II.

A Hall in Asambeg's *Palace.*

Enter Asambeg; *he unlocks a door, and* Paulina
    comes forth.

    Asam. Be your own guard: obsequiousness
    and service
Shall win you to be mine. Of all restraint
For ever take your leave, no threats shall awe you,
No jealous doubts of mine disturb your freedom,
No fee'd spies wait upon your steps: your virtue,
And due consideration in yourself
Of what is noble, are the faithful helps
I leave you, as supporters, to defend you
From falling basely.
    Paul. This is wondrous strange:
Whence flows this alteration?
    Asam. From true judgment;
And strong assurance, neither grates of iron,
Hemm'd in with walls of brass, strict guards,
    high birth,
The forfeiture of honour, nor the fear
Of infamy or punishment, can stay
A woman slaved to appetite, from being
False, and unworthy.
    Paul. You are grown satirical

Against our sex. Why, sir, I durst produce
Myself in our defence, and from you challenge
A testimony that's not to be denied,
All fall not under this unequal censure.
I, that have stood your flatteries, your threats,
Born up against your fierce temptations ; scorn'd
The cruel means you practised to supplant me,[1]
Having no arms to help me to hold out,
But love of piety, and constant goodness ;
If you are unconfirm'd, dare again boldly,
Enter into the lists, and combat with
All opposites man's malice can bring forth
To shake me in my chastity, built upon
The rock of my religion.

   Asam. I do wish
I could believe you ; but, when I shall shew you
A most incredible example of
Your frailty, in a princess, sued and sought to
By men of worth, of rank, of eminence ; courted
By happiness itself, and her cold temper
Approved by many years ; yet she to fall,
Fall from herself, her glories, nay, her safety,
Into a gulf of shame and black despair ;
I think you'll doubt yourself, or, in beholding
Her punishment, for ever be deterr'd
From yielding basely.

   Paul. I would see this wonder ;
'Tis, sir, my first petition.

   Asam. And thus granted :
Above, you shall observe all.   [*Exit Paulina.*

Enter MUSTAPHA.

   Musta. Sir, I sought you,
And must relate a wonder. Since I studied,

---

   [1] —— *to* supplant *me,*] A Latinism—to trip up, to overthrow, &c.

And knew what man was, I was never witness
Of such invincible fortitude as this Christian
Shews in his sufferings : all the torments that
We could present him with, to fright his constancy,
Confirm'd, not shook it; and those heavy chains,
That eat into his flesh, appear'd to him
Like bracelets made of some loved mistress' hairs
We kiss in the remembrance of her favours.
I am strangely taken with it, and have lost
Much of my fury.
 Asam. Had he suffer'd poorly,
It had call'd on my contempt; but manly patience,
And all-commanding virtue, wins upon
An enemy. I shall think upon him.—Ha !

   Enter Aga,[2] *with a black box.*

So soon return'd ! This speed pleads in excuse
Of your late fault, which I no more remember.
What's the grand signior's pleasure ?
 Aga. 'Tis enclosed here.
The box too that contains it may inform you
How he stands affected : I am trusted with
Nothing but this, On forfeit of your head,
She must have a speedy trial.
 Asam. Bring her in

 [2] *Enter* Aga,] I suppose the reader will be inclined to ex-
claim with Asambeg, " So soon return'd !" for from Tunis to
Constantinople is an interval *humanè commodum.* I have neither
enter d, nor proposed to enter, into any disquisitions on the
preservation of the unities of time and place, which must be a
work of absolute supererogation in criticizing an author who
totally forgot or disregarded them. Massinger is not more ir-
regular than his contemporaries ; indeed he is less so than most
of them ; but, in all cases, I am persuaded that he followed his
story, without entertaining much anxiety as to the time which
it might occupy, or the various changes of situation which it
might require.

In black, as to her funeral : [*Exit Aga.*] 'tis the
    colour
Her fault wills her to wear, and which, in justice,
I dare not pity. Sit, and take your place :
However in her life she has degenerated,
May she die nobly, and in that confirm
Her greatness and high blood!

Solemn music. Re-enter the Aga, *with the* Capiaga
    leading in Donusa *in black, her train born up*
    by Carazie *and* Manto. *A Guard attending.*
    Paulina *enters above.*

    Musta. I now could melt—
But soft compassion leave me.
    Mant. I am affrighted
With this dismal preparation. Should the enjoying
Of loose desires find ever such conclusions,
All women would be Vestals.
    Don. That you clothe me
In this sad livery of death, assures me
Your sentence is gone out before, and I
Too late am call'd for, in my guilty cause
To use qualification or excuse——
Yet must I not part so with mine own strengths,[3]
But borrow, from my modesty, boldness, to
Enquire by whose authority you sit
My judges, and whose warrant digs my grave
In the frowns you dart against my life?
    Asam. See here,
This fatal sign and warrant! This, brought to
A general, fighting in the head of his

---

[3] *Yet must I not part so with mine own* strengths,] The modern
editors read *strength,* which does not convey Massinger's meaning, and, indeed, is scarcely sense in this place : but they did
not understand the word. *Strengths* are castles, strong places,
and metaphorically *defences,* as here.

Victorious troops, ravishes from his hand
His even then conquering sword; this, shewn unto
The sultan's brothers, or his sons, delivers
His deadly anger; and, all hopes laid by,
Commands them to prepare themselves for heaven;
Which would stand with the quiet of your soul,
To think upon, and imitate.

   Don. Give me leave
A little to complain; first, of the hard
Condition of my fortune, which may move you,
Though not to rise up intercessors for me,
Yet, in remembrance of my former life,
(This being the first spot tainting mine honour,)
To be the means to bring me to his presence:
And then I doubt not, but I could allege
Such reasons in mine own defence, or plead
So humbly, (my tears helping,) that it should
Awake his sleeping pity.

   Asam. 'Tis in vain.
If you have aught to say, you shall have hearing;
And, in me, think him present.

   Don. I would thus then
First kneel, and kiss his feet; and after, tell him
How long I had been his darling; what delight
My infant years afforded him; how dear
He prized his sister in both bloods, my mother:
That she, like him, had frailty, that to me
Descends as an inheritance; then conjure him,
By her blest ashes, and his father's soul,
The sword that rides upon his thigh, his right
    hand
Holding the sceptre and the Othoman fortune,
To have compassion on me.

   Asam. But suppose
(As I am sure) he would be deaf, what then
Could you infer?

   Don. I, then, would thus rise up,

And to his teeth tell him he was a tyrant,
A most voluptuous and insatiable epicure
In his own pleasures; which he hugs so dearly,
As proper and peculiar to himself,
That he denies a moderate lawful use
Of all delight to others. And to thee,
Unequal judge, I speak as much, and charge thee,
But with impartial eyes to look into
Thyself, and then consider with what justice
Thou canst pronounce my sentence. Unkind
    nature,
To make weak women servants, proud men masters!
Indulgent Mahomet, do thy bloody laws
Call my embraces with a Christian death,
Having my heat and May of youth, to plead
In my excuse? and yet want power to punish
These that, with scorn, break through thy cobweb
    edicts,
And laugh at thy decrees? To tame their lusts
There's no religious bit: let her be fair,
And pleasing to the eye, though Persian, Moor,
Idolatress, Turk, or Christian, you are privileged,
And freely may enjoy her. At this instant,
I know, unjust man, thou hast in thy power
A lovely Christian virgin; thy offence
Equal, if not transcending mine: why, then,
(We being both guilty,) dost thou not descend
From that usurp'd tribunal, and with me
Walk hand in hand to death?
   Asam. She raves; and we
Lose time to hear her: Read the law.
   Don. Do, do;
I stand resolved to suffer.
   Aga. [reads.] *If any virgin, of what degree, or
quality soever, born a natural Turk, shall be con-
victed of corporal looseness, and incontinence with any*

Christian, she is, by the decree of our great prophet,
Mahomet, to lose her head.

Asam. Mark that, then tax our justice !

Aga. Ever provided, That if she, the said offender,
by any reasons, arguments, or persuasion, can win
and prevail with the said Christian offending with her,
to alter his religion, and marry her, that then the
winning of a soul to the Mahometan sect, shall acquit
her from all shame, disgrace, and punishment what-
soever.

Don. I lay hold on that clause, and challenge
  from you
The privilege of the law.

Must. What will you do ?

Don. Grant me access and means, I'll under-
  take
To turn this Christian Turk, and marry him :
This trial you cannot deny.

Musta. O base !
Can fear to die make you descend so low
From your high birth, and brand the Othoman
  line
With such a mark of infamy ?

Asam. This is worse
Than the parting with your honour. Better suffer
Ten thousand deaths, and without hope to have
A place in our great prophet's paradise,
Than have an act to aftertimes remember'd,
So foul as this is.

Musta. Cheer your spirits, madam ;
To die is nothing, 'tis but parting with
A mountain of vexations.

Asam. Think of your honour :
In dying nobly, you make satisfaction
For your offence, and you shall live a story
Of bold heroic courage.

Don. You shall not fool me
Out of my life : I claim the law, and sue for
A speedy trial ; if I fail, you may
Determine of me as you please.
    Asam. Base woman !
But use thy ways, and see thou prosper in them ;
For, if thou fall again into my power,
Thou shalt in vain, after a thousand tortures,
Cry out for death, that death which now thou
    fliest from.
Unloose the prisoner's chains. Go, lead her on,
To try the magic of her tongue. I follow :
                    [*Exeunt all but Asambeg.*
I'm on the rack—descend, my best Paulina.
                    [*Exit with Paulina.*

SCENE III.

A Room in the Prison.

Enter FRANCISCO *and* Gaoler.

    Fran. I come not empty-handed ; I will pur-
        chase
Your favour at what rate you please. There's
        gold.
    Gaol. 'Tis the best oratory. I will hazard
A check for your content.—Below, there !
    Vitel. [*below.*] Welcome !
Art thou the happy messenger, that brings me
News of my death ?
    Gaol. Your hand.   [*Plucks up Vitelli.*
    Fran. Now, if you please,
A little privacy.
    Gaol. You have bought it, sir ;
Enjoy it freely.   [*Exit.*
    Fran. O, my dearest pupil !

Witness these tears of joy, I never saw you,
'Till now, look lovely ; nor durst I ever glory
In the mind of any man I had built up
With the hands of virtuous and religious precepts,
Till this glad minute. Now you have made
    good
My expectation of you. By my order,
All Roman Cæsars, that led kings in chains,
Fast bound to their triumphant chariots, if
Compared with that true glory and full lustre
You now appear in ; all their boasted honours,
Purchased with blood and wrong, would lose their
    names,
And be no more remember'd !
   Vitel. This applause,
Confirm'd in your allowance, joys me more
Than if a thousand full-cramm'd theatres
Should clap their eager hands, to witness that
The scene I act did please, and they admire it.
But these are, father, but beginnings, not
The ends, of my high aims. I grant, to have
    master'd
The rebel appetite of flesh and blood,
Was far above my strength ; and still owe for it
To that great Power that lent it : but, when I
Shall make't apparent the grim looks of Death
Affright me not, and that I can put off
The fond desire of life, (that, like a garment,
Covers and clothes our frailty,) hastening to
My martyrdom, as to a heavenly banquet,
To which I was a choice invited guest ;
Then you may boldly say, you did not plough,
Or trust the barren and ungrateful sands
With the fruitful grain of your religious counsels.
   Fran. You do instruct your teacher. Let the
    sun
Of your clear life, that lends to **good men light,**

But set as gloriously as it did rise,
(Though sometimes clouded,) you may write *nil
    ultra*
To human wishes.
   Vitel. I have almost gain'd
The end o' the race, and will not faint or tire now.

   Re-enter Gaoler *with* Aga.

   Aga. Sir, by your leave,—nay, stay not,[4] [*to
    the Gaoler, who goes out.*] I bring comfort.
The viceroy, taken with the constant bearing
Of your afflictions; and presuming too
You will not change your temper, does command
Your irons should be ta'en off. [*They take off
    his irons.*] Now arm yourself
With your old resolution; suddenly
You shall be visited. You must leave the room
    too,
And do it without reply.
   Fran. There's no contending:
Be still thyself, my son.
          [*Exeunt Aga and Francisco.*
   Vitel. 'Tis not in man

   Enter DONUSA, *followed at a distance by* ASAM-
BEG, MUSTAPHA, *and* PAULINA.

To change or alter me.
   Paul. Whom do I look on?
My brother? 'tis he!—but no more, my tongue;
Thou wilt betray all.   [*Aside.*
   Asam. Let us hear this temptress:
The fellow looks as he would stop his ears
Against her powerful spells.

   [4] ————— *nay,* stay *not,*] So the old copy
reads. Coxeter and M. Mason read, *stare* not: but they did
not see that this was addressed to the Gaoler.

Paul. He is undone else.   [*Aside.*

Vitel. I'll stand the encounter—charge me
    home.

Don. I come, sir,   [*Bows herself.*
A beggar to you, and doubt not to find
A good man's charity, which if you deny,
You are cruel to yourself; a crime a wise man
(And such I hold you) would not willingly
Be guilty of: nor let it find less welcome,
Though I, a creature you contemn, now shew
        you
The way to certain happiness; nor think it
Imaginary or fantastical,
And so not worth the acquiring, in respect
The passage to it is nor rough nor thorny;
No steep hills in the way which you must climb up,
No monsters to be conquer'd, no enchantments
To be dissolved by counter charms, before
You take possession of it.

Vitel. What strong poison
Is wrapp'd up in these sugar'd pills?

Don. My suit is,
That you would quit your shoulders of a burthen,
Under whose ponderous weight you wilfully
Have too long groan'd, to cast those fetters off,
With which, with your own hands, you chain your
        freedom:
Forsake a severe, nay, imperious mistress,
Whose service does exact perpetual cares,
Watchings, and troubles; and give entertainment
To one that courts you, whose least favours are
Variety, and choice of all delights
Mankind is capable of.

Vitel. You speak in riddles.
What burthen, or what mistress, or what fetters,
Are those you point at?

Don. Those which your religion,

The mistress you too long have served, compels you[5]
To bear with slave-like patience.
   Vitel. Ha!
   Paul. How bravely
That virtuous anger shews!
   Don. Be wise, and weigh[6]
The prosperous success of things; if blessings
Are donatives from heaven, (which, you must grant,
Were blasphemy to question,) and that
They are call'd down and pour'd on such as are
Most gracious with the great Disposer of them,
Look on our flourishing empire, if the splendor,
The majesty, and glory of it dim not
Your feeble sight; and then turn back, and see
The narrow bounds of yours, yet that poor remnant
Rent in as many factions and opinions
As you have petty kingdoms;—and then, if
You are not obstinate against truth and reason,
You must confess the Deity you worship
Wants care or power to help you.
   Paul. Hold out now,
And then thou art victorious.   [*Aside.*
   Asam. How he eyes her!
   Musta. As if he would look through her.

---

    5   —— ——— *compels* you] Coxeter dropt
the last word at the press. Mr. M. Mason omits it of course,
though the passage is not sense without it. In the next speech,
for *that* virtuous anger, he reads *the* &c. There are other
errors and omissions, which are here rectified and supplied.

   6 *Don. Be wise, and weigh* &c.] Part of this speech is taken,
but with great skill, from Minucius Felix; indeed it was the
leading argument, and constantly directed, for the two first ages
of the church, against the Christians; after the Reformation, the
church of Rome took it up, and pointed it with equal propriety,
and, indeed, with equal success, against the Protestants.

Asam. His eyes flame too,
As threatening violence.
    Vitel. But that I know
The devil, thy tutor, fills each part about thee,
And that I cannot play the exorcist
To dispossess thee, unless I should tear
Thy body limb by limb, and throw it to
The Furies, that expect it; I would now
Pluck out that wicked tongue, that hath blas-
        phemed
The great Omnipotency, at whose nod
The fabric of the world shakes. Dare you bring
Your juggling prophet in comparison with
That most inscrutable and infinite Essence,
That made this All, and comprehends his work!—
The place is too profane to mention him
Whose only name is sacred.[7] O Donusa!
How much, in my compassion, I suffer,
That thou, on whom this most excelling form,
And faculties of discourse,[8] beyond a woman,
Were by his liberal gift conferr'd, shouldst still
Remain in ignorance of him that gave it!
I will not foul my mouth to speak the sorceries
Of your seducer, his base birth, his whoredoms,
His strange impostures; nor deliver how
He taught a pigeon to feed in his ear,
Then made his credulous followers believe

---

[7] *The place is too profane to mention him*
Whose only name *is sacred.*] i. e. whose name is the sole
or only one that is sacred : a mode of expression frequently
adopted by our old writers.
    [8] *And faculties of* discourse,] i. e. of reason. See Vol. I. p.
148. It is to be regretted, that so just and noble a speech as
this assuredly is, should be debased by the insertion of the contemptible fable with which it concludes : that fable, however,
was gravely delivered by contemporary historians and divines;
Massinger, therefore, though he may perhaps be arraigned for
want of taste, cannot fairly be charged with over credulity.

It was an angel, that instructed him
In the framing of his Alcoran—pray you, mark
   me.
  Asam. These words are death, were he in nought
   else guilty.
  Vitel. Your intent to win me[9]
To be of your belief, proceeded from
Your fear to die. Can there be strength in that
Religion, that suffers us to tremble
At that which every day, nay hour, we haste to?
  Don. This is unanswerable, and there's some-
   thing tells me
I err in my opinion.
  Vitel. Cherish it,
It is a heavenly prompter; entertain
This holy motion, and wear on your forehead
The sacred badge he arms his servants with;[1]
You shall, like me, with scorn look down upon
All engines tyranny can advance to batter
Your constant resolution. Then you shall
Look truly fair, when your mind's pureness an-
   swers
Your outward beauties.
  Don. I came here to take you,
But I perceive a yielding in myself
To be your prisoner.
  Vitel. 'Tis an overthrow,
That will outshine all victories. O Donusa,
Die in my faith, like me; and 'tis a marriage

  [9] Vitel. *Your intent to win me*] A hemistich preceding this,
is lost; it was probably an ejaculatory remark from Paulina.
  [1] ————— *and wear on your forehead*
The sacred badge he arms his servants with;] This is a peri-
phrasis of baptism, familiar to the Catholic writers. It may
neither be unamusing, nor uninstructive, for the reader to compare this scene with the third act of *the Virgin-Martyr :* he will
find many passages strikingly similar.

At which celestial angels shall be waiters,
And such as have been sainted welcome us:
Are you confirm'd?
    Don. I would be; but the means
That may assure me?
    Vitel. Heaven is merciful,
And will not suffer you to want a man
To do that sacred office, build upon it.
    Don. Then thus I spit at Mahomet.
    Asam. [*coming forward.*] Stop her mouth:
In death to turn apostata! I'll not hear
One syllable from any.—Wretched creature!
With the next rising sun prepare to die.—
Yet, Christian, in reward of thy brave courage,
Be thy faith right or wrong, receive this favour;
In person I'll attend thee to thy death:
And boldly challenge all that I can give,
But what's not in my grant, which is—to live.
                                        [*Exeunt.*

ACT V. SCENE I.

A Room in the Prison.

Enter VITELLI *and* FRANCISCO.

    Fran. You are wondrous brave[2] and jocund.
    Vitel. Welcome, father.
Should I spare cost, or not wear cheerful looks
Upon my wedding day, it were ominous,
And shew'd I did repent it; which I dare not,

    [2] *Fran. You are wondrous* brave *and jocund.*] i. e. as has been
already observed, richly, splendidly apparelled.

It being a marriage, howsoever sad
In the first ceremonies that confirm it,
That will for ever arm me against fears,
Repentance, doubts, or jealousies, and bring
Perpetual comforts, peace of mind, and quiet
To the glad couple.
  Fran. I well understand you;
And my full joy to see you so resolved
Weak words cannot express. What is the hour
Design'd for this solemnity?
  Vitel. The sixth:
Something before the setting of the sun,
We take our last leave of his fading light,
And with our soul's eyes seek for beams eternal.
Yet there's one scruple with which I am much
Perplex'd and troubled, which I know you can
Resolve me of.
  Fran. What is't?
  Vitel. This, sir; my bride,
Whom I first courted, and then won, not with
Loose lays, poor flatteries, apish compliments,
But sacred and religious zeal, yet wants
The holy badge that should proclaim her fit
For these celestial nuptials: willing she is,
I know, to wear it, as the choicest jewel,
On her fair forehead; but to you, that well
Could do that work of grace, I know the viceroy
Will never grant access. Now, in a case
Of this necessity, I would gladly learn,
Whether, in me, a layman, without orders,
It may not be religious and lawful,
As we go to our deaths, to do that office?
  Fran. A question in itself with much ease
    answer'd:
Midwives, upon necessity, perform it;
And knights that, in the Holy Land, fought for
The freedom of Jerusalem, when full

Of sweat and enemies' blood, have made their
    helmets [3]
The fount, out of which with their holy hands
They drew that heavenly liquor : 'twas approved
    then
By the holy church, nor must I think it now,
In you, a work less pious.
    Vitel. You confirm me ;
I will find a way to do it. In the mean time,
Your holy vows assist me !
    Fran. They shall ever
Be present with you.
    Vitel. You shall see me act
This last scene to the life.
    Fran. And though now fall,
Rise a bless'd martyr.
    Vitel. That's my end, my all.   [*Exeunt.*

SCENE II.

A Street.

Enter GRIMALDI, Master, Boatswain, *and* Sailors.

    Boatsw. Sir, if you slip this opportunity,
Never expect the like.
    Mast. With as much ease now
We may steal the ship out of the harbour, captain,
As ever gallants, in a wanton bravery,
Have set upon a drunken constable,
And bore him from a sleepy rug-gown'd watch :
Be therefore wise.

    [3] *Have made their* helmets &c.] There is an instance of this
in Tasso, and, probably, the particular one which the poet had
in view : the observation, however, as a general one, is perfectly just, and consonant with history.

Grim. I must be honest too.
And you shall wear that shape, you shall observe
    me,
If that you purpose to continue mine.
Think you ingratitude can be the parent
To our unfeign'd repentance? Do I owe
A peace within here, kingdoms could not purchase,
To my religious creditor, to leave him
Open to danger, the great benefit
Never remembered! no; though in her bottom
We could stow up the tribute of the Turk;
Nay, grant the passage safe too; I will never
Consent to weigh an anchor up, till he,
That only must, commands it.
    Boatsw. This religion
Will keep us slaves and beggars.
    Mast. The fiend prompts me
To change my copy: plague upon't! we are
    seamen;
What have we to do with't, but for a snatch or so,
At the end of a long Lent?*

        Enter FRANCISCO.

    Boatsw. Mum: see who is here.
    Grim. My father!
    Fran. My good convert. I am full
Of serious business which denies me leave
To hold long conference with you: only thus
    much
Briefly receive; a day or two, at the most,

---

  * *At the end of a long* Lent?] Massinger alludes to the custom
which all good Catholics had (and, indeed, still have) of confessing themselves at Easter. Good-Friday and Easter Sunday
are almost the only days on which the French and Italian sailors
ever think of repairing to a confessional.

Shall make me fit to take my leave of Tunis,
Or give me lost for ever.
 Grim. Days nor years,
Provided that my stay may do you service,
But to me shall be minutes.
 Fran. I much thank you:
In this small scroll you may in private read
What my intents are; and, as they grow ripe,
I will instruct you further: in the mean time
Borrow your late distracted looks and gesture;
The more dejected you appear, the less
The viceroy must suspect you.
 Grim. I am nothing,
But what you please to have me be.
 Fran. Farewell, sir.
Be cheerful, master, something we will do,
That shall reward itself in the performance;
And that's true prize indeed.
 Mast. I am obedient.
 Boatsw. And I: there's no contending.
   [*Exeunt Grim. Mast. Boatsw. and Sailors.*
 Fran. Peace to you all!
Prosper, thou Great Existence, my endeavours,
As they religiously are undertaken,
And distant equally from servile gain,

  Enter PAULINA, CARAZIE, *and* MANTO.

Or glorious ostentation!—I am heard,
In this blest opportunity, which in vain
I long have waited for. I must shew myself.
O, she has found me! now if she prove right,
All hope will not forsake us.
 Paul. Further off;
And in that distance know your duties too.
You were bestow'd on me as slaves to serve me,

And not as spies to pry into my actions,
And after, to betray me. You shall find
If any look of mine be unobserved,
I am not ignorant of a mistress' power,
And from whom I receive it.

   Car. Note this, Manto,
The pride and scorn with which she entertains us,
Now we are made her's by the viceroy's gift!
Our sweet condition'd princess, fair Donusa,
Rest in her death wait on her! never used us
With such contempt. I would he had sent me
To the gallies, or the gallows, when he gave me
To this proud little devil.

   Mant. I expect
All tyrannous usage, but I must be patient;
And though, ten times a day, she tears these locks,
Or makes this face her footstool, 'tis but justice.

   Paul. 'Tis a true story of my fortunes, father.
My chastity preserved by miracle,
Or your devotions for me; and, believe it,
What outward pride soe'er I counterfeit,
Or state, to these appointed to attend me,
I am not in my disposition alter'd,
But still your humble daughter, and share with
    you
In my poor brother's sufferings:—all hell's tor-
    ments
Revenge it on accurs'd Grimaldi's soul,
That, in his rape of me, gave a beginning
To all the miseries that since have follow'd!

   Fran. Be charitable, and forgive him, gentle
    daughter.
He's a changed man, and may redeem his fault
In his fair life hereafter. You must bear too
Your forced captivity, for 'tis no better,
Though you wear golden fetters, and of him,
Whom death affrights not, learn to hold out nobly.

Paul. You are still the same good counsellor.

Fran. And who knows,

(Since what above is purposed, is inscrutable,)

But that the viceroy's extreme dotage on you

May be the parent of a happier birth

Than yet our hopes dare fashion.   Longer conference

May prove unsafe for you and me ; however

(Perhaps for trial) he allows you freedom.—

                              [*Delivers a paper.*

From this learn therefore what you must attempt,

Though with the hazard of yourself : heaven
guard you,

And give Vitelli patience ! then I doubt not

But he will have a glorious day, since some

Hold truly,—such as suffer, overcome. [*Exeunt.*

SCENE III.

A Hall in Asambeg's *Palace.*

Enter ASAMBEG, MUSTAPHA, Aga, *and* Capiaga.

Asam. What we commanded, see perform'd ;
and fail not

In all things to be punctual.

Aga. We shall, sir. [*Exeunt Aga and Capiaga.*

Musta. 'Tis strange, that you should use such
circumstance

To a delinquent of so mean condition.

Asam. Had he appeared in a more sordid shape

Than disguised greatness ever deign'd to mask in,

The gallant bearing of his present fortune

Aloud proclaims him noble.

Musta. If you doubt him

To be a man built up for great employments,

And, as a cunning spy, sent to explore
The city's strength, or weakness, you by torture
May force him to discover it.
    Asam. That were base;
Nor dare I do such injury to virtue
And bold assured courage; neither can I
Be won to think, but if I should attempt it,
I shoot against the moon. He that hath stood
The roughest battery, that captivity
Could ever bring to shake a constant temper;
Despised the fawnings of a future greatness,
By beauty, in her full perfection, tender'd;
That hears of death as of a quiet slumber,
And from the surplusage of his own firmness,
Can spare enough of fortitude, to assure
A feeble woman; will not,' Mustapha,
Be alter'd in his soul for any torments
We can afflict his body with.
    Musta. Do your pleasure:
I only offer'd you a friend's advice,
But without gall or envy to the man
That is to suffer. But what do you determine
Of poor Grimaldi? the disgrace call'd on him,
I hear, has run him mad.
    Asam. There weigh the difference
In the true temper of their minds. The one,
A pirate, sold to mischiefs, rapes, and all
That make a slave relentless and obdurate,
Yet, of himself wanting the inward strengths
That should defend him, sinks beneath compassion
Or pity of a man: whereas this merchant,

---

⁵ *A feeble woman; will* not, *Mustapha*,] For *not*, the old copy
reads *now*. Instead of correcting this palpable error of the
press, the modern editors add to it a word of no authority, and
thus produce a verse of surprising harmony:

A feeble woman; will now, *Mustapha*, never.

Acquainted only with a civil[6] life ;
Arm'd in himself, intrench'd and fortified
With his own virtue, valuing life and death
At the same price, poorly does not invite
A favour, but commands us do him right ;
Which unto him, and her we both once honour'd
As a just debt, I gladly pay ;—they enter.
Now sit we equal hearers.

[6] *Acquainted only with a* civil *life ;*] *Civil*, in Massinger, as well as in his contemporaries, alludes to the political regulations, customs, and habits, of the city, as distinguished from the court ; sometimes, indeed, it takes a wider range, and comprises a degree of civilization or moral improvement, as opposed to a state of barbarism, or pure nature.

Wherever *civil* occurs in Shakspeare, Steevens interprets, or rather misinterprets, it by " grave, solemn, decent," &c. That it sometimes bears those meanings cannot be denied, but then it is always in reference to citizenship, or to that state of orderly society which is swayed by wise and well-balanced institutions : in its abstract sense it would frequently have no meaning, or at least, none that was worthy of Shakspeare : e. g.

" You, lord archbishop,—
" Whose see is by a *civil* peace maintain'd."
Second Part of Henry IV.

That is, (says Steevens,) a " grave and decent" peace. What is that ?

Again :

" Why should this desert silent be ?
" For it is unpeopled ? No :
" Tongues I'll hang on every tree,
" That shall *civil* sayings show."   *As you like it.*

" That is, grave and solemn sayings !" No, surely : sayings collected from an intercourse with civil life.

A dreadful music. Enter at one door, the Aga, Janizaries, VITELLI, FRANCISCO, *and* GAZET; *at the other,* DONUSA, *(her train born up),* PAULINA, CARAZIE, *and* MANTO.

Musta. I shall hear
And see, sir, without passion; my wrongs arm me.
Vitel. A joyful preparation! To whose bounty
Owe we our thanks for gracing thus our hymen?
The notes, though dreadful to the ear, sound here
As our epithalamium were sung
By a celestial choir, and a full chorus
Assured us future happiness. These that lead me
Gaze not with wanton eyes upon my bride,
Nor for their service are repaid by me
With jealousies or fears; nor do they envy
My passage to those pleasures from which death
Cannot deter me. Great sir, pardon me:
Imagination of the joys I haste to
Made me forget my duty; but the form
And ceremony past, I will attend you,
And with our constant resolution feast you;
Not with coarse cates, forgot as soon as tasted,
But such as shall, while you have memory,
Be pleasing to the palate.
Fran. Be not lost
In what you purpose.   [*Exit.*
Gaz. Call you this a marriage!
It differs little from hanging; I cry at it.
Vitel. See, where my bride appears! in what
     full lustre!
As if the virgins that bear up her train
Had long contended to receive an honour
Above their births, in doing her this service.
Nor comes she fearful to meet those delights,
Which, once past o'er, immortal pleasures follow.
I need not, therefore, comfort or encourage

Her forward steps; and I should offer wrong
To her mind's fortitude, should I but ask
How she can brook the rough high-going sea,
Over whose foamy back our ship, well rigg'd
With hope and strong assurance, must transport
     us.
Nor will I tell her, when we reach the haven,
Which tempests shall not hinder, what loud
     welcome
Shall entertain us; nor commend the place,
To tell whose least perfection would strike dumb
The eloquence of all boasted in story,
Though join'd together.
     Don. 'Tis enough, my dearest,
I dare not doubt you; as your humble shadow,
Lead where you please, I follow.
     Vitel. One suit, sir,
And willingly I cease to be a beggar;
And that you may with more security hear it,
Know, 'tis not life I'll ask, nor to defer
Our deaths, but a few minutes.
     Asam. Speak; 'tis granted.
     Vitel. We being now to take our latest leave,
And grown of one belief, I do desire
I may have your allowance to perform it,
But in the fashion which we Christians use
Upon the like occasions.
     Asam. 'Tis allow'd of.
     Vitel. My service: haste, Gazet, to the next
     spring,
And bring me of it.
     Gaz. Would I could as well
Fetch you a pardon; I would not run but fly,
And be here in a moment.   [*Exit.*
     Musta. What's the mystery
Of this? discover it.
     Vitel. Great sir, I'll tell you.

Each country hath its own peculiar rites:
Some, when they are to die, drink store of wine,
Which, pour'd in liberally, does oft beget
A bastard valour, with which arm'd, they bear
The not-to-be declined charge of death
With less fear and astonishment: others take
Drugs to procure a heavy sleep, that so
They may insensibly receive the means
That casts them in an everlasting slumber;
Others——

Re-enter GAZET, *with water.*

   O welcome!
Asam. Now the use of yours?
Vitel. The clearness of this is a perfect sign
Of innocence: and as this washes off
Stains and pollutions from the things we wear;
Thrown thus upon the forehead, it hath power
To purge those spots that cleave upon' the mind,
     [Sprinkles it on her face.
If thankfully received.
Asam. 'Tis a strange custom.
Vitel. How do you entertain it, my Donusa?
Feel you no alteration, no new motives,
No unexpected aids, that may confirm you
In that to which you were inclined before?
 Don. I am another woman;—till this minute
I never lived, nor durst think how to die.
How long have I been blind! yet on the sudden,
By this blest means, I feel the films of error
Ta'en from my soul's eyes. O divine physician!
That hast bestow'd a sight on me, which Death,
Though ready to embrace me in his arms,

---

[7] ———— *that cleave* upon *the mind,*] So the old copy: the modern editors, with as little judgment as necessity, read, cleave *unto* the mind.

Cannot take from me : let me kiss the hand
That did this miracle, and seal my thanks
Upon those lips from whence these sweet words
            vanish'd,
That freed me from the cruellest of prisons,
Blind ignorance and misbelief. False prophet !
Impostor Mahomet !——
    Asam. I'll hear no more,
You do abuse my favours ; sever them :
Wretch, if thou hadst another life to lose,
This blasphemy deserved it ;—instantly
Carry them to their deaths.
    Vitel. We part now, blest one,
To meet hereafter in a kingdom, where
Hell's malice shall not reach us.
    Paul. Ha ! ha ! ha !
    Asam. What means my mistress ?
    Paul. Who can hold her spleen,
When such ridiculous follies are presented,
The scene, too, made religion ? O, my lord,
How from one cause two contrary effects
Spring up upon the sudden !
    Asam. This is strange.
    Paul. That which hath fool'd her in her death,
            wins me,
That hitherto have barr'd myself from pleasure,
To live in all delight.
    Asam. There's music in this.
    Paul. I now will run as fiercely to your arms
As ever longing woman did, born high
On the swift wings of appetite.
    Vitel. O devil !
    Paul. Nay, more ; for there shall be no odds
            betwixt us,
I will turn Turk.[8]

---

    [8] *I will* turn Turk.
        Gaz. *Most of your tribe do so,*
        When they begin in whore.] To turn *Turk*, was a figurative

Gaz. Most of your tribe do so,
When they begin in whore.   [*Aside.*
   Asam. You are serious, lady ?
   Paul. Serious !—but satisfy me in a suit
That to the world may witness that I have
Some power upon you, and to morrow challenge
Whatever's in my gift; for I will be
At your dispose.
   Gaz. That's ever the subscription
To a damn'd whore's false epistle.   [*Aside.*
   Asam. Ask this hand,
Or, if thou wilt, the heads of these. I am rapt
Beyond myself with joy. Speak, speak, what is it ?
   Paul. But twelve short hours reprieve for this
         base couple.
   Asam. The reason, since you hate them ?
   Paul. That I may
Have time to triumph o'er this wretched woman.
I'll be myself her guardian ; I will feast,
Adorned in her choice and richest jewels :
Commit him to what guards you please. Grant
      this,
I am no more mine own, but yours.
   Asam. Enjoy it ;
Repine at it who dares : bear him safe off
To the black tower, but give him all things
      useful :
The contrary was not in your request ?
   Paul. I do contemn him.
   Don. Peace in death denied me !

expression for a change of condition, or opinion. It should be
observed, that Gazet wantonly perverts the phrase, which is
used in its literal acceptation by Paulina.
      9   ———— *I will be*
   At your dispose.] Mr. M. Mason, for no other reason, as
appears, than that of spoiling the metre, alters this to
                  ——————— *I will be*
   At your disposal.

Paul. Thou shalt not go in liberty to thy grave;
For one night a sultana is my slave.
  Musta. A terrible little tyranness!
  Asam. No more;
Her will shall be a law.   Till now ne'er happy!
                                            [*Exeunt.*

SCENE IV.

A Street.

Enter FRANCISCO, GRIMALDI, Master, Boatswain,
and Sailors.

  Grim. Sir, all things are in readiness; the Turks,
That seized upon my ship, stow'd under hatches;
My men resolved and cheerful. Use but means
To get out of the ports,* we will be ready
To bring you aboard, and then (heaven be but
        pleased)
This, for the viceroy's fleet!
  Fran. Discharge your parts;
In mine I'll not be wanting: Fear not, master;
Something will come along to fraught your bark,
That you will have just cause to say you never
Made such a voyage.
  Must. We will stand the hazard.
  Fran. What's the best hour?
  Boatsw. After the second watch.
  Fran. Enough; each to his charge.
  Grim. We will be careful.   [*Exeunt.*

  * *To get out of the* ports,] i. e. the *gates* of the city. See
Vol. I. p. 8.

SCENE V.

A Room in Asambeg's *Palace.*

Enter PAULINA, DONUSA, CARAZIE, *and*
MANTO.

Paul. Sit, madam, it is fit that I attend you;
And pardon, I beseech you, my rude language,
To which the sooner you will be invited,
When you shall understand, no way was left me
To free you from a present execution,
But by my personating that which never
My nature was acquainted with.
   Don. I believe you.
   Paul. You will, when you shall understand I
      may
Receive the honour to be known unto you
By a nearer name :—and, not to rack you further,
The man you please to favour is my brother;
No merchant, madam, but a gentleman
Of the best rank in Venice.
   Don. I rejoice in't;
But what's this to his freedom ? for myself,
Were he well off, I were secure.
   Paul. I have
A present means, not plotted by myself,
But a religious man, my confessor,
That may preserve all, if we had a servant
Whose faith we might rely on.
   Don. She, that's now
Your slave, was once mine; had I twenty lives,
I durst commit them to her trust.
   Mant. O madam !
I have been false,—forgive me: I'll redeem it

By any thing, however desperate,
You please to impose upon me.
    Paul. Troth, these tears,
I think, cannot be counterfeit; I believe her,
And, if you please, will try her.
    Don. At your peril;
There is no further danger can look towards me.
    Paul. This only then—canst thou use means
        to carry
This bake-meat to Vitelli?
    Mant. With much ease;
I am familiar with the guard; beside,
It being known it was I that betray'd him,[1]
My entrance hardly will of them be question'd.
    Paul. About it then. Say, that 'twas sent to
        him
From his Donusa; bid him search the midst of it,
He there shall find a cordial.
    Mant. What I do
Shall speak my care and faith.   [*Exit.*
    Don. Good fortune with thee!
    Paul. You cannot eat?
    Don. The time we thus abuse
We might employ much better.
    Paul. I am glad
To hear this from you. As for you, Carazie,
If our intents do prosper, make choice, whether
You'll steal away with your two mistresses,
Or take your fortune.
    Car. I'll be gelded twice first;
Hang him that stays behind.
    Paul. I wait you, madam.

    [1] *It being known it was I that betray'd* him,] Besides making several petty alterations in this line, Coxeter subjoined *him* to it, which is not found in the old copy. This is retained, as either that or *you* seems necessary to complete the sense: his imaginary improvements I have removed.

Were but my brother off, by the command
Of the doting viceroy there's no guard dare stay
    me;
And I will safely bring you to the place,
Where we must expect him.
 Don. Heaven be gracious to us! [*Exeunt.*

SCENE VI.

A Room in the Black Tower.

Enter VITELLI, Aga, *and Guard, at the door.*

 Vitel. Paulina to fall off thus! 'tis to me
More terrible than death, and, like an earthquake,
Totters this walking building, such I am;
And in my sudden ruin would prevent,
By choaking up at once my vital spirits,
This pompous preparation for my death.
But I am lost;[2] that good man, good Francisco,
Deliver'd me a paper, which till now
I wanted leisure to peruse. [*Reads the Paper.*
 Aga. This Christian
Fears not, it seems, the near approaching sun,
Whose second rise he never must salute.

Enter MANTO *with the baked-meat.*

 1 *Guard.* Who's that?
 2 *Guard.* Stand.
 Aga. Manto!
 Mant. Here's the viceroy's ring,
Gives warrant to my entrance; yet you may
Partake of any thing I shall deliver.

---

 [2] *But* I am lost;] i. e. I forget myself.

'Tis but a present to a dying man,
Sent from the princess that must suffer with him.
    Aga. Use your own freedom.
    Mant. I would not disturb
This his last contemplation.
    Vitel. O, 'tis well!
He has restored all, and I at peace again
With my Paulina.
    Mant. Sir, the sad Donusa,
Grieved for your sufferings, more than for her
        own,
Knowing the long and tedious pilgrimage
You are to take, presents you with this cordial,
Which privately she wishes you should taste of;
And search the middle part, where you shall find
Something that hath the operation to
Make death look lovely.
    Vitel. I will not dispute
What she commands, but serve it.   [*Exit.*
    Aga. Prithee, Manto,
How hath the unfortunate princess spent this
        night,
Under her proud new mistress?
    Mant. With such patience
As it o'ercomes the other's insolence,
Nay, triumphs o'er her pride. My much haste now
Commands me hence; but, the sad tragedy past,
I'll give you satisfaction to the full
Of all hath pass'd, and a true character
Of the proud Christian's nature.   [*Exit.*
    Aga. Break the watch up;
What should we fear i'the midst of our³ own
        strengths?
'Tis but the basha's jealousy. Farewell, soldiers.
        [*Exeunt.*

    ³ *What should we fear in the midst of our own* strengths? &c.] i. e.
our own fortresses. See p. 199.

SCENE VII.

An upper Room in the same.

Enter VITELLI *with the baked-meat.*

Vitel. There's something more in this than
    means to cloy
A hungry appetite, which I must discover.
She will'd me search the midst: thus, thus I
    pierce it.
—Ha! what is this? a scroll bound up in pack-
    thread!
What may the mystery be?   [*Reads.*

  *Son, let down this packthread at the west window
of the castle. By it you shall draw up a ladder of
ropes, by which you may descend: your dearest
Donusa with the rest of your friends below attend
you. Heaven prosper you!*

O best of men! he that gives up himself
To a true religious friend, leans not upon
A false deceiving reed, but boldly builds
Upon a rock; which now with joy I find
In reverend Francisco, whose good vows,
Labours, and watchings, in my hoped-for free-
    dom,
Appear a pious miracle. I come,
I come with confidence; though the descent
Were steep as hell, I know I cannot slide,
Being call'd down by such a faithful guide.
                                        [*Exit.*

SCENE VIII.

A Room in Asambeg's *Palace.*

Enter ASAMBEG, MUSTAPHA, *and* Janizaries.

Asam. Excuse me, Mustapha, though this night
to me
Appear as tedious as that treble one
Was to the world, when Jove on fair Alcmena
Begot Alcides. Were you to encounter
Those ravishing pleasures, which the slow-paced
hours
(To me they are such) bar me from, you would,
With your continued wishes, strive to imp[4]
New feathers to the broken wings of time,
And chide the amorous sun, for too long dalliance
In Thetis' watery bosom.
Musta. You are too violent
In your desires, of which you are yet uncertain;
Having no more assurance to enjoy them,
Than a weak woman's promise, on which wise men
Faintly rely.
Asam. Tush! she is made of truth;

---

[4] —————————— *to imp*
New feathers to the broken wings of time,] *To* imp, says the
compiler of *the Faulconer's Dictionary,* " is to insert a feather
into the wing of a hawk, or other bird, in the place of one that
is broken." To this practice our old writers, who seem to have
been, in the language of the present day, keen sportsmen, perpetually allude. There is a passage in Tomkis's *Albumazar,*
which would be admired even in the noblest scenes of Shakspeare:

    " How slow the day slides on! when we desire
    " Time's haste, he seems to lose a match with lobsters;
    " And when we wish him stay, he *imps his wings,*
    " *With feathers plumed with thought!*"

And what she says she will do, holds as firm
As laws in brass, that know no change: [*A
    chamber shot off.*[5]] What's this?
Some new prize brought in, sure—

Enter Aga *hastily.*

                              Why are thy looks
So ghastly? Villain, speak!
    Aga. Great sir, hear me,
Then after, kill me:—we are all betray'd.
The false Grimaldi, sunk in your disgrace,
With his confederates, has seized his ship,
And those that guarded it stow'd under hatches.
With him the condemn'd princess, and the
    merchant,
That, with a ladder made of ropes, descended
From the black tower, in which he was enclosed,
And your fair mistress——
    Asam. Ha!
    Aga. With all their train,
And choicest jewels, are gone safe aboard:

[5] *A* chamber *shot off.*] Such is the marginal direction in the
old copy. The modern editors, in kindness to their readers'
ignorance, have considerately expunged the word *chamber*,
and inserted *piece* (it should have been *great gun*) in its place.
Yet a little while, and we shall happily purge our language of
every unfashionable expression. *Chambers* occur continually in
our old writers; they are, as Mr. Malone says, small pieces
of ordnance, such as are still fired in the Park on rejoicing
days. From the marginal direction, it seems as if the theatres,
in our author's time, were provided with one or more of these
pieces: and indeed, it appears from Jonson's *Execration upon
Vulcan*, that the Globe playhouse was set on fire by the discharge of this holiday artillery:

    "——— the Globe, the glory of the Bank,
    " I saw with two poor *chambers* taken in,
    " And razed, ere thought could urge, this might have been."
                    * R 2

Their sails spread forth, and with a fore-right
    gale[6]
Leaving our coast, in scorn of all pursuit,
As a farewell, they shew'd a broadside to us.[7]
  Asam. No more.
  Musta. Now note your confidence!
  Asam. No more.
O my credulity! I am too full
Of grief and rage to speak. Dull, heavy fool!
Worthy of all the tortures that the frown
Of thy incensed master can throw on thee,

---

[6] ——————— *and with a* fore-right *gale*] The old
copy has *a fore-gale.* Mr. M. Mason saw that the measure was
defective, and proposed to read *a right fore-gale.* I prefer the
lection which I have inserted in the text, as it is a common
expression, and has indeed been already used by the poet himself. Thus, in *the Bondman :*

    " ——————— sink him with
    " A *fore-right gale* of liberty."

[7] *As a farewell, they* shew'd a broadside *to us.*] I take this opportunity of observing, that our old dramatic writers were extremely well acquainted with nautical terms ; this was owing
to the avidity with which voyages were read by all descriptions
of people. Great effects were then produced by small means,
and created a wonderful interest in the public mind : the writers,
too, of these popular works entered into them with their whole
soul, and gave a fullness and precision to their narratives
which are not always to be found in those of the present day.
I know not how I have been drawn on so far ; but I meant to
say that, from some cause or other, (perhaps from what I last
hinted at,) maritime language is not so generally understood now
as it was two centuries ago. There is scarcely a nautical expression in Shakspeare which is not illustrated into obscurity, or
misinterpreted. With respect to the expression which gave
rise to these remarks, I shall only observe, (not to puzzle the
reader with terms which he would perhaps ill-understand,) that
to shew a broadside to an enemy, argues the highest degree of
confidence and security ; and is here adduced with great propriety to prove that the fugitives thought themselves out of the
danger of pursuit.—They *bore up in the wind ;* which checked
their course.

Without one man's compassion! I will hide
This head among the desarts, or some cave
Fill'd with my shame and me ; where I alone
May die without a partner in my moan. [*Exeunt.*

[8] The quantity of action in this play is the very cause of the
forced contrivances which are to be found in it : yet, however
extravagant in its plan, or improbable in its conduct, it contains
many beautiful sentiments and interesting situations. There was
no such call for some of the licentiousness which stains it.
After all, its conclusion is favourable to the cause of virtue.
The final influence of truth is seen in the conversion of Donusa ;
and the force of conscience in the reclaiming of Vitelli and the
Renegado. Massinger seems to have pleased himself with the
discrimination of their repentance, Act V. sc. iii.; and it may
be remarked in general, that when his plots are unhappy, or
his action confused, he makes amends by the superior care
bestowed on certain of his characters.

The Renegado is described as impious, atheistical, sacrilegious, vindictive, licentious, and cruel. Accordingly, his remorse
is of a violent nature. He is abject and forlorn, despairs of the
power of heaven itself to save him, and appears frantic with
imaginations of horror. He is superstitious too, (a true mark of
nature thus agitated,) and will only be comforted if he can
atone to the holy man in person whose administration of the
sacred rites he had profaned. And when this is dexterously
contrived by Francisco, his protestations of penance are as
tumultuously uttered as they are gloomily conceived. Inflic-
tions the most severe shall be his pleasures ; the stripes of iron
whips, but gentle touches of a saving hand ; and his whole
life, one continued atonement to his native faith, which he had
renounced.

The recovery of the tender but misguided Vitelli is of a different kind. At first he is pleased with the success of his pursuit,
talks lightly of virtue, and is resolved to proceed with his indulgence. But he is soon checked by the appearance of his confessor, acknowledges his error, earnestly asks forgiveness, avows
the struggle between his passions and his duty, but promises
submission, and keeps his promise. In his conference with
Donusa (an impressive scene) he shews himself superior to the
enticements which yet he deeply feels; and the satisfaction of
conscience, now secure from a relapse, gives him constancy in
prison, and amid the prospect of death. He rises to a sacred
vehemence in favour of his religion, and converts Donusa herself.

This incident, though but slightly managed, reminds us of *the Virgin-Martyr*, and in both plays we may observe a similar use of religious terms and ecclesiastical questions, which, with the language and events of the Roman Martyrologies, seem to be familiar to Massinger.

The Jesuit is represented in a manner highly flattering to his order. Pious, sagacious, charitable, disinterested, and without ostentation, he watches over the welfare of his charge, and directs all the proceedings to the desired conclusion.

The Turkish characters are not ill-drawn. The women are wanton, capricious, and stick at nothing to accomplish their ends. The men are shrewd and interested, haughty and violent, and of course become alternately fawning and ferocious.

The chief lesson to be drawn from this play is, to be on our guard against the effects of vicious habits. Gross sins make repentance a terror. The return to duty is most easy and consoling, when the departure from it has been neither long nor wilful :

———— *breve sit quod turpiter audes.*

THE

PARLIAMENT OF LOVE.

THE PARLIAMENT OF LOVE.] A Comedy of this name was entered on the books of the Stationers' Company, June 29, 1660; and a manuscript play so called, and said to be written by W. Rowley, was in the number of those destroyed by Mr. Warburton's servant. I suspect this to be the drama before us. It is, beyond all possibility of doubt, the genuine work of Massinger. and was licensed for the stage by Sir H. Herbert on the 3d of June, 1624. I have already mentioned my obligations to Mr. Malone for the use of the manuscript, with permission to insert it in the present Edition, of which it forms no inconsiderable ornament: it is here given with the most scrupulous fidelity, not a word, not a syllable, being altered or omitted, except in one or two instances, where the inadvertence of the old copyist had occasioned a palpable blunder, of which the remedy was as certain as the discovery was easy.

It would not have required much pains, or the exertion of much ingenuity, to supply most of the chasms occasioned by the defect of the manuscript, which are here pointed out by short lines: but it seemed the safer method to present them as they stood. The reader may now be confident that all is genuine, and exercise his skill in filling up the vacant spaces, in a manner most consonant to his own opinion of the drift of the author. He must not flatter himself with the hope of further aids; for unless another manuscript of this play should be discovered, (of which there is little probability,) no subsequent researches will add an iota to what is now before him. Such, unfortunately, is the decayed state of the present, that with every precaution which the most anxious concern could suggest, it crumbled under the inspection: a repetition, therefore, of my labours, which I scarcely think will be lightly undertaken, will produce nothing but disappointment; since many lines, and fragments of lines, which are faithfully copied in the succeeding pages, will be found in it no more.

I cannot entertain a doubt but that this curious relic will be perused with uncommon interest; at least, with all that perfect novelty can give: since it is highly probable, that not a single line of it has been read by any person now in existence.

The plot is founded upon those celebrated Courts or Parliaments of Love, said to be holden in France during the twelfth, thirteenth, and fourteenth centuries, for the discussion of amorous questions, and the distribution of rewards and punishments among faithful and perfidious lovers.

The origin of these institutions is due to the lively imagination of the Troubadours: petty discussions on points of gallantry, which probably took place between them and their mistresses, are magnified, in their romantic writings, into grave and solemn debates, managed with all the form and ceremony of provincial councils, by the most distinguished personages of both sexes.

In their tales this does not look amiss : when the whole business of the world is love, every thing connected with it assumes an air of importance ; but, unfortunately, these reveries of a warm fancy have found admittance into general history, where the improbability and folly of them become instantly apparent. Nothing, in short, can be more mean and absurd than the causes proposed for judgment, except, perhaps, it be the sentences of this motley tribunal.

In France, the existence of these Parliaments has been discussed with much warmth. Monsieur de Chasteuil, a Provençal, and therefore interested in the honour of his country, collected from the Troubadours and their followers a number of anecdotes on the subject, which he moulded into a consistent and entertaining narrative : it wanted, however, the foundation of truth, and was controverted in all its parts by Monsieur de Haitze. The question is of little interest to us : those, however, who feel any degree of curiosity on the subject, may consult the Abbé de Sade,* who has stated the arguments on both sides with that candour and perspicuity which are visible in every page of his entertaining work.

De Sade himself, though he laughs at the pretensions of the Troubadours, is yet inclined to think that Courts or Parliaments of Love were sometimes held ; though not with the state and formality ascribed to them by the historians of Provence. He mentions a celebrated one at Troyes, where the countess of Champagne† presided ; and he gives a few of the *arrets*, or decrees, which emanated from it : these are still more frivolous than those of the Troubadours, and in no age of the world could have been received without derision and contempt.

After all, the reality of these tribunals was not doubted in Massinger's time, nor in the ages preceding it : he had therefore sufficient authority for his fable. Add too, that he has given the establishment a dignity which renders its decisions of importance. A *dame de chateau* issuing her ridiculous *arrets* (for so they were styled) excites little notice ; but a great and victorious monarch sitting in judgment, attended by his peers, and surrounded with all the pomp of empire, is an imposing object. Nor are the causes selected, altogether unworthy of the tribunal : it is not a miserable question, " whether lovers must needs be jealous," " whether love can consist with matrimony"‡ &c. which is to

---

* *Mémoires pour la Vie de François Pétrarque,* Tom II. *notes,* p. 44.

† Mr. Godwin says—" the queen of France ;" but he seems to have posted through de Sade, as Yorick and his pupil did through Europe—" at a prodigious rate."

‡ *Mémoires pour la Vie de Pétrarque,* Tom II. *notes,* p. 60.

be heard ; but injuries of a serious nature, and which can only be redressed by a court of this peculiar kind. In a word, a Parliament of Love, if ever respectable, is only so, as convoked in this delightful drama.

As the list of the dramatis personæ is destroyed, we are reduced to guess at the period in which the supposed events of this drama took place : luckily, there is not much room for deliberation, since the king's speech, on his first appearance, confines it to Charles VIII. That monarch led his army into Italy on the 6th of October 1494, and entered Naples in triumph on the 20th of February in the following year: thus, says Mezerai, " in four months this young king marched through all Italy, was received every where as their sovereign lord, without using any force, only sending his harbingers to mark out his lodgings, and conquered the whole kingdom of Naples, excepting only Brindes, in fifteen days."

Charles was the gayest monarch that ever sat upon the throne of France : he was fond of masques, revels, dances, and the society of the ladies, to a culpable degree ; Massinger, therefore, could not have found a fitter prince for the establishment of a Parliament of Love. During a treaty with Lodowick Sforza, (father of Francis Duke of Milan,) on which the security of his conquests in a great measure depended, he was so impatient to return to his favourite amusements, that he broke through all restraint, and before any of its stipulations were put in execution, " went away," continues the honest historian, " to dance, masquerade, and make love." By this precipitation he lost all the fruit of his victories ; for Sforza did not perform one article of the treaty.

This play was acted at the Cockpit in Drury Lane. I have been sparing of my observations, being desirous (as far as was consistent with my plan) that it might enjoy the reader's undivided attention.

DRAMATIS PERSONÆ,

AS FAR AS THEY APPEAR IN THE REMAINING
SCENES OF THIS PLAY.

Charles VIII. *king of* France.
Duke of Orleans.
Duke of Nemours.
Chamont, *a nobleman ; once guardian to* Bellisant.
Philamour, ⎱ *counsellors.*
Lafort, ⎰
Montrose, *a noble gentleman, in love with* Bellisant.
Cleremond, *in love with* Leonora.
Clarindore, ⎱
Perigot, ⎬ *wild courtiers.*
Novall, ⎰
Dinant, *physician to the court.*

Bellisant, *a noble lady.*
Lamira, *wife to* Chamont.
Beaupré, (*supposed* Calista,) *wife to* Clarindore.
Leonora.
Clarinda, *wife to* Dinant.

Other Courtiers, Priest, Officers, Servants, &c.

SCENE, Paris, *and the adjacent country.*

THE

PARLIAMENT OF LOVE.

ACT I. SCENE IV.

A Room in Bellisant's *House.*

Enter CHAMONT *and* BELLISANT.

Cham. - - - - - - - - - -
- - - - - - - - - - - - - -
I did[1] discharge the trust imposed upon me,
Being your guardian.
    Bell. 'Tis with truth acknowledged.
    Cham. The love I then bore to you, and desire
To do you all good offices of a friend,
Continues with me, nay, increases, lady ;
And, out of this assurance, I presume,

---

[1] *I did*, &c.] Here the fragment begins. It is not possible to
say how much of this act is lost, as the manuscript is not paged ;
but, perhaps, two or three scenes. One must have taken place
between Chamont and Beaupré, in which the latter disclosed her
history ; another, perhaps, between Cleremond and Leonora ;
the assemblage of the " guests" at Bellisant's house probably
formed a third, and the present conference, in which she quits
her guests, to attend on Chamont, may be the fourth. The
reader will please to observe, that all this is conjecture, and
given for nothing more. To facilitate references, it is necessary
to fix on some determinate number : the ultimate choice, however, is of no great moment, though I flatter myself it cannot
be far from the truth. Very little of this scene appears to be
lost ; Chamont is here, perhaps, in his first speech.

What, from a true heart, I shall now deliver,
Will meet a gentle censure.
   Bell. When you speak,
Whate'er the subject be, I gladly hear.
   Cham. To tell you of the greatness of your state,
And from what noble stock you are derived,
Were but impertinence, and a common theme,
Since you well know both. What I am to speak of,
Touches you nearer; therefore, give me leave
To say, that, howsoever your great bounties,
Continual feasting, princely entertainments,
May gain you the opinion of some few
Of a brave generous spirit, (the best harvest
That you can hope for from such costly seed,)
You cannot yet, amongst the multitude,
(Since, next unto the princes of the blood,
The eyes of all are fix'd on you,) but give
Some wounds, which will not close without a scar,
To your fair reputation, and good name;
In suffering such a crew of riotous gallants,
Not of the best repute, to be so frequent
Both in your house and presence: this, 'tis rumour'd,
Little agrees with the curiousness[2] of honour,
Or modesty of a maid.
   Bell. Not to dwell long
Upon my answer, I must thank your goodness,
And provident care, that have instructed me
What my revenues are, by which I measure
How far I may expend; and yet I find not
That I begin to waste; nor would I add
To what I now possess. I am myself;
And for my fame, since I am innocent here,
This, for the world's opinion!
   Cham. Take heed, madam.

---

   [2] *Little agrees with the* curiousness *of honour,*] i. e. the punctilious nicety of honour: in this sense the word often occurs.

That [world's][3] opinion, which you slight, confirms
This lady for immodest, and proclaims
Another for a modest; whereas the first
Ne'er knew what loose thoughts were, and the
  praised second
Had never a cold dream.
 Bell. I dare not argue:
But what means to prevent this?
 Cham. Noble marriage.
 Bell. Pardon me, sir; and do not think I scorn
Your grave advice, which I have ever followed,
Though not pleased in it.——
Would you have me match with wealth? I need
  it not:
Or hunt for honour, and increase of titles?
In truth, I rest ambitious of no greater
Than what my father left.   Or do you judge
My blood to run so high, that 'tis not in
Physic to cool me? I yet feel no such heat:
But when, against my will, it grows upon me,
I'll think upon your counsel.
 Cham. If you resolve, then,
To live a virgin, you have -   -   -   -
To which you may retire, and ha-   -   -   -
To -   -   -   -   -   -   -   -   -   -   -   -
In -   -   -   -   -   -   -   -   -   -   -   -
And live cont-   -   -   -
 Bell. What proof
Should I give of my continence, if I lived
Not seen, nor seeing any? Spartan Helen,
Corinthian Lais, or Rome's Messaline,
So mew'd up, might have died as they were born,
By lust untempted: no, it is the glory
Of chastity to be tempted, tempted home too,

 [3] *That* [world's] *opinion, which you slight, &c.*] I have ventured to complete the metre by inserting the word between
brackets, which was probably overlooked by the transcriber.

The honour else is nothing! I would be
The first example to convince, for liars,
Those poets, that with sharp and bitter rhymes
Proclaim aloud, that chastity has no being,
But in a cottage : and so confident
I am in this to conquer, that I will
Expose myself to all assaults ; see masques,
And hear bewitching sonnets; change discourse
With one that, for experience, could teach Ovid
To write, a better way, his *Art of Love :*
Feed high, and take and give free entertain-
       ment,
Lend Cupid eyes, and new artillery,
Deny his mother for a deity ;
Yet every burning shot he made at me,
Meeting with my chaste thoughts, should lose
       their ardour ;
Which when I have o'ercome, malicious men
Must, to their shame, confess 'its possible,
For a young lady, (some say fair,) at court,
To keep her virgin honour.
    Cham. May you prosper
In this great undertaking! I'll not use
A syllable to divert you: but must be
A suitor in another kind.
    Bell. Whate'er it be,
'Tis granted.
    Cham. It is only to accept
A present from me.
    Bell. Call you this a suit?
    Cham. Come in, Calista.

-*Enter* BEAUPRÉ, *disguised as a Moorish Slave.*

                          This is one I would
Bestow upon you.
    Bell. 'Tis the handsomest.

I e'er saw of her country; she hath neither
Thick lips, nor rough curl d hair.
    Cham. Her manners, lady,
Upon my honour, better her good shape :
She speaks our language too, for being surprised
In Barbary, she was bestow'd upon
A pirate of Marseilles,[4] with whose wife
She lived five years, and learn'd it; there I
    bought her,
As pitying her hard usage ; if you please
To make her yours, you may.
    Bell. With many thanks.
Come hither, pretty one; fear not, you shall find
    me
A gentle mistress.
    Beau. With my care and service,
I'll study to preserve you such.
    Beli. Well answered.
Come, follow me; we'll instantly to court,
And take my guests along.
    Cham. They wait you, madam.   [*Exeunt.*

SCENE V.

A State-room in the Palace.

Flourish. Enter CHARLES, ORLEANS, NEMOURS,
PHILAMOUR, *and* LAFORT.

    Char. What solitude does dwell about our
    court !
Why this dull entertainment? Have I march'd
Victorious through Italy, enter'd Rome,

---

    [4] *A pirate of* Marseilles,] *Marseilles* here, as in *the Unnatural
Combat,* is a trissyllable.

Like a triumphant conqueror, set my foot
Upon the neck of Florence, tamed the pride
Of the Venetians, scourged those petty tyrants,
That -   -   -   -   -   den of the world, to be
-   -   -   -   home, nay, my house neglected!
   (*New Speaker.*) - - - the courtiers would
    appear
-   -   -   -   -   -   therefore they presumed
- - - - - - - - - - - - -
   (*New Speaker.*) - - - - the ladies, sir,
-   -   -   -   -   -   that glad time
-   -   -   -   -   -   -   -   -   the choice.

Enter BELLISANT, LEONORA, LAMIRA, CLA-
RINDA, CHAMONT, MONTROSE, CLEREMOND,
CLARINDORE, PERIGOT, NOVALL, *and other
Courtiers.*

  Phil. Here they come.
  Ladies. All happiness to your majesty!
  Courtiers. And victory sit ever on your sword!
  Char. Our thanks to all.
But wherefore come you in divided troops,
As if the mistresses would not accept
Their servants' guardship,[5] or the servants,
    slighted,
Refuse to offer it? You all wear sad looks:

   [5] *But wherefore come you in divided troops,*
     As if the mistresses *would not accept*
     Their servants' *gua⸱dship,* &c.] *Servant* and *mistress*, as I have
already observed, signified, in the language of Massinger's time,
a lover and the object of his affection. Let me now call the
reader's attention to the exquisite melody of this speech:
nothing is forced, nothing is inverted; plainness and simplicity
are all the aids of which the poet has availed himself, yet a more
perfect specimen of flowing, elegant, and rhythmical modulation
is not to be found in the English language. The sprightliness,
energy, and spirit which pervade the remainder of this scene are
worthy of all praise.

On Perigot appears not that blunt mirth
Which his face used to promise ; on Montrose
There hangs a heavy dulness ; Cleremond
Droops e'en to death, and Clarindore hath lost
Much of his sharpness ; nay, these ladies too,
Whose sparkling eyes did use to fire the court
With various inventions of delight,
Part with their splendour.   What's the cause ? from whence
Proceeds this alteration ?
   Peri. I am troubled
With the toothach, or with love, I know not
      whether ;
There is a worm in both.   [*Aside.*
   Clarin. It is their pride.
   Bell. Or your unworthiness.
   Cler. The honour that
The French dames held for courtesy, above
All ladies of the earth, dwells not in these,
That glory in their cruelty.
   Leon. The desert
The chevaliers of France were truly lords of,
And which your grandsires really did possess,
At no part you inherit.
   Bell. Ere they durst
Presume to offer service to a lady,
In person they perform'd some gallant acts
The fame of which prepared them gracious hear-
      ing,
Ere they made their approaches : what coy she,
      then,
Though great in birth, not to be parallell'd
For nature's liberal bounties, both set off
With fortune's trappings, wealth; but, with de-
      light,
Gladly acknowledged such a man her servant,
To whose heroic courage, and deep wisdom,
                  * S 2

The flourishing commonwealth, and thankful
    king,
Confess'd themselves for debtors? Whereas, now,
If you have travelled Italy, and brought home
Some remnants of the language, and can set
Your faces in some strange and ne'er-seen posture,
Dance a lavolta,[6] and be rude and saucy;
Protest, and swear, and damn, (for these are
    acts
That most think grace them,) and then view
    yourselves
In the deceiving mirror of self-love,
You do conclude there hardly is a woman
That can be worthy of you.
   Mont. We would grant
We are not equal to our ancestors
In noble undertakings, if we thought,
In us a free confession would persuade you,
Not to deny your own most wilful errors:
And where you tax us[7] for unservice, lady,
I never knew a soldier yet, that could
Arrive into your favour: we may suffer
The winter's frost, and scorching summer's heat,
When the hot lion's breath singeth the fields,
To seek out victory; yet, at our return,
Though honour'd in our manly wounds, well taken,
You say they do deform us, and the loss
Of much blood that way, renders us unfit
To please you in your chambers.
   Clarin. I must speak
A little in the general cause: Your beauties

<hr />

  [6] *Dance a* lavolta,] For this dance (for which the courtiers
of England as well as of France were indebted to Italy) see *the
Great Duke of Florence.*

  [7] *And* where *you tax us,* &c.] *Where* is used for whereas: a
practice so common with Massinger, and indeed with all our old
writers, that it is unnecessary to produce any example of it.

Are charms that do enchant so - - - -
- - - - - - - - - - - - - - -
Knowing that we are fastened in your toils;
In which to struggle, or strive to break out,
Increases the captivity. Never Circe,
Sated with such she purposed to transform,
Or cunning Siren, for whose fatal music
Nought but the hearer's death could satisfy,
Knew less of pity. Nay, I dare go further,[8]
And justify your majesty hath lost
More resolute and brave courageous spirits
In this same dull and languishing fight of love,
Than e'er your wars took from you.
     Char. No reply :——
This is a cause we will determine of,
And speedily redress : Tamed Italy,
With fear, confesses me a warlike king,
And France shall boast I am a prince of love.
Shall we, that keep perpetual parliaments
For petty suits, or the least injury
Offer'd the goods or bodies of our subjects,
Not study a cure for the sickness of the mind,
Whose venomous contagion hath infected
Our bravest servants, and the choicest beauties
Our court is proud of? These are wounds require
A kingly surgeon, and the honour worthy
By us to be accepted.
     Phil. It would add
To the rest of your great actions.

---

[8] *Nay, I dare go further, &c.*] A passage very similar to this
occurs in the *Little French Lawyer* :

     " I have heard that some of our late kings
     " For the lie, wearing of a mistress' favours,
     " Have lost as many gallant gentlemen
     " As might have met the Great Turk in the field,
     " With confidence of a glorious victory."

Laf. But the means
Most difficult, I fear.
    Cham. You shall do more, sir,
If you perform this, than I e'er could read
The sons of Saturn, that by lot divided
The government of the air, the sea, and hell,
Had spirit to undertake
    Char. Why, this more fires me;
And now partake of my design. With speed
Erect a place of justice near the court,
Which we'll have styled, the PARLIAMENT OF
      LOVE:
Here such whose humble service is not consider'd
By their proud mistresses, freely may complain;
And shall have hearing and redress.
    Nov. O rare!
    Peri. I like this well.
    Char. And ladies that are wrong'd
By such as do profess themselves their servants,
May cite them hither, and their cause deliver'd
Or by their own tongues, or fee'd advocates,
Find sudden satisfaction.
    Nov. What a rascal
Was I to leave the law! I might have had
Clients and clients. Ne'er was such a time
For any smooth-chinn'd advocate.
    Peri. They will get the start
Of the ladies' spruce physicians, starve their
      chaplains,
Though never so well timber'd.
    Char. 'Tis our will,
Nor shall it be disputed. Of this court,
Or rather, sanctuary of pure lovers,
My lord of Orleans, and Nemours, assisted
By the messieurs Philamour and Lafort, are
      judges.

You have worn Venus's colours from your youth,
And cannot, therefore, but be sensible
Of all her mysteries: what you shall determine,
In the way of penance, punishment, or reward,
Shall - - - the trial; a month we grant you
- - - - - - - amours, which expired,
- - - - make your complaints, and be assured
- - - impartial hearing; this determined,
- - - - - - rest of our affairs. [*Exeunt.*

ACT II. SCENE I.

A Room in Clarindore's *House.*

Enter CLARINDORE, MONTROSE, PERIGOT, *and*
NOVALL.

Peri. I do not relish
The last part of the king's speech, though I was
Much taken with the first.
Nov. Your reason, tutor?
Peri. Why, look you, pupil; the decree, that
women
Should not neglect the service of their lovers,
But pay them from the exchequer they were born
with,
Was good and laudable; they being created
To be both tractable and tactable,
When they are useful: but to have it order'd,
All women that have stumbled in the dark,
Or given, by owl-light, favours, should complain,
Is most intolerable: I myself shall have,
Of such as trade in the streets, and scaped my
pockets,

Of progress laundresses, and marketwomen,
When the king's pleasure's known, a thousand
    bills
Preferr'd against me.
    Clarin. This is out of season:
Nothing to madam Bellisant, that, in public,
Hath so inveigh'd against us.
    Nov. She's a Fury,
I dare no more attempt her.
    Peri. I'll not venture
To change six words with her for half her state,
Or stay, till she be trimm'd,[9] from wine and
    women,
For any new monopoly.
    Mont. I will study
How to forget her, shun the tempting poison
Her looks, and magic of discourse, still offer,
And be myself again: since there's no hope,
'Twere madness to pursue her.
    Peri. There are madams
Better brought up, 'tis thought, and wives that
    dare not
Complain in parliament; there's safe trading,
    pupil:
And, when she finds she is of all forsaken,
Let my lady Pride repent in vain, and mump,
And envy others' markets.
    Clarin. May I ne'er prosper
But you are three of the most fainting spirits,
That ever I conversed with! You do well

---

9 *Or stay, till she be* trimm'd, *from wine and women,*] This word
is very indistinct in the manuscript; I copied it with my best
care, but still doubt whether it be the one given by the author.
Tamed, has been proposed to me; but this recedes too far from
the MS. After all, the expression admits of a sense, which
suits the context—till she be *trimm'd,* may, without much violence to the language, mean—till she be in the *humour.*

To talk of progress laundresses, punks, and
    beggars ;
The wife of some rich tradesman with three teeth,
And twice so many hairs :—truck with old ladies,
That nature hath given o'er, that owe their doctors
For an artificial life, that are so frozen,
That a sound plague cannot thaw them ; but
    despair,
I give you over : never hope to take
A velvet petticoat up, or to commit
With an Italian cutwork smock, when torn too.
   Mont. And what hopes nourish you ?
   Clarin. Troth, mine are modest.
I am only confident to win the lady
You dare not look on, and now, in the height
Of her contempt and scorn, to humble her,
And teach her at what game her mother play'd,
When she was got ; and, cloy'd with those poor
    toys,
As I find her obedient and pleasing,
I may perhaps descend to marry her :
Then, with a kind of state, I take my chair,[1]
Command a sudden muster of my servants,
And, after two or three majestic hums,
It being known all is mine, peruse my writings,
Let out this manor, at an easy rate,
To such a friend, lend this ten thousand crowns,
For the redemption of his mortgaged land,
Give to each by-blow I know mine, a farm,
Erect - - - - - - this in conse- - -
- - - - - - - - - - - - - - - -
That pleased me in my youth, but now grown stale.
These things first ordered by me, and confirm'd

---

[1] *Then, with a kind of state, I take my chair, &c.*] This is imi-
tated from the soliloquy of Malvolio, in *Twelfth Night ;* which
is itself an imitation of the reverie of Alnaschar, in *the Arabian
Nights Entertainment.*

By Bellisant, my wife, I care not much
If, out of her own lands, I do assign her
Some pretty jointure.
    Peri. Talk'st thou in thy sleep?
    Nov. Or art thou mad?
    Clarin. A little elevated
With the assurance of my future fortune:
Why do you stare and grin? I know this must be,
And I will lay three thousand crowns, within
A month I will effect this.
    Mont. How!
    Clarin. Give proof
I have enjoy'd fair Bellisant, evident proof
I have pluck'd her virgin rose, so long preserved,
Not, like a play-trick, with a chain or ring[2]
Stolen by corruption, but, against her will,
Make her confess so much.
    Mont. Impossible.
    Clarin. Then the disgrace be mine, the profit
      yours.
If that you think her chastity a rock
Not to be moved or shaken, or hold me
A flatterer of myself, or overweener,
Let me pay for my foolery.
    Peri. I'll engage
Myself for a thousand.
    Nov. I'll not out for a second.
    Mont. I would gladly lose a third part for
      assurance
No virgin can stand constant long.
    Clarin. Leave that
To the trial: let us to a notary,
Draw the conditions, see the crowns deposited,

---

    [2] *Not, like a play-trick, with a chain or ring*
   Stolen by corruption, &c.] Here is an allusion, perhaps, to
the bracelet of Imogen: the trick, however, of which Clarindore speaks, is found in many of our old dramas.

And then I will not cry, St. Dennis for me![3]
But—Love, blind archer, aid me!
 Peri. Look you thrive;
I would not be so jeer'd and hooted at,
As you will be else.
 Clarin. I will run the hazard.   [*Exeunt.*

SCENE II.

A Room in Leonora's *House.*

Enter LEONORA *and a* Servant.

 Serv. He will not be denied.
 Leon. Slave, beat him back.
I feed such whelps!——
 Serv. Madam, I rattled him,
Rattled him home.
 Leon. Rattle him hence, you rascal,
Or never see me more.

Enter CLEREMOND.

 Serv. He comes: a sword!
What would you have me do? Shall I cry murder,
Or raise the constable?
 Leon. Hence, you shaking coward!
 Serv. I am glad I am so got off: here's a round
   sum   [*Looking at his money.*
For a few bitter words! Be not shook off, sir;
I'll see none shall disturb you.   [*Exit.*
 Cler. You might spare
These frowns, good lady, on me; they are useless,
I am shot through and through with your disdain,

_____

[3] ————— *St. Dennis for me!*] The **war-cry**
of the French soldiers.

And on my heart the darts of scorn so thick,
That there's no vacant place left to receive
Another wound; their multitude is grown
My best defence, and do confirm me that
You cannot hurt me further.
  Leon. Wert thou not
Made up of impudence, and slaved to folly,
Did any drop of noble blood remain
In thy lustful veins, hadst thou or touch, or relish,
Of modesty, civility, or manners,
Or but in thy deformed outside only
Thou didst retain the essence of a man,
- - - - - - - so many - - -
- - - - - - - - - - - - - -
And loathing to thy person, thou wouldst not
Force from a blushing woman that rude language,
Thy baseness first made me acquainted with.
  Cler. Now saint-like patience guard me!
  Leon. I have heard
Of mountebanks, that to vent their drugs and oils,
Have so enured themselves to poison, that
They could digest a venom'd toad, or spider,
Better than wholesome viands: in the list
Of such I hold thee; for that bitterness
Of speech, reproof, and scorn, by her delivered
Whom thou professest to adore, and shake at,
Which would deter all mankind but thyself,
Do nourish in thee saucy hopes, with pleasure.
  Cler. Hear but my just defence.
  Leon. Yet, since thou art
So spaniel-like affected, and thy dotage
Increases from abuse and injury,
That way I'll once more feast thee. Of all men
I ever saw yet, in my settled judgment,
Spite of thy barber, tailor, and perfumer,
And thine adulterate and borrow'd helps,
Thou art the ugliest creature; and when trimm'd up

To the height, as thou imagin'st, in mine eyes,
A leper with a clap-dish, (to give notice
He is infectious,)[4] in respect of thee,
Appears a youg Adonis.
    Cler. You look on me
In a false glass, madam.
    Leon. Then thy dunghill mind,
Suitable to the outside, never yet
Produced one gentle thought, knowing her want
Of faculties to put it into act.
Thy courtship, as absurd as any zany's,
After a practised manner ; thy discourse,

---

[4] *A leper with a clap-dish, (to give notice*
    He is infectious,)] This explains the origin of the custom,
to which our old writers have such frequent allusions.
    The leprosy was once very common here ; this the writers on
the subject properly attribute to the want of linen, of fresh
meat and vegetables, and above all, to the sloth in which the
poor, in winter, vegetated in their most filthy hovels. Our old
poets seldom mention a leper, without noticing, at the same
time, his constant accompaniments, the cup and clapper. Thus
Henryson :
        " Thus shalt thou go begging fro hous to hous,
        " With *cuppe* and *clapper*, like a *Lazarous.*"
                            Testament of Cresseide.
    The *clapper* was not, as some imagine, an instrument solely
calculated for making a noise ; it was simply the cover of the
cup or *dish*, which the poor wretch opened and shut with a
loud clap, at the doors of the well-disposed. Cleanliness and a
wholesome diet have eradicated this loathsome disease amongst
us ; but it still exists in many parts of the continent, where I
have seen little communities of the infected, begging by the road
side with a clap-dish, which they continue to strike, as for-
merly, on the appearance of a traveller. In England the clap-
dish was impudently assumed by vagrants, sturdy-beggars, &c.
who found it (as Farquhar says of the title of captain) " convenient for travelling," as the terror or pity which the sound
of it excited was well calculated to draw contributions from
the public.

Though full of bombast phrase, never brought
        matter
Worthy the laughing at, much less the hearing.—
But I grow weary ; for, indeed, to speak thee,
Thy ills I mean, and speak them to the full,
Would tire a thousand women's voluble tongues,
And twice so many lawyers'—for a farewell,
I'll sooner clasp an incubus, or hug
A fork'd-tongued adder, than meet thy embraces,
Which, as the devil, I fly from.
    Cler. Now you have spent
The utmost of your spleen, I would not say
Your malice, set off to the height with fiction,
Allow me leave, (a poor request, which judges
Seldom deny unto a man condemn'd,)
A little to complain : for, being censured,
Or to extenuate, or excuse my guilt,
Were but to wash an Ethiop. How oft, with tears,
When the inhuman porter has forbid
My entrance by your most severe commands,
Have these eyes wash'd your threshold ! Did
        there ever
Come novelty to Paris, rich or rare,
Which but as soon as known was not presented,
Howe'er with frowns refused? Have I not
        brought
The braveries of France[5] before your window,
To fight at barriers, or to break a lance,
Or, in their full career, to take the ring,[6]

---

[5] *The braveries of France,*] See *the Bondman,* p. 12.
[6] *In their full career to take the ring,*] For this amusement
we are probably indebted to the French. As long as it continued in vogue it was attended with no inconsiderable degree of
parade, and usually made a part of those magnificent spectacles
given on public occasions. A ring of a very small diameter,
was suspended by a string from a kind of gibbet, of which the

To do you honour? and then, being refused
To speak my grief, my arms, my impresses,
The colours that I wore, in a dumb sorrow
Express'd how much I suffer'd in the rigour
Of your displeasure.
    Leon. Two months hence I'll have
The - - - - - -
    Cler. Stay, best madam,
I am growing to a period.
    Leon. Pray you do;
I here shall take a nap else, 'tis so pleasing.
    Cler. Then only this : the voice you now con-
      temn,
You once did swear was musical; you have met
    too
These lips in a soft encounter, and have brought
An equal ardour with you : never lived
A happier pair of lovers. I confess,
After you promised marriage, nothing wanting
But a few days expired, to make me happy,
My violent impatience of delay
Made me presume, and with some amorous force,
To ask a full fruition of those pleasures
Which sacred Hymen to the world makes lawful,
Before his torch was lighted; in this only,
You justly can accuse me.

horizontal beam moved on a swivel. At this the competitors
ran with their spears couched, with loose reins, and as the
public regulations have it, " as much speed as the horses have."
The object was to carry off the ring on the point of the spear,
which was light, taper, and adapted to the purpose. It was of
difficult attainment, for from an account of a match made by
King Edward VI. seventeen against seventeen, of which he
has left a description, it appears that " in one hundred and
twenty courses the *ring* was carried off but *three* times. *King
Edward's Journal,* p. 26. The victor was usually rewarded
with a ring set with precious stones, and bestowed by the Lady
of the Day.

Leo. Dar'st thou think
That this offence can ever find a pardon,
Unworthy as thou art!
    Cler. But you most cruel,
That, in your studied purpose of revenge,
Cast both divine and human laws behind you,
And only see their rigour, not their mercy.
Offences of foul shape, by holy writ
Are warranted remission, provided
That the delinquent undergo the penance
Imposed upon him by his confessor:
But you, that should be mine, and only can
Or punish or absolve me, are so far
From doing me right, that you disdain to hear
    me.
    Leon. Now I may catch him in my long-wish'd
    toils ;
My hate help me to work it! [*Aside.*]—To what
    purpose,
Poor and pale spirited man, should I expect
From thee the satisfaction of a wrong,
Compared to which, the murder of a brother
Were but a gentle injury?
    Cler. Witness, heaven,
All blessings hoped by good men, and all tortures
The wicked shake at, no saint left unsworn by,
That, uncompell'd, I here give up myself
Wholly to your devotion: if I fail
To do whatever you please to command,
To expiate my trespass to your honour,
So that, the task perform'd, you likewise swear,
First to forgive, and after marry me,
May I endure more sharp and lingering tor-
    ments
Than ever tyrants found out! may my friends
With scorn, not pity, look upon my sufferings,

And at my last gasp, in the place of hope,
Sorrow, despair, possess me!
    Leon. You are caught,
Most miserable fool, but fit to be so ;—
And 'tis but justice that thou art delivered
Into her power that's sensible of a wrong,
And glories to revenge it.   Let me study
What dreadful punishment, worthy my fury,
I shall inflict upon thee ; all the malice
Of injured women help me! Death? that's no-
        thing,
'Tis, to a conscious wretch, a benefit,
And not a penance ; else, on the next tree,
For sport's sake I would make thee hang thyself.
    Cler. What have I done ?
    Leon. What cannot be recall'd.
To row for seven years in the Turkish gallies ?
A flea-biting ! To be sold to a brothel,
Or a common bagnio ? that's a trifle too !
- - - - Furies, - - - - - -
The lashes of their whips pierce through the
        mind.
I'll imitate them :—I have it too.
    Cler. Remember
You are a woman.
    Leon. I have heard thee boast,
That of all blessings in the earth next me,
The number of thy trusty, faithful friends,
Made up thy happines: out of these, I charge
        thee,
And by thine own repeated oaths conjure thee,
To kill the best deserver.   Do not start ;
I'll have no other penance.   Then to practise,
To find some means he that deserves thee best,
By undertaking something others fly from :
This done, I am thine.
    Cler. But hear me.

Leon. Not a syllable:
And till then, never see me.   [*Exit.*
    Cler. I am lost,
Foolishly lost and sunk by mine own baseness:
I'll say only,
With a heart-breaking patience, yet not rave,
Better the devil's than a woman's slave.   [*Exit.*

SCENE III.

A Room in Bellisant's *House.*

Enter CLARINDORE *and* BEAUPRÉ.

Clarin. Nay, prithee, good Calista—
    Beau. As I live, sir,
She is determined to be private, and charged me,
Till of herself she broke up her retirement,
Not to admit a visitant.
    Clarin. Thou art a fool,
And I must have thee learn to know thy strength;
There never was a sure path to the mistress,
But by her minister's help, which I will pay for:
                              [*Gives her his purse.*
But yet this is but trash; hark in thine ear—
By Love! I like thy person, and will make
Full payment that way; be thou wise.
    Beau. Like me, sir!
One of my dark complexion!
    Clarin. I am serious:
The curtains drawn, and envious light shut out,
The soft touch heightens appetite, and takes
        more
Than colour, Venus' dressing, in the day time,
But never thought on in her midnight revels.
Come, I must have thee mine.

Beau. But how to serve you?

Clarin. Be speaking still my praises to thy lady,
How much I love and languish for her bounties:
You may remember[7] too, how many madams
Are rivals for me, and, in way of caution,
Say you have heard, when I was wild, how
    dreadful
My name was to a profess'd courtezan,
Still asking more than she could give—

Enter BELLISANT.

Beau. My lady!
Bell. Be within call:—
        [*Aside, to the Servants within.*
        How now, Clarindore,
Courting my servant! Nay, 'tis not my envy—
You now express yourself a complete lover,
That, for variety's sake, if she be woman,
Can change discourse with any.
Clarin. All are foils
I practise on, but when you make me happy
In doing me that honour: I desired
To hear her speak in the Morisco tongue;
Troth, 'tis a pretty language.
Bell. Yes, to dance to:—
Look to those sweetmeats.   [*Exit Beauprè.*
Clarin. How! by heaven, she aims
To speak with me in private!   [*Aside.*
Bell. Come, sit down;
Let's have some merry conference.
Clarin. In which - - - -
It - - - - - - - ` - - - -

---

[7] *You may* remember *too*,] i. e. put her in mind. See *the Bondman,* p. 86.

         * T 2

That my whole life employ'd to do you service,
At no part can deserve.

    Bell. If you esteem it
At such a rate, do not abuse my bounty,
Or comment on the granted privacy, further
Than what the text may warrant ; so you shall
Destroy what I have built.

    Clarin. I like not this.   [*Aside.*

    Bell. This new erected Parliament of Love,
It seems, has frighted hence my visitants :
How spend Montrose and Perigot their hours ?
Novall and Cleremond vanish'd in a moment ;
I like your constancy yet.

    Clarin. That's good again ;
She hath restored all : [*Aside.*] —Pity them, good
        madam ;
The splendour of your house and entertainment,
Enrich'd with all perfections by yourself,
Is too, too glorious for their dim eyes :
You are above their element ; modest fools,
That only dare admire ! and bar them from
Comparing of these eyes to the fairest flowers,
Giving you Juno's majesty, Pallas' wit,
Diana's hand, and Thetis' pretty foot ;
Or, when you dance, to swear that Venus leads
The Loves and Graces from the Idalian green,
And such hyperboles stolen out of playbooks,
They would stand all day mute, and, as you were
Some curious picture only to be look'd on,
Presume no further.

    Bell. Pray you, keep your distance,
And grow not rude.

    Clarin. Rude, lady ! manly boldness
Cannot deserve that name ; I have studied you,
And love hath made an easy gloss upon
The most abstruse and hidden mysteries
Which you may keep conceal'd. You well may
        praise

A bashful suitor, that is ravish'd with
A feather of your fan, or if he gain
A riband from your shoe, cries out, *Nil ultra !*
  Bell. And what would satisfy you?
  Clarin. Not such poor trifles,
I can assure you, lady. Do not I see
You are gamesome, young, and active? that you
    love
A man that, of himself, comes boldly on,
That will not put your modesty to trouble,
To teach him how to feed, when meat's before him?
That knows that you are flesh and blood, a creature,
And born with such affections, that, like me,
Now I have opportunity, and your favour,
Will not abuse my fortune? Should I stand now
Licking my fingers, cry Ah me! then kneel,
And swear you were a goddess, kiss the skirts
Of your proud garments, when I were gone, I
    am sure
I should be kindly laugh'd at for a coxcomb;
The story made the subject of your mirth,
At your next meeting, when you sit in council,
Among the beauties.
  Bell. Is this possible?
All due respect forgotten!
  Clarin. Hang respect!
Are we not alone? See, I dare touch this hand,
And without adoration unglove it.
A spring of youth is in this palm; here Cupid,
The moisture turn'd to diamonds, heads his
    arrows :
The far-famed English Bath, or German Spa,
One drop of this will purchase. Shall this nectar
Run useless, then, to waste? or - - - these lips,
That open like the morn, breathing perfumes
On such as dare approach them, be untouch'd?
They must—nay, 'tis in vain to make resistance,—

Be often kiss'd and tasted :—You seem angry
At - - - I have displeased you.
   Bell. [*to the Servants within.*] - - - - - -
And come prepared, as if some Africk monster,
By force, had broke into my house.

   Enter Servants *with drawn swords.*

   Clarin. How's this?
   Bell. Circle him round with death, and if he
     stir,
Or but presume to speak, till I allow it,
His body be the navel to the wheel,
In which your rapiers, like so many spokes,
Shall meet and fix themselves.
   Clarin. Were I off with life,
This for my wager!   [*Aside.*
   Bell. Villain, shake and tremble
At my just anger! Which, of all my actions,
Confined in virtuous limits, hath given life
And birth to this presumption? Hast thou ever
Observed in me a wanton look or gesture,
Not suiting with a virgin? Have I been
Prodigal in my favours, or given hopes,
To nourish such attempts? swear, and swear truly,
What in thy soul thou think'st of me.
   Clarin. As of one
Made up of chastity; and only tried,
Which I repent, what this might work upon you.
   Bell. The intent deserves not death; but, sirrah,
     know
'Tis in my power to look thee dead.
   Clarin. 'Tis granted.
   Bell. I am not so cruel; yet, for this insolence,
Forbear my house for ever: if you are hot,
You, ruffian-like, may force a parting kiss,
As from a common gamester.

Clarin. I am cool :—
She's a virago.   [*Aside.*
   Bell. Or you may go boast,
How bravely you came on, to your companions ;
I will not bribe your silence : no reply.—
Now thrust him headlong out of doors, and see
He never more pass my threshold.   [*Exit.*
   Clarin. This comes of
My daring : all hell's plagues light on the proverb
That says, *Faint heart*——but it is stale.
   Serv. Pray you walk, sir,
We must shew you the way else.
   Clarin. Be not too officious.
I am no bar* for you to try your strength on.—
Sit quietly by this disgrace I cannot :
Some other course I must be forced to take,
Not for my wager now, but honour's sake.
                                             [*Exeunt.*

ACT III. SCENE I.

A Room in Chamont's *House.*

Enter CHAMONT, PERIGOT, NOVALL, DINANT,
      LAMIRA, *and* CLARINDA.

   Peri. 'Twas prince-like entertainment.
   Cham. You o'erprize it.
   Din. Your cheerful looks made every dish a
      feast,
And 'tis that crowns a welcome.
   Lam. For my part,

   * *I am no bar for you to try, your strength on.*] Alluding to
the threats of the servants " to quoit him down stairs." Pitch-
ing the *bar* is still a game at which the rustics *try their strength.*

I hold society and honest mirth
The greatest blessing of a civil life.

Cla. Without good company, indeed, all dainties
Lose their true relish, and, like painted grapes,
Are only seen, not tasted.

Nov. By this light,
She speaks well too! I'll have a fling at her:
She is no fit electuary for a doctor:
A coarser julap may well cool his worship;
This cordial is for gallants.   [*Aside.*

Cham. Let me see,
The night grows old: pray you often be my guests.
Such as dare come unto a - - - table,
Although not crack'd with curious delicates,
Have liberty to command it as their own:
I may do the like with you, when you are married.

Peri. Yes, 'tis likely,
When there's no forage to be had abroad,
Nor credulous husbands left to father children
Of bachelors' begetting; when court wives
Are won to grant variety is not pleasing,
And that a friend at a pinch is useless to them,
I - - - - - - - - but till then
- - - - - - - - - - - - - -

Cham. You have a merry time of't;——
But we forget ourselves:—Gallants, good night.
Good master doctor, when your leisure serves,
Visit my house; when we least need their art,
Physicians look most lovely.

Din. All that's in me,
Is at your lordship's service. Monsieur Perigot,
Monsieur Novall, in what I may be useful,
Pray you command me.

Nov. We'll wait on you home.

Din. By no means, sir; good night.
          [*Exeunt all but Novall and Perigot.*

Nov. The knave is jealous.

Peri. 'Tis a disease few doctors cure themselves of.

Nov. I would he were my patient!

Peri. Do but practise
To get his wife's consent, the way is easy.

Nov. You may conclude so; for myself, I grant
I never was so taken with a woman,
Nor ever had less hope.

Peri. Be not dejected;
Follow but my directions, she's your own:
I'll set thee in a course that shall not fail.—
I like thy choice; but more of that hereafter:
Adultery is a safe and secret sin;
The purchase of a maidenhead seldom quits
The danger and the labour: build on this,
He that puts home shall find all women coming,
The frozen Bellisant ever excepted.
Could you believe the fair wife of Chamont,
A lady never tainted in her honour,
Should, at the first assault, (for till this night
I never courted her,) yield up the fort
That she hath kept so long?

Nov. 'Tis wondrous strange.
What winning language used you?

Peri. Thou art a child;
'Tis action, not fine speeches, take a woman.
Pleasure's their heaven; and he that gives as-
surance
That he hath strength to tame their hot desires,
Is the prevailing orator: she but saw me
Jump over six join'd stools, and after cut
Some forty capers; tricks that never miss,[9]

---

[9] ——————— tricks *that never miss,* &c.]
" He, indeed, danced well:
" A turn o' the toe, with a lofty *trick* or two,
" To argue nimbleness and a strong back,
" Will go far with a madam." *The Custom of the Country.*

In a magnificent masque, to draw the eyes
Of all the beauties in the court upon me,
But straight she wrung my hand, trod on my toe,
And said my mistress could not but be happy
In such an able servant. I replied
Bluntly, I was ambitious to be hers;
And she, nor coy nor shy, straight entertain'd me:
I begg'd a private meeting, it was granted,
The time and place appointed.
    Nov. But remember,
Chamont is your friend.
    Peri. Now out upon thee, puisne!
As if a man so far e'er loved that title,
But 'twas much more delight and tickling to him,
To hug himself, and say, This is my cuckold!
    Nov. But did he not observe thee?
    Peri. Though he did,
As I am doubtful, I will not desist;
The danger will endear the sport.

       Enter CLARINDORE.

    Nov. Forbear;
Here's Clarindore.
    Peri. We will be merry with him;
I have heard his entertainment. Join but with
      me,
And we will jeer this self-opinion'd fool
Almost to madness.
    Nov. He's already grown
Exceeding melancholy, and some say
That's the first step to frenzy.
    Peri. I'll upon him.—
Save you, good monsieur! no reply? grown proud
Of your success? it is not well -   -   -   -
    Clar. 'Tis come out; these goslings
Have heard of my -   -   -   -   -   -

Nov. We gratulate,
Though we pay for't, your happy entrance to
The certain favours, nay, the sure possession,
Of madam Bellisant.
   Clarin. The young whelp too!—
'Tis well, exceeding well.
   Peri. 'Tis so, with you, sir;
But bear it modestly, faith it will become you:
And being arrived at such a lordly revenue,
As this your happy match instates you with,
Two thousand crowns from me, and from Novall,
Though we almost confess the wager lost,
Will be a small addition.
   Nov. You mistake him;
Nor do I fear, out of his noble nature,
But that he may be won to license us
To draw our venture.
   Clarin. Spend your frothy wits,
Do, do; you snarl, but hurt not.
   Nov. O, give leave
To losers for to speak.
   Peri. 'Tis a strange fate
Some men are born to, and a happy star
That reign'd at your nativity! it could not be
     else,
A lady of a constancy like a rock,
Not to be moved, and held impregnable,
Should yield at the first assault!
   Nov. 'Tis the reward
Of a brave daring spirit.
   Peri. Tush! we are dull;
Abuse our opportunities.
   Clarin. Have you done yet?
   Peri. When he had privacy of discourse, he
     knew
How to use that advantage; did he stand

Fawning, and crouching? no; he ran up boldly,
Told her what she was born to, ruffled her,
Kiss'd her, and toused her :—all the passages
Are at court already; and, 'tis said, a patent
Is granted him, if any maid be chaste,
For him to humble her, and a new name given him,
The scornful-virgin tamer.
   Clarin. I may tame
Your buffoon tongues, if you proceed.
   Nov. No anger.
I have heard that Bellisant was so taken with
Your manly courage, that she straight prepared
    you
A sumptuous banquet.
   Peri. Yet his enemies
Report it was a blanket.
   Nov. Malice, malice!
She was shewing him her chamber too, and call'd
    for
Perfumes, and cambric sheets.
   Peri. When, see the luck on't!
Against her will, her most unmannerly grooms,
For so 'tis rumour'd, took him by the shoulders,
And thrust him out of doors.
   Nov. Faith, sir, resolve us;
How was it? we would gladly know the truth,
To stop the mouth of calumny.
   Clarin. Troth, sir, I'll tell you:
One took me by the nose thus,—and a second
Made bold with me thus—but one word more, you shall
    you shall
Feel new expressions—and so, my gentle boobies,
Farewell, and be hang'd!   [*Exit.*
   Nov. We have nettled him.
   Peri. Had we stung him to death, it were but
    justice,
An overweening braggard!

Nov. This is nothing
To the doctor's wife.
 Peri. Come, we'll consult of it,
And suddenly.
 Nov. I feel a woman's longing
Till I am at it.
 Peri. Never fear; she's thine own, boy.
          [*Exeunt.*

SCENE II.

A Street.

Enter CLEREMOND.

 Cler. What have my sins been, heaven? yet
   thy great pleasure
Must not be argued. Was wretch ever bound
On such a black adventure, in which only
To wish to prosper is a greater curse
Than to - - - - - - - - - me
Of reason, understanding, and true judgment.
'Twere a degree of comfort to myself
I were stark mad; or, like a beast of prey,
Prick'd on by griping hunger, all my thoughts
And faculties were wholly taken up
To cloy my appetite, and could look no further:
But I rise up a new example of
Calamity, transcending all before me;
And I should gild my misery with false comforts,
If I compared it with an Indian slave's,
That, with incessant labour to search out
Some unknown mine, dives almost to the centre;
And, if then found, not thank'd of his proud master.
But this, if put into an equal scale
With my unparallell'd fortune, will weigh nothing;
For from a cabinet of the choicest jewels

That mankind e'er was rich in, whose least gem
All treasure of the earth, or what is hid
In Neptune's watery bosom, cannot purchase,
I must seek out the richest, fairest, purest,
And when by proof 'tis known it holds the value,
A soon as found destroy it. O most cruel!
And yet, when I consider of the many
That have profess'd themselves my friends, and vow'd
Their lives were not their own, when my en-
    gagements
Should summon them to be at my devotion,
Not one endures the test ; I almost grow
Of the world's received opinion, that holds
Friendship but a mere name, that binds no further
Than to the altar[1]—to retire with safety.
Here comes Montrose.

Enter MONTROSE and BEAUPRÉ.

                    What sudden joy transports him ?
I never saw man rapt so.
    Mon. Purse and all,
And 'tis too little, though it were cramm'd full
With crowns of the sun.[2] O blessed, blessed
    paper !
But made so by the touch of her fair hand.
What shall I answer? Say, I am her creature.
Or, if thou canst find out a word, that may

---

[1]   ———— <i>that binds no further</i>
Than to the altar—] An allusion to the saying of Pericles, that
he would support the interests of his friend μεχρι ϐωμου, as <i>far as
the altar</i> ; i. e. as far as his respect for the gods would give him
leave. Cleremond is, at once, absurd and impious.
    [2] ——— crowns of the sun.] See Vol. I. p. 133.

Express subjection in an humbler style,
Use it, I prithee; add too, her commands
Shall be with as much willingness perform'd,
As I in this fold, this, receive her favours.

 Beau. I shall return so much.

 Mont. And that two hours
Shall bring me to attend her.

 Beau. With all care
And circumstance of service from yourself,
I will deliver it.

 Mont. I am still your debtor. [*Exit Beaupré.*

 Cler. I read the cause now clearly; I'll slip by:
For though, even at this instant, he should prove
Himself, which others' falsehood makes me doubt,
That constant and best friend I go in quest of,
It were inhuman in their birth to strangle
His promising hopes of comfort.

 Mont. Cleremond
Pass by me as a stranger! at a time too
When I am fill'd with such excess of joy,
So swollen and surfeited with true delight,
That had I not found out a friend, to whom
I might impart them, and so give them vent,
In their abundance they would force a passage,
And let out life together! Prithee, bear,
For friendship's sake, a part of that sweet burthen
Which I shrink under; and when thou hast read
Fair Bellisant subscribed, so near my name too,
Observe but that,—thou must, with me, confess,
There cannot be room in one lover's heart
Capacious enough to entertain
Such multitudes of pleasures.

 Cler. I joy with you,
Let that suffice, and envy not your blessings;
May they increase! Farewell, friend.

 Mont. How! no more?
By the snow-white hand that writ these characters,

It is a breach to courtesy and manners,
So coldly to take notice of his good,
Whom you call friend! See further: here she writes
That she is truly sensible of my sufferings,
And not alone vouchsafes to call me servant,
But to employ me in a cause that much
Concerns her in her honour; there's a favour!
Are you yet stupid?—and that, two hours hence,
She does expect me in the private walks
Neighbouring the Louvre: cannot all this move
      you?
I could be angry. A tenth of these bounties
But promised to you from Leonora,
To witness my affection to my friend,
In his behalf, had taught me to forget
All mine own miseries.
   Cler. Do not misinterpret
This coldness in me; for alas! Montrose,
I am a thing so made up of affliction,
So every way contemn'd, that I conclude
My sorrows are infectious; and my company,
Like such as have foul ulcers running on them,
To be with care avoided. May your happiness,
In the favour of the matchless Bellisant,
Hourly increase! and—my best wishes guard you!
'Tis all that I can give.
   Mont. You must not leave me.
   Cler. Indeed I must and will; mine own en-
      gagements
Call me away.
   Mont. What are they? I presume
There cannot be a secret of that weight,
You dare not trust me with; and should you
      doubt me,
I justly might complain that my affection
Is placed unfortunately.
   Cler. I know you are honest;

And this is such a business, and requires
Such sudden execution, that it cannot
Fall in the compass of your will, or power,
To do me a friend's office. In a word,
On terms that near concern me in mine honour,
I am to fight the quarrel, mortal too,
The time some two hours hence, the place ten miles
Distant from Paris; and when you shall know
I yet am unprovided of a second,
You will excuse my sudden parting from you.
Farewell, Montrose!
 Mont. Not so; I am the man
Will run the danger with you; and must tell you,
That, while I live, it was a wrong to seek
Another's arm to second you. Lead the way;
My horse stands ready.
 Cler. I confess 'tis noble,
For you to offer this, but it were base
In me to accept it.
 Mont. Do not scorn me, friend.
 Cler. No; but admire and honour you; and from that
Serious consideration, must refuse
The tender of your aid. France knows you valiant,
And that you might, in single opposition,
Fight for a crown; but millions of reasons
Forbid me your assistance. You forget
Your own designs; being, the very minute
I am to encounter with mine enemy,
To meet your mistress, such a mistress too,
Whose favour you so many years have sought:
And will you then, when she vouchsafes access,
Nay more, invites you, check at her fair offer?
Or shall it be repeated, to my shame,

VOL. II.   U *

For my own ends I robb'd you of a fortune
Princes might envy? Can you even hope
She ever will receive you to her presence,
If you neglect her now?—Be wise, dear friend,
And, in your prodigality of goodness,
Do not undo yourself. Live long and happy,
And leave me to my dangers.

    Mont. Cleremond,
I have with patience heard you, and consider'd
The strength of your best arguments; weigh'd
      the dangers
I run in mine own fortunes: but again,
When I oppose the sacred name of friend
Against those joys I have so long pursued,
Neither the beauty of fair Bellisant,
Her wealth, her virtues, can prevail so far,
In such a desperate case as this, to leave you.—
To have it to posterity recorded,
At such a time as this I proved true gold,
And current in my friendship, shall be to me
A thousand mistresses, and such embraces
As leave no sting behind them; therefore, on:
I am resolved, unless you beat me off,
I will not leave you.

    Cler. Oh! here is a jewel
Fit for the cabinet of the greatest monarch!
But I of all men miserable——

    Mont. Come, be cheerful;
Good fortune will attend us.

    Cler. That, to me,
To have the greatest blessing, a true friend,
Should be the greatest curse!—Be yet advised.

    Mont. It is in vain.

    Cler. That e'er I should have cause
To wish you had loved less!

    Mont. The hour draws on:
We'll talk more as we ride.

    Cler. Of men most wretched!   [*Exeunt.*

SCENE III.

A Room in Bellisant's *House.*

Enter BELLISANT *and* BEAUPRÉ.

Bell. Nay, pray you, dry your eyes, or your
    sad story,
Whose every accent still, methinks, I hear,
'Twas with such passion, and such grief deliver'd,
Will make mine bear your's company. All my
    fear is,
The rigorous repulse this worst of men,
False, perjured Clarindore—I am sick to name
    him—
Received at his last visit, will deter him
From coming again.
    Beau. No; he's resolved to venture;
And has bribed me, with hazard of your anger,
To get him access, but in another shape:[3]
The time prefix'd draws near too.
    Bell. 'Tis the better.   [*Knocking within.*
One knocks.
    Beau. I am sure 'tis he.
    Bell. Convey him in;
But do it with a face of fear: [*Exit Beaupré.*
                 I cannot
Resolve yet with what looks to entertain him.
You Powers that favour innocence, and revenge
Wrongs done by such as scornfully deride
Your awful names, inspire me!   [*Walks aside.*

[3] ——————— *but in another* shape:] i.e. as
has been before observed, in another dress.

* U 2

Re-enter BEAUPRÉ *with* CLARINDORE *disguised.*

Beau. Sir, I hazard
My service, in this action.
   Clarin. Thou shalt live
To be the mistress of thyself and others,
If that my projects hit: all's at the stake now ;
And as the die falls, I am made most happy,
Or past expression wretched.
   Bell. Ha! who's that?
What bold intruder usher you? This rudeness !—
From whence? what would he?
   Beau. He brings letters, madam,
As he says, from lord Chamont.
   Clarin. How her frowns fright me !
   Bell. From lord Chamont? Are they of such
      import,
That you, before my pleasure be enquired,
Dare bring the bearer to my private chamber?
No more of this : your packet, sir?
   Clarin. The letters
Deliver'd to my trust and faith are writ
In such mysterious and dark characters,
As will require the judgment of your soul,
More than your eye, to read and understand them.
   Bell. What riddle's this? [*Discovering Clarin.*]
      —Ha ! am I then contemn'd?
Dare you do this, presuming on my soft
And gentle nature ?—Fear not, I must shew
A seeming anger. [*Aside to Beaupré.*]—What new
      boist'rous courtship,
After your late loose language, and forced kiss,
Come you to practise? I know none beyond it.
If you imagine that you may commit
A rape in mine own house, and that my servants
Will stand tame lookers on——

Clarin. If I bring with me
One thought, but of submission and sorrow,
Or nourish any hope, but that your goodness
May please to sign my pardon, may I perish
In your displeasure! which, to me, is more
Than fear of hell hereafter. I confess,
The violence I offered to your sweetness,
In my presumption, with lips impure,
To force a touch from yours, a greater crime
Than if I should have mix'd lascivious flames
With those chaste fires that burn at Dian's altar.
That 'twas a plot of treason to your virtues,
To think you could be tempted, or believe
You were not fashion'd in a better mould,
And made of purer clay, than other women.
Since you are, then, the phœnix of your time,
And e'en now, while you bless the earth, partake
Of their angelical essence, imitate
Heaven's aptness to forgive, when mercy's sued
        for,
And once more take me to your grace and favour.
    Bell. What charms are these! What an en-
        chanting tongue!
What pity 'tis, one that can speak so well,
Should, in his actions, be so ill!
    Beau. Take heed,
Lose not yourself.
    Bell. So well, sir, you have pleaded,
And like an advocate, in your own cause,
That, though your guilt were greater, I acquit you,
The fault no more remember'd; and for proof,
My heart partakes in my tongue, thus seal your
        pardon;   [*Kisses him,*
And with this willing favour (which forced from
        me,
Call'd on my anger) make atonement with you.

Clarin. If I dream now, O, may I never wake,
But slumber thus ten ages !

Bell. Till this minute,
You ne'er to me look'd lovely.

Clarin. How !

Bell. Nor have I
E'er seen a man, in my opinion, worthy
The bounty I vouchsafe you ; therefore fix here,
And make me understand that you can bear
Your fortune modestly.

Clarin. I find her coming :
This kiss was but the prologue to the play,
And not to seek the rest, were cowardice.
Help me, dissimulation ! [*Aside.*]—Pardon, madam,
Though now, when I should put on cheerful looks,
In being blest with what I durst not hope for,
I change the comic scene, and do present you
With a most tragic spectacle.

Bell. Heaven avert
This prodigy ! What mean you ?

Clarin. To confirm,
In death, how truly I have loved.   I grant
Your favours done me, yield this benefit,
As to make way for me to pass in peace
To my long rest ; what I have tasted from you,
Informs me only of the much I want :
For in your pardon, and the kiss vouchsafed me,
You did but point me out a fore-right way
To lead to certain happiness, and then will'd me
To move no further. Pray you, excuse me, there-
    fore,
Though I desire to end a lingering torment.
And, if you please, with your fair hand, to make me
A sacrifice to your chastity, I will meet
The instrument you make choice of, with more
    fervour

Than ever Cæsar did, to hug the mistress,
He doated on, plumed Victory : but if that
You do abhor the office, as too full
Of cruelty, and horror, yet give leave,
That, in your presence, I myself may be
Both priest and offering.   [*Draws his sword.*
    Bell. Hold, hold, frantic man !
The shrine of love shall not be bathed in blood.
Women, though, fair, were made to bring forth
        men,
And not destroy them ; therefore, hold, I say !
I had a mother, and she look'd upon me
As on a true epitome of her youth :
Nor can I think I am forbid the comfort
To bring forth little models of myself,
If heaven be pleased (my nuptial joys perform'd)
To make me fruitful.
    Clarin. Such celestial music
Ne'er blest these ears. O! you have argued better
For me, than I could for myself.
    Bell. For you !
What, did I give you hope to be my husband ?
    Clarin. Fallen off again !   [*Aside.*
    Bell. Yet since you have given sure proof
Of love and constancy, I'll unmask those thoughts,
That long have been conceal'd ; I am yours, but
        how ?
In an honourable way.
    Clarin. I were more than base,
Should I desire you otherwise.
    Bell. True affection
Needs not a contract : and it were to doubt me,
To engage me further ; yet, my vow expired,
Which is, to live a virgin for a year,
Challenge my promise.
    Clarin. For a year ! O, madam !
Play not the tyranness ; do not give me hopes,

And in a moment change them to despair.
A year! alas, this body, that's all fire,
If you refuse to quench it with your favour,
Will in three days be cinders; and your mercy
Will come too late then. Dearest lady, marriage
Is but a ceremony; and a hurtful vow
Is in the breach of it better commended,
Than in the keeping. O! I burn, I burn;
And if you take not pity, I must fly
To my last refuge.   [*Offers to stab himself.*
    Bell. Hold! Say I could yield
This night, to satisfy you to the full,
And you should swear, until the wedding day,
To keep the favours I now grant conceal'd;
You would be talking.
    Clarin. May my tongue rot out, then!
    Bell. Or boast to your companions of your
        conquest,
And of my easiness.
    Clarin. I'll endure the rack first.
    Bell. And, having what you long for, cast
        me off,
As you did madam Beaupré.
    Clarin. May the earth
First gape, and swallow me!
    Bell. I'll press you no further.
Go in, your chamber's ready; if you have
A bedfellow, so: but silence I enjoin you,
And liberty to leave you when I please:
I blush, if you reply.
    Clarin. Till now ne'er happy!   [*Exit.*
    Beau. What means your ladyship?
    Bell. Do not ask, but do
As I direct you: though as yet we tread
A rough and thorny way, faint not; the ends
I hope to reach shall make a large amends.
                              [*Exeunt.*

ACT IV. SCENE I.

A Room in Dinant's *House.*

Enter Novall *and* Dinant.

Din. You are welcome first, sir; and that
    spoke, receive
A faithful promise, all that art, or long
Experience, hath taught me, shall enlarge
Themselves for your recovery.
    Nov. Sir, I thank you,
As far as a weak, sick, and unable man
Has power to express; but what wants in my
    tongue,
My hand (for yet my fingers feel no gout)
Shall speak in this dumb language.
                    [Gives him his purse.
    Din. You are too magnificent.
    Nov. Fie! no, sir; health is, sure, a precious
    jewel,
We cannot buy it too dear.
    Din. Take comfort, sir;
I find not, by your urine, nor your pulse,
Or any outward symptom, that you are
In any certain danger.
    Nov. Oh! the more my fear:
Infirmities that are known are - - - cured,
But when the causes of them are conceal'd,
As these of mine are, doctor, they prove mortal:
Howe'er, I'll not forget you while I live,
Do but your parts.
    Din. Sir, they are at your service.

I'll give you some preparatives, to instruct me
Of your inward temper ; then, as I find cause,
Some gentle purge.
 Nov. Yes, I must purge ; I die else :
But where, dear doctor, you shall not find out.
This is a happy entrance, may it end well !
I'll mount your nightcap, Doddipol.   [*Aside.*
 Din. In what part,
(We are sworn to secrecy, and you must be free,)
Do you find your greatest agony ?
 Nov. Oh ! I have
Strange motions on the sudden;villainous tumours,
That rise, then fall, then rise again ; oh, doctor !
Not to be shewn or named.
 Din. Then, in my judgment,
You had best leave Paris: choose some fresher air;
That does help much in physic.
 Nov. By no means.
Here, in your house, or no where, you must cure
  me :
The eye of the master fats the horse ; and when
His doctor's by, the patient may drink wine
In a fit of a burning fever : for your presence
Works more than what you minister. Take
  physic,
Attended on by ignorant grooms, mere strangers
To your directions, I must hazard life,
And you your reputation ! whereas, sir,
I hold your house a college of your art,
And every boy you keep, by you instructed,
A pretty piece of a Galenist: then the females,
From your most fair wife to your kitchen drudge,
Are so familiar with your learned courses,
That, to an herb, they know to make thin broth :
Or, when occasion serves, to cheer the heart,
And such ingredient I shall have most need of,

How many cocks o' the game make a strong
      culiis,
Or pheasant's eggs a caudle.
   Din. I am glad
To hear you argue with such strength.

   Enter CLARINDA, *and whispers* DINANT.

   Nov. A flash, sir:
But now I feel my fit again.—She is
Made up of all perfection ; any danger
That leads to the enjoying so much sweetness
Is pleasure at the height : I am ravish'd with
The mere imagination. Oh happiness!— [*Aside.*
   Din. How's this! One from the duke Nemours?
   Cla. Yes, sir.
   Din. 'Tis rank :
The sight of my wife hath forced him to forget
To counterfeit: [*Aside.*]—I now guess at your
      sickness,
And if I fit you not——
   Cla. The gentleman stays you.
   Din. I come to him presently; in the mean
      time, wife,
Be careful of this monsieur: nay, no coyness,
You may salute him boldly; his pale lips
Enchant not in the touch.
   Nov. Her's do, I'm sure.
   Din. Kiss him again.
   Cla. Sir, this is more than modest.
   Din. Modest ! why, fool, desire is dead in him :
Call it a charitable, pious work,
If it refresh his spirits.
   Nov. Yes, indeed, sir.
I find great ease in it.
   Din. Mark that ! and would you
Deny a sick man comfort? meat's against

- - - - - physic, must be granted too,
- - - - wife - - - - you shall,
In person, wait on him ; nay, hang not off,
I say you shall : this night, with your own hands,
I'll have you air his bed, and when he eats
Of what you have prepared, you shall sit by him,
And, with some merry chat, help to repair
Decayed appetite ; watch by him when he slum-
     bers ;
Nay, play his page's part : more, I durst trust you,
Were this our wedding day, you yet a virgin,
To be his bedfellow ; for well I know
Old Priam's impotence, or Nestor's hernia is
Herculean activeness, if but compared
To his debility : put him to his oath,
He'll swear he can do nothing.
    Nov. Do ! O no, sir ;
I am past the thought of it.
    Din. But how do you like
The method I prescribe ?
    Nov. Beyond expression :
Upon the mere report I do conceive
Hope of recovery.
    Cla. Are you mad ?
    Din. Peace, fool.
This night you shall take a cordial to strengthen
Your feeble limbs :—'twill cost ten crowns a
    draught.
    Nov. No matter, sir.
    Din To morrow you shall walk
To see my garden ; then my wife shall shew you
The choice rooms of my house; when you are weary,
Cast yourself on her couch.
    Nov. Oh, divine doctor !
What man in health would not be sick, on purpose
To be your patient ?
    Din. Come, sir, to your chamber ;

And now I understand where your disease lies,
(Nay, lead him by the hand,) doubt not I'll cure
you.   [*Exeunt.*

SCENE II.

An open part of the Country near Paris.

Enter CLEREMOND *and* MONTROSE.

Cler. This is the place.
Mont. An even piece of ground,
Without advantage; but be jocund, friend :
The honour to have entered first the field,
However we come off, is ours.[4]
Cler. I need not,
So well I am acquainted with your valour,
To dare, in a good cause, as much as man,
Lend you encouragement; and should I add,
Your power to do, which Fortune, howe'er blind,
Hath ever seconded, I cannot doubt
But victory still sits upon your sword,
And must not now forsake you.
Mont. You shall see me
Come boldly up; nor will I shame your cause,
By parting with an inch of ground not bought
With blood on my part.
Cler. 'Tis not to be question'd :
That which I would entreat, (and pray you grant
    it,)

4 *The honour to have enter'd first the field,*
  However we come of, is ours.] Thus Fletcher :
" *Cler.* I'm first in the field, that honour's gain'd of our side;
" Pray heaven, I may get off as honourably !"
                        The Little French Lawyer.
It is observable, that several of the names which occur in *the
Parliament of Love* are found also in Fletcher's play; though
their plots have nothing in common.

Is, that you would forget your usual softness,
Your foe being at your mercy ; it hath been
A custom in you, which I dare not praise,
Having disarm'd your enemy of his sword,
To tempt your fate, by yielding it again ;
Then run a second hazard.
    Mont. When we encounter
A noble foe, we cannot be too noble.
    Cler. That I confess ; but he that's now to
        oppose you,
I know for an archvillain ; one that hath lost
All feeling of humanity, one that hates
Goodness in others, 'cause he's ill himself ;
A most ungrateful wretch, (the name's too
        gentle,
All attributes of wickedness cannot reach him,)
Of whom to have deserved, beyond example,
Or precedent of friendship, is a wrong
Which only death can satisfy.
    Mont. You describe
A monster to me.
    Cler. True, Montrose, he is so.
Afric, though fertile of strange prodigies,
Never produced his equal ! be wise, therefore,
And if he fall into your hands, dispatch him :
Pity to him is cruelty. The sad father,
That sees his son stung by a snake to death,
May, with more justice, stay his vengeful hand,
And let the worm[5] escape, than you vouchsafe
       him
A minute to repent : for 'tis a slave

---

[5] *And let the* worm *escape,*] i. e. the *snake* mentioned in the preceding line. *Worm,* which is pure Saxon, was once the general term for all reptiles of the serpent kind ; indeed, it is still so, in many parts of England. The word occurs so frequently in this sense, among the writers of Massinger's time, that it appears unnecessary to produce instances of it.

So sold to hell and mischief; that a traitor
To his most lawful prince, a church-robber,
A parricide, who, when his garners are
Cramm'd with the purest grain, suffers his parents,
Being old, and weak, to starve for want of bread ;
Compared to him, are innocent.
 Mont. I ne'er heard
Of such a cursed nature ; if long-lived,
He would infect mankind : rest you assured,
He finds from me small courtesy.
 Cler. And expect
As little from him : blood is that he thirsts for,
Not honourable wounds.
 Mont. I would I had him
Within my sword's length !
 Cler. Have thy wish : Thou hast !
      [*Cleremond draws his sword.*
Nay, draw thy sword, and suddenly ; I am
That monster, temple-robber, parricide,
Ingrateful wretch ; friend-hater, or what else
Makes up the perfect figure of the devil,
Should he appear like man. Banish amazement,
And call thy ablest spirits up to guard thee.
From him that's turn'd a Fury. I am made
Her minister, whose cruelty but named,
Would with more horror strike the pale-cheek'd
   stars,
Than all those dreadful words which conjurers use,
To fright their damn'd familiars. Look not on me
As I am Cleremond ; I have parted with
The essence that was his, and entertain'd
The soul of some fierce tigress, or a wolf's
New-hang'd for human slaughter, and tis fit :
I could not else be an apt instrument
To bloody Leonora.
 Mont. To my knowledge
I never wrong'd her.

Cler. Yes, in being a friend
To me she hated, my best friend ; her malice
Would look no lower :—and for being such,
By her commands, Montrose, I am to kill thee.
Oh, that thou hadst, like others, been all words,
And no performance ! or that thou hadst made
Some little stop in thy career of kindness !
Why wouldst thou, to confirm the name of friend,
Despise the favours of fair Bellisant,
And all those certain joys that waited for thee ?
Snatch at this fatal offer of a second,
Which others fled from ?—'Tis in vain to mourn
        now,
When there's no help ; and therefore, good
        Montrose,
Rouse thy most manly parts, and think thou
        stand'st now
A champion for more than king or country ;
Since, in thy fall, goodness itself must suffer.
Remember too, the baseness of the wrong
- - - friendship ; let it edge thy sword,
And kill compassion in thee ; and forget not
I will take all advantages : and so,
Without reply, have at thee !

            [*They fight. Cleremond falls.*
    Mont. See, how weak
An ill cause is ! you are already fallen :
What can you look for now ?
    Cler. Fool, use thy fortune :
And so he counsels thee, that, if we had
Changed places, instantly would have cut thy
        throat,
Or digg'd thy heart out.
    Mont. In requital of
That savage purpose, I must pity you ;
Witness these tears, not tears of joy for conquest,
But of true sorrow for your misery.

Live, O live, Cleremond, and, like a man,
Make use of reason, as an exorcist,
To cast this devil out, that does abuse you ;
This fiend of false affection.

Cler. Will you not kill me?
You are then more tyrannous than Leonora.
An easy thrust will do it : you had ever
A charitable hand ; do not deny me,
For our old friendship's sake : no ! will't not be?
There are a thousand doors to let out life ;
You keep not guard of all : and I shall find,
By falling headlong from some rocky cliff,
Poison, or fire, that long rest which your sword
Discourteously denies me.   [*Exit.*

Mont. I will follow ;
And something I must fancy, to dissuade him
From doing sudden violence on himself :
That's now my only aim ; and that to me,
Succeeding well, is a true victory.   [*Exit.*

SCENE III.

Paris.   *An outer Room in* Chamont's *House.*

Enter CHAMONT *disguised, and* DINANT.

Din. Your lady tempted too !
Cham. And tempted home ;
Summon'd to parley, the fort almost yielded,
Had not I stepp'd in to remove the siege :
But I have countermined his works, and if
You second me, will blow the letcher up,
And laugh to see him caper.

Din. Any thing :
Command me as your servant, to join with you ;
VOL. II.   X

All ways are honest we take, to revenge us
On these lascivious monkies of the court,
That make it their profession to dishonour
Grave citizens' wives; nay, those of higher rank,
As 'tis, in your's, apparent. My young rambler,
That thought to cheat me with a feign'd disease,
I have in the toil already; I have given him,
Under pretence to make him high and active,
A cooler :—I dare warrant it will yield
Rare sport to see it work; I would your lordship
Could be a spectator.
 Cham. It is that I aim at:
And might I but persuade you to dispense
A little with your candour,[6] and consent
To make your house the stage, on which we'll
  act
A comic scene; in the pride of all their hopes,
We'll shew these shallow fools sunk-eyed despair,
And triumph in their punishment.
 Din. My house,
Or whatsoever else is mine, shall serve
As properties to grace it.
 Cham. In this shape, then,
Leave me to work the rest.
 Din. Doubt not, my lord,
You shall find all things ready.   [*Exit.*

Enter PERIGOT.

 Cham. This sorts well
With my other purposes. Perigot! to my wish.
Aid me, invention!
 Peri. Is the quean fallen off?
I hear not from her?—'tis the hour and place

 6 *With your* candour,] i. e. honour; See *the Guardian.*
A. iii. S. 1.

That she appointed.
What have we here? This fellow has a pimp's face,
And looks as if he were her call, her fetch——
With me?
    Cham. Sir, from the party,
The lady you should truck with, the lord's wife
Your worship is to dub, or to make free
Of the company of the horners.
    Peri. Fair Lamira?
    Cham. The same, sir.
    Peri. And how, my honest squire o'dames?[7] I see
Thou art of her privy council.
    Cham. Her grant holds, sir.
    Peri. O rare! But when?
    Cham. Marry, instantly.
    Peri. But where?
    Cham. She hath outgone the cunning of a woman,
In ordering it both privately and securely :
You know Dinant, the doctor?
    Peri. Good.
    Cham. His house
And him she has made at her devotion, sir.
Nay, wonder not ; most of these empirics
Thrive better by connivance in such cases,
Than their lame practice : framing some dis-
    temper,
The fool, her lord——
    Peri. Lords may be what they please ;
I question not their patent.
    Cham. Hath consented.
That this night, privately, she shall take a clyster ;
Which he believes the doctor ministers,
And never thinks of you.
    Peri. A good wench still.

---

    [7] *And how, my honest squire o' dames ?*] See *the Emperor of the
East.*

           * X 2

Cham. And there, without suspicion——
Peri. Excellent!
I make this lord my cuckold?
    Cham. True ; and write
The reverend drudging doctor, my copartner,
And fellow bawd: next year we will have him
       warden
Of our society.
    Peri. There! there! I shall burst,
I am so swollen with pleasure ; no more talking,
Dear keeper of the vaulting door ;[8] lead on.
    Cham. Charge you as boldly.
    Peri. Do not fear; I have
A staff to taint, and bravely.[9]

---

[8] *Dear* keeper of the vaulting door;] To *keep the door,* was one of the thousand synonyms of a bawd or pander. To this the distracted Othello alludes in his passionate speech to Emilia :

    " —————————— you, mistress,
    " That have the office opposite to saint Peter,
    " And *keep the gate of* hell!"

[9] Peri. *Do not fear ; I have*
    A staff to taint, *and bravely.*] This is a very uncommon word in its present application; nor can I be certain that I comprehend its precise meaning. To break a staff or spear, in the tilts and tournaments of our ancestors, was an honourable achievement; but then (as appears from " the Ordinances made by the earl of Worcester, constable of England in 1466, and renewed in 1562") it was to be done in a particular manner, and " as it ought to bee broken." How a spear ought to be broken, is not said ; nor was the information perhaps necessary at the time. It seems, however, that it should be as near the middle as possible; for, if it were within a foot of the coronel or extremity, it was then " to bee adjudged as no speare broken, but a fayre attaynt." *Nugæ Antiquæ,* Vol. I. p. 4. I meet with the word in *Every Man out of His Humour,* the only place, with the exception of the work just quoted, where I recollect ever to have seen it : and there, too, it is used in a derogatory sense, " He has a good riding face, and he can sit a horse well; he will *taint* a staff well at tilt."

Cham. Save the splinters,
If it break in the encounter.
   Peri. Witty rascal!   [*Exeunt.*

SCENE IV.

A Room in Bellisant's *House.*

Enter CLARINDORE, BELLISANT, *and* BEAUPRÉ.

   Clarin. Boast of your favours, madam!
   Bell. Pardon, sir,
My fears, since it is grown a general custom,
In our hot youth, to keep a catalogue
Of conquests this way got; nor do they think
Their victory complete, unless they publish,
To their disgrace, that are made captives to them,
How far they have prevail'd.
   Clarin. I would have such rascals
First gelded, and then hang'd.
   Bell. Remember too, sir,
To what extremities your love had brought you;
And, since I saved your life, I may, with justice,
By silence charge you to preserve mine honour;
Which, howsoever to my conscious self
I am tainted, foully tainted, to the world
I am free from all suspicion.
   Clarin. Can you think
I'll do myself that wrong? although I had
A lawyer's mercenary tongue, still moving,
- - - -le this precious carcanet, these jewels,
- - of your magnificence, would keep me
A Pythagorean, and ever silent.
No, rest secure, sweet lady; and excuse
My sudden and abrupt departure from you:

And if the fault makes forfeit of your grace,
A quick return shall ransome and redeem it.
   Bell. Be mindful of your oaths.
                      [Walks aside with Beaupré.
   Clarin. I am got off,
And leave the memory of them behind me.
Now, if I can find out my scoffing gulls,
Novall and Perigot, besides my wager,
Which is already sure, I shall return
Their bitter jests, and wound them with my
     tongue,
Much deeper than my sword. Oh! but the oaths
I have made to the contrary, and her credit,
Of which I should be tender:—tush! both hold
With me an equal value. The wise say,
That the whole fabric of a woman's lighter
Than wind or feathers: what is then her fame?
A kind of nothing;—not to be preserved
With the loss of so much money: 'tis sound
     doctrine,
And I will follow it.   *[Exit.*
   Bell. Prithee, be not doubtful;
Let the wild colt run his course.
   Beau. I must confess
I cannot sound the depth of what you purpose,
But I much fear——
   Bell. That he will blab; I know it,
And that a secret scalds him: that he suffers
Till he hath vented what I seem to wish
He should conceal;—but let him, I am arm'd
     for't.   *[Exeunt.*

SCENE V.

A Room in Dinant's *House.*

Enter CHAMONT, DINANT, LAMIRA, CLARINDA,
and Servants.

Cham. For Perigot, he's in the toil ne'er
    doubt it.
O, had you seen how his veins swell'd with lust,
When I brought him to the chamber! how he
    gloried,
And stretch'd his limbs, preparing them for action;
And, taking me to be a pander, told me
'Twas more delight to have a lord his cuckold,
Than to enjoy my lady!—there I left him
In contemplation, greedily expecting
Lamira's presence; but, instead of her,
I have prepared him other visitants.——
You know what you have to do?
    1 *Serv.* Fear not, my lord,
He shall curvet, I warrant him, in a blanket.
    2 *Serv.* We'll discipline him with dog-whips, and
    take off
His rampant edge.
    Cham. His life; save that—remember,
You cannot be too cruel.
    Din. For his pupil,
My wife's Inamorato, if cold weeds,
Removed but one degree from deadly poison,
Have not forgot their certain operation,
You shall see his courage cool'd; and in that
    temper,
Till he have howl'd himself into my pardon,
I vow to keep him.

Nov. [within.] Ho, doctor! master doctor!
Din. The game's afoot; we will let slip: conceal
Yourselves a little.   [*Exeunt all but Dinant.*

Enter NOVALL.

Nov. Oh! a thousand agues
Play at barley-break in my bones; my blood's a
    pool
On the sudden frozen, and the isicles
Cut every vein: 'tis here, there, every where;
Oh dear, dear, master doctor!
    Din. I must seem
Not to understand him; 'twill increase his torture.—   [*Aside.*
How do you, sir? has the potion wrought? do
    you feel
An alteration? have your swellings left you?
Is your blood still rebellious?
    Nov. Oh, good doctor,
I am a ghost! I have nor flesh, nor blood,
Nor heat, nor warmth, about me.
    Din. Do not dissemble;
I know you are high and jovial.
    Nov. Jovial! doctor;
No, I am all amort, as if I had lain
Three days in my grave already.
    Din. I will raise you:
For, look you, sir, you are a liberal patient,
Nor must I, while you can be such, part with you;
'Tis against the laws of our college. Pray you,
    mark me;
I have with curiosity consider'd
Your constitution to be hot and moist,
And that at your nativity Jupiter
And Venus were in conjunction, whence it follows,

By necessary consequence, you must be
A most insatiate letcher.
   Nov. Oh! I have been,
I have been, I confess: but now I cannot
Think of a woman.
   Din. For your health you must, sir,
Both think, and see, and touch; you're but a
      dead man else.
   Nov. That way, I am already.
   Din. You must take,
And suddenly, ('tis a conceal'd receipt,)
A buxom, juicy wench.
   Nov. Oh! 'twill not down, sir;
I have no swallow for't.
   Din. Now, since I would
Have the disease as private as the cure,
(For 'tis a secret,) I have wrought my wife
To be both physic and physician,
To give you ease :—will you walk to her?
   Nov. Oh! doctor,
I cannot stand; in every sense about me
I have the palsy, but my tongue.
   Din. Nay then,
You are obstinate, and refuse my gentle offer;
Or else 'tis foolish modesty :—Come hither,
Come, my Clarinda,

     Re-enter CLARINDA.

          'tis not common courtesy;
Comfort the gentleman.
   Nov. This is ten times worse.
   Cham. [*within*] He does torment him rarely.
   Din. She is not coy, sir.
What think you, is not this a pretty foot,
And a clean instep? I will leave the calf

For you to find and judge of: here's a hand too;
Try it, the palm is moist; the youthful blood
Runs strong in every azure vein: the face too
Ne'er knew the help of art; and, all together,
May serve the turn, after a long sea-voyage,
For the captain's self.

    Nov. I am a swabber, doctor,
A bloodless swabber; have not strength enough
To cleanse her poop.

    Din. Fie! you shame yourself,
And the profession of your rutting gallants,
That hold their doctors' wives as free for them,
As some of us do our apothecaries'!

    Nov. Good sir, no more.

    Din. Take her aside; cornute me;
I give you leave: what should a quacksalve
A fellow that does deal with drugs, as I do,
That has not means to give her choice of gowns,
Jewels, and rich embroidered petticoats,
Do with so fair a bedfellow? she being fashion'd
To purge a rich heir's reins, to be the mistress
Of a court gallant? Did you not tell her so?

    Nov. I have betray'd myself! I did, I did.

    Din. And that rich merchants, advocates, and
        doctors,
Howe'er deserving from the commonwealth,
On forfeit of the city's charter, were
Predestined cuckolds?

    Nov. Oh, some pity, doctor!
I was an heretic, but now converted.
Some little, little respite!

    Din. No, you town-bull;
- - - -venge all good men's wrongs,
And now will play the tyrant. To dissect thee,
Eat thy flesh off with burning corrosives,
Or write with aquafortis in thy forehead,

Thy last intent to wrong my bed, were justice;
And to do less were foolish pity in me:
I speak it, ribald!
Nov. Perigot! Perigot!
Woe to thy cursed counsel.

Re-enter CHAMONT *and* LAMIRA.

Cham. Perigot!
Did he advise you to this course?
Nov. He did.
Cham. And he has his reward for't.
Peri. [*within.*] Will you murder me!
Serv. [*within.*] Once more, aloft with him.
Peri. [*within.*] Murder! murder! murder!

Re-Enter Servants, *with* PERIGOT *in a blanket.*

Cham. What conceal'd bake-meats have you
    there? a present?
Is it goat's flesh? It smells rank.
1 *Serv.* We have had
Sweet work of it, my lord.
2 *Serv.* I warrant you 'tis tender,
It wants no cooking; yet, if you think fit,
We'll bruise it again.
Peri. As you are Christians, spare me!
I am jelly within already, and without
Embroidered all o'er with statute lace.[*]
What would you more?
Nov. My tutor in the gin, too!

[*] *Embroidered all o'er with* statute *lace.*] Meaning, I believe,
that his skin was so torn, that it hung down in stripes like the
narrow worsted laces allowed by *statute.* There is a passage in
Beaumont and Fletcher, which appears to support the sense
given here.' "Jag him, gentlemen," says the Captain. "I'll
have him cut to the kell, then down the seams. O for a
whip to make him *galloon laces!*" *Philaster.* The expression
occurs in Shirley: "We were of your acquaintance once, sir,

This is some comfort : he is as good as drench'd ;[2]
And now we'll both be chaste.

    Cham. What, is't a cat
You have encounter'd, monsieur, you are scratch'd
    so ?
My lady, sure, forgot to pare her nails,
Before your soft embraces.

    Din. He has ta'en great pains :
What a sweat he's in !

    Cham. O ! he's a master-dancer,
Knows how to caper into a lady's favour :
One lofty trick more, dear monsieur.

    Nov. That I had
But strength enough to laugh at him ! blanketted
    like a dog,
And like a cut-purse whipt ! I am sure that now,
He cannot jeer me.

    Peri. May not a man have leave
To hang himself?

    Cham. No ; that were too much mercy.
Live to be wretched ; live to be the talk
Of the conduit, and the bakehouse.[3] I will have
    thee
Pictured as thou art now, and thy whole story
Sung to some villainous tune in a lewd ballad ;
And make thee so notorious to the world,
That boys in the streets shall hoot at thee : come,
    Lamira,

---

when we sold garters and *statute lace.*" *Doubtful Heir.* Here
it evidently means some coarse manufactory. In the reign of
Elizabeth many sumptuary laws passed. Among the rest, one,
in 1571, for obliging all but the nobility and people of fortune,
to wear *statute caps,* i. e. caps of wool, knit and drest in England, upon penalty of ten groats.

    [2] *He is as good as drench'd ;*] i. e. as impotent as if, like me,
he had been physicked by Dinant.

    [3] *Of the* conduit, *and the* bakehouse.] These, in the age of
Massinger, were the general redezvous of gossips of both
sexes : they are still so, in most country towns.

And triumph o'er him.—Dost thou see this lady,
My wife, whose honour foolishly thou thought'st
To undermine, and make a servant to
Thy brutish lusts, laughing at thy affliction?
And, as a sign she scorns thee, set her foot
Upon thy head? Do so :—'Sdeath! but resist,
Once more you caper.
    Peri. I am at the stake,
And must endure it.
    Cham. Spurn him, too.
    Lam. Troth, sir,
I do him too much grace.
    Cham. Now, as a schoolboy
Does kiss the rod that gave him chastisement,
To prove thou art a slave, meet, with thy lips,
This instrument that corrects thee.
    Peri. Have you done yet?
    Din. How like a pair of crest-fallen jades they
      look now!
    Cla. They are not worth our scorn.
    Peri. O pupil, pupil!
    Nov. Tutor, I am drench'd: let us condole
      together.
    Cham. And where's the tickling itch now, my
      dear monsieur,
To say, *This lord's my cuckold!*—I am tired :
That we had fresh dogs to hunt them!

Enter CLARINDORE.

    Clarin. - - - - -
- - - - - - - - - - - - - - -
- - - - I am acquainted with the story;
The doctor's man has told me all.
    Din. Upon them.
    Peri. Clarindore! worst of all :—for him to
      know this,
Is a second blanketting to me.

Nov. I again
Am drench'd to look on him.
   Clarin. How is't? nay, bear up;
You that commend adultery, I am glad
To see it thrive so well. Fie, Perigot!
Dejected? Haply thou wouldst have us think,
This is the first time that thou didst curvet,
And come aloft in a blanket. By St. Dennis!
Here are shrewd scratches too; but nothing to
A man of resolution, whose shoulders
Are of themselves armour of proof, against
A bastinado, and will tire ten beadles.
   Peri. Mock on; know no mercy.
   Clarin. Thrifty young men!
What a charge is saved in wenching! and 'tis
      timely——
A certain wager of three thousand crowns
Is lost, and must be paid, my pair of puppies:
The coy dame, Bellisant, hath stoop'd! bear wit-
      ness
This chain and jewels you have seen her wear.
The fellow, that her grooms kick'd down the stairs,
Hath crept into her bed; and, to assure you
There's no deceit, she shall confess so much,
I have enjoy'd her.
   Cham. Are you serious?
   Clarin. Yes, and glory in it.
   Cham. Nay then, give over fooling.——
Thou liest, and art a villain, a base villain,
To slander her.
   Clarin. You are a lord, and that
Bids me forbear you; but I will make good
Whatever I have said.
   Cham. I'll not lose time
To change words with thee. The king hath or-
      dain'd
A Parliament of Love to right her wrongs,
To which I summon thee.   *[Exit.*

Clarin. Your worst: I care not.—Farewell,
    babions!   [*Exit.*
  Din. Here was a sudden change!
Nay, you must quit my house: shog on, kind
    patient,
And, as you like my physic, when you are
Rampant again, you know I have that can cool you.
Nay, monsieur Perigot, help your pupil off too,
Your counsel brought him on. Ha! no reply?
Are you struck dumb? If you are wrong'd, com-
    plain.
  Peri. We shall find friends to right us.
  Din. And I justice,
The cause being heard; I ask no more. Hence!
    vanish!   [*Exeunt.*

ACT V. SCENE I.

A Court of Justice.

Enter CHAMONT, PHILAMOUR, *and* LAFORT.

  Phil. Montrose slain! and by Cleremond!
  Cham. 'Tis too true.
  Laf. But wondrous strange, that any difference,
Especially of such a deadly nature,
Should e'er divide so eminent a friendship.
  Phil. The miracle is greater, that a lady,
His most devoted mistress, Leonora,
Against the usual softness of her sex,
Should with such violence and heat pursue
Her amorous servant; since I am inform'd

That he was apprehended by her practice,[4]
And, when he comes to trial for his life,
She'll rise up his accuser.

Cham. So 'tis rumour'd :
And that's the motive that young Cleremond
Makes it his humble suit, to have his cause
Decided in the Parliament of Love ;
For he pretends the bloody quarrel grew
From grounds that claim a reference to that place:
Nor fears he, if you grant him equal hearing,
But, with unanswerable proof, to render
The cruel Leonora tainted with
A guilt beyond his.

Laf. The king is acquainted
Already with the accident; besides,
He hath vouchsafed to read divers petitions
Preferr'd on several causes ; one against
Monsieur Dinant, his doctor, by Novall ;
A second, in which madam Bellisant
Complains 'gainst Clarindore ; there is a bill too,
Brought in by Perigot, against your lordship ;
All which, in person, he resolves to hear,
Then, as a judge, to censure.   [*A flourish within.*

Phil. See the form !
Choice musick ushers him.

Cham. Let us meet the troop,
And mix with them.

Phil. 'Twill poize your expectation.   [*Exeunt.*

---

[4] *That he was apprehended by her* practice,] i. e. by her artifice.   This word is frequently found in Massinger, and his contemporaries, in the sense of an insidious trick, or stratagem.
The circumstance of Leonora instigating her lover to murder
his friend, and then giving him up to justice, is adopted, with
some variations, from Marston's *Dutch Courtezan.*

Loud music. Enter CHARLES *followed by* OR-
LEANS, NEMOURS, CHAMONT, LAFORT, *and*
PHILAMOUR. *A* Priest *with the image of* CUPID:
then enter CLEREMOND, CLARINDORE, PERI-
GOT, NOVALL, BELLISANT, LEONORA, BEAUPRÉ,
LAMIRA, CLARINDA, *and* Officers. MONTROSE
*is brought forward on a bier, and placed before
the bar.*

Char. Let it not seem a wonder, nor beget
An ill opinion in this fair assembly,
That here I place this statue; 'tis not done,
Upon the forfeit of our grace, that you
Should, with a superstitious reverence,
Fall down and worship it: nor can it be
Presumed, we hope, young Charles, that justly
        holds
The honour'd title of *most Christian King*,
Would ever nourish such idolatrous thoughts.
'Tis rather to instruct deceived mankind,
How much pure Love, that has his birth in heaven,
And scorns to be received a guest, but in
A noble heart prepared to entertain him,
Is, by the gross misprision of weak men,
Abused and injured. That celestial fire,
Which hieroglyphically is described
In this his bow, his quiver, and his torch,
First warm'd their bloods, and after gave a name
To the old heroic spirits: such as Orpheus,
That drew men, differing little then from beasts,
To civil government; or famed Alcides,
The tyrant-queller, that refused the plain
And easy path leading to vicious pleasures,
And ending in a precipice deep as hell,
To scale the ragged cliff,[5] on whose firm top

[5] *To scale the ragged cliffs,*] This expressive epithet is from
Scripture, as are many of Massinger's. See Is. c. ii. v. 21.
VOL. II.   * Y

Virtue and Honour, crown'd with wreaths of stars,
Did sit triumphant.   But it will be answer'd,
(The world decaying in her strength,) that now
We are not equal to those ancient times,
And therefore 'twere impertinent and tedious
To cite more precedents of that reverend age,
But rather to endeavour, as we purpose,
To give encouragement, by reward, to such
As with their best nerves imitate that old good-
  ness;
And, with severe correction, to reform
The modern vices.—Begin; read the bills.
 Peri. Let mine be first, my lord; 'twas first
  preferr'd.
 Bell. But till my cause be heard, our whole sex
  suffers—
 Off. Back! keep back, there!
 Nov. Prithee, gentle officer,
Handle me gingerly, or I fall to pieces,
Before I can plead mine.
 Peri. I am bruised -   -   -
 Omnes. Justice! justice!
 Char. Forbear these clamours, you shall all be
  heard:
And, to confirm I am no partial judge,
By lottery decide it;⁶ here's no favour.——
Whose bill is first, Lafort? [*the names are drawn.*]
 Laf. 'Tis Cleremond's.
 Char. The second?
 Laf. Perigot's; the third Novall's.
 Nov. Our cases are both lamentable, tutor.
 Peri. And I am glad they shall be heard toge-
  ther;
We cannot stand asunder.

 ⁶ *By lottery decide it;*]
   " Let high-sighted tyranny range on,
   " Till each man drop *by lottery.*" *Julius Cæsar.*

Char. What's the last?

Laf. The injured lady Bellisant's.

Char. To the first, then;
And so proceed in order.

Phil. Stand to the bar.   [*Cler. comes forward.*

Leon. Speak, Cleremond, thy grief, as I will
    mine.

Peri. A confident little pleader! were I in case,
I would give her a double fee.

Nov. So would I, tutor.

Off. Silence! silence!

Cler. Should I rise up to plead my innocence,
Though, with the favour of the court, I stood
Acquitted to the world, yea, though the wounds
Of my dead friend, (which, like so many mouths
With bloody tongues, cry out aloud against me,)
By your authority, were closed; yet here,
A not to be corrupted judge, my conscience,
Would not alone condemn me, but inflict
Such lingering tortures on me, as the hangman,
Though witty in his malice, could not equal.
I therefore do confess a guilty cause,
Touching the fact, and, uncompell'd, acknowledge
Myself the instrument of a crime the sun,
Hiding his face in a thick mask of clouds,
As frighted with the horror, durst not look on.
But if your laws with greater rigour punish
Such as invent a mischief, than the organs
By whom 'tis put in act, (they truly being
The first great wheels by which the lesser move,)
Then stand forth, Leonora; and I'll prove
The white robe of my innocence tainted with
But one black spot of guilt, and even that one
By thy hand cast on me; but thine, died o'er,
Ten times in grain, in hell's most ugly colours.

Leon. The fellow is distracted: see how he
    raves!

* Y 2

Now as I live, if detestation of
His baseness would but give me leave, I should
Begin to pity him.
    Cler. Frontless impudence,
And not to be replied to! Sir, to you,
And these subordinate ministers of yourself,
I turn my speech: to her I do repent
I e'er vouchsafed a syllable. My birth[7]
Was noble as 'tis ancient, nor let it relish
Of arrogance, to say my father's care,
With curiousness and cost, did train me up
In all those liberal qualities that commend
A gentleman: and when the tender down
Upon my chin told me I was a man,
I came to court; there youth, ease, and example,
First made me feel the pleasing pains of love:
And there I saw this woman; saw, and loved her
With more than common ardour: for that deity,

[7]   —————— *My birth*
Was noble as 'tis ancient, &c.] Sir H. Herbert (for Mr.
Malone supposes this to be the presentation copy, and to have
remained in his hands) has taken several liberties with this play.
In some places, where the expressions appeared too free, he has
drawn his pen through them; in others, he has struck out lines,
under the idea, perhaps, of compressing the sense, kindly sup-
plying a connecting word or two from his own stores; and in
others, he has been content with including the objectionable
passages between brackets. In the latter there is not much
harm, but the former is a sore evil: for as I do not deem very
highly of Sir Henry's taste, nor indeed of his judgment, the
endeavours to recover the genuine text from the blot spread
over it, has been attended with a very considerable degree of
trouble; it has, however, been generally successful.

    If I thought that innovations, hazarded without knowledge
to direct them, could be objects of curiosity, I would give the
reader this speech as it stands in *the new version:*—but it is not
worth his care. 1805.

    I am now enabled to speak with certainty respecting the
hand-writing of the MS. The fortunate discovery of the corrected copy of *the Duke of Milan* proves it to be Massinger's.

(Such our affection makes him,) whose dread
    power
- - - - - - - - - - - - -
- - - - the choicest arrow, headed with
Not loose but loyal flames, which aim'd at me,
Who came with greedy haste to meet the shaft,
- - - -ing, that my captive heart was made
- - - - - - - - - Love's divine artillery,
- - - - preserved - - - no relation.
But the shot made at her was not, like mine,
Of gold, nor of pale lead that breeds disdain ;
Cupid himself disclaims it : I think rather,
As by the sequel 'twill appear, some Fury
From burning Acheron snatch'd a sulphur brand,
That smoak'd with hate, the parent of red murder,
And threw it in her bosom. Pardon me,
Though I dwell long upon the cause that did
Produce such dire effects ; and, to omit,
For your much patience' sake, the cunning trap
In which she caught me, and, with horrid oaths,
Embark'd me in a sea of human blood,
I come to the last scene——
    Leon. 'Tis time ; for this
Grows stale and tedious.
    Cler. When, I say, she had,
To satisfy her fell rage, as a penance,
Forced me to this black deed, her vow, too, given,
That I should marry her, and she conceal me ;
When to her view I brought the slaughter'd body
Of my dear friend, and labour'd with my tears
To stir compunction in her, aided too
By the sad object, which might witness for me,
At what an over-rate I had made purchase
Of her long-wish'd embraces ; then, great sir,—
But that I had a mother, and there may be
Some two or three of her - - - sex less faulty,
I should affirm she was the perfect image

Of the devil, her tutor, that had left hell empty,
To dwell in wicked woman.
    Leon. Do; rail on.
    Cler. For not alone she gloried in my sufferings,
Forswore what she had vow'd, refused to touch
       me,
Much less to comfort me, or give me harbour;
But, instantly, ere I could recollect
My scatter'd sense, betray'd me to your justice,
Which I submit to; hoping, in your wisdom,
That as, in me, you lop a limb of murder,
You will, in her, grub up the root. I have said, sir.
    Leon. Much, I confess, but much to little purpose.
And though, with your rhetorical flourishes,
You strive to gild a rotten cause, the touch
Of reason, fortified by truth, deliver'd
From my unletter'd tongue, shall shew it dust;
And so to be contemn'd: You have trimm'd up
All your deservings, should I grant them such,
With more care than a maiden of threescore
Does hide her wrinkles, which, if she encounter
The rain, the wind, or sun, the paint wash'd off,
Are to dim eyes discover'd. I forbear
The application, and in a plain style
Come roundly to the matter. 'Tis confess'd,
This pretty, handsome, gentleman, (for thieves
Led to the gallows are held proper men,
And so I now will call him,) would needs make
       me
The mistress of his thoughts; nor did I scorn,
For truth is truth, to grace him as a servant.
Nay, he took pretty ways to win me too,
For a court novice; every year I was
His Valentine, and, in an anagram,
My name worn in his hat; he made me banquets,
As if he thought that ladies, like to flies,

Were to be caught with sweetmeats ; quarrell'd
    with
My tailor, if my gown were not the first
Of that edition ; beat my shoemaker,
If the least wrinkle on my foot appear'd,
As wronging the proportion ; and, in time,
Grew bolder, usher'd me to masques, and - - -
Or else paid him that wrote them ; - - -
With such a deal of p- - - - - - -
And of good rank, are taken with such gambols :
In a word, I was so ; and a solemn contract
Did pass betwixt us ; and the day appointed,
That should make our embraces warrantable,
And lawful to the world : all things so carried,
As he meant nought but honourable love.
   Char. A pretty method.
   Phil. Quaintly, too, deliver'd.
   Leon. But, when he thought me sure, he then
    gave proof
That foul lust lurk'd in the fair shape of love;
For, valuing neither laws divine, nor human,
His credit, nor my fame, with violence born
On black-sail'd wings of loose and base desires,
As if his natural parts had quite forsook him,
And that the pleasures of the marriage bed
Were to be reap'd with no more ceremony
Than brute beasts couple,—I yet blush to speak it,
He tempted me to yield my honour up
To his libidinous twines ; and, like an atheist,
Scoff'd at the form and orders of the church ;
Nor ended so, but, being by me reproved,
He offer'd violence ; but was prevented.
   Char. Note, a sudden change.
   Laf. 'Twas foul in Cleremond.
   Leon. I, burning then with a most virtuous anger,
Razed from my heart the memory of his name,

Reviled, and spit at him; and knew 'twas justice
That I should take those deities he scorn'd,
Hymen and Cupid, into my protection,
And be the instrument of their revenge :
And so I cast him off, scorn'd his submission,
His poor and childish whinings, will'd my servants
To shut my gates against him : but, when neither
Disdain, hate, nor contempt, could free me from
His loathsome importunities, (and fired too,
To wreak mine injured honour,) I took gladly
Advantage of his execrable oaths
To undergo what penance I enjoin'd him;
Then, to the terror of all future ribalds,
That make no difference between love and lust,
Imposed this task upon him. I have said, too :
Now, when you please, a censure.

 Char. She has put
The judges to their whisper.

 Nov. What do you think of these proceedings,
  tutor ?

 Peri. The truth is,
I like not the severity of the court;
Would I were quit, and in an hospital,
I could let fall my suit !

 Nov. 'Tis still your counsel.

 Char. We are resolved, and with an equal hand
Will hold the scale of justice; pity shall not
Rob us of strength and will to draw her sword,
Nor passion transport us : let a priest
And headsman be in readiness ;—do you start,
To hear them named ? Some little pause we grant
  you,
To take examination of yourselves,
What either of you have deserved, and why
These instruments of our power are now thought
  useful :
You shall hear more, anon.——

Cler. I like not this.   [*Aside.*
Leon. A dreadful preparation ! I confess
It shakes my confidence.   [*Aside.*
Clarin. I presumed this court
Had been in sport erected ; but now find,
With sorrow to the strongest hopes I built on,
That 'tis not safe to be the subject of
The   -   -   -   of kings.
(New Speaker.) To the second cause.
Laf. -   -   -   Perigot's.
Nov. Nay, take me along too ;
And, since that our complaints differ not much,
Dispatch us both together. I accuse
This devilish doctor.
Peri. I, this wicked lord.
Nov. 'Tis known I was an able, lusty man,
Fit to get soldiers to serve my king
And country in the wàrs ; and howsoever
'Tis said I am not valiant of myself,
I was a striker, one that could strike home too ;
And never did beget a girl, though drunk.
To make this good, I could produce brave boys,
That others father, twigs of mine own grafting,
That loved a drum at four, and ere full ten,
Fought battles for the parish they were born in ;
And such by-blows, old stories say, still proved
Fortunate captains : now, whereas, in justice,
I should have had a pension from the state
For my good service, this ingrateful doctor,
Having no child, and never like to have one,
Because, in pity of his barrenness,
I plotted how to help him to an heir,
Has, with a drench, so far disabled me,
That the great Turk may trust me with his virgins,
And never use a surgeon. Now consider,
If this be not hard measure, and a wrong to
Little Dan Cupid, if he be the god

Of coupling, as 'tis said ; and will undo,
If you give way to this, all younger brothers
That carry their revenue in their breeches.—
Have I not nick'd it, tutor ?   [*Aside to Peri.*
    Peri. To a hair, boy :
Our bills shall pass, ne'er fear it. [*Aside.*]—For
    my case,
It is the same, sir ; my intent as noble
As was my pupil's.
    Cham. Plead it not again, then :
It takes much from the dignity of the court
But to give audience to such things as these,
That do, in their defence, condemn themselves,
And need not an accuser.   To be short, sir,
And in a language as far from obsceneness,
As the foul cause will give me leave, be pleased
To know thus much : This hungry pair of flesh-flies,
And most inseparable pair of coxcombs,
Though born of divers mothers, twins in baseness,
Were frequent at my table, had free welcome
And entertainment fit for better men ;
In the return of which, this thankful monsieur
Tempted my wife, seduced her, at the least
To him it did appear so ; which discover'd,
And with what treacheries he did abuse
My bounties, treading underneath his feet
All due respect of hospitable rights,
Or the honour of my family ; though the intent
Deserved a stab, and at the holy altar,
I borrow'd so much of your power to right me,
As to make him caper.
    Din. For this gallant, sir,
I do confess I cool'd him, spoil'd his rambling ;
Would all such as delight in it, were served so !
And since you are acquainted with the motives
That did induce me to it, I forbear
A needless repetition.

Cham. 'Tis not worth it.
The criminal judge is fitter to take   -   -   -
Of pleas of this base nature.   Be   -   -   -   -
An injured lady, for whose wrong   -   -   -   -
I see the statue of the god of love
Drop down tears of compassion, his sad mother,
And fair-cheek'd Graces, that attend on her,
Weeping for company, as if that all
The ornaments upon the Paphian shrine
Were, with one gripe, by sacrilegious hands,
Torn from the holy altar : 'tis a cause, sir,
That justly may exact your best attention ;
Which if you truly understand and censure,
You not alone shall right the present times,
But bind posterity to be your debtor.
Stand forth, dear madam :—
                              [*Bellisant comes forward.*
                              Look upon this face,
Examine every feature and proportion,
And you with me must grant, this rare piece
      finish'd,
Nature, despairing e'er to make the like,
Brake suddenly the mould in which 'twas fashion'd.
Yet, to increase your pity, and call on
Your justice with severity, this fair outside
Was but the cover of a fairer mind.
Think, then, what punishment he must deserve,
And justly suffer, that could arm his heart
With such impenetrable flinty hardness,
To injure so much sweetness.
    Clarin. I must stand
The fury of this tempest, which already
Sings in my ears.
    Bell. Great sir, the too much praise
This lord, my guardian once, has shower'd upon
      me,
Could not but spring up blushes in my cheeks,

If grief had left me blood enough to speak
My humble modesty : and so far I am
From being litigious, that though I were robb'd
Of my whole estate, provided my fair name
Had been unwounded, I had now been silent,
But since the wrongs I undergo, if smother'd,
Would injure our whole sex, I must lay by
My native bashfulness, and put on boldness,
Fit to encounter with the impudence
Of this bad man, that from his birth hath been
So far from nourishing an honest thought,
That the abuse of virgins was his study,
And daily practice. His forsaking of
His wife, distressed Beaupré; his lewd wager
With these, companions like himself, to abuse me;
His desperate resolution, in my presence,
To be his own assassin ; to prevent which,
Foolish compassion forced me to surrender
The life of life, my honour, I pass over :
I'll only touch his foul ingratitude,
To scourge which monster, if your laws provide
          not
A punishment with rigour, they are useless.
Or if the sword, the gallows, or the wheel,
Be due to such as spoil us of our goods ;
Perillus' brazen bull, the English rack,
The German pincers, or the Scotch oil'd-boots,
Though join'd together, yet come short of torture,
To their full merit, those accursed wretches,
That steal our reputations, and good names,
As this base villain has done mine :—Forgive me,
If rage provoke me to uncivil language ;
The cause requires it. Was it not enough
That, to preserve thy life, I lost my honour,
- - - - in recompense of such a gift
- - - - - publish it, to my disgrace ?
- - - - - - whose means, unfortunate I,

Whom, but of late, the city, nay, all France,
Durst bring in opposition for chaste life,
With any woman in the Christian world,
Am now become a by-word, and a scorn,
In mine own country.
   Char. As I live, she moves me.
Is this true, Clarindore?
   Nov. Oh! 'tis very true, sir;
He bragg'd of it to me.
   Peri. And me.
Nay, since we must be censured, we'll give evi-
     dence;
'Tis comfort to have fellows in affliction:
You shall not 'scape, fine monsieur.
   Clarin. Peace, you dog-bolts!—
Sir, I address myself to you, and hope
You have preserved one ear for my defence,
The other freely given to my accuser:
This lady, that complains of injury,
If she have any, was herself the cause
That brought it to her; for being young, and rich,
And fair too, as you see, and from that proud,
She boasted of her strength, as if it were not
In the power of love to undermine the fort
On which her chastity was strongly raised:
I, that was bred a courtier, and served
Almost my whole life under Cupid's ensigns,
Could not, in justice, but interpret this
As an affront to the great god of love,
And all his followers, if she were not brought
To due obedience: these strong reasons, sir,
Made me to undertake her.   How I woo'd,
Or what I swore, it skills* not; (since 'tis said,
And truly, Jupiter and Venus smile
At lovers' perjuries;) to be brief, she yielded,

---

   * *It* skills *not;*] It *signifies* not.   See Vol. I. p. 239.

And I enjoy'd her: if this be a crime,
And all such as offend this pleasant way
Are to be punish'd, I am sure you would have
Few followers in the court: you are young your-
      self, sir,
And what would you in such a cause?——
   Laf. Forbear.
   Phil. You are rude and insolent.
   Clarin. Good words, gentle judges.
I have no oil'd tongue; and I hope my bluntness
Will not offend.
   Char. But did you boast your conquest
Got on this lady?
   Clarin. After victory;
A little glory in a soldier's mouth
Is not uncomely; love being a kind of war too:
And what I did achieve, was full of labour
As his that wins strong towns, and merits triumphs.
I thought it could not but take from my honour,
(Besides the wager of three thousand crowns
Made sure by her confession of my service,)
If it had been conceal'd.
   Char. Who would have thought
That such an impudence could e'er have harbour
In the heart of any gentleman? In this,
Thou dost degrade thyself of all the honours
Thy ancestors left thee, and, in thy base nature,
'Tis too apparent that thou art a peasant.
Boast of a lady's favours! this confirms
Thou art the captain of that   -   -   -   -
That glory in their sins, and   -   -   -   -
With name of courtship; such as dare bely
Great women's bounties, and repuls'd and scorn'd,
Commit adultery with their good names,
And never touch their persons. I am sorry,
For your sake, madam, that I cannot make
Such reparation for you in your honour

As I desire ; for, if I should compel him
To marry you, it were to him a blessing,
To you a punishment ; he being so unworthy :
I therefore do resign my place to you ;
Be your own judge ; whate'er you shall deter-
    mine,
By my crown, I'll see perform'd.
    Clarin. I am in a fine case,
To stand at a woman's mercy.   [*Aside.*
    Bell. Then thus, sir :
I am not bloody, nor bent to revenge ;
And study his amendment, not his ruin :
Yet, since you have given up your power to me,
For punishment, I do enjoin him to
Marry this Moor.
    Clarin. A devil ! hang me rather.
    Char. It is not to be alter'd.
    Clarin. This is cruelty
Beyond expression,   -   -   I have a wife.
    Cham. Ay, too good for thee. View her well,
And then, this varnish from her face wash'd off,
Thou shalt find Beaupré.
    Clarin. Beaupré !
    Bell. Yes, his wife, sir,
But long by him with violence cast off :
And in this shape she served me ; all my studies
Aiming to make a fair atonement for her,
To which your majesty may now constrain him.
    Clarin. It needs not ; I receive her, and ask
        pardon
Of her and you.
    Bell. On both our parts 'tis granted.
This was your bedfellow, and fill'd your arms,
When you thought you embraced me : I am yet
A virgin ; nor had ever given consent,
In my chaste house, to such a wanton passage,
But that I knew that her desires were lawful.—

But now no more of personated passion:
This is the man I loved, [*pointing to the bier.*] that
    I loved truly,
However I dissembled; and, with him,
Dies all affection in me. So, great sir,
Resume your seat.
    Char. An unexpected issue,
Which I rejoice in. Would 'twere in our power
To give a period to the rest, like this,
And spare our heavy censure! but the death
Of good Montrose forbids it. Cleremond,
Thou instantly shall marry Leonora;
Which done, as suddenly thy head cut off,
And corpse interr'd, upon thy grave I'll build
A room of eight feet square, in which this lady,
For punishment of her cruelty, shall die
An anchoress.
    Leon. I do repent, and rather
Will marry him, and forgive him.
    Clarin. Bind her to
Her word, great sir; Montrose lives; this a plot
To catch this obstinate lady.
    Leon. I am glad
To be so cheated.
    Mont. [*rises from the bier.*] - - - lady,
- - - - - - deceived; do not repent
Your good opinion of me when thought dead.
Nor let not my neglect to wait upon you,
Considering what a business of import
Diverted me, be thought unpardonable.
    Bell. For my part 'tis forgiven; and thus I seal
- - - - - - - - - - -
    Char. Nor are we averse
To your desires; may you live long, and happy!
    Nov. Mercy to us, great sir.
    Peri. We will become
Chaste and reform'd men.

Cham. and Din. We both are suitors,
On this submission, for your pardon, sir.
   Char. Which we in part will grant: but, to deter
Others, by their example, from pursuing
Unlawful lusts, that think adultery
A sport to be oft practised; fix on them
Two satyrs' heads; and so, in capital letters
Their foul intents writ on their breasts, we'll
    have them
Led thrice through Paris; then, at the court gate,
To stand three hours, where Clarindore shall
    make
His recantation for the injury
Done to the lady Bellisant; and read
A sharp invective, ending with a curse
Against all such as boast of ladies' favours:
Which done, both truly penitent, my doctor
Shall use his best art to restore your strength,
And render Perigot a perfect man.——
So break we up Love's PARLIAMENT, which, we
    hope,
Being for mirth intended, shall not meet with
An ill construction; and if then, fair ladies,[9]
You please to approve it, we hope you'll invite
Your friends to see it often, with delight.
                       [Exeunt.[1]

[9] ——————————*fair ladies,*] After this, the
manuscript adds, " and gracious spectators," which, as a foolish
interpolation, I have dropped.
  [1] This is a beautiful fragment, and is every where strongly
marked with Massinger's manner; the same natural flow of
poetry, the same unforced structure of his lines, and easy fall of
period; the same fond use of mythology; and, what is more
convincing than all the rest, the same intimate and habitual
reference to his own thoughts and expressions elsewhere. I wish
it could be added that there are no marks of licentiousness:
the only consolation for the uneasiness occasioned by it is,
that proper punishments are at last inflicted on the offenders;

and we hail the moral, which aims at the suppression of " unlawful lusts."

As to the history connected with it, it is very slender ;
Charles talks of his conquests in Italy ; but his chief business
is to decree the " Parliament of Love." After this he disap-
pears, and various gallantries take place, which are only meant
to create employment for the court, and are adjudged by him
in the last act.

The principal point of curiosity is the chivalrous institution
of courts, where " disdained lovers" and " wronged ladies"
might seek redress of amorous grievances. And this is already
enquired into by the Editor.

The characters are lively and amusing ; but in Montrose it
seems to have been Massinger's intention to describe the united
force of love and friendship. He is both lofty and tender, and
possesses a sort of unconscious greatness, which shews itself in
disinterested and magnanimous actions rather than in words.
We tremble for him in the conversation preceding the combat
with Cleremond, and are at length made happy with the success of the device which induces the reluctant Bellisant to confess her love.

THE

ROMAN ACTOR,

THE ROMAN ACTOR.] This Tragedy was licensed by Sir H. Herbert, October 11th, 1626, and given to the press in 1629.

The plot is founded on the life of Domitian, as recorded by Suetonius, Dio, and others. Coxeter and Mr. M. Mason say that the poet has been very true to history ; but they say it, as usual, without knowledge : he has, as in *the Duke of Milan*, adopted a few leading circumstances, and had recourse to his invention for the rest.

This Play was successful in the representation ; and appears to have been well received by the critics of those times, since it is preceded by commendatory copies of verses from Ford, Harvey, May, Taylor, and others. Taylor, an admirable actor, who played the part of Paris, calls it " the best of many good ;" and Massinger himself declares, that " he ever held it as the most perfect birth of his Minerva."* The judgment of an author is not always to be taken upon his own works. He has his partialities and his prejudices, and, like other parents, sees beauties which are not immediately apparent to an indifferent spectator. *The Roman Actor*, though a very excellent piece, will scarcely be ranked at this day above *the Unnatural Combat*, *the Duke of Milan*, or *the Bondman*.

This Tragedy was revived by Betterton, who took for himself the part of Paris, in which he was highly celebrated. It was again brought on the stage, with a few trifling alterations, in 1722, but I know not with what success. The old title page says, that it had been " divers times acted, with good allowance, at the private Play-house in the Black Friars, by the King's Majesty's servants."

---

* Too much stress has been laid on this expression ; it is proper, in adverting to it, to consider how few dramatic pieces Massinger had produced, when it was used.

TO

My much honoured and most true Friends,

SɪR PHILLIP KNYVET, KNT. AND BART.

AND TO

SɪR THOMAS JEAY, KNT.

AND

THOMAS BELLINGHAM,

OF NEWTIMBER, IN SUSSEX, ESQ.

*How much I acknowledge myself bound for your so many,
and extraordinary favours conferred upon me, as far as it
is in my power, posterity shall take notice: I were most
unworthy of such noble friends, if I should not, with all
thankfulness, profess and own them. In the composition of
this Tragedy you were my only supporters, and it being now
by your principal encouragement to be turned into the world,
it cannot walk safer than under your protection. It hath
been happy in the suffrage of some learned and judicious
gentlemen when it was presented, nor shall they find cause, I
hope, in the perusal, to repent them of their good opinion of
it. If the gravity and height of the subject distaste such as
are only affected with jigs and ribaldry, (as I presume it
will,) their condemnation of me and my poem, can no way
offend me: my reason teaching me, such malicious and ignorant detractors deserve rather contempt than satisfaction. I
ever held it the most perfect birth of my Minerva; and
therefore in justice offer it to those that have best deserved of
me; who, I hope, in their courteous acceptance will render
it worth their receiving, and ever, in their gentle construction
of my imperfections, believe they may at their pleasure dispose
of him, that is wholly and sincerely*

devoted to their service,

PHILIP MASSINGER.

DRAMATIS PERSONÆ.   ACTORS' NAMES.

Domitianus Cæsar,	J. Lowin.*
Paris, the ROMAN ACTOR,	J. Taylor.
Ælius Lamia,	T. Pollard.
Junius Rusticus, } *senators,*	Rob. Benfield.
Palphurius Sura,	W. Patricke.
Fulcinius,	
Parthenius, Cæsar's *freedman.*	R. Sharpe.
Aretinus, Cæsar's *spy,*	E. Swanstone.
Stephanos,† Domitilla's *freedman.*	
Æsopus, } *players,*	R. Robinson.
Latinus,	C. Greville.
Philargus, *a rich miser*; *father to*	
Parthenius,	A. Smith.
Ascletario, *an astrologer.*	
Sejeius, } *conspirators,*	G. Vernon.‡
Entellus,	J. Horne.‡
Domitia, *wife of* Ælius Lamia,	J. Tompson.
Domitilla, *cousin-german to* Cæsar,	J. Hunnieman.
Julia, *daughter of* Titus,	W. Trigge.
Cænis, Vespasian's *concubine,*	A. Gough.
A Lady.	

*Tribunes, Lictors, Centurions, Soldiers, Hangmen,
Servants, Captives.*

SCENE, Rome.

* *John Lowin,* &c.] All that is known of this excellent actor (as well as of most of those who follow) is collected with great care by Mr. Malone, and inserted in his *Historical View of the English Stage;* to which I refer the reader.

† *Stephanos.*] So Massinger spells his name; it should, however, be Stephanus.

‡ George Vernon and James Horne have no characters assigned them in the list of persons presented; probably they played Sejeius and Entellus, whose names have not hitherto been given among the dramatis personæ; though they appear in the second scene of the last act.

THE

ROMAN ACTOR.

ACT I. SCENE I.

The Theatre.

Enter PARIS, LATINUS, *and* ÆSOPUS.

Æsop. What do we act to day?
Lat. Agave's frenzy,
With Pentheus' bloody end.
Par. It skills not what;[1]
The times are dull, and all that we receive
Will hardly satisfy the day's expense.
The Greeks, to whom we owe the first invention
Both of the buskin'd scene, and humble sock,
That reign in every noble family,
Declaim against us : and our theatre,[2]

---

[1] *Par. It* skills not] i. e. matters not. So in *the Custom of
the Country :*

  " —————— ————— Some pursue
  " The murderer ; yet if he scape, it *skills not ;*
  " Were I a prince, I would reward him for't."

[2]   —————— ——— *and our* theatre,
  Great Pompey's work, &c.] The old copy reads *amphitheatre,*
for which I have taken the liberty to substitute *theatre.* Massinger could not be ignorant that the former was not " the work
of Pompey ;" nor that a building appropriated solely to com-
bats of gladiators, wild beasts, &c. was not properly adapted to
the scenical exhibitions of Paris and his associates. Not to

Great Pompey's work, that hath given full delight
Both to the eye and ear of fifty thousand
Spectators in one day, as if it were
Some unknown desart, or great Rome unpeopled,
Is quite forsaken.
 Lat. Pleasures of worse natures
Are gladly entertained ; and they that shun us,
Practise, in private, sports the stews would blush
   at.
A litter born by eight Liburnian slaves,
To buy diseases from a glorious strumpet,
The most censorious of our Roman gentry,
Nay, of the garded robe,[3] the senators,
Esteem an easy purchase.
 Par. Yet grudge us,[4]
That with delight join profit, and endeavour
To build their minds up fair, and on the stage
Decipher to the life what honours wait
On good and glorious actions, and the shame

insist that the *work* for which Pompey was so celebrated, was a
theatre, (as we learn from Tacitus and others,) I would just observe, that the redundancy of the old reading furnishes no slight
proof that the confusion of terms did not arise from the poet,
but his transcriber.
 What Massinger says of the theatre, is applied by Addison,
in his letter from Rome, to the Coliseo :—

   " ———— which *unpeopled Rome,*
   " And held uncrowded nations in its womb."

 [3] *Nay of the* garded *robe,*] i. e. the laced or bordered robe.
—The *Laticlavus.* M. MASON.

 [4] Paris. *Yet grudge us,*
 That with delight join profit, &c.] Paris here applies, plea-
santly enough to himself, what was said of a very different
character :
   Hos inter sumptus, sestertia Quintiliano,
   Ut multum, duo sufficient.

On the whole, it is amusing to hear him and his associates talk
in the high moral strain of Seneca and Juvenal.

That treads upon the heels of vice, the salary
Of six *sestertii.*
Æsop. For the profit, Paris,
And mercenary gain, they are things beneath us;
Since, while you hold your grace and power with
   Cæsar,
We, from your bounty, find a large supply,
Nor can one thought of want ever approach us.
 Par. Our aim is glory, and to leave our names
To aftertime.
 Lat. And, would they give us leave,
There ends all our ambition.
 Æsop. We have enemies,
And great ones too, I fear. 'Tis given out lately,
The consul Aretinus, Cæsar's spy,
Said at his table, ere a month expired,
For being gall'd in our last comedy,
He'd silence us for ever.
 Par. I expect
No favour from him; my strong Aventine[5] is,
That great Domitian, whom we oft have cheer'd
In his most sullen moods, will once return,
Who can repair, with ease, the consul's ruins.
 Lat. 'Tis frequent in the city,[6] he hath sub-
  dued
The Catti and the Daci, and, ere long,
The second time will enter Rome in triumph.

---

[5] ———— *my strong* Aventine] i. e. my
security, my defence. The Aventine was a post of great
strength. It is used in the same metaphorical sense by others
of our old dramatists. Thus Fletcher:

 " ————· Ferrand's fled,
 " And with small strength, into the castle's tower,
 " The only *Aventine* that now is left him."
        The Double Marriage.

[6] *Lat.* '*Tis frequent in the city,*] A Latinism; 'tis common,
currently reported, &c.

Enter two Lictors.

Par. Jove hasten it? With us?—I now believe
The consul's threats, Æsopus.
    1 *Lict.* You are summon'd
To appear to day in senate.
    2 *Lict.* And there to answer
What shall be urged against you.
    Par. We obey you.
Nay, droop not, fellows; innocence should be bold.
We, that have personated in the scene
The ancient heroes, and the falls of princes,
With loud applause; being to act ourselves,
Must do it with undaunted confidence.
Whate'er our sentence be, think 'tis in sport:
And, though condemn'd, let's hear it without
        sorrow,
As if we were to live again to morrow,'
    1 *Lict.* 'Tis spoken like yourself.

Enter Ælius Lamia, Junius Rusticus, *and*
        Palphurius Sura.

    Lam. Whither goes Paris?
    1 *Lict.* He's cited to the senate.
    Lat. I am glad the state is
So free from matters of more weight and trouble,
That it has vacant time to look on us.

------

7 *As if we were to live again to morrow.*] This line is wholly
omitted by Mr. M. Mason! To a culpable negligence, this " most
accurate of editors" joins a gross ignorance of history. He reads,
just below, *Enter Ælius, Lamia, Junius Rusticus, Palphurius, and
Sura !* He has not even the excuse of being misled by Coxeter
here, for the copulative between Palphurius and Sura is his own
ingenious addition.

Par. That reverend place, in which the affairs
    of kings
And provinces were determined, to descend
To the censure of a bitter word, or jest,
Dropp'd from a poet's pen! Peace to your lordships!
We are glad that you are safe.
    [*Exeunt Lictors, Paris, Latinus, and Æsopus.*
    Lam. What times are these!
To what 's Rome fallen! may we, being alone,
Speak our thoughts freely of the prince and state,
And not fear the informer?
    Rust. Noble Lamia,
So dangerous the age is, and such bad acts
Are practised every where, we hardly sleep,
Nay, cannot dream with safety.[8] All our actions
Are call'd in question; to be nobly born
Is now a crime; and to deserve too well,
Held capital treason. Sons accuse their fathers,
Fathers their sons; and, but to win a smile
From one in grace at court, our chastest matrons
Make shipwreck of their honours. To be virtuous
Is to be guilty. They are only safe
That know to sooth the prince's appetite,
And serve his lusts.
    Sura. 'Tis true; and 'tis my wonder,
That two sons of so different a nature
Should spring from good Vespasian. We had a
    Titus,
Styl'd, justly, " the Delight of all Mankind,"
Who did esteem that day lost in his life,
In which some one or other tasted not
Of his magnificent bounties. One that had
A ready tear, when he was forced to sign
The death of an offender: and so far

---

[8] In this speech, as well as in some of those that follow,
Massinger had *Sejanus* in view. He frequently treads very
closely on Jonson's heels.

From pride, that he disdain'd not the converse
Even of the poorest Roman.
    Lam. Yet his brother,
Domitian, that now sways the power of things,'
Is so inclined to blood, that no day passes
In which some are not fasten'd to the hook,
Or thrown down from the Gemonies.' His freedmen
Scorn the nobility, and he himself,
As if he were not made of flesh and blood,
Forgets he is a man.
    Rust. In his young years,
He shew'd what he would be when grown to
      ripeness:
His greatest pleasure was, being a child,
With a sharp-pointed bodkin to kill flies,
Whose rooms now men supply. For his escape
In the Vitellian war, he raised a temple
To Jupiter, and proudly placed his figure
In the bosom of the god: and, in his edicts,
He does not blush, or start, to style himself

---

   ⁹ *Domitian, that now sways the* power of things,] A Latinism
—that now sways the world, *rerum potestas.*
   ¹ *Or* thrown down from the Gemonies.] For this pure and
classical expression, the modern editors have foolishly substi-
tuted,

       Or thrown from the Tarpeian rock!

I say foolishly, because, from their impertinent alteration, they
appear to take the fastening to the hook, and the throwing from
the Gemonies to be modes of execution: whereas they were
expressions of indignity to the sufferer *after* death. The Gemonies (*Scalæ Gemoniæ*) were abrupt and rugged precipices on
the Aventine, where the bodies of state criminals were flung,
and whence, after they had been exposed to the insults of the
rabble, they were dragged to the Tiber, which flowed at the
foot of the hill.
   I have already observed, that Massinger is only known to
those who read him in the old editions, and every page, and
every line of Coxeter and Mr. M. Mason, support and confirm
the observation.

(As if the name of emperor were base)
Great Lord and God Domitian.

    Sura. I have letters
He's on his way to Rome, and purposes
To enter with all glory. The flattering senate
Decrees him divine honours ; and to cross it,
Were death with studied torments :—for my part,[2]
I will obey the time ; it is in vain
To strive against the torrent.

    Rust. Let's to the curia,
And, though unwillingly, give our suffrages,
Before we are compell'd.

    Lam. And since we cannot
With safety use the active, let's make use of
The passive fortitude, with this assurance,
That the state, sick in him, the gods to friend,[3]
Though at the worst, will now begin to mend.

                             [Exeunt.

---

[2] ——————————— *for my part,*
  I will obey the time ; it is in vain
  To strive against the torrent.] Massinger has confounded the
character of Sura with that of Crispus. It is needless, however,
to dwell on such inaccuracies, since none will consult the dramatic poet for the true characters of those eventful times. In
the preceding speech, he represents Domitian as delighting
" to kill flies in his childhood." This is directly in the face of
history. Suetonius says that he *began his reign* with killing flies.
His childhood was sufficiently innocent.

[3] —————— *the* gods to friend,] i. e. συν θεοις, with the
protection of heaven : a very common expression in our old
poets. Thus Spenser :

    " So forward on his way, with *God to friend,*
    " He passed forth———

SCENE II.

A Room in Lamia's *House.*

Enter DOMITIA *and* PARTHENIUS.

Dom. To me this reverence !
Parth. I pay it, lady,
As a debt due to her that's Cæsar's mistress :
For understand with joy, he that commands
All that the sun gives warmth to, is your servant;
Be not amazed, but fit you to your fortunes.
Think upon state and greatness, and the honours
That wait upon Augusta, for that name,
Ere long, comes to you :—still you doubt your
          vassal—   [*Presents a letter.*
But, when you've read this letter, writ and sign'd
With his imperial hand, you will be freed
From fear and jealousy ; and, I beseech you,
When all the beauties of the earth bow to you,
And senators shall take it for an honour,
As I do now, to kiss these happy feet ;   [*Kneels.*
When every smile you give is a preferment,
And you dispose of provinces to your creatures,
Think on Parthenius.
     Dom. Rise.   I am transported,
And hardly dare believe what is assured here.
The means, my good Parthenius, that wrought
          Cæsar,
Our god on earth, to cast an eye of favour.
Upon his humble handmaid ?
     Parth. What, but your beauty ?
When nature framed you for her masterpiece,
As the pure abstract of all rare in woman,
She had no other ends but to design you

To the most eminent place. I will not say
(For it would smell of arrogance, to insinuate
The service I have done you) with what zeal
I oft have made relation of your virtues,
Or how I've sung your goodness, or how Cæsar
Was fired with the relation of your story :
I am rewarded in the act, and happy
In that my project prosper'd.
  Dom. You are modest:
And were it in my power, I would be thankful.
If that, when I was mistress of myself,
And, in my way of youth, pure and untainted,[*]
The emperor had vouchsafed to seek my favours,
I had with joy given up my virgin fort,
At the first summons, to his soft embraces :
But I am now another's, not mine own.
You know I have a husband :—for my honour,
I would not be his strumpet ; and how law
Can be dispensed with to become his wife,
To me's a riddle.
  Parth. I can soon resolve it :
When power puts in his plea the laws are silenced.
The world confesses one Rome, and one Cæsar,
And as his rule is infinite, his pleasures
Are unconfined ; this syllable, his *will*,
Stands for a thousand reasons.
  Dom. But with safety,
Suppose I should consent, how can I do it?
My husband is a senator, of a temper
Not to be jested with.

Enter LAMIA.

Parth. As if he durst

---

[*] *And in my way of youth, pure and untainted,*] See *a Very*
Woman, Vol. IV.

Be Cæsar's rival !—here he comes ; with ease
I will remove this scruple.

    Lam. How ! so private !
My own house made a brothel ! [*Aside.*]—Sir,
    how durst you,
Though guarded with your power in court, and
    greatness,
Hold conference with my wife? As for you, minion,
I shall hereafter treat——

    Parth. You are rude and saucy,
Nor know to whom you speak.

    Lam. This is fine, i'faith !
Is she not my wife ?

    Parth. Your wife ! But touch her, that respect
    forgotten
That's due to her whom mightiest Cæsar favours,
And think what 'tis to die. Not to lose time,
She's Cæsar's choice : it is sufficient honour
You were his taster in this heavenly nectar ;
But now must quit the office.

    Lam. This is rare !
Cannot a man be master of his wife
Because she's young and fair, without a patent ?
I in my own house am an emperor,
And will defend what's mine. Where are my
    knaves ?
If such an insolence escape unpunish'd——

    Parth. In yourself, Lamia,—Cæsar hath forgot
To use his power, and I, his instrument,
In whom, though absent, his authority speaks,
Have lost my faculties !   [*Stamps.*

    Enter a Centurion *with* Soldiers.

    Lam. The guard ! why, am I
Design'd for death?

Dom. As you desire my favour,
Take not so rough a course.
    Parth. All your desires
Are absolute commands : Yet give me leave
To put the will of Cæsar into act.
Here's a bill of divorce between your lordship
And this great lady : if you refuse to sign it,
And so as if you did it uncompell'd,
Won to't by reasons that concern yourself,
Her honour too untainted, here are clerks,
Shall in your best blood write it new, till torture
Compel you to perform it.
    Lam. Is this legal ?[5]
    Parth. Monarchs that dare not do unlawful
        things,
Yet bear them out, are constables, not kings.
Will you dispute ?
    Lam. I know not what to urge
Against myself, but too much dotage on her,
Love, and observance.
    Parth. Set it under your hand,
That you are impotent, and cannot pay

---

⁵ *Lam. Is this legal ?*
Parth. Monarchs, that dare not do unlawful things,] In Coxeter
and Mr. M. Mason's editions these lines are thus printed :

> *Lam. Is this legal ?*
> New works *that dare not, &c.*

On which the latter says : " I considered this passage for some
time as irretrievable, for there is a mistake not only in the
words, but in the person also to whom they are attributed ;"
and he proceeds with great earnestness and gravity to rectify
the mistake. All this " consideration" might have been saved
by a glance at the old copies, which read precisely as I have
given it. True it is, that Coxeter found the nonsense which
they have printed, in the quarto ; but the error seems to have
been quickly discovered and removed, since it occurs but in
one of the numerous copies which I have had occasion to consult.

The duties of a husband; or, that you are mad;
Rather than want just cause, we'll make you so.
Dispatch, you know the danger else ;—deliver it,
Nay, on your knee.— Madam, you now are free,
And mistress of yourself.

 Lam. Can you, Domitia,
Consent to this?

 Dom. 'Twould argue a base mind
To live a servant, when I may command.
I now am Cæsar's: and yet, in respect
I once was yours, when you come to the palace,
Provided you deserve it in your service,
You shall find me your good mistress.[6] Wait me,
  Parthenius;
And now farewell, poor Lamia !

     [*Exeunt all but Lamia.*

 Lam. To the gods
I bend my knees, (for tyranny hath banish'd
Justice from men,) and as they would deserve
Their altars, and our vows, humbly invoke them,
That this my ravish'd wife may prove as fatal
To proud Domitian, and her embraces
Afford him, in the end, as little joy
As wanton Helen brought to him of Troy! [*Exit.*

 [6] *You shall find me your good* mistress.] **That is, your** *patroness.* This was the language of the times, and is frequently
found in our old writers: it occurs again in the dedication to
the Emperor of the East.

S C E N E   III.

The Curia or Senate-house.

Enter Lictors, ARETINUS, FULCINIUS, RUSTICUS,
SURA, PARIS, LATINUS, *and* ÆSOPUS.

    Aret. Fathers conscript,[7] may this our meeting
      be
Happy to Cæsar and the commonwealth!
    Lict. Silence!
    Aret. The purpose of this frequent senate
Is, first, to give thanks to the gods of Rome,
That, for the propagation of the empire,
Vouchsafe us one to govern it, like themselves.
In height of courage, depth of understanding,
And all those virtues, and remarkable graces,
Which make a prince most eminent, our Domitian
Transcends the ancient Romans: I can never
Bring his praise to a period.   What good man,
That is a friend to truth, dares make it doubtful,
That he hath Fabius' staidness, and the courage
Of bold Marcellus, to whom Hannibal gave
The style of Target, and the Sword of Rome?
But he has more, and every touch more Roman;
As Pompey's dignity, Augustus' state,
Antony's bounty, and great Julius' fortune,
With Cato's resolution.   I am lost
In the ocean of his virtues: in a word,
All excellencies of good men meet in him,
But no part of their vices.

    [7] *Aret.* *Fathers conscript,* &c.] The customary form of
opening the debate: it occurs in Jonson's *Catiline.* *Frequent
senate,* which is found in the next speech, is a Latinism for a full
house.

Rust. This is no flattery!

Sura. Take heed, you'll be observed.

Aret. 'Tis then most fit

That we, (as to the father of our country,[8]

Like thankful sons, stand bound to pay true service

For all those blessings that he showers upon us,)

Should not connive, and see his government

Depraved and scandalized by meaner men,

That to his favour and indulgence owe

Themselves and being.

    Par. Now he points at us.

    Aret. Cite Paris, the tragedian.

    Par. Here.

    Aret. Stand forth.

In thee, as being the chief of thy profession,

I do accuse the quality of treason,[9]

As libellers against the state and Cæsar.

    Par. Mere accusations are not proofs, my lord;

In what are we delinquents?

    Aret. You are they

That search into the secrets of the time,

And, under feign'd names, on the stage, present

Actions not to be touch'd at; and traduce

Persons of rank and quality of both sexes,

And, with satirical, and bitter jests,

Make even the senators ridiculous

To the plebeians.

---

    [8] *That we, (as to the father* &c.] We should certainly read *who* instead of *as.* M. MASON.

    There is an ellipsis of *who :* but the text is right.

    [9] *In thee, as being the chief of thy profession,*

I do accuse the quality of treason.] *Quality,* though used in a general sense for any occupation, calling, or condition of life, yet seems more peculiarly appropriated, by our old writers, to that of a player. See *the Picture ;* Vol. III.

Par. If I free not myself,
And, in myself, the rest of my profession,
From these false imputations, and prove
That they make that a libel which the poet
Writ for a comedy, so acted too ;
It is but justice that we undergo
The heaviest censure.
    Aret. Are you on the stage,
You talk so boldly ?
    Par. The whole world being one,
This place is not exempted ; and I am
So confident in the justice of our cause,
That I could wish Cæsar, in whose great name
All kings are comprehended, sat as judge,
To hear our plea, and then determine of us.—
If, to express a man sold to his lusts,
Wasting the treasure of his time and fortunes
In wanton dalliance, and to what sad end
A wretch that's so given over does arrive at ;
Deterring careless youth, by his example,
From such licentious courses ; laying open
The snares of bawds, and the consuming arts
Of prodigal strumpets, can deserve reproof ;
Why are not all your golden principles,
Writ down by grave philosophers to instruct us
To choose fair virtue for our guide, not pleasure,
Condemn'd unto the fire ?
    Sura. There's spirit in this.
    Par. Or if desire of honour was the base
On which the building of the Roman empire
Was raised up to this height ; if, to inflame
The noble youth with an ambitious heat
T' endure the frosts of danger, nay, of death,
To be thought worthy the triumphal wreath
By glorious undertakings, may deserve
Reward, or favour from the commonwealth ;
Actors may put in for as large a share

As all the sects of the philosophers:
They with cold precepts[1] (perhaps seldom read)
Deliver, what an honourable thing
The active virtue is: but does that fire
The blood, or swell the veins with emulation,
To be both good and great, equal to that
Which is presented on our theatres?
Let a good actor, in a lofty scene,
Shew great Alcides honour'd in the sweat
Of his twelve labours; or a bold Camillus,
Forbidding Rome to be redeem'd with gold
From the insulting Gauls; or Scipio,
After his victories, imposing tribute
On conquer'd Carthage: if done to the life,
As if they saw their dangers, and their glories,
And did partake with them in their rewards,
All that have any spark of Roman in them,
The slothful arts laid by, contend to be
Like those they see presented.

    Rust. He has put
The consuls to their whisper.[2]

    Par. But, 'tis urged
That we corrupt youth, and traduce superiors.

---

[1] *They with cold precepts, &c.*] This is judiciously expanded from Horace:

> *Segnius irritant animos, demissa per aurem,*
> *Quam quæ sunt oculis subjecta fidelibus, et quæ*
> *Ipse sibi tradit spectator.*

[2] Rust. *He has put &c.*] Massinger never scruples to repeat himself. We have just had this expression in *the Parliament of Love:*

> " —— ———— she has put
> " The judges to their whiper."

The learned reader will discover several classical allusions in the ensuing speech, and, indeed, in every part of this drama: these I have not always pointed out; though I would observe, in justice to Massinger, that they are commonly made with skill and effect, and without that affectation of literature elsewhere so noticeable.

When do we bring a vice upon the stage,
That does go off unpunish'd ? Do we teach,
By the success of wicked undertakings,
Others to tread in their forbidden steps?
We shew no arts of Lydian panderism,
Corinthian poisons, Persian flatteries,
But mulcted so in the conclusion, that
Even those spectators that were so inclined,
Go home changed men. And, for traducing such
That are above us, publishing to the world
Their secret crimes, we are as innocent
As such as are born dumb. When we present
An heir, that does conspire against the life
Of his dear parent, numbering every hour
He lives, as tedious to him ; if there be,
Among the auditors, one whose conscience tells
    him
He is of the same mould,—WE CANNOT HELP IT.
Or, bringing on the stage a loose adulteress,
That does maintain the riotous expense
Of him that feeds her greedy lust, yet suffers
The lawful pledges of a former bed
To starve the while for hunger ; if a matron,
However great in fortune, birth, or titles,
Guilty of such a foul unnatural sin,
Cry out, 'Tis writ for me,—WE CANNOT HELP IT.
Or, when a covetous man's express'd, whose wealth
Arithmetic cannot number, and whose lordships
A falcon in one day cannot fly over ;
Yet he so sordid in his mind, so griping,
As not to afford himself the necessaries
To maintain life ; if a patrician,
(Though honour'd with a consulship,) find himself
Touch'd to the quick in this,—WE CANNOT HELP
    IT.
Or, when we show a judge that is corrupt,
And will give up his sentence, as he favours

The person, not the cause; saving the guilty,
If of his faction, and as oft condemning
The innocent, out of particular spleen;
If any in this reverend assembly,
Nay, even yourself, my lord, that are the image
Of absent Cæsar, feel something in your bosom
That puts you in remembrance of things past,
Or things intended,—'TIS NOT IN US TO HELP IT.
I have said, my lord : and now, as you find cause,
Or censure us, or free us with applause,
    Lat. Well pleaded, on my life! I never saw him
Act an orator's part before.
    Æsop. We might have given
Ten double fees to Regulus, and yet
Our cause deliver'd worse.   [*A shout within.*

Enter PARTHENIUS.

    Aret. What shout is that?
    Parth. Cæsar, our lord, married to conquest, is
Return'd in triumph.
    Ful. Let's all haste to meet him.
    Aret. Break up the court; we will reserve to him
The censure of this cause.
    All. Long life to Cæsar!   [*Exeunt.*

SCENE IV.

The Approach to the Capitol.

Enter JULIA, CÆNIS, DOMITILLA, and DOMITIA.

    Cænis. Stand back—the place is mine.
    Jul. Yours! Am I not

Great Titus' daughter, and Domitian's niece?
Dares any claim precedence?
  Cænis. I was more:
The mistress of your father, and, in his right,
Claim duty from you.
  Jul. I confess, you were useful
To please his appetite.
  Dom. To end the controversy,
For I'll have no contending, I'il be bold
To lead the way myself.
  Domitil. You, minion!
  Dom. Yes;
And all, ere long, shall kneel to catch my favours.
  Jul. Whence springs this flood of greatness?
  Dom. You shall know
Too soon, for your vexation, and perhaps
Repent too late, and pine with envy, when
You see whom Cæsar favours.
  Jul. Observe the sequel.

Enter Captains *with laurels,* DOMITIAN *in his
triumphant chariot,* PARTHENIUS, PARIS, LATI-
NUS, *and* ÆSOPUS, *met by* ARETINUS, SURA,
LAMIA, RUSTICUS, FULCINIUS, Soldiers, *and
Captives.*

  Cæs. As we now touch the height of human
     glory,
Riding in triumph to the capitol,
Let these, whom this victorious arm hath made
The scorn of fortune, and the slaves of Rome,
Taste the extremes of misery. Bear them off
To the common prisons, and there let them prove
How sharp our axes are.
              [*Exeunt Soldiers with Captives.*
  Rust. A bloody entrance!   [*Aside.*
  Cæs. To tell you you are happy in your prince,

Were to distrust your love, or my desert;
And either were distasteful: or to boast
How much, not by my deputies, but myself,
I have enlarged the empire; or what horrors
The soldier, in our conduct, hath broke through,
Would better suit the mouth of Plautus' braggart,
Than the adored monarch of the world.
 Sura. This is no boast!   [*Aside.*
 Cæs. When I but name the Daci,
And gray-eyed Germans, whom I have subdued,
The ghost of Julius will look pale with envy,
And great Vespasian's and Titus' triumph,
(Truth must take place of father and of brother,)
Will be no more remember'd. I am above
All honours you can give me; and the style
Of Lord and God, which thankful subjects give
 me,
Not my ambition, is deserved.
 Aret. At all parts
Celestial sacrifice is fit for Cæsar,
In our acknowledgment.
 Cæs. Thanks, Aretinus;
Still hold our favour. Now, the god of war,
And famine, blood, and death, Bellona's pages,
Banish'd from Rome to Thrace, in our good
 fortune,
With justice he may taste the fruits of peace,
Whose sword hath plough'd the ground, and
 reap'd the harvest
Of your prosperity. Nor can I think
That there is one among you so ungrateful,
Or such an enemy to thriving virtue,
That can esteem the jewel he holds dearest,
Too good for Cæsar's use.
 Sura. All we possess—
 Lam. Our liberties—
 Ful. Our children—

Par. Wealth——

Aret. And throats,

Fall willingly beneath his feet.

Rust. Base flattery!

What Roman can endure this!   [*Aside.*

Cæs. This calls[3] on

My love to all, which spreads itself among you.

The beauties of the time! [*seeing the ladies.*]

   Receive the honour

To kiss the hand which, rear'd up thus, holds

   thunder;

To you 'tis an assurance of a calm.

Julia, my niece, and Cænis, the delight

Of old Vespasian; Domitilla, too,

A princess of our blood.

Rust. 'Tis strange his pride

Affords no greater courtesy to ladies

Of such high birth and rank.

Sura. Your wife's forgotten.

Lam. No, she will be remember'd, fear it not;

She will be graced, and greased.

Cæs. But, when I look on

Divine Domitia, methinks we should meet

(The lesser gods applauding the encounter)

As Jupiter, the Giants lying dead

On the Phlegræan plain, embraced his Juno.

Lamia, it is your honour that she's mine.

Lam. You are too great to be gainsaid.

Cæs. Let all

That fear our frown, or do affect our favour,

Without examining the reason why,

---

³ *This calls* &c.] This passage is so strangely pointed in the modern editions, that it clearly appears to have been misunderstood. They read,

  This calls on

 My love to all, which spreads itself among you,

 The beauties of the time. Receive &c.

Salute her (by this kiss I make it good)
With the title of Augusta.
   Dom. Still your servant.
   All. Long live Augusta, great Domitian's
      empress!
   Cæs. Paris, my hand.
   Par. [*kissing it.*] The gods still honour Cæsar!
   Cæs. The wars are ended, and, our arms laid
      by,
We are for soft delights. Command the poets
To use their choicest and most rare invention,
To entertain the time, and be you careful
To give it action: we'll provide the people
Pleasures of all kinds.—My Domitia, think not
I flatter, though thus fond.—On to the capitol:
'Tis death to him that wears a sullen brow.
This 'tis to be a monarch, when alone
He can command all, but is awed by none.
                [*Exeunt.*

ACT II. SCENE I.

A State Room in the Palace.

Enter PHILARGUS *in rags, and* PARTHENIUS.

   Phil. My son to tutor me! Know your obe-
      dience,
And question not my will.
   Parth. Sir, were I one,
Whom want compell'd to wish a full possession
Of what is yours; or had I ever number'd[4]

---

  4   ——————— *or had I ever number'd*
   Your years,] This was accounted a high degree of unna-
turalness and impiety among all nations: *patrios inquirere in*

Your years, or thought you lived too long, with
    reason
You then might nourish ill opinions of me:
Or did the suit that I prefer to you
Concern myself, and aim'd not at your good,
You might deny, and I sit down with patience,
And after never press you.
    Phil. In the name of Pluto,
What would'st thou have me do?
    Parth. Right to yourself;
Or suffer me to do it. Can you imagine
This nasty hat, this tatter'd cloak, rent shoe,
This sordid linen, can become the master
Of your fair fortunes? whose superfluous means,
Though I were burthensome, could clothe you in
The costliest Persian silks, studded with jewels,
The spoils of provinces, and every day
Fresh change of Tyrian purple.
    Phil. Out upon thee!
My monies in my coffers melt to hear thee.
Purple! hence, prodigal! Shall I make my mercer,
Or tailor heir, or see my jeweller purchase?
No, I hate pride.
    Parth. Yet decency would do well.
Though, for your outside, you will not be alter'd,
Let me prevail so far yet, as to win you
Not to deny your belly nourishment;
Neither to think you've feasted, when 'tis cramm'd
With mouldy barley-bread, onions and leeks,
And the drink of bondmen, water.
    Phil. Wouldst thou have me
Be an Apicius, or a Lucullus,
And riot out my state in curious sauces?

---

annos is reckoned by Ovid among the prominent causes which
provoked Jupiter to destroy the old world by a deluge. See
p. 347.

Wise nature with a little is contented;
And, following her, my guide, I cannot err.
    Parth. But you destroy her in your want of care
(I blush to see, and speak it) to maintain her
In perfect health and vigour; when you suffer,
Frighted with the charge of physic, rheums,
    catarrhs,
The scurf, ach in your bones, to grow upon you,
And hasten on your fate with too much sparing:
When a cheap purge, a vomit, and good diet,
May lengthen it. Give me but leave to send
The emperor's doctor to you.
    Phil. I'll be borne first,
Half rotten, to the fire that must consume me!
His pills, his cordials, his electuaries,
His syrups, julaps, bezoar stone, nor his
Imagined unicorn's horn, comes in my belly;
My mouth shall be a draught first, 'tis resolved.
No; I'll not lessen my dear golden heap,
Which, every hour increasing, does renew
My youth and vigor; but, if lessen'd, then,
Then my poor heart-strings crack. Let me en-
    joy it,
And brood o'er't, while I live, it being my life,
My soul, my all: but when I turn to dust,
And part from what is more esteem'd, by me,
Than all the gods Rome's thousand altars smoke to,
Inherit thou my adoration of it,
And, like me, serve my idol.   [*Exit.*
    Parth. What a strange torture
Is avarice to itself! what man, that looks on
Such a penurious spectacle, but must
Know what the fable meant of Tantalus,
Or the ass whose back is crack'd with curious
    viands,
Yet feeds on thistles. Some course I must take,
To make my father know what cruelty
He uses on himself.

Enter PARIS.

Par. Sir, with your pardon,
I make bold to enquire the emperor's pleasure;
For, being by him commanded to attend,
Your favour may instruct us what's his will
Shall be this night presented.
    Parth. My loved Paris,
Without my intercession, you well know,
You may make your own approaches, since his ear
To you is ever open.
    Par. I acknowledge
His clemency to my weakness, and, if ever
I do abuse it, lightning strike me dead !
The grace he pleases to confer upon me,
(Without boast I may say so much,) was never
Employ'd to wrong the innocent, or to incense
His fury.
    Parth. 'Tis confess'd : many men owe you
For provinces they ne'er hoped for; and their lives,
Forfeited to his anger :—you being absent,
I could say more.
    Par. You still are my good patron ;
And, lay it in my fortune to deserve it,
You should perceive the poorest of your clients
To his best abilities thankful.
    Parth. I believe so.
Met you my father?
    Par. Yes, sir, with much grief,
To see him as he is. Can nothing work him
To be himself?
    Parth. O, Paris, 'tis a weight
Sits heavy here ; and could this right hand's loss
Remove it, it should off : but he is deaf
To all persuasion.
    Par. Sir, with your pardon,

I'll offer my advice: I once observed,
In a tragedy of ours,[5] in which a murder
Was acted to the life, a guilty hearer,
Forced by the terror of a wounded conscience,
To make discovery of that which torture
Could not wring from him. Nor can it appear
Like an impossibility, but that
Your father, looking on a covetous man
Presented on the stage, as in a mirror,
May see his own deformity, and loath it.
Now, could you but persuade the emperor
To see a comedy we have, that's styled
The Cure of Avarice, and to command
Your father to be a spectator of it,
He shall be so anatomized in the scene,
And see himself so personated, the baseness
Of a self-torturing miserable wretch
Truly described, that I much hope the object
Will work compunction in him.

  Parth. There's your fee;
I ne'er bought better counsel. Be you in readiness,
I will effect the rest.

  Par. Sir, when you please;
We'll be prepared to enter.—Sir, the emperor.
          [*Exit.*

  [5]*Enter* CÆSAR, ARETINUS, *and Guard.*

  Cæs. Repine at us!

[5] ————— ———— *I once observed,*
In a tragedy of ours, &c.]
  " ————— —— I have heard,
  " That guilty creatures, sitting at a play,
  " Have by the very cunning of the scene,
  " Been struck so to the soul, that presently
  " They have proclaim'd their malefactions;
  " For murder, though it have no tongue, will speak
  " With most miraculous organ." *Hamlet.*
  Enter CÆSAR, &c.] Coxeter seldom attempts to specify the

Aret. 'Tis more, or my informers,
That keep strict watch upon him, are deceived
In their intelligence : there is a list
Of malcontents, as Junius Rusticus,
Palphurius Sura, and this Ælius Lamia,
That murmur at your triumphs, as mere pageants ;
And, at their midnight meetings, tax your justice,
(For so I style what they call tyranny,)
For Pætus Thrasea's death, as if in him
Virtue herself were murder'd : nor forget they
Agricola, who, for his service done
In the reducing Britain to obedience,
They dare affirm to be removed with poison ;
And he compell'd to write you a coheir
With his daughter, that his testament might stand,
Which, else, you had made void. Then your much
          love
To Julia your niece, censured as incest,
And done in scorn of Titus, your dead brother :
But the divorce Lamia was forced to sign
To her you honour with Augusta's title,
Being only named, they do conclude there was
A Lucrece once, a Collatine, and a Brutus ;
But nothing Roman left now but, in you,
The lust of Tarquin.
    Cæs. Yes, his fire, and scorn
Of such as think that our unlimited power
Can be confined. Dares Lamia pretend
An interest to that which I call mine ;
Or but remember she was ever his,

place of action without falling into error ; and **Mr. M. Mason,**
who, in despite of his " accuracy," labours, like Falstaff, under
" the malady of not marking," constantly and closely follows
him. They call this " Scene the second," and change the
ground " from a chamber to a palace ;" notwithstanding that
the emperor enters while Paris is yet speaking, and Parthenius
continues on the stage.

That's now in our possession? Fetch him hither.
                              [*Exit Guard.*
I'll give him cause to wish he rather had
Forgot his own name, than e'er mention'd her's.
Shall we be circumscribed? Let such as cannot
By force make good their actions, though wicked,
Conceal, excuse, or qualify their crimes!
What our desires grant leave and privilege to,
Though contradicting all divine decrees,
Or laws confirm'd by Romulus and Numa,
Shall be held sacred.
    Aret. You should, else, take from
The dignity of Cæsar.
    Cæs. Am I master
Of two and thirty legions, that awe
All nations of the triúmphed world,
Yet tremble at our frown, to yield account
Of what's our pleasure, to a private man!
Rome perish first, and Atlas's shoulders shrink,
Heaven's fabric fall, (the sun, the moon, the stars
Losing their light and comfortable heat,)
Ere I confess that any fault of mine
May be disputed!
    Aret. So you preserve your power,
As you should, equal and omnipotent here,
With Jupiter's above.
                [*Parthenius kneeling, whispers Cæsar.*
    Cæs. Thy suit is granted,
Whate'er it be, Parthenius, for thy service
Done to Augusta.——Only so? a trifle:
Command him hither. If the comedy fail
To cure him, I will minister something to him
That shall instruct him to forget his gold,
And think upon himself.
    Parth. May it succeed well,
Since my intents are pious!   [*Exit.*
    Cæs. We are resolved

What course to take; and, therefore, Aretinus,
Enquire no further. Go you to my empress,
And say I do entreat (for she rules him
Whom all men else obey) she would vouchsafe
The music of her voice at yonder window,
When I advance my hand, thus. I will blend
                              [*Exit Aretinus.*
My cruelty with some scorn, or else 'tis lost.
Revenge, when it is unexpected, falling
With greater violence; and hate clothed in smiles,
Strikes, and with horror, dead the wretch that
        comes not
Prepared to meet it.--

Re-enter Guard with LAMIA.

                        Our good Lamia, welcome.
So much we owe you for a benefit,
With willingness on your part conferr'd upon us,
That 'tis our study, we that would not live
Engaged to any for a courtesy,
How to return it.
    Lam. 'Tis beneath your fate
To be obliged, that in your own hand grasp
The means to be magnificent,
    Cæs. Well put off;
But yet it must not do: the empire, Lamia,
Divided equally, can hold no weight,
If balanced with your gift in fair Domitia——
You, that could part with all delights at once,
The magazine of rich pleasures being contain'd
In her perfections,—uncompell'd, deliver'd
As a present fit for Cæsar. In your eyes,
With tears of joy, not sorrow, 'tis confirm'd
You glory in your act.
    Lam. Derided too!
Sir, this is more—
                    * B b 2

Cæs. More than I can requite;
It is acknowledged, Lamia. There's no drop
Of melting nectar I taste from her lip,
But yields a touch of immortality
To the blest receiver; every grace and feature,
Prized to the worth, bought at an easy rate,
If purchased for a consulship. Her discourse
So ravishing, and her action so attractive,
That I would part with all my other senses,
Provided I might ever see and hear her.
The pleasures of her bed I dare not trust
The winds or air with; for that would draw
    down,
In envy of my happiness, a war
From all the gods, upon me.
        Lam Your compassion
To me, in your forbearing to insult
On my calamity, which you make your sport,
Would more appease those gods you have pro-
    voked,
Than all the blasphemous comparisons
You sing unto her praise.

DOMITIA *appears at the window.*

Cæs. I sing her praise!
'Tis far from my ambition to hope it;
It being a debt she only can lay down,
And no tongue else discharge.
                    [*He raises his hand. Music above.*
                    Hark! I think, prompted
With my consent that you once more should
    hear her,
She does begin. An universal silence
Dwell on this place! 'Tis death, with lingering
    torments,
To all that dare disturb her.—

A song *by* DOMITIA.

     —Who can hear this,
And fall not down and worship? In my fancy,
Apollo being judge, on Latmos' hill
Fair-hair'd Calliope, on her ivory lute,
(But something short of this,) sung Ceres' praises,
And grisly Pluto's rape on Proserpine.
The motions of the spheres are out of time,[7]
Her musical notes but heard.   Say, Lamia, say,
Is not her voice angelical?
  Lam. To your ear:
But I, alas! am silent.
  Cæs. Be so ever,
That without admiration canst hear her!
Malice to my felicity strikes thee dumb,
And, in thy hope, or wish, to repossess
What I love more than empire, I pronounce thee
Guilty of treason.—Off with his head! do you stare?
By her that is my patroness, Minerva,
Whose statue I adore of all the gods,
If he but live to make reply, thy life
Shall answer it!
  [*The Guard leads off Lamia, stopping his mouth.*
     My fears of him are freed now;
And he that lived to upbraid me with my wrong,
For an offence he never could imagine,

---

7 *The motions of the spheres are out of* time,] For *time*, Mr. M.
Mason chooses to read, *tune.* In this capricious alteration he is
countenanced by some of the commentators on Shakspeare, who,
as well as himself, might have spared their pains; since it appears from numberless examples that the two words were once
synonymous. *Time*, however, was the more ancient and common term: nor was it till long after the age of Massinger, that
the use of it, in the sense of harmony, was entirely superseded
by that of *tune.*

In wantonness removed.—Descend, my dearest;
Plurality of husbands shall no more
Breed doubts or jealousies in you: [*Exit Dom.
above.*] 'tis dispatch'd,
And with as little trouble here, as if
I had kill'd a fly.

Enter DOMITIA, *ushered in by* ARETINUS, *her
train born up by* JULIA, CÆNIS, *and* DOMI-
TILLA.

           Now you appear, and in
That glory you deserve! and these, that stoop
To do you service, in the act much honour'd!
Julia, forget that Titus was thy father;
Cænis, and Domitilla, ne'er remember
Sabinus or Vespasian.   To be slaves
To her is more true liberty, than to live
Parthian or Asian queens.   As lesser stars,
That wait on Phœbe in her full of brightness,
Compared to her, you are.   Thus, thus I seat you
By Cæsar's side, commanding these, that once
Were the adored glories of the time,
To witness to the world they are your vassals,
At your feet to attend you.
   Dom. 'Tis your pleasure,
And not my pride.   And yet, when I consider
That I am yours, all duties they can pay
I do receive as circumstances due
To her you please to honour.

   Re-enter PARTHENIUS *with* PHILARGUS.

   Parth. Cæsar's will
Commands you hither, nor must you gainsay it.
   Phil. Lose time to see an interlude! must I
     pay too,
For my vexation?

Parth. Not in the court:
It is the emperor's charge.
 Phil. I shall endure
My torment then the better.
 Cæs. Can it be
This sordid thing, Parthenius, is thy father?
No actor can express him: I had held
The fiction for impossible in the scene,
Had I not seen the substance.—Sirrah, sit still,
And give attention; if you but nod,
You sleep for ever.—Let them spare the prologue,
And all the ceremonies proper to ourself,
And come to the last act—there, where the cure
By the doctor is made perfect. The swift minutes
Seem years to me, Domitia, that divorce thee
From my embraces: my desires increasing
As they are satisfied, all pleasures else
Are tedious as dull sorrows. Kiss me again:
If I now wanted heat of youth, these fires,
In Priam's veins, would thaw his frozen blood,
Enabling him to get a second Hector
For the defence of Troy.
 Dom. You are wanton!
Pray you, forbear. Let me see the play.
 Cæs. Begin there.

Enter PARIS, *like a doctor of physic, and* ÆSOPUS:
 LATINUS *is brought forth asleep in a chair, a key
 in his mouth.*

 *Æsop. O master doctor, he is past recovery;
A lethargy hath seized him; and, however
His sleep resemble death, his watchful care
To guard that treasure he dares make no use of,
Works strongly in his soul.*
 *Par. What's that he holds
So fast between his teeth?*

Æsop. The key that opens
His iron chests, cramm'd with accursed gold,
Rusty with long imprisonment. There's no duty
In me, his son, nor confidence in friends,
That can persuade him to deliver up
That to the trust of any.
    Phil. He is the wiser:
We were fashion'd in one mould.
    Æsop. He eats with it ;
And when devotion calls him to the temple
Of Mammon,[8] *whom, of all the gods, he kneels to,*
That held thus still, his orisons are paid:
Nor will he, though the wealth of Rome were
      pawn'd
For the restoring of't, for one short hour
Be won to part with it.
    Phil. Still, still myself!
And if like me he love his gold, no pawn
Is good security.
    Par. I'll try if I can force it----
It will not be. His avaricious mind,
Like men in rivers drown'd, make him gripe fast,
To his last gasp, what he in life held dearest ;
And, if that it were possible in nature,
Would carry it with him to the other world.
    Phil. As I would do to hell, rather than leave it.
    Æsop. Is he not dead?
    Par. Long since to all good actions,
Or to himself, or others, for which wise men
Desire to live. You may with safety pinch him,
Or under his nails stick needles, yet he stirs not ;
Anxious fear to lose what his soul doats on,
Renders his flesh insensible. We must use
Some means to rouse the sleeping faculties

---

[8] *Of Mammon &c.*]   There seems a want of judgment in the
introduction of Mammon, (a deity unknown to the Romans,)
when Plutus would have served the turn as well.

Of his mind; there lies the lethargy. Take a
*   trumpet,[9]*
And blow it into his ears; 'tis to no purpose;
The roaring noise of thunder cannot wake him:—
And yet despair not; I have one trick left yet.
Æsop. *What is it?*
Par. *I will cause a fearful dream*
To steal into his fancy, and disturb it
With the horror it brings with it, and so free
His body's organs.
Dom. 'Tis a cunning fellow;
If he were indeed a doctor, as the play says,[1]
He should be sworn my servant; govern my
    slumbers,
And minister to me waking.
Par. *If this fail,*   [A chest brought in.
I'll give him o'er. So; with all violence
Rend ope this iron chest, for here his life lies
Bound up in fetters, and in the defence
Of what he values higher, 'twill return,
And fill each vein and artery.—Louder yet !

[9] ——————————— *Take a trumpet*
And blow it in his ears; 'tis to no purpose;]
    Qui vix cornicines exaudiet, atque tubarum
    Concentus.   JUV. SAT. X.

And Jonson:
    "Sir, speak out:
    "You may be louder yet; a culverin
    "Discharged into his ear, would hardly bore it." *The Fox.*

[1] *If he were* indeed *a doctor, as the play says,*] Indeed, which
completes the verse, is omitted by both the modern editors; as
are many other words in this little interlude, which I have
silently brought back. Domitia adds, "He should be *sworn my
servant.*" This was less a Roman than an English custom. In
Massinger's time the attendants of the great, who were main-
tained in considerable numbers, took *an oath of fidelity* on their
entrance into office.

—*'Tis open, and already he begins*
To stir ; mark with what trouble.

[Latinus stretches himself.

    Phil. As you are Cæsar,
Defend this honest, thrifty man! they are thieves,
And come to rob him.

    Parth Peace! the emperor frowns.

    Par. So ; now pour out the bags upon the table ;
Remove his jewels, and his bonds.—Again,
Ring a second golden peal. His eyes are open ;
He stares as he had seen Medusa's head,
And were turn'd marble.—Once more.

    Lat. Murder! murder!
They come to murder me.   My son in the plot ?
Thou worse than parricide ! if it be death
To strike thy father's body, can all tortures
The Furies in hell practise, be sufficient
For thee, that dost assassinate my soul ?—
My gold ! my bonds ! my jewels ! dost thou envy
My glad possession of them for a day ;
Extinguishing the taper of my life
Consumed unto the snuff ;

    Par. Seem not to mind him.

    Lat. Have I, to leave thee rich, denied myself
The joys of human being ; scraped and hoarded
A mass of treasure, which had Solon seen,
The Lydian Crœsus had appear'd to him
Poor as the beggar Irus ? And yet I,
Solicitous to increase it, when my entrails
Were clemm'd⁹ with keeping a perpetual fast,

---

  ⁹ *Were* clemm'd *with keeping a perpetual fast,*] To be *clemm'd,*
not *clamm'd,* (as Steevens quotes it from the miserable text of
Coxeter and M. Mason,) is to have the entrails shrunk up with
hunger, so as to cling together: thus Marston ;

  " Now lions *half-clemm'd entrails* roar for food."

                        Antonio and Mellida.

Was deaf to their loud windy cries, as fearing,
Should I disburse one penny to their use,
My heir might curse me.   And, to save expense
In outward ornaments, I did expose
My naked body to the winter's cold,
And summer's scorching heat : nay, when diseases
Grew thick upon me, and a little cost
Had purchased my recovery, I chose rather
To have my ashes closed up in my urn,
By hasting on my fate, than to diminish
The gold my prodigal son, while I am living,
Carelessly scatters.
    Æsop. Would you'd dispatch and die once ![3]
Your ghost should feel in hell, THAT *is my slave*
Which was your master.
    Phil. Out upon thee, varlet !
    Par. And what then follows all your carke and
        caring,
And self-affliction? When your starved trunk is
Turn'd to forgotten dust, this hopeful youth
Urines upon your monument, ne'er remembering
How much for him you suffer'd; and then tells,
To the companions of his lusts and riots,
The hell you did endure on earth, to leave him
Large means to be an epicure, and to feast

Metaphorically, to be starved. Thus Jonson : " Hard is their fate, when the valiant must either beg or *clem.*" Again, " I cannot eat stones and turf: What ! will he *clem* me and my followers ? ask him, an he will *clem* me." *Poetaster.*

    [3] *Æsop. Would you'd dispatch and die once !*] This line is incorrectly given in both the modern editions. Coxeter dropt a word, and M. Mason inserted one at random, which spoiled at once the measure and the sense. He reads,

        Would you dispatch and die at once.

Once is used by Massinger, and his contemporaries, for final, that is, *once for all.*

His senses all at once, a happiness
You never granted to yourself. Your gold, then,
Got with vexation, and preserved with trouble,
Maintains the public stews, panders, and ruffians,
That quaff damnations to your memory,[4]
For living so long here.

    Lat. *It will be so ; I see it—*
O, that I could redeem the time that's past !
I would live and die like myself ; and make true
    use
Of what my industry purchased.

    Par. *Covetous men,*
Having one foot in the grave, lament so ever :
But grant that I by art could yet recover
Your desperate sickness, lengthen out your life
A dozen of years ; as I restore your body
To perfect health, will you with care endeavour
To rectify your mind ?

    Lat. *I should so live then,*
As neither my heir should have just cause to think
I lived too long, for being close-handed to him,
Or cruel to myself.

    Par. *Have your desires.*
Phœbus assisting me, I will repair
The ruin'd building of your health ; and think not
You have a son that hates you ; the truth is,
This means, with his consent, I practised on you
To this good end : it being a device,
In you to shew the Cure of Avarice.

        [Exeunt Paris, Latinus, and Æsopus.

    Phil. An old fool, to be gull'd thus ! had he
      died

---

  [4] *That quaff damnations to your memory, &c.*] Thus Pope :

    " At best, it falls to some ungracious son,
    " Who cries, my father's d——d, and all's my own !"

As I resolve to do, not to be alter'd,
It had gone off twanging.

Cæs. How approve you, sweetest,
Of the matter and the actors?

Dom. For the subject,[5]
I like it not; it was filch'd out of Horace.
—Nay, I have read the poets:—but the fellow
That play'd the doctor, did it well, by Venus;
He had a tuneable tongue, and neat delivery:
And yet, in my opinion, he would perform
A lover's part much better.   Prithee, Cæsar,
For I grow weary, let us see, to morrow,
Iphis and Anaxarete.

Cæs. Any thing
For thy delight, Domitia; to your rest,
Till I come to disquiet you: wait upon her.
There is a business that I must dispatch,
And I will straight be with you.
          [*Exeunt Aret. Dom. Julia, Cænis, and Domitil.*

Parth. Now, my dread sir,
Endeavour to prevail.

Cæs. One way or other
We'll cure him, never doubt it. Now, Philargus,
Thou wretched thing, hast thou seen thy sordid
          baseness,
And but observed what a contemptible creature
A covetous miser is? Dost thou in thyself
Feel true compunction, with a resolution
To be a new man?

Phil. This crazed body's Cæsar's;
But for my mind——

Cæs. Trifle not with my anger.

---

[5] **Dom.** *For the subject,*
I like it not ; it was filch'd out of Horace.] I differ from **Domitia.**
There is uncommon spirit and beauty in this little interlude.
The outline indeed, as the lady observes, is from **Horace**; but
it is filled up with a masterly pencil.

Canst thou make good use of what was now
        presented;
And imitate, in thy sudden change of life,
The miserable rich man, that express'd
What thou art to the life?
    Phil. Pray you, give me leave
To die as I have lived. I must not part with
My gold; it is my life: I am past cure.
    Cæs. No; by Minerva, thou shalt never more
Feel the least touch of avarice. Take him hence,
And hang him instantly. If there be gold in
        hell,
Enjoy it:—thine here, and thy life together,
Is forfeited.
    Phil. Was I sent for to this purpose?
    Parth. Mercy for all my service; Cæsar,
        mercy!
    Cæs. Should Jove plead for him, 'tis resolved
        he dies,
And he that speaks one syllable to dissuade me;
And therefore tempt me not. It is but justice:
Since such as wilfully would hourly die,
Must tax themselves, and not my cruelty.
                                    [*Exeunt.*

ACT III. SCENE I.

A Room in the Palace.

Enter JULIA, DOMITILLA, *and* STEPHANOS.

    Jul. No, Domitilla; if you but compare
What I have suffered with your injuries,
(Though great ones, I confess,) they will appear
Like molehills to Olympus.

Domitil. You are tender
Of your own wounds, which makes you lose the
    feeling
And sense of mine. The incest he committed
With you, and publicly profess'd, in scorn
Of what the world durst censure, may admit
Some weak defence, as being borne headlong to it,
But in a manly way, to enjoy your beauties :
Besides, won by his perjuries, that he would
Salute you with the title of Augusta,
Your faint denial show'd a full consent,
And grant to his temptations. But poor I,
That would not yield, but was with violence
    forced
To serve his lusts, and in a kind Tiberius
At Capreæ never practised, have not here
One conscious touch to rise up my accuser ;
I, in my will, being innocent.
    Steph. Pardon me,
Great princesses, though I presume to tell you,
Wasting your time in childish lamentations,
You do degenerate from the blood you spring
    from :
For there is something more in Rome expected
From Titus' daughter, and his uncle's heir,
Than womanish complaints, after such wrongs
Which mercy cannot pardon. But, you'll say,
Your hands are weak, and should you but at-
    tempt
A just revenge on this inhuman monster,
This prodigy of mankind, bloody Domitian
Hath ready swords at his command, as well
As islands to confine you, to remove
His doubts, and fears, did he but entertain
The least suspicion you contrived or plotted
Against his person.

Jul. 'Tis true, Stephanos;
The legions that sack'd Jerusalem,
Under my father Titus, are sworn his,
And I no more remember'd.
    Domitil. And to lose
Ourselves by building on impossible hopes,
Were desperate madness.
    Steph. You conclude too fast.
One single arm, whose master does contemn
His own life, holds a full command o'er his,
Spite of his guards.[6] I was your bondman, lady,
And you my gracious patroness; my wealth
And liberty your gift; and, though no soldier,
To whom or custom or example makes
Grim death appear less terrible, I dare die
To do you service in a fair revenge:
And it will better suit your births and honours
To fall at once, than to live ever slaves
To his proud empress, that insults upon
Your patient sufferings. Say but you, *Go on!*
And I will reach his heart, or perish in
The noble undertaking.
    Domitil. Your free offer
Confirms your thankfulness, which I acknow-
    ledge
A satisfaction for a greater debt
Than what you stand engaged for; but I must
    not,
Upon uncertain grounds, hazard so grateful
And good a servant. The immortal Powers
Protect a prince, though sold to impious acts,

---

    [6] *One single arm, whose master does contemn*
     His own life, holds a full command o'er his,
    Spite of his guards.] The same thought is expressed with
more energy in *the Fatal Dowry*:
      " I am desperate of my life, and command your's."

And seem to slumber, till his roaring crimes
Awake their justice ; but then, looking down,
And with impartial eyes, on his contempt
Of all religion, and moral goodness,
They, in their secret judgments, do determine
To leave him to his wickedness, which sinks
  him,
When he is most secure.'

Jul. His cruelty
Increasing daily, of necessity
Must render him as odious to his soldiers,
Familiar friends, and freedmen, as it hath done
Already to the senate : then forsaken
Of his supporters, and grown terrible
Even to himself, and her he now so doats on,
We may put into act what now with safety
We cannot whisper.

Steph. I am still prepared
To execute, when you please to command me :
Since I am confident he deserves much more
That vindicates his country from a tyrant,*
Than he that saves a citizen.

Enter CÆNIS.

Jul. O, here's Cænis.
Domitil. Whence come you ?
Cænis. From the empress, who seems moved

---

7 A noble sentiment, beautifully expressed. How much superior are these manly and rational observations, to the slavish
maxims found in *Hamlet, the Maid's Revenge,* &c.? It is true,
they are derived from a purer code than any with which
Domitilla was acquainted ; but which, however, was not more
open to Massinger than to his contemporaries.

8 ——————*from* a tyrant,] The old copies read
tirannie. I have not removed Coxeter's emendation from the
text ; though it seems, by no means, necessary.

In that you wait no better. Her pride's grown
To such a height, that she disdains the service
Of her own women; and esteems herself
Neglected, when the princesses of the blood,
On every coarse employment, are not ready
To stoop to her commands.

    Domitil. Where is her Greatness?

    Cœnis. Where you would little think she could
      descend
To grace the room or persons.

    Jul. Speak, where is she?

    Cœnis. Among the players; where, all state
      laid by,
She does enquire who acts this part, who that,
And in what habits? blames the tirewomen
For want of curious dressings;— and, so taken
She is with Paris the tragedian's shape,[9]
That is to act a lover, I thought once
She would have courted him.

    Domitil. In the mean time
How spends the emperor his hours?

    Cœnis. As ever
He hath done heretofore; in being cruel
To innocent men, whose virtues he calls crimes.
And, but this morning, if't be possible,
He hath outgone himself, having condemn'd,
At Aretinus his informer's suit,
Palphurius Sura, and good Junius Rusticus,
Men of the best repute in Rome for their
Integrity of life; no fault objected,
But that they did lament his cruel sentence
On Pætus Thrasea, the philosopher,
Their patron and instructor.

[9] ——————— *and so taken*
    She is with Paris the tragedian's shape,] See p. 38.

Steph. Can Jove see this,
And hold his thunder!
  Domitil. Nero and Caligula
Only commanded mischiefs; but our Cæsar
Delights to see them.
  Jul. What we cannot help,
We may deplore with silence.
  Cænis. We are call'd for
By our proud mistress.
  Domitil. We awhile must suffer.
  Steph. It is true fortitude to stand firm against
All shocks of fate, when cowards faint and die
In fear to suffer more calamity.   [*Exeunt.*

SCENE II.

Another Room in the same.

Enter CÆSAR *and* PARTHENIUS.

  Cæs. They are then in fetters?
  Parth. Yes, sir, but——
  Cæs. But what?
I'll have thy thoughts; deliver them.
  Parth. I shall, sir :
But still submitting to your god-like pleasure,
Which cannot be instructed——
  Cæs. To the point.
  Parth. Nor let your sacred majesty believe
Your vassal, that with dry eyes look'd upon
His father dragg'd to death by your command,
Can pity these, that durst presume to censure
What you decreed.
  Cæs. Well; forward.
  Parth. 'Tis my zeal
                    * C c 2

Still to preserve your clemency admired,
Temper'd with justice, that emboldens me
To offer my advice. Alas! I know, sir,
These bookmen, Rusticus and Palphurius Sura,
Deserve all tortures : yet, in my opinion,
They being popular senators, and cried up
With loud applauses of the multitude,
For foolish honesty, and beggarly virtue,
'Twould relish more of policy, to have them
Made away in private, with what exquisite tor-
     ments
You please,—it skills not,—than to have them
     drawn
To the Degrees[1] in public ; for 'tis doubted
That the sad object may beget compassion
In the giddy rout, and cause some sudden uproar
That may disturb you.
     Cæs. Hence, pale-spirited coward !
Can we descend so far beneath ourself,
As or to court the people's love, or fear
Their worst of hate ? Can they, that are as dust
Before the whirlwind of our will and power,
Add any moment to us ? Or thou think,
If there are gods above, or goddesses,
But wise Minerva, that's mine own, and sure,
That they have vacant hours to take into
Their serious protection, or care,
This many-headed monster ? Mankind lives
In few, as potent monarchs, and their peers ;
And all those glorious constellations
That do adorn the firmament, appointed,

---

[1] *To the* Degrees, &c.] To the *Scalæ Gemoniæ*, mentioned
before (p. 336.) Coxeter printed *Decrees ;* but the old copy
reads as above. The word is used by Jonson :
     " Their bodies thrown into the Gemonics,
     " The expulsed Apicata finds them there ;
     " Whom when she saw lie spread on the *Degrees*," &c.

Like grooms, with their bright influence to attend
The actions of kings and emperors,
They being the greater wheels that move the less.
Bring forth those condemn'd wretches ;—[*Exit.*
    Parthenius.]—let me see
One man so lost, as but to pity them,
And though there lay a million of souls
Imprison'd in his flesh, my hangmen's hooks
Should rend it off, and give them liberty.
Cæsar hath said it.

Re-enter PARTHENIUS, *with* ARETINUS, *and Guard;*
  Executioners dragging in JUNIUS RUSTICUS
  and PALPHURIUS SURA, *bound back to back.*

  Aret. 'Tis great Cæsar's pleasure,
That with fix'd eyes you carefully observe
The people's looks. Charge upon any man
That with a sigh or murmur does express
A seeming sorrow for these traitors' deaths.
You know his will, perform it.
  Cæs. A good bloodhound,
And fit for my employments.
  Sura. Give us leave
To die, fell tyrant.
  Rust. For, beyond our bodies,
Thou hast no power.
  Cæs. Yes; I'll afflict your souls,
And force them groaning to the Stygian lake,
Prepared for such to howl in, that blaspheme
The power of princes, that are gods on earth.
Tremble to think how terrible the dream is
After this sleep of death.
  Rust. To guilty men
It may bring terror; not to us, that know
What 'tis to die, well taught by his example

For whom we suffer. In my thought I see
The substance of that pure untainted soul
Of Thrasea, our master, made a star,
That with melodious harmony invites us
(Leaving this dunghill Rome, made hell by thee)
To trace his heavenly steps, and fill a sphere
Above yon crystal canopy.
 Cæs. Do invoke him
With all the aids his sanctity of life
Have won on the rewarders of his virtue;
They shall not save you.—Dogs, do you grin?
  torment them.
 [*The Executioners torment them, they still smiling.*
So, take a leaf of Seneca now, and prove
If it can render you insensible
Of that which but begins here. Now an oil,
Drawn from the Stoic's frozen principles,
Predominant over fire, were useful for you.
Again, again. You trifle. Not a groan!——
Is my rage lost? What cursed charms defend
  them!
Search deeper, villains. Who looks pale, or thinks
That I am cruel?
 Aret. Over-merciful:
'Tis all your weakness, sir.
 Parth. I dare not shew
A sign of sorrow; yet my sinews shrink,
The spectacle is so horrid.   [*Aside.*
 Cæs. I was never
O'ercome till now. For my sake roar a little,
And shew you are corporeal, and not turn'd
Aerial spirits.—Will it not do? By Pallas,
It is unkindly done to mock his fury
Whom the world styles Omnipotent! I am tor-
  tured
In their want of feeling torments. Marius' story,

That does report him to have sat unmoved,
When cunning surgeons ripp'd his arteries
And veins, to cure his gout, compared to this,
Deserves not to be named. Are they not dead?
If so, we wash an Æthiop.
 Sura. No; we live.
 Rust. Live to deride thee, our calm patience
  treading
Upon the neck of tyranny. That securely,
As 'twere a gentle slumber, we endure
Thy hangman's studied tortures, is a debt
We owe to grave philosophy, that instructs us
The flesh is but the clothing of the soul,
Which growing out of fashion, though it be
Cast off, or rent, or torn, like ours, 'tis then,
Being itself divine, in her best lustre.
But unto such as thou, that have[2] no hopes
Beyond the present, every little scar,
The want of rest, excess of heat or cold,
That does inform them only they are mortal,
Pierce through and through them.
 Cæs. We will hear no more.
 Rust. This only, and I give thee warning of it:
Though it is in thy will to grind this earth
As small as atoms, they thrown in the sea too,
They shall seem re-collected to thy sense:—
And, when the sandy building of thy greatness
Shall with its own weight totter, look to see me
As I was yesterday, in my perfect shape;
For I'll appear in horror.
 Cæs. By my shaking
I am the guilty man, and not the judge,
Drag from my sight these cursed ominous wizards,
That, as they are now, like to double-faced Janus,

<hr>

[2] ———————— *that* have *no hopes*] Coxeter and
M. Mason very incorrectly read, *that* hast *no hopes.*

Which way soe'er I look, are Furies to me.
Away with them! first shew them death, then
        leave
No memory of their ashes. I'll mock Fate.
    [*Exeunt Executioners with Rusticus and Sura.*[3]
Shall words fright him victorious armies circle?
No, no; the fever does begin to leave me;

Enter DOMITIA, JULIA, *and* CÆNIS; STEPHANOS
        following.

Or, were it deadly, from this living fountain
I could renew the vigour of my youth,
And be a second Virbius.[4] O my glory!
My life! command![5] my all!
    Dom. As you to me are.
                     [*Embracing and kissing.*
I heard you were sad; I have prepared you
        sport
Will banish melancholy. Sirrah, Cæsar,
(I hug myself for't,) I have been instructing
The players how to act; and to cut off
All tedious impertinence, have contracted
The tragedy into one continued scene.

    [3] [*Exeunt* Executioners *with Rusticus and* Sura.] After *Sura*,
Coxeter and M. Mason add, *Stephanos following.* This sending
a man out before he comes in, is another instance of the surprising attention which Massinger experienced from the former
editors. The quarto reads as it stands here.
    [4] *And be a second* Virbius.] The name given to Hippolytus
after he was restored to life by Æsculapius. He was so called,
say the critics, *quòd inter* viros bis *fuerit.* See *the Æneid*, lib.
vii. v. 765.
    [5] *My life! command! my all!*] i. e. my power! my all! This
is the reading of the old copies, and undoubtedly genuine: the
modern editors (I know not why) choose to read, *My life!
command my all!* which the reply of Domitia proves to be rank
nonsense.

I have the art of't, and am taken more
With my ability that way, than all knowledge
I have but of thy love.
 Cæs. Thou art still thyself,
The sweetest, wittiest,——
 Dom. When we are abed
I'll thank your good opinion. Thou shalt see
Such an Iphis of thy Paris !'—and, to humble
The pride of Domitilla, that neglects me,
(Howe'er she is your cousin,) I have forced her
To play the part of Anaxarete——
You are not offended with it?
 Cæs, Any thing
That does content thee yields delight to me:
My faculties and powers are thine.
 Dom. I thank you:
Prithee let's take our places. Bid them enter
Without more circumstance.

 After a short flourish, enter PARIS *as* IPHIS.

      How do you like
That shape?' methinks it is most suitable
To the aspéct of a despairing lover
The seeming late-fallen, conterfeited tears
That hang upon his cheeks, was my device.

---

 6   ——— *Thou shalt see*
Such an Iphis of thy Paris! &c.] The story of Iphis and
Anaxarete is beautifully told by Ovid, in the fourteenth book
of his *Metamorphosis,* (v. 698, *et seq.*) to which I refer the reader,
as it is too long to be extracted. Massinger has followed his
leader *pari passu;* and indeed the elegance and spirit which he
has infused into these little interludes, cannot be too highly
commended.
 7   ——— *How do you like*
That shape?] the Roman actors played in masks, one of
which Domitia calls a shape. M. MASON.
That a mask was called a *shape* I never heard before. The

Cæs. And all was excellent,
Dom. Now hear him speak.
    Iphis. *That she is fair, (and that an epithet*
Too foul to express her,) or descended nobly,
Or rich, or fortunate, are certain truths
In which poor Iphis glories. But that these
Perfections, in no other virgin found,
Abused, should nourish cruelty and pride
In the divinest Anaxarcte,
Is, to my love-sick, languishing soul, a riddle;
And with more difficulty to be dissolv'd,
Than that the monster Sphinx, from the steep rock,
Offer'd to Œdipus. Imperious Love,
As at thy ever-flaming altars Iphis,
Thy never-tired votary, hath presented,
With scalding tears, whole hecatombs of sighs,
Preferring thy power, and thy Paphian mother's,
Before the Thunderer's, Neptune's, or Pluto's
(That, after Saturn, did divide the world,
And had the swdy of things, yet were compell'd
By thy inevitable shafts to yield,
And fight under thy ensigns) be auspicious
To this last trial of my sacrifice
Of love and service !
    Dom. Does he not act it rarely?
Observe with what a feeling he delivers
His orisons to Cupid ; I am rapt with't.
    Iphis. *And from thy never-emptied quiver take*
A golden arrow,[9] *to transfix her heart,*

---

fact is, that *shape* is a theatrical word, and, in the language of
the property-man, means, as has been already observed, the
whole of the dress.

    [8] *And with more difficulty to be* dissolv'd,] So the old copies.
Coxeter and M. Mason read *solved.* See Vol. I. p. 321.

    [9]   Iphis. *And from thy never-emptied quiver take*
    A golden arrow, &c.] For this expression, which, like a few
others, occurs somewhat too frequently, see Vol. I.p. 19.

And force her love like me ; or cure my wound
With a leaden one, that may beget in me
Hate and forgetfulness of what's now my idol——
But I call back my prayer ; I have blasphemed
In my rash wish : 'tis I that am unworthy ;
But she all merit, and may in justice challenge,
From the assurance of her excellencies,
Not love but adoration. Yet, bear witness,
All-knowing Powers ! I bring along with me,
As faithful advocates to make intercession,
A loyal heart with pure and holy flames,
With the foul fires of lust never polluted.
And, as I touch her threshold, which with tears,
My limbs benumb'd with cold, I oft have wash'd,
With my glad lips I kiss this earth, grown proud
With frequent favours from her delicate feet.

    Dom. By Cæsar's life he weeps! and I forbear
Hardly to keep him company.

    Iphis. *Blest ground, thy pardon,*
If I profane it with forbidden steps.
I must presume to knock—and yet attempt it
With such a trembling reverence, as if
My hands [were now][1] *held up for expiation*

---

[1] *My hands* [were now] *held up for expiation*] **I am very**
doubtful of the genuineness of this line. Of the old copies **of**
this tragedy (of which there is but one edition) some read,
      My hands held up, or expiation,
and others,
      My hands held up, for expiation.
It is evident, from the comma, that there is an error somewhere,
which was discovered at the press, and attempted to be removed :
but as it has happened more than once in these plays, only exchanged for another. My addition is harmless : but if I could
have ventured so far, I should have read,
      My hands held up in prayer, *or expiation,*
      To &c.
As the line stands in Coxeter and Mr. M. Mason, it is impossible to read it as verse, or any thing like verse.

To the incensed gods to spare a kingdom.
Within there, ho! something divine come forth
To a distressed mortal.

Enter LATINUS *as a* Porter.

Port. *Ha! Who knocks there?*
Dom. What a churlish look this knave has!
Port. *Is't you, sirrah?*
Are you come to pule and whine? Avaunt, and
*   quickly;*
Dog-whips shall drive you hence, else.
Dom. Churlish devil!
But that I should disturb the scene, as I live
I would tear his eyes out.
Cæs. 'Tis in jest, Domitia.
Dom. I do not like such jesting : if he were not
A flinty-hearted slave, he could not use
One of his form so harshly. How the toad swells
At the other's sweet humility!
Cæs. 'Tis his part:
Let them proceed.
Dom. A rogue's part will ne'er leave him.
Iphis. *As you have, gentle sir, the happiness*
(When you please) to behold the figure of
The masterpiece of nature, limn'd to the life,
In more than human Anaxarete,
Scorn not your servant, that with suppliant hands
Takes hold upon your knees, conjuring you,
As you are a man, and did not suck the milk
Of wolves, and tigers, or a mother of
A tougher temper, use some means these eyes,
Before they are wept out, may see your lady.
Will you be gracious, sir?
Port. *Though I lose my place for't,*
I can hold out no longer.

Dom. Now he melts,
There is some little hope he may die honest.
Port, *Madam!*

Enter DOMITILLA *as* ANAXARETE.

Anax. *Who calls? What object have we here?*
Dom. Your cousin keeps her proud state still;
     I think
I have fitted her for a part.
     Anax. *Did I not charge thee*
I ne'er might see this thing more?
     Iphis. *I am, indeed,*
What thing you please; a worm that you may
     tread on :
Lower I cannot fall to shew my duty,
Till your disdain hath digg'd a grave to cover
This body with forgotten dust ; and, when
I know your sentence, cruellest of women !
I'll, by a willing death, remove the object
That is an eyesore to you.
     Anax. *Wretch, thou dar'st not :*
That were the last and greatest service to me
Thy doting love could boast of. What dull fool
But thou could nourish any flattering hope,
One of my height in youth, in birth and fortune,
Could e'er descend to look upon thy lowness,
Much less consent to make my lord of one
I'd not accept, though offer'd for my slave?
My thoughts stoop not so low.
     Dom. There's her true nature :
No personated scorn.
     Anax. *I wrong my worth,*
Or to exchange a syllable or look
With one so far beneath me.
     Iphis. *Yet take heed,*
Take heed of pride, and curiously consider,

How brittle the foundation is, on which
You labour to advance it.   Niobe,
Proud of her numerous issue, durst contemn
Latona's double burthen ; but what follow'd ?
She was left a childless mother, and mourn'd to
        marble.
The beauty you o'erprize so, time or sickness
Can change to loath'd deformity ; your wealth
The prey of thieves ; queen Hecuba, Troy fired,
Ulysses' bondwoman : *but the love I bring you*
Nor time, nor sickness, violent thieves, nor fate,
Can ravish from you.
    Dom. Could the oracle
Give better counsel !
    Iphis. *Say, will you relent yet,*
Revoking your decree that I should die ?
Or, shall I do what you command ? resolve ;
I am impatient of delay.

----

² —————*Queen Hecuba, Troy fired,*
Ulysses' bondwoman :] These two half-lines are entirely mis-
placed, and should not be inserted here ; they afterwards occur
in the second volume, to which passage they belong. M. Mason.

    This is the most unaccountable notion that ever was taken
up. *The Roman Actor* was not only written but printed many
years before *the Emperor of the East;* how, then, could any
lines or " half lines" be inserted into it from a piece which was
not yet in existence ! It required Mr. M. Mason's own words to
convince me that he could range through Massinger, even in his
desultory way, without discovering his propensity to repeat
himself; which is so obtrusive as to form one of the most cha-
racteristic traits of his manner. With respect to the two half
lines, they are where they should be, and are referred to in the
verse which follows. It may amuse the reader to see this passage as " it occurs again."!

        " You are read in story, call to your remembrance
        " What the great Hector's mother, Hecuba,
        " Was to Ulysses, Ilium sack'd."

The identity may admit of some question——but enough of this
deplorable folly.

Anax. Dispatch then :
I shall look on your tragedy unmoved,
Peradventure laugh at it ; for it will prove
A comedy to me.
   Dom. O devil ! devil !
   Iphis. *Then thus I take my last leave.* All the
      curses
Of lovers fall upon you ; and, hereafter,
When any man, like me contemn'd, shall study,
In the anguish of his soul, to give a name
To a scornful, cruel mistress, let him only
Say, This most bloody woman is to me,
As Anaxarete was to wretched Iphis !——
Now feast your tyrannous mind, and glory in
The ruins you have made : for Hymen's bands,
That should have made us one, this fatal halter
For ever shall divorce us : at your gate,
As a trophy of your pride and my affliction,
I'll presently hang myself.
   Dom. Not for the world —
                        [*Starts from her seat.*
Restrain him, as you love your lives !
   Cæs. Why are you
Transported thus, Domitia? 'tis a play;
Or, grant it serious, it at no part merits
This passion in you.
   Par. I ne'er purposed, madam,
To do the deed in earnest; though I bow
To your care and tenderness of me.
   Dom. Let me, sir,
Entreat your pardon ; what I saw presented,
Carried me beyond myself.
   Cæs. To your place again,
And see what follows.
   Dom. No, I am familiar
With the conclusion ; besides, upon the sudden
I feel myself much indisposed.

Cæs. To bed then;
I'll be thy doctor.
Aret. There is something more
In this than passion,—which I must find out,
Or my intelligence freezes.
Dom. Come to me, Paris,
To morrow, for your reward.
[*Exeunt all but Domitilla and Stephanos.*
Steph. Patroness, hear me;
Will you not call for your share? Sit down with this,
And, the next action, like a Gaditane[3] strumpet,
I shall look to see you tumble!
Domitil. Prithee be patient.
I, that have suffer'd greater wrongs, bear this;
And that, till my revenge, my comfort is.
[*Exeunt.*

ACT IV. SCENE I.

A Room in the Palace.

Enter PARTHENIUS, JULIA, DOMITILLA, *and* CÆNIS.

Parth. Why, 'tis impossible.—Paris!
Jul. You observed not,
As it appears, the violence of her passion,

[3] Like a *Gaditane* strumpet,] These "tumblers," who came from the neighbourhood of the modern Cadiz, are frequently noticed by the Roman writers, for the indecency of their gestures: the dance which appears to have so scandalized them was, beyond question, the Fandango, which is even now sufficiently licentious in the remote parts of Spain.

When personating Iphis, he pretended,
For your contempt, fair Anaxarete,
To hang himself.

    Parth. Yes, yes, I noted that;
But never could imagine it could work her
To such a strange intemperance of affection,
As to doat on him.

    Domitil. By my hopes, I think not
That she respects, though all here saw, and
      mark'd it;
Presuming she can mould the emperor's will
Into what form she likes, though we, and all
The informers of the world, conspired to cross it.

    Cæn. Then with what eagerness, this morning,
      urging
The want of health and rest, she did entreat
Cæsar to leave her!

    Domitil. Who no sooner absent,
But she calls, *Dwarf!* (so in her scorn she styles
      me,)
Put on my pantofles ; fetch pen and paper,
I am to write :—and with distracted looks,
In her smock, impatient of so short delay
As but to have a mantle thrown upon her,
She seal'd—I know not what, but 'twas indorsed,
To my loved Paris.

    Jul. Add to this, I heard her
Say, when a page received it, *Let him wait me,*
And carefully, in the walk call'd our Retreat,
Where Cæsar, in his fear to give offence,
Unsent for, never enters.

    Parth. This being certain,
(For these are more than jealous suppositions,)
Why do not you, that are so near in blood,
Discover it?

    Domitil. Alas! you know we dare not.
'Twill be received for a malicious practice,

To free us from that slavery which her pride
Imposes on us. But, if you would please
To break the ice, on pain to be sunk ever,
We would aver it.
    Parth. I would second you,
But that I am commanded with all speed
To fetch in[2] Ascletario the Chaldæan ;
Who, in his absence, is condemn'd of treason,
For calculating the nativity
Of Cæsar, with all confidence fortelling,
In every circumstance, when he shall die
A violent death.   Yet, if you could approve
Of my directions, I would have you speak
As much to Aretinus, as you have
To me deliver'd : he in his own nature
Being a spy, on weaker grounds, no doubt,
Will undertake it ; not for goodness' sake,
(With which he never yet held correspondence,)
But to endear his vigilant observings
Of what concerns the emperor, and a little
To triumph in the ruins of this Paris,
That cross'd him in the senate-house.—

Enter ARETINUS.

                                   Here he comes,
His nose held up ; he hath something in the wind,
Or I much err, already.   My designs
Command me hence, great ladies ; but I leave
My wishes with you.   [*Exit.*
    Aret. Have I caught your Greatness
In the trap, my proud Augusta !
    Domitil. What is't raps him?
    Aret. And my fine Roman Actor ! Is't even so?
No coarser dish to take your wanton palate,

---

    [2] *To* fetch in] i. e. to seize ; a frequent expression.

Save that which, but the emperor, none durst
    taste of!
'Tis very well.   I needs must glory in
This rare discovery: but the rewards
Of my intelligence bid me think, even now,
By an edict from Cæsar, I have power
To tread upon the neck of slavish Rome,
Disposing offices and provinces
To my kinsmen, friends, and clients.
   Domitil. This is more
Than usual with him.
   Jul. Aretinus!
   Aret. How!
No more respect and reverence tender'd to me,
But *Aretinus!* 'Tis confess'd that title,
When you were princesses, and commanded all,
Had been a favour; but being, as you are,
Vassals to a proud woman, the worst bondage,
You stand obliged with as much adoration
To entertain him, that comes arm'd with strength
To break your fetters, as tann'd galley-slaves
Pay such as do redeem them from the oar.
I come not to entrap you; but aloud
Pronounce that you are manumized: and to make
Your liberty sweeter, you shall see her fall,
This empress,—this Domitia,—what you will,—
That triumph'd in your miseries.
   Domitil. Were you serious,
To prove your accusation I could lend
Some help.
   Cæn. And I.
   Jul. And I.
   Aret. No atom to me.—
My eyes and ears are every where; I know all,
To the line and action in the play that took her:
Her quick dissimulation to excuse
Her being transported, with her morning passion.

I bribed the boy that did convey the letter,
And, having perused it, made it up again :
Your griefs and angers are to me familiar.
—That Paris is brought to her,⁴ and how far
He shall be tempted.

    Domitil. This is above wonder.

    Aret. My gold can work much stranger miracles,
Than to corrupt poor waiters. Here, join with
        me—   *[Takes out a petition.*
'Tis a complaint to Cæsar. This is that
Shall ruin her, and raise you. Have you set
      your hands
To the accusation?

    Jul. And will justify
What we've subscribed to.

    Cæn. And with vehemence.

    Domitil. I will deliver it.

    Aret. Leave the rest to me then.

        Enter Cæsar, *with his Guard.*

    Cæs. Let our lieutenants bring us victory,
While we enjoy the fruits of peace at home :
And being secured from our intestine foes,
(Far worse than foreign enemies,) doubts and fears,
Though all the sky were hung with blazing me-
      teors,
Which fond astrologers give out to be
Assured presages of the change of empires,
And deaths of monarchs, we, undaunted yet,
Guarded with our own thunder, bid defiance
To them and fate; we being too strongly arm'd
For them to wound us.

    Aret. Cæsar!

    ⁵ — *That Paris is brought to her,* &c.] A line preceding this
seems to have been lost at the press : the drift of it is not difficult to guess; but I have not meddled with the old copies.

Jul. As thou art
More than a man—
 Cæn. Let not thy passions be
Rebellious to thy reason—
 Domitil. But receive   [*Delivers the petition.*
This trial of your constancy, as unmoved
As you go to or from the capitol,
Thanks given to Jove for triumphs.
 Cæs. Ha!
 Domitil. Vouchsafe
A while to stay the lightning of your eyes,
Poor mortals dare not look on.
 Aret. There's no vein
Of yours that rises with high rage, but is
An earthquake to us.
 Domitil. And, if not kept closed
With more than human patience, in a moment
Will swallow us to the centre.
 Cæn. Not that we
Repine to serve her, are we her accusers.
 Jul. But that she's fallen so low.
 Aret. Which on sure proofs
We can make good.
 Domitil. And shew she is unworthy
Of the least spark of that diviner fire
You have conferr'd upon her.
 Cæs. I stand doubtful,
And unresolved what to determine of you.
In this malicious violence you have offer'd
To the altar of her truth and pureness to me,
You have but fruitlessly labour'd to sully
A white robe of perfection, black-mouth'd envy
Could belch no spot on.—But I will put off
The deity you labour to take from me,
And argue out of probabilities with you,
As if I were a man. Can I believe
That she, that borrows all her light from me,

And knows to use it, would betray her darkness
To your intelligence ; and make that apparent,
Which, by her perturbations in a play,
Was yesterday but doubted, and find none
But you, that are her slaves, and therefore hate
    her,
Whose aids she might employ to make way for
    her?
Or Aretinus, whom long since she knew
To be the cabinet counsellor, nay, the key
Of Cæsar's secrets ? Could her beauty raise her
To this unequall'd height, to make her fall.
The more remarkable? or must my desires
To her, and wrongs to Lamia, be revenged
By her, and on herself, that drew on both?
Or she leave our imperial bed, to court
A public actor?
    Aret. Who dares contradict
These more than human reasons, that have power
To clothe base guilt in the most glorious shape
Of innocence?
    Domitil. Too well she knew the strength
And eloquence of her patron to defend her,
And thereupon presuming, fell securely ;
Not fearing an accuser, nor the truth
Produced against her, which your love and favour
Will ne'er discern from falsehood.
    Cæs. I'll not hear
A syllable more that may invite a change
In my opinion of her. You have raised
A fiercer war within me by this fable,
Though with your lives you vow to make it
    story,
Than if, and at one instant, all my legions
Revolted from me, and came arm'd against me.
Here in this paper are the swords predestined
For my destruction ; here the fatal stars.

That threaten more than ruin; this the Death's
  head
That does assure me, if she can prove false,
That I am mortal, which a sudden fever
Would prompt me to believe, and faintly yield to.
But now in my full confidence what she suffers,
In that, from any witness but myself,
I nourish a suspicion she's untrue,
My toughness returns to me. Lead on, monsters,
And, by the forfeit of your lives, confirm
She is all excellence, as you all baseness;
Or let mankind, for her fall, boldly swear
There are no chaste wives now, nor ever were.[6]
           [Exeunt.

SCENE II.

A private Walk in the Gardens of the Palace.

Enter DOMITIA, PARIS, *and* Servants.

Dom. Say we command, that none presume to
  dare,
On forfeit of our favour, that is life,
Out of a saucy curiousness, to stand
Within the distance of their eyes or ears,
Till we please to be waited on. [*Exeunt Servants.*
        And, sirrah,
Howe'er you are excepted, let it not
Beget in you an arrogant opinion
'Tis done to grace you.
  Par. With my humblest service

---

 [6] *Or let mankind, for her fall, boldly swear*
  There are no chaste *wives now, nor ever* were.] The " godlike
Cæsar" forgets that the *chastity* of Domitia had long ceased to
be a matter of doubt.

I but obey your summons, and should blush else,
To be so near you.
    Dom. 'Twould become you rather
To fear the greatness of the grace vouchsafed
    you
May overwhelm you; and 'twill do no less,
If, when you are rewarded, in your cups
You boast this privacy.
    Par. That were, mightiest empress,
To play with lightning.
    Dom. You conceive it right.
The means to kill or save is not alone
In Cæsar circumscribed; for, if incensed,
We have our thunder too, that strikes as deadly.
    Par. 'Twould ill become the lowness of my
    fortune,
To question what you can do, but with all
Humility to attend what is your will,
And then to serve it.
    Dom. And would not a secret,
Suppose we should commit it to your trust,
Scald you to keep it?
    Par. Though it raged within me
Till I turn'd cinders, it should ne'er have vent.
To be an age a dying, and with torture,
Only to be thought worthy of your counsel,[7]
Or actuate what you command to me,[8]

---

[7] *Only to be thought worthy of your* counsel,] The modern editors, who appear not to have understood the word, read *council* for *counsel:* but the latter is right. It means *secrecy*, and so it is frequently used, not only by Massinger, but by all the writers of his time:

      " But what they did there is *counsel* to me,
      " Because they lay late the next day."   *Old Ballad.*

See Vol. I. p. 281.

[8] *Or* actuate *what you command to me,*] Here *actuate* is used for *act*, as *act* is used by some of our best poets, and Pope among the rest, but with less propriety, for *actuate.*

A wretched obscure thing, not worth your know-
    ledge,
Were a perpetual happiness.
  Dom. We could wish
That we could credit thee, and cannot find
In reason, but that thou, whom oft I have seen
To personate a gentleman, noble, wise,
Faithful, and gainsome, and what virtues else
The poet pleases to adorn you with;
But that (as vessels still partake the odour'
Of the sweet precious liquors they contain'd)
Thou must be really, in some degree,
The thing thou dost present.—Nay, do not
    tremble;
We seriously believe it, and presume
Our Paris is the volume in which all
Those excellent gifts the stage hath seen him
    graced with,
Are curiously bound up.
  Par. The argument
Is the same, great Augusta, that I, acting
A fool, a coward, a traitor, or cold cynic,
Or any other weak and vicious person,
Of force I must be such. O, gracious madam,
How glorious soever, or deform'd,
I do appear in the scene, my part being ended,
And all my borrow'd ornaments put off,
I am no more, nor less, than what I was
Before I enter'd.
  Dom. Come, you would put on
A wilful ignorance, and not understand

---

9   ———— (*as vessels still partake the odour*
Of the sweet precious liquors they contain'd)]

    Quæ semel est imbuta recens servabit odorem
    Testa diu.   HOR.

What 'tis we point at. Must we in plain language,
Against the decent modesty of our sex,
Say that we love thee, love thee to enjoy thee;
Or that in our desires thou art preferr'd,
And Cæsar but thy second? Thou in justice,
If from the height of majesty we can
Look down upon thy lowness, and embrace it,
Art bound with fervor to look up to me.

    Par. O, madam! hear me with a patient ear,
And be but pleased to understand the reasons
That do deter me from a happiness
Kings would be rivals for. Can I, that owe
My life, and all that's mine, to Cæsar's bounties,
Beyond my hopes or merits, shower'd upon me,
Make payment for them with ingratitude,
Falsehood, and treason! Though you have a shape
Might tempt Hippolitus, and larger power
To help or hurt than wanton Phædra had,
Let loyalty and duty plead my pardon,
Though I refuse to satisfy.

    Dom. You are coy,
Expecting I should court you. Let mean ladies
Use prayers and entreaties to their creatures
To rise up instruments to serve their pleasures;
But for Augusta so to lose herself,
That holds command o'er Cæsar and the world,
Were poverty of spirit. Thou must—thou shalt:
The violence of my passion knows no mean,
And in my punishments, and my rewards,
I'll use no moderation. Take this only,
As a caution from me; threadbare chastity
Is poor in the advancement of her servants,
But wantonness magnificent; and 'tis frequent
To have the salary of vice weigh down
The pay of virtue. So, without more trifling,
Thy sudden answer.

Par. In what a strait am I brought in !¹
Alas ! I know that the denial's death ;
Nor can my grant, discover'd, threaten more.
Yet, to die innocent, and have the glory
For all posterity to report, that I
Refused an empress, to preserve my faith
To my great master ; in true judgment, must
Show fairer, than to buy a guilty life
With wealth and honour. 'Tis the base I build on:
I dare not, must not, will not.
 Dom. How ! contemn'd ?
Since hopes, nor fears, in the extremes, prevail not,
I must use a mean. [*Aside.*]—Think who 'tis sues
  to thee.
Deny not that yet, which a brother may
Grant to a sister : as a testimony

Enter Cæsar, Aretinus, Julia, Domitilla,
 Cænis, *and a Guard, behind.*

I am not scorn'd, kiss me ;—kiss me again :
Kiss closer. Thou art now my Trojan Paris,
And I thy Helen.
 Par. Since it is your will.
 Cæs. And I am Menelaus : but I shall be
Something I know not yet.
 Dom. Why lose we time

 ¹ *Par.* In *what a strait am I brought* in !]   Coxeter and M.
Mason read,
  Oh! *what a strait am I brought in!*
This is, perhaps, a better mode of expression; but we should
confound all times, if we thus modernised every phrase which
appears uncouth to our eyes and ears: add too, that similar
redundancies are to be found in almost every page of our old
writers, and above all, in Massinger.   An instance occurs just
below :
   —————————— of *which, if again*
  I could be ignorant of, &c.

And opportunity? These are but salads
To sharpen appetite: let us to the feast,
                [*Courting Paris wantonly.*
Where I shall wish that thou wert Jupiter,
And I Alcmena; and that I had power
To lengthen out one short night into three,
And so beget a Hercules.
   Cæs. [*Comes forward.*] While Amphitrio
Stands by, and draws the curtains.
   Par. Oh!——   [*Falls on his face.*
   Dom. Betray'd!
   Cæs. No; taken in a net of Vulcan's filing,
Where, in myself, the theatre of the gods
Are sad spectators, not one of them daring
To witness, with a smile, he does desire
To be so shamed for all the pleasure that
You've sold your being for! What shall I name
     thee?
Ingrateful, treacherous, insatiate, all
Invectives which, in bitterness of spirit,
Wrong'd men have breathed out against wicked
     women,
Cannot express thee! Have I raised thee from
Thy low condition to the height of greatness,
Command, and majesty, in one base act
To render me, that was, before I hugg'd
     thee,[2]
An adder, in my bosom, more than man,
A thing beneath a beast! Did I force these
Of mine own blood, as handmaids to kneel to
Thy pomp and pride, having myself no thought
But how with benefits to bind thee mine;

[2] *To render me that was, before I hugg'd thee,*] This and the two following lines have been hitherto printed and pointed in a very unintelligible manner. **Mr. M.** Mason tried to reform them, but failed: the simple removal of a bracket in the old copies restores them to sense.

And am I thus rewarded! Not a knee,
Nor tear, nor sign of sorrow for thy fault?
Break, stubborn silence: what canst thou al-
      lege
To stay my vengeance?
      Dam. This. Thy lust compell'd me
To be a strumpet, and mine hath return'd it
In my intent and will, though not in act,
To cuckold thee.
      Cæs. O, impudence! take her hence,
And let her make her entrance into hell,
By leaving life with all the tortures that
Flesh can be sensible of. Yet stay. What
      power
Her beauty still holds o'er my soul, that wrongs
Of this unpardonable nature cannot teach me
To right myself, and hate her!—Kill her.—
      Hold!
O that my dotage should increase from that
Which should breed detestation! By Minerva,
If I look on her longer, I shall melt,
And sue to her, my injuries forgot,
Again to be received into her favour;
Could honour yield to it! Carry her to her[3]
      chamber;
Be that her prison, till in cooler blood
I shall determine of her.
      [*Exit Guard with Domitia.*
      Aret. Now step I in,
While he's in this calm mood, for my reward.—
Sir, if my service hath deserved—
      Cæs. Yes, yes:
And I'll reward thee. Thou hast robb'd me of

---

[3] *Carry her to* her *chamber; &c.*] Mr. M. Mason reads *my*
chamber, strangely enough; but, indeed, this whole scene is
very carelessly given by him.

All rest and peace, and been the principal means
To make me know that, of which if again
I could be ignorant of, I would purchase it

Re-enter Guard.

With the loss of empire: Strangle him; take these
    hence too,
And lodge them in the dungeon. Could your
    reason,
Dull wretches, flatter you with hope to think
That this discovery, that hath shower'd upon me
Perpetual vexation, should not fall
Heavy on you? Away with them!—stop their
    mouths;
I will hear no reply.

       [Exit Guard with Aretinus, Julia, Cænis,
        and Domitilla.
               —O, Paris, Paris!
How shall I argue with thee? how begin
To make thee understand, before I kill thee,
With what grief and unwillingness 'tis forced
    from me?
Yet, in respect I have favour'd thee, I'll hear
What thou canst speak to qualify or excuse
Thy readiness to serve this woman's lust;
And wish thou couldst give me such satisfaction,
As I might bury the remembrance of it.
Look up: we stand attentive.
    Par. O, dread Cæsar!
To hope for life, or plead in the defence
Of my ingratitude, were again to wrong you.
I know I have deserved death; and my suit is,
That you would hasten it: yet, that your highness,
When I am dead, (as sure I will not live,)
May pardon me, I'll only urge my frailty,
Her will, and the temptation of that beauty

Which you could not resist. How could poor I,
    then,
Fly that which follow'd me, and Cæsar sued for?
This is all. And now your sentence.
    Cæs. Which I know not
How to pronounce. O that thy fault had been
But such as I might pardon! if thou hadst
In wantonness, like Nero, fired proud Rome,
Betray'd an army, butcher'd the whole senate,
Committed sacrilege, or any crime
The justice of our Roman laws calls death,
I had prevented any intercession,
And freely sign'd thy pardon.
    Par. But for this,
Alas! you cannot, nay, you must not, sir;
Nor let it to posterity be recorded,
That Cæsar, unrevenged, suffer'd a wrong,
Which, if a private man should sit down with it,
Cowards would baffle him.
    Cæs. With such true feeling
Thou arguest against thyself, that it
Works more upon me, than if my Minerva,
The grand protectress of my life and empire,
On forfeit of her favour, cried aloud,
Cæsar, show mercy! and, I know not how,
I am inclined to it. Rise. I'll promise nothing;
Yet clear thy cloudy fears, and cherish hopes.
What we must do, we shall do: we remember
A tragedy we oft have seen with pleasure,
Call'd *the False Servant.*
    Par. Such a one we have, sir.
    Cæs. In which a great lord[4] takes to his pro-
    tection

<hr/>

[4] *Cæs. In which a great lord,* &c.] The modern editions give
this speech and the next to Paris. The blunder, which is palpable enough, originated with Coxeter, and " the most accurate"
of all editors unfortunately followed him.

A man forlorn, giving him ample power
To order and dispose of his estate
In's absence, he pretending then a journey :
But yet with this restraint that, on no terms,
(This lord suspecting his wife's constancy,
She having play'd false to a former husband,)
The servant, though solicited, should consent,
Though she commanded him to quench her
  flames.

 Par. That was, indeed, the argument.
 Cæs. And what
Didst thou play in it?

 Par. The *False Servant*, sir.
 Cæs. Thou didst, indeed. Do the players wait
  without?
 Par. They do, sir, and prepared to act the story
Your majesty mention'd.
 Cæs. Call them in. Who presents
The injured lord!

  Enter ÆSOPUS, LATINUS, *and a* Lady.

 Æsop. 'Tis my part, sir.
 Cæs. Thou didst not
Do it to the life ; we can perform it better.
Off with my robe and wreath : since Nero scorn'd
  not
The public theatre, we in private may
Disport ourselves. This cloak and hat, without
Wearing a beard, or other property,
Will fit the person.
 Æsop. Only, sir, a foil,
The point and edge rebated, when you act,
To do the murder. If you please to use this,
And lay aside your own sword.
 Cæs. By no means.
In jest nor earnest this parts never from me,

We'll have but one short scene—That, where the
          lady
In an imperious way commands the servant
To be unthankful to his patron : when
My cue's to enter, prompt me :—Nay, begin,
And do it sprightly : though but a new actor,
When I come to execution, you shall find
No cause to laugh at me.
      Lat. In the name of wonder,
What's Cæsar's purpose !
      Æsop. There is no contending.
      Cæs. Why, when?[5]
      Par. I am arm'd :
And, stood grim Death now in my view, and his
Inevitable dart aim'd at my breast,
His cold embraces should not bring an ague
To any of my faculties, till his pleasures
Were served and satisfied ; which done, Nestor's
          years
To me would be unwelcome.   [*Aside.*
      Lady. *Must we entreat,*
That were born to command? or court a servant,
That owes his food and clothing to our bounty,
For that, which thou ambitiously shouldst kneel for?
Urge not, in thy excuse, the favours of
Thy absent lord, or that thou stand'st engaged
For thy life to his charity ; nor thy fears
Of what may follow, it being in my power
To mould him any way.
      Par. *As you may me,*
In what his reputation is not wounded,
Nor I, his creature, in my thankfulness suffer.

---

      [5] *Why, when?*] This is marked by the editors as an imperfect
speech : it is, however, complete ; and occurs continually in our
old dramas, as a mark of impatience.

I know you're young, and fair; be virtuous too,
And loyal to his bed, that hath advanced you
To the height of happiness.
    Lady. *Can my love-sick heart*
Be cured with counsel? or durst reason ever
Offer to put in an exploded plea
In the court of Venus? My desires admit not
The least delay; and therefore instantly
Give me to understand what I must trust to:
For, if I am refused, and not enjoy
Those ravishing pleasures from thee, I run mad for,
I'll swear unto my lord, at his return,
(Making what I deliver good with tears,)
That brutishly thou wouldst have forced from me
What I make suit for. And then but imagine
What 'tis to die, with these words, slave and
      traitor,
With burning corsives[6] *writ upon thy forehead,*
And live prepared for't.
    Par. *This he will believe*
Upon her information, 'tis apparent;
And then I'm nothing: and of two extremes,
Wisdom says, choose the less. [Aside.]—*Rather than*
     fall
Under your indignation, I will yield:
This kiss, and this, confirms it.
    Æsop. Now, sir, now.
    Cæs. I must take them at it?
    Æsop. Yes, sir; be but perfect.
    Cæs. O villain! thankless villain!—I should
     talk now;
But I've forgot my part. But I can do:
Thus, thus, and thus!   [*Stabs Paris.*

    [6] *With burning* corsives *writ upon thy forehead,*] See *the Emperor of the East*, Vol. III.

Par. Oh! I am slain in earnest.

Cæs. 'Tis true; and 'twas my purpose, my good
      Paris:
And yet, before life leave thee, let the honour
I've done thee in thy death bring comfort to
      thee.
If it had been within the power of Cæsar,
His dignity preserved, he had pardon'd thee:
But cruelty of honour did deny it.
Yet, to confirm I loved thee, 'twas my study,
To make thy end more glorious, to distinguish
My Paris from all others; and in that
Have shewn my pity. Nor would I let thee fall
By a centurion's sword, or have thy limbs
Rent piecemeal by the hangman's hook, however
Thy crime deserved it: but, as thou didst live
Rome's bravest actor, 'twas my plot that thou
Shouldst die in action, and to crown it, die,
With an applause enduring to all times,
By our imperial hand.—His soul is freed
From the prison of his flesh; let it mount upward!
And for this trunk, when that the funeral pile
Hath made it ashes, we'll see it enclosed
In a golden urn; poets adorn his hearse
With their most ravishing sorrows, and the stage
For ever mourn him, and all such as were
His glad spectators, weep his sudden death,
The cause forgotten in his epitaph.

      [*Sad music; the Players bear off Paris'
      body, Cæsar and the rest following.*

ACT V. SCENE I.

A Room in the Palace, with an image of Minerva.

Enter PARTHENIUS, STEPHANOS, *and Guard.*

 Parth. Keep a strong guard upon him, and
  admit not
Access to any, to exchange a word
Or syllable with him, till the emperor pleases
To call him to his presence.—[*Exit Guard.*]—The
  relation
That you have made me, Stephanos, of these late
Strange passions in Cæsar, much amaze me.
The informer Aretinus put to death
For yielding him a true discovery
Of the empress' wantonness; poor Paris kill'd first,
And now lamented; and the princesses
Confined to several islands; yet Augusta,
The machine on which all this mischief moved,
Received again to grace!
 Steph. Nay, courted to it:
Such is the impotence' of his affection!
Yet, to conceal his weakness, he gives out
The people made suit for her, whom they hate more
Than civil war, or famine.   But take heed,
My lord, that, nor in your consent nor wishes,
You lend or furtherance or favour to
The plot contrived against her: should she prove it,
Nay, doubt it only, you are a lost man,
Her power o'er doating Cæsar being now
Greater than ever.

 7 *Such is the* impotence *of his affection!*] i. e. the ungovern-
ableness, the uncontrollable violence.   See Vol. I. p. 174.

Parth. 'Tis a truth I shake at ;
And, when there's opportunity——
   Steph. Say but, Do,
I am yours, and sure.
   Parth. I'll stand one trial more,
And then you shall hear from me.
   Steph. Now observe
The fondness of this tyrant, and her pride.
                   [They stand aside.

     Enter Cæsar *and* Domitia.

   Cæs. Nay, all's forgotten.
   Dom. It may be, on your part.
   Cæs. Forgiven too, Domitia :—'tis a favour
That you should welcome with more cheerful looks.
Can Cæsar pardon what you durst not hope for,
That did the injury, and yet must sue
To her, whose guilt is wash'd off by his mercy,
Only to entertain it ?
   Dom. I ask'd none ;
And I should be more wretched to receive
Remission for what I hold no crime,
But by a bare acknowledgment, than if,
By slighting and contemning it, as now,
I dared thy utmost fury. Though thy flatterers
Persuade thee, that thy murders, lusts, and rapes,
Are virtues in thee ; and what pleases Cæsar,
Though never so unjust, is right and lawful ;
Or work in thee a false belief that thou
Art more than mortal ; yet I to thy teeth,
When circled with thy guards, thy rods, thy axes,
And all the ensigns of thy boasted power,
Will say, Domitian, nay, add to it Cæsar,
Is a weak, feeble man, a bondman to
His violent passions, and in that my slave ;
Nay, more my slave than my affections made me
To my loved Paris.

Cæs. Can I live and hear this?
Or hear, and not revenge it? Come, you know
The strength that you hold on me, do not use it
With too much cruelty; for though 'tis granted
That Lydian Omphale had less command
O'er Hercules, than you usurp o'er me,
Reason may teach me to shake off the yoke
Of my fond dotage.
    Dom. Never; do not hope it:
It cannot be. Thou being my beauty's captive,
And not to be redeem'd, my empire's larger
Than thine, Domitian, which I'll exercise
With rigour on thee, for my Paris' death.
And, when I've forced those eyes, now red with
      fury,
To drop down tears, in vain spent to appease me,
I know thy fervour such to my embraces,
Which shall be, though still kneel'd for, still
      denied thee,
That thou with languishment shalt wish my actor
Did live again, so thou mightst be his second
To feed upon those delicates, when he's sated.'
    Cæs. O my Minerva!
    Dom. There she is, [*Points to the statue.*] in-
    voke her:
She cannot arm thee with ability
To draw thy sword on me, my power being greater:
Or only say to thy centurions,
Dare none of you do what I shake to think on,
And, in this woman's death, remove the Furies
That every hour afflict me?—Lamia's wrongs,
When thy lust forced me from him, are, in me,
At the height revenged; nor would I outlive Paris,

    ³ *To feed upon those delicates,* when he's sated.] So the old
copies: but the modern editors, laudably solicitous for the sense,
as well as the metre, of their author, concur in reading,
    To feed upon those delicates, when he were *sated!*

But that thy love, increasing with my hate,
May add unto thy torments; so, with all
Contempt I can, I leave thee.   [*Exit.*
 Cæs. I am lost;
Nor am I Cæsar. When I first betray'd
The freedom of my faculties and will
To this imperious Siren, I laid down
The empire of the world, and of myself,
At her proud feet. Sleep all my ireful powers!
Or is the magic of my dotage such,
That I must still make suit to hear those charms
That do increase my thraldom! Wake, my anger!
For shame, break through this lethargy, and appear
With usual terror, and enable me,
Since I wear not a sword to pierce her heart,
Nor have a tongue to say this, *Let her die,*
Though 'tis done with a fever-shaken hand,
    [*Pulls out a table-book.*
To sign her death. Assist me, great Minerva,
And vindicate thy votary! [*writes*] So; she's now
Among the list of those I have proscribed,
And are, to free me of my doubts and fears,
To die to morrow.
 Steph. That same fatal book
Was never drawn yet, but some men of rank
Were mark'd out for destruction.   [*Exit.*
 Parth. I begin
To doubt myself.
 Cæs. Who waits there?
 Parth. [*coming forward.*] Cæsar.
 Cæs. So!
These, that command arm'd troops, quake at my
  frowns,
And yet a woman slights them. Where's the wizard
We charged you to fetch in?
 Parth. Ready to suffer
What death you please to appoint him.

Cæs. Bring him in.
We'll question him ourself.

Enter Tribunes, *and Guard with* ASCLETARIO.

                        Now, you, that hold
Intelligence with the stars, and dare prefix
The day and hour in which we are to part
With life and empire, punctually foretelling
The means and manner of our violent end;
As you would purchase credit to your art,
Resolve me, since you are assured of us,
What fate attends yourself?

    Ascle. I have had long since
A certain knowledge, and as sure as thou
Shalt die to morrow, being the fourteenth of
The kalends of October, the hour five;
Spite of prevention, this carcass shall be
Torn and devour'd by dogs;—and let that stand
For a firm prediction.

    Cæs. May our body, wretch,
Find never nobler sepulchre, if this
Fall ever on thee! Are we the great disposer
Of life and death, yet cannot mock the stars
In such a trifle? Hence with the impostor;
And having cut his throat, erect a pile,
Guarded with soldiers, till his cursed trunk
Be turn'd to ashes: upon forfeit of
Your life, and theirs, perform it.

    Ascle. 'Tis in vain;
When what I have foretold is made apparent,
Tremble to think what follows.

    Cæs. Drag him hence,
       [*The Tribunes and Guard bear off Ascletario.*
And do as I command you. I was never
Fuller of confidence; for, having got
The victory of my passions, in my freedom

From proud Domitia, (who shall cease to live,
Since she disdains to love,) I rest unmoved :
And, in defiance of prodigious meteors,
Chaldeans' vain predictions, jealous fears
Of my near friends and freedmen, certain hate
Of kindred and alliance, or all terrors
The soldiers' doubted faith, or people's rage
Can bring to shake my constancy, I am arm'd.
That scrupulous thing styled conscience is sear'd
            up,
And I insensible of all my actions,
For which, by moral and religious fools,
I stand condemn'd, as they had never been.
And, since I have subdued triumphant love,
I will not deify pale captive fear,
Nor in a thought receive it : for, till thou,
Wisest Minerva, that from my first youth
Hast been my sole protectress, dost forsake me,
Not Junius Rusticus' threaten'd apparition,[9]
Nor what this soothsayer but even now foretold,
Being things impossible to human reason,
Shall in a dream disturb me. Bring my couch, there:
A sudden but a secure drowsiness
Invites me to repose myself. [*A couch brought in.*]
            Let music,
With some choice ditty, second it :—[*Exit Par-
            thenius.*]—the mean time,
Rest there, dear book, which open'd, when I wake,
            [*Lays the book under his pillow.*[1]
Shall make some sleep for ever.
            [*Music and a song. Cæsar sleeps.*

[9] *Nor Junius Rusticus'* threaten'd apparition,] See p. 379.
[1] [*Lays the book under his pillow.*] Nothing (as I have more
than once had occasion to observe) can be more careless than
the stage-directions in the modern editions. Here they both
make Cæsar fall asleep in the midst of his speech, which, never-
theless they both suffer him to continue !

Re-enter PARTHENIUS *and* DOMITIA.

Dom. Write my name
In his bloody scroll, Parthenius! the fear's idle:
He durst not, could not.
    Parth. I can assure nothing;
But I observed, when you departed from him,
After some little passion, but much fury,
He drew it out: whose death he sign'd, I know
    not;
But in his looks appear'd a resolution
Of what before he stagger'd at.   What he hath
Determined of is uncertain, but too soon
Will fall on you, or me, or both, or any,
His pleasure known to the tribunes and centu-
    rions,
Who never use to enquire his will, but serve it.
Now, if, out of the confidence of your power,
The bloody catalogue being still about him,
As he sleeps you dare peruse it, or remove it,
You may instruct yourself, or what to suffer,
Or how to cross it.
    Dom. I would not be caught
With too much confidence.   By your leave, sir.
    Ha!
No motion!—you lie uneasy, sir,
Let me mend your pillow.   [*Takes away the book.*
    Parth. Have you it?
    Dom. 'Tis here.
    Cæs. Oh!
    Parth. You have waked him: softly, gracious
    madam,
While² we are unknown; and then consult at
    leisure.   [*Exeunt.*

  ²   ——————— *softly, gracious madam,*
While *we are unknown,*] i. e. *until:* a very common ac-

Dreadful music.   The Apparitions of JUNIUS RUS-
TICUS *and* PALPHURIUS SURA *rise, with bloody
swords in their hands ; they wave them over the
head of* CÆSAR, *who seems troubled in his sleep,
and as if praying to the image of Minerva, which
they scornfully seize, and then disappear with it.*

Cæs. [*starting.*] Defend me, goddess, or this
        horrid dream
Will force me to distraction! whither have
These Furies born thee? Let me rise and follow.
I am bath'd o'er with the cold sweat of death,
And am deprived of organs to pursue
These sacrilegious spirits. Am I at once
Robb'd of my hopes and being? No, I live—
                        [*Rises distractedly.*
Yes, live, and have discourse,[3] to know myself
Of gods and men forsaken. What accuser
Within me cries aloud, I have deserved it,
In being just to neither? Who dares speak this?
Am I not Cæsar?—How! again repeat it?
Presumptuous traitor, thou shalt die!—What
        traitor?
He that hath been a traitor to himself,
And stands convicted here. Yet who can sit
A competent judge o'er Cæsar? Cæsar. Yes,
Cæsar by Cæsar's sentenced, and must suffer ;

ceptation of the word in our old writers. So Beaumont and
Fletcher :

> " I may be convey'd into your chamber, I'll lie
> " Under your bed *while* midnight." *Wit at several Weapons.*

And Waller :

> " Blessings may be repeated *while* they cloy ;
> " But shall we starve because fruition's joy ?"

[3] *Yes, live, and have* discourse,] i. e. reason or judgment. See
Vol. I. p. 148.

Minerva cannot save him.   Ha! where is she?[4]
Where is my goddess? vanish'd! I am lost
  ther.
No; 'twas no dream, but a most real truth,
That Junius Rusticus and Palphurius Sura,
Although their ashes were cast in the sea,
Were by their innocence made up again,
And in corporeal forms but now appear'd,
Waving their bloody swords above my head,
As at their deaths they threaten'd.   And me-
  thought,
Minerva, ravish'd hence, whisper'd that she
Was, for my blasphemies, disarm'd by Jove,
And could no more protect me.   Yes, 'twas so,
     [*Thunder and lightning.*
His thunder does confirm it, against which,
Howe'er it spare the laurel, this proud wreath

Enter three Tribunes.

Is no assurance. Ha! come you resolved
To be my executioners?
 1 *Trib.* Allegiance
And faith forbid that we should lift an arm
Against your sacred head.
 2 *Trib.* We rather sue
For mercy.
 3 *Trib.* And acknowledge that in justice
Our lives are forfeited for not performing
What Cæsar charged us.

   4 —————— *Ha! where is she?*
 Where is my goddess?] This attachment of Domitian to Minerva is an historical fact.   He chose her at an early period of
his life for his protectress, multiplied her statues to a great
extent, and had always a strong reliance on her favour.   If the
reader wishes for more on the subject, he may turn to the editor's translation of Juvenal, Sat. VII.

1 *Trib.* Nor did we transgress it
In our want of will or care ; for, being but men,
It could not be in us to make resistance,
The gods fighting against us.

Cæs. Speak, in what
Did they express their anger? we will hear it,
But dare not say, undaunted.

1 *Trib.* In brief thus, sir:
The sentence given by your imperial tongue,
For the astrologer Ascletario's death,
With speed was put in execution.

Cæs. Well.

1 *Trib.* For, his throat cut, his legs bound, and
   his arms
Pinion'd behind his back, the breathless trunk
Was with all scorn dragg'd to the field of Mars,
And there, a pile being raised of old dry wood,
Smear'd o'er with oil and brimstone, or what
   else
Could help to feed or to increase the fire,
The carcass was thrown on it ; but no sooner
The stuff, that was most apt, began to flame,
But suddenly, to the amazement of
The fearless soldier, a sudden flash
Of lightning, breaking through the scatter'd
   clouds,
With such a horrid violence forced its passage,
And, as disdaining all heat but itself,
In a moment quench'd the artificial fire :
And before we could kindle it again,
A clap of thunder follow'd with such noise,
As if then Jove, incensed against mankind,
Had in his secret purposes determined
An universal ruin to the world.
This horror past, not at Deucalion's flood
Such a stormy shower of rain (and yet that word is
Too narrow to express it) was e'er seen :

Imagine rather, sir, that with less fury
The waves rush down the cataracts of Nile;
Or that the sea, spouted into the air
By the angry Orc,⁵ endangering tall ships
But sailing near it, so falls down again.———
Yet here the wonder ends not, but begins:
For, as in vain we labour'd to consume
The wizard's body, all the dogs of Rome,
Howling and yelling like to famish'd wolves,
Brake in upon us; and though thousands were
Kill'd in th' attempt, some did ascend the pile,
And with their eager fangs seized on the carcass.
   Cæs. But have they torn it?
   1 *Trib.* Torn it, and devour'd it.
   Cæs. I then am a dead man, since all predictions
Assure me I am lost.   O, my loved soldiers,
Your emperor must leave you! yet, however
I cannot grant myself a short reprieve,
I freely pardon you.   The fatal hour
Steals fast upon me: I must die this morning
By five,⁹ my soldiers; that's the latest hour
You e'er must see me living.
   1 *Trib.* Jove avert it!
In our swords lies your fate, and we will guard it.
   Cæs. O no, it cannot be; it is decreed
Above, and by no strength here to be alter'd.
Let proud mortality but look on Cæsar,
Compass'd of late with armies, in his eyes
Carrying both life and death, and in his arms

---

   ⁵ *By the angry Orc,*]   A fabulous sea monster, depicted on
most of the marine charts of Massinger's time.   The whale of
our old Romances.
   6   ——————— *I must die this* morning,
   By five, &c.]   It may be just necessary, for the sake of the
mere English reader, to observe that Massinger makes use of the
Roman manner of computation: *five in the morning,* therefore,
answers to our eleven o'clock.

Fathoming the earth; that would be styled a
    God,
And is, for that presumption, cast beneath
The low condition of a common man,
Sinking with mine own weight.
    1 *Trib.* Do not forsake
Yourself, we'll never leave you.
    2 *Trib.* We'll draw up
More cohorts of your guard, if you doubt treason.
    Cæs. They cannot save me. The offended gods,
That now sit judges on me, from their envy
Of my power and greatness here, conspire against
    me.
    1 *Trib.* Endeavour to appease them.
    Cæs. 'Twill be fruitless :
I am past hope of remission. Yet, could I
Decline this dreadful hour of five, these terrors,
That drive me to despair, would soon fly from me :
And could you but till then assure me——[6]
    1 *Trib.* Yes, sir;
Or we'll fall with you, and make Rome the urn
In which we'll mix our ashes.
    Cæs. 'Tis said nobly :
I am something comforted : howe'er, to die
Is the full period of calamity.   [*Exeunt.*

---

[6] *And could you but* till then *assure me.* ——] i. e. till five. *Till
then,* which is absolutely necessary to the sense, as well as the
metre, is omitted by Mr. M. Mason,

SCENE II.

Another Room in the Palace.

Enter PARTHENIUS, DOMITIA, JULIA, CÆNIS, DOMITILLA, STEPHANOS, SEJEIUS, *and* ENTELLUS.

Parth. You see we are all condemn'd; there's
    no evasion;
We must do, or suffer.
    Steph. But it must be sudden;
The least delay is mortal.
    Dom. Would I were
A man, to give it action!
    Domitil. Could I make my approaches, though
    my stature
Does promise little, I have a spirit as daring
As her's that can reach higher.
    Steph. I will take
That burthen from you, madam. All the art is,
To draw him from the tribunes that attend him;
For, could you bring him but within my sword's
    reach,
The world should owe her freedom from a tyrant
To Stephanos.
    Sej. You shall not share alone
The glory of a deed that will endure
To all posterity.
    Ent. I will put in
For a part, myself.
    Parth. Be resolv'd, and stand close.
I have conceived a way, and with the hazard
Of my life I'll practise it, to fetch him hither.
But then no trifling.

Steph. We'll dispatch him, fear not:
A dead dog never bites.

Parth. Thus then at all.

[*Exit; the rest conceal themselves.*

Enter CÆSAR *and the* Tribunes.

Cæs. How slow-paced are these minutes! in
    extremes,
How miserable is the least delay!
Could I imp[8] feathers to the wings of time,
Or with as little ease command the sun
To scourge his coursers up heaven's eastern
    hill,
Making the hour to tremble at, past recalling,
As I can move this dial's tongue to six ;[9]
My veins and arteries, emptied with fear,
Would fill and swell again. How do I look?
Do you yet see Death about me?

  1 *Trib.* Think not of him ;
There is no danger: all these prodigies
That do affright you, rise from natural causes ;
And though you do ascribe them to yourself,
Had you ne'er been, had happened.

  Cæs. 'Tis well said,
Exceeding well, brave soldier. Can it be,
That I, that feel myself in health and strength,
Should still believe I am so near my end,
And have my guards about me? perish all
Predictions! I grow constant they are false,
And built upon uncertainties.

  1 *Trib.* This is right ;
Now Cæsar's heard like Cæsar.

---

  [8] *Could I* imp *feathers, &c.*] See p. 230.
  [9] *As I can move this dial's tongue to* six ;] i. e. to the hour of
noon ; see above, p. 418.

Cæs. We will to
The camp, and having there confirm'd the soldier
With a large donative, and increase of pay,
Some shall——I say no more.

Re-enter PARTHENIUS.

Parth. All happiness,
Security, long life, attend upon
The monarch of the world !
Cæs. Thy looks are cheerful.
Parth. And my relation full of joy and wonder.
Why is the care of your imperial body,
My lord, neglected, the fear'd hour being past,
In which your life was threaten'd?
Cæs. Is't past five ?
Parth. Past six, upon my knowledge ; and, in
    justice,
Your clock-master should die, that hath deferr'd
Your peace so long.   There is a post new lighted,
That brings assured intelligence, that your legions
In Syria have won a glorious day,
And much enlarged your empire.   I have kept
    him
Conceal'd, that you might first partake the pleasure
In private, and the senate from yourself
Be taught to understand how much they owe
To you and to your fortune.
Cæs. Hence, pale fear, then !
Lead me, Parthenius.
1 Trib. Shall we wait you ?
Cæs. No.
After losses guards are useful.   Know your
    distance.   [*Exeunt Cæsar and Parthenius.*
2 Trib. How strangely hopes delude men ! as
    I live,
The hour is not yet come.

1 *Trib.* Howe'er, we are
To pay our duties, and observe the sequel.
      [*Exeunt Tribunes. Domitia and the rest
            come forward.*
Dom. I hear him coming. Be constant.

Re-enter CÆSAR *and* PARTHENIUS.

Cæs. Where, Parthenius,
Is this glad messenger?
Steph. Make the door fast.—Here;
A messenger of horror.
Cæs. How! betray'd?
Dom. No; taken, tyrant.
Cæs. My Domitia
In the conspiracy!
Parth. Behold this book.
Cæs. Nay, then I am lost. Yet, though I am
            unarm'd,
I'll not fall poorly.   [*Overthrows Stephanos.*
Steph. Help me.
Ent. Thus, and thus!
Sej. Are you so long a falling? } *They stab him.*
Cæs. 'Tis done basely.   [*Falls, and dies.*
Parth. This for my father's death.
Dom. This for my Paris.
Jul. This for thy incest.
Domitil. This for thy abuse
Of Domitilla.   [*They severally stab him.*
Tribunes. [*within.*] Force the doors!

Enter Tribunes.

                              O Mars!
What have you done?
Parth. What Rome shall give us thanks for.
Steph. Dispatch'd a monster.
                  * F f 2

424 THE ROMAN ACTOR.THE ROMAN ACTOR.

1 *Trib.* Yet he was our prince,
However wicked; and, in you, this murder,—
Which whosoe'er succeeds him will revenge:
Nor will we, that serv'd under his command,
Consent that such a monster as thyself,
(For in thy wickedness Augusta's title
Hath quite forsook thee,) thou, that wert the
     ground
Of all these mischiefs, shall go hence unpunish'd.
Lay hands on her, and drag her to her sentence.—
We will refer the hearing to the senate,
Who may at their best leisure censure you.
Take up his body: he in death hath paid
For all his cruelties. Here's the difference;
Good kings are mourn'd for after life; but ill,
And such as govern'd only by their will,
And not their reason, unlamented fall;
No good man's tear shed at their funeral.

    [*Exeunt; the Tribunes bearing the body of Cæsar.*[1]

[1] In this Tragedy Massinger seems to have aimed at something
particularly dignified and lofty. I do not know that he has
quite succeeded. The failure, however, arises not so much from
the subject as the characters. The portrait of Domitian, which
is too disgusting to excite much interest, might have been re-
lieved by some of those touches of accidental virtue which sometimes straggled across his vices; or the vices themselves might
have been made to enliven each other by contrast. History
would have supplied both these resources. But Massinger has
been content to represent him in the least varied part of his life,
when lust and cruelty had swallowed up all his faculties, extinguished every remembrance of virtue, and reduced him to a
loathsome mass of filth and fury. Now and then, indeed, we
meet with more movement and interest. During the tortures of
Rusticus and Sura (the horror of which reminds us of *the Virgin
Martyr*) the force of conscience is made to appear for a moment;
and while his assassination is preparing, he is fatally secure,
then falls into terror; is confident once more, and is presently
dispatched. The characters of the women are scarcely better
than that of Domitian. Their love is licentiousness; nor is
Domitilla, whose case would have allowed it, sufficiently distin-

guished from the rest. But the vengeance implored by Lamia
against his wife is well conducted. It is aptly fulfilled by herself in the progress of her own debaucheries.

Indeed Massinger's chief attention is bestowed on Paris. In
his favour the voice of history is raised far above the truth;
and in a scene of extraordinary animation he is made to defend
himself and the stage with all the dignity of patriotism, and the
intrepidity of conscious rectitude. Here we may reasonably
suppose the writer to have had some nearer meaning; and the
charge of Aretinus, and the refutation of it, Act I. Sc. iii. may
strengthen the suspicion expressed in the account given of *the
Bondman*. Another of these personal circumstances strikes us
at the very opening of this play. Paris had the wealth and the
honours of Rome at his command, but Massinger had too good
reason to complain that the " times were dull," and that the
profits of his profession hardly satisfied " the day's expense."

A word must be said of the " episodes," as they have been
termed. Mr. M. Mason has pronounced them tedious, and
Davies allows them to be incumbrances. It was their duty to
enquire whether the plot is assisted by them. If they had done
this with care, they must have found that the interlude ordered
for Philargus is the occasion of his death, and therefore con-
tributes to the assassination of Domitian through the vengeance
of Parthenius, who stabs him in the name of his murdered father.
It also begins the passion of Domitia for Paris, and hastens the
catastrophe, through her alienation from the emperor. The
other interludes promote the last effect only; but all of them
are more or less connected with the main subject, which they
tend to enliven and relieve. The only forgetfulness I observe,
is in the last act. The princesses are " confined to several
islands;" yet they appear without further notice, and partake
in the assassination of Domitian. However, this is very unusual
with Massinger, who is generally exact in arranging his subject,
and accounting for the minutest incidents of it.

A word more of the two conspirators, whose names have not
hitherto appeared among the dramatis personæ. Coxeter had
referred the reader to Suetonius for the materials of this play,
and asserted that Massinger had strictly copied him. This seems
to have satisfied Mr. M. Mason, who either did not look into
Suetonius, or, if he did, was prudently silent about characters
which he could not find. But Sejeius (Sigerius) and Entellus
are as much historical persons as Parthenius or any other. They
are expressly mentioned in this very affair by Dio Cassius, who
furnishes other particulars adopted by Massinger, and not to be
found in Suetonius. The first of them indeed he calls Sigerus;
but the true name has been recovered from Martial, who couples

it with that of Parthenius, lib. iv. 79. If the commentator be right, (or rather Grotius, to whom he refers,) Sigerius is also quoted by Tertullian as a name of boldness: but the edition which I use reads, *Stephanis atque Partheniis audaciores.* At all events, the passage informs us that the actors in this conspiracy were long remembered in Rome; where, however, was no want of names eminent in this bloody way. Indeed, insurrection was now taking a wider range ; and the Cassii, the Nigri, and the Albini had begun to eclipse the murderous fame of their humbler predecessors.

If, as I sincerely hope, the reader loves to see the pure and peaceful manners of Christianity amidst those scenes of treachery and blood, he will be gratified with the argument which led to the above allusion : *Unde qui inter duas lauros obsident Cæsarem?* (It is pleasing to discover the laurels of Augustus at the door of Pertinax,)*Unde qui faucibus ejus exprimendis palæstricam*exercent? Unde qui armati palatium irrumpunt, omnibus Stephanis atque Partheniis audaciores ? De Romanis, ni fallor, id est, de non Christianis. Apol. ad Gentes.*

---

* This allusion is explained by Victor's account of the murder of Commodus : *ab immisso validissimo palæstrita compressis faucibus expiravit.*

THE

GREAT DUKE OF FLORENCE.

THE GREAT DUKE OF FLORENCE.] "The Great Duke" was licensed by Sir H. Herbert " for the Queen's servants," July 5th, 1627. This, Mr. Malone conjectures, with every appearance of probability, to be the " COMICAL HISTORY" before us. The plot, if not Italian, is raised, perhaps, on the slight materials afforded by our old chroniclers in the life of Edgar, materials which we have since seen worked up by Mason into the beautiful drama of *Elfrida.*

This Play was not committed to the press till 1636, when it was preceded by two commendatory copies of verses by G. Donne and J. Ford. Though highly, and, indeed, deservedly, popular, it was not reprinted : this may be attributed, in some measure, to the growing discontent of the times, which perversely turned aside from scenes like these, to dwell with fearful anxiety on those of turbulence and blood.

It was acted " by her Majesty's servants at the Phœnix, in Drury Lane ;" where, the title adds, it was " often presented."

TO

The truly honoured, and my noble Favourer,

Sir ROBERT WISEMAN, Knt.*

OF THORRELL'S-HALL, IN ESSEX.

SIR,

AS I dare not be ungrateful for the many benefits you have heretofore conferred upon me, so I have just reason to fear that my attempting this way to make satisfaction (in some measure) for so due a debt, will further engage me. However, examples encourage me. The most able in my poor quality have made use of Dedications in this nature, to make the world take notice (as far as in them lay) who and what they were that gave supportment and protection to their studies, being more willing to publish the doer, than receive a benefit in a corner. For myself, I will freely, and with a zealous thankfulness, acknowledge, that for many years I had but faintly subsisted, if I had not often tasted of your bounty. But it is above my strength and faculties to celebrate to the desert your noble inclination, and that made actual, to raise up, or, to speak more properly, to rebuild the ruins of demolished poesie. But that is a work reserved, and will be, no doubt, undertaken, and finished, by one that can to the life express it. Accept, I beseech you, the tender of my service, and in the list of those you have obliged to you, contemn not the name of

Your true and faithful honourer,

PHILIP MASSINGER.

* Sir Robert Wiseman was the eldest son of Richard Wiseman, a merchant of London, who having acquired an ample fortune retired into Essex, in which county he possessed considerable estates, where he died in 1618, and was succeeded by Sir Robert. The friend of Massinger was the oldest of fourteen children, and a man of an amiable character. He died unmarried the 11th May, 1641, in his 65th year. GILCHRIST.

DRAMATIS PERSONÆ.

Cozimo,* *duke of* Florence.
Giovanni, *nephew to the duke.*
Sanazarro, *the duke's favourite.*
Carolo Charomonte, Giovanni's *tutor.*
Contarino, *secretary to the duke.*
Alphonso,
Hippolito, } *counsellors of state.*
Hieronimo,
Calandrino, *a merry fellow, servant to* Giovanni.
Bernardo.
Caponi, } *servants to* Charomonte.
Petruchio,
A Gentleman.

Fiorinda, *dutchess of* Urbin.
Lidia, *daughter to* Charomonte.
Calaminta, *servant to* Fiorinda.
Petronella, *a foolish servant to* Lidia.

Attendants, Servants, &c.

SCENE, *partly in* Florence, *and partly at the residence of* Charomonte *in the country.*

---

* *Cozimo,*] Coxeter spells this Cozim*a,* and Mr. M. Mason blindly follows him, as usual. It stands right in the old copy.

THE

GREAT DUKE OF FLORENCE.

ACT I. SCENE I.

The Country. A Room in Charomonte's House.

Enter CHAROMONTE *and* CONTARINO.

Char. You bring your welcome with you.
Cont. Sir, I find it
In every circumstance.
Char. Again most welcome.
Yet, give me leave to wish (and pray you, excuse
    me,
For I must use the freedom I was born with)
The great duke's pleasure had commanded you
To my poor house upon some other service;
Not this you are design'd to: but his will
Must be obey'd, howe'er it ravish from me
The happy conversation of one
As dear to me as the old Romans held
Their household Lars, whom[1] they believed had
    power
To bless and guard their families.
Cont. 'Tis received so
On my part, signior; nor can the duke

---

[1] *Their household Lars,* whom *they believed* &c.] Mr. M. Mason
chooses to read, of his own authority,
    Their household Lars, who, *they believed,* &c.

But promise to himself as much as may
Be hoped for from a nephew. And'twere weakness
In any man to doubt, that Giovanni,[2]
Train'd up by your experience and care
In all those arts peculiar and proper
To future greatness, of necessity
Must in his actions, being grown a man,
Make good the princely education
Which he derived from you.
  Char. I have discharged,
To the utmost of my power, the trust the duke
Committed to me, and with joy perceive
The seed of my endeavours was not sown
Upon the barren sands, but fruitful glebe,
Which yields a large increase: my noble charge,
By his sharp wit, and pregnant apprehension,
Instructing those that teach him; making use,
Not in a vulgar and pedantic form,
Of what's read to him, but 'tis straight digested,
And truly made his own. His grave discourse,
In one no more indebted unto years,
Amazes such as hear him: horsemanship,
And skill to use his weapon, are by practice
Familiar to him: as for knowledge in
Music, he needs it not, it being born with him;
All that he speaks being with such grace deliver'd,
That it makes perfect harmony.

 [2] *In any man to doubt that* Giovanni,] Giovanni is here used
as a quadrisyllable. This is incorrect, and shews that Massinger
had studied the language in books only: no Italian would or
could pronounce it in this manner. He makes the same mistake
in the name of the dutchess; Fiorinda is a trisyllable, yet he
adopts the division of poor Calandrino, and constantly pro-
nounces it Fi-o-rin-da; see p. 451. I observe the same mode of
pronunciation in Shirley: in *the Gentleman of Venice*, Giovanni
is almost always a quadrisyllable. Ford, more of a scholar
perhaps, adopts a similar method.

Cont. You describe
A wonder to me.
 Car. Sir, he is no less;
And that there may be nothing wanting that
May render him complete, the sweetness of
His disposition so wins on all
Appointed to attend him, that they are
Rivals, even in the coarsest office, who
Shall get precedency to do him service;
Which they esteem a greater happiness,
Than if they had been fashion'd and built up
To hold command o'er others.
 Cont. And what place
Does he now bless with his presence?
 Char. He is now
Running at the ring,[4] at which he's excellent.
He does allot for every exercise
A several hour; for sloth, the nurse of vices,
And rust of action, is a stranger to him.
But I fear I am tedious, let us pass,
If you please, to some other subject, though I
   cannot
Deliver him as he deserves.
 Cont. You have given him
A noble character.
 Char. And how, I pray you,
(For we, that never look beyond our villas,
Must be inquisitive,) are state affairs
Carried in court?
 Cont. There's little alteration:
Some rise, and others fall, as it stands with
The pleasure of the duke, their great disposer.
 Char. Does Lodovico Sanazarro hold
Weight, and grace with him?

[3] ——————— *He is now*
Running at the ring,] See p. 258.

Cont. Every day new honours
Are shower'd upon him, and without the envy
Of such as are good men; since all confess
The service done our master in his wars
'Gainst Pisa and Sienna may with justice
Claim what's conferr'd upon him.
    Char. 'Tis said nobly;
For princes never more make known their wisdom,
Than when they cherish goodness where they
    find it:
They being men, and not gods, Contarino,
They can give wealth and titles, but no virtues;
That is without their power. When they advance,
Not out of judgment, but deceiving fancy,
An undeserving man, howe'er set off
With all the trim of greatness, state, and power,
And of a creature even grown terrible
To him from whom he took his giant form,
This thing is still a comet, no true star;
And when the bounties feeding his false fire
Begin to fail, will of itself go out,
And what was dreadful, proves ridiculous.
But in our Sanazarro 'tis not so,
He being pure and tried gold; and any stamp
Of grace, to make him current to the world,
The duke is pleased to give him, will add honour
To the great bestower; for he, though allow'd
Companion to his master, still preserves
His majesty in full lustre.
    Cont. He, indeed,
At no part does take from it, but becomes
A partner of his cares, and eases him,
With willing shoulders, of a burthen which
He should alone sustain.
    Char. Is he yet married?
    Cont. No, signior, still a bachelor; howe'er
It is apparent that the choicest virgin

For beauty, bravery, and wealth, in Florence,
Would, with her parents glad consent, be won,
Were his affection and intent but known,
To be at his devotion.
   Char. So I think too.
But break we off—here comes my princely
   charge.

    Enter GIOVANNI *and* CALANDRINO.

Make your approaches boldly; you will find
A courteous entertainment.   [*Cont. kneels.*
   Giov. Pray you, forbear
My hand, good signior; 'tis a ceremony
Not due to me. 'Tis fit we should embrace
With mutual arms.
   Cont. It is a favour, sir,
I grieve to be denied.
   Giov. You shall o'ercome:
But 'tis your pleasure, not my pride, that grants
   it.
Nay, pray you, guardian, and good sir, put on:
How ill it shews to have that reverend head
Uncover'd to a boy!
   Char. Your excellence
Must give me liberty to observe the distance
And duty that I owe you.
   Giov. Owe me duty!
I do profess (and when I do deny it,
Good fortune leave me!) you have been to me
A second father, and may justly challenge,
For training up my youth in arts and arms,
As much respect and service, as was due
To him that gave me life. And did you know, sir,
Or will believe from me, how many sleeps
Good Charomonte hath broken, in his care
To build me up a man, you must confess

Chiron, the tutor to the great Achilles,
Compared with him, deserves not to be named.
And if my gracious uncle, the great duke,
Still holds me worthy his consideration,
Or finds in me aught worthy to be loved,
That little rivulet flow'd from this spring;
And so from me report him.

    Cont. Fame already
Hath fill'd his highness' ears with the true story
Of what you are, and how much better'd by him.
And 'tis his purpose to reward the travail
Of this grave sir, with a magnificent hand.
For, though his tenderness hardly could consent
To have you one hour absent from his sight,
For full three years he did deny himself
The pleasure he took in you, that you, here,
From this great master, might arrive unto
The theory of those high mysteries
Which you, by action, must make plain in court.
'Tis, therefore, his request, (and that, from him,
Your excellence must grant a strict command,)
That instantly (it being not five hours riding)
You should take horse and visit him. These his
    letters
Will yield you further reasons. [*Delivers a packet.*

    Cal. To the court!
Farewell the flower,[4] then, of the country's gar-
    land.
This is our sun, and when he's set, we must not
Expect or spring or summer, but resolve
For a perpetual winter.

    Char. Pray you, observe
               [*Giovanni reading the letters.*
The frequent changes in his face.

---

    4 *Farewell* the flower, *then*, of the country's garland.] I sup-
pose this to be the title of one of those innumerable *livres bleus*
that fluttered about the town in our author's time.

Cont. As if
His much unwillingness to leave your house
Contended with his duty.
 Char. Now he appears
Collected and resolved.
 Giov. It is the duke!
The duke, upon whose favour all my hopes
And fortunes do depend. Nor must I check
At his commands for any private motives
That do invite my stay here, though they are
Almost not to be master'd. My obedience,
In my departing suddenly, shall confirm
I am his highness' creature; yet, I hope
A little stay to take a solemn farewell
Of all those ravishing pleasures I have tasted
In this my sweet retirement, from my guardian,
And his incomparable daughter, cannot meet
An ill construction.
 Cont. I will answer that:
Use your own will.
 Giov. I would speak to you, sir,
In such a phrase as might express the thanks
My heart would gladly pay; but——
 Char. I conceive you:
And something I would say; but I must do it
In that dumb rhetoric which you make use of;
For I do wish you all——I know not how,
My toughness melts, and, spite of my discretion,
I must turn woman.   [*Embraces Giovanni.*
 Cont. What a sympathy
There is between them!
 Cal. Were I on the rack,
I could not shed a tear. But I am mad,
And, ten to one, shall hang myself for sorrow,
Before I shift my shirt. But hear you, sir,
(I'll separate you,) when you are gone, what will
Become of me?

Giov. Why, thou shalt to court with me.

[*Takes Char. aside.*

Cal. To see you worried ?

Cont. Worried, Calandrino !

Cal. Yes, sir : for, bring this sweet face to the court,
There will be such a longing 'mong the madams,
Who shall engross it first, nay, fight and scratch for't,
That, if they be not stopp'd, for entertainment
They'll kiss his lips off. Nay, if you'll scape so,
And not be tempted to a further danger,
These succubæ are so sharp set, that you must
Give out you are an eunuch.

Cont. Have a better
Opinion of court-ladies, and take care
Of your own stake.

Cal. For my stake, 'tis past caring.
I would not have a bird of unclean feathers
Handsel his lime twig,—and so much for him :
There's something else that troubles me.

Cont. What's that ?

Cal. Why, how to behave myself in court, and tightly.
I have been told the very place transforms men,
And that not one of a thousand, that before
Lived honestly in the country on plain salads,
But bring him thither, mark me that, and feed him
But a month or two with custards and court cake-bread,
And he turns knave immediately.—I'd be honest ;
But I must follow the fashion, or die a beggar.

Giov. And, if I ever reach my hopes, believe it,
We will share fortunes.

Char. This acknowledgement

Enter LIDIA.

Binds me your debtor ever.—Here comes one
In whose sad looks you easily may read
What her heart suffers, in that she is forced
To take her last leave of you.
    Cont. As I live,
A beauty without parallel!
    Lid. Must you go, then,
So suddenly?
    Giov. There's no evasion, Lidia,
To gain the least delay, though I would buy it
At any rate.   Greatness, with private men
Esteem'd a blessing, is to me a curse;
And we, whom, for our high births, they con-
      clude
The only freemen, are the only slaves.
Happy the golden mean! had I been born
In a poor sordid cottage, not nurs'd up
With expectation to command a court,
I might, like such of your condition, sweetest,
Have ta'en a safe and middle course, and not,
As I am now, against my choice, compell'd
Or to lie grovelling on the earth, or raised
So high upon the pinnacles of state,
That I must either keep my height with danger,
Or fall with certain ruin.
    Lid. Your own goodness
Will be your faithful guard.
    Giov. O, Lidia!——
    Cont. So passionate![5]   [*Aside.*
    Giov. For, had I been your equal,
I might have seen and liked with mine own eyes,

---

[5] *So* passionate!] So full of sorrow, so deeply affected. In
this sense the word perpetually occurs in our old writers.

And not, as now, with others ; I might still,
And without observation, or envy,
As I have done, continued my delights
With you, that are alone, in my esteem,
The abstract of society : we might walk
In solitary groves, or in choice gardens ;
From the variety of curious flowers
Contemplate nature's workmanship, and wonders:
And then, for change, near to the murmur of
Some bubbling fountain, I might hear you sing,
And, from the well-tuned accents of your tongue,
In my imagination conceive
With what melodious ·harmony a quire
Of angels sing above their Maker's praises.
And then with chaste discourse, as we return'd,
Imp[6] feathers to the broken wings of time :—
And all this I must part from.
    Cont. You forget
The haste imposed upon us.
    Giov. One word more,
And then I come. And after this, when, with
Continued innocence of love and service,
I had grown ripe for Hymeneal joys,
Embracing you, but with a lawful flame,
I might have been your husband.
    Lid. Sir, I was,
And ever am, your servant; but it was,
And 'tis, far from me in a thought to cherish
Such saucy hopes. If I had been the heir
Of all the globes and sceptres mankind bows to,
At my, best you had deserved me ; as I am,
Howe'er unworthy, in my virgin zeal
I wish you, as a partner of your bed,
A princess equal to you ; such a one
That may make it the study of her life,

   [6] Imp *feathers to the broken wings of time:*—] See p. 230.

With all the obedience of a wife, to please you.
May you have happy issue, and I live
To be their humblest handmaid !
   Giov. I am dumb,
And can make no reply.
   Cont. Your excellence
Will be benighted.
   Giov. This kiss, bathed in tears,
May learn you what I should say.
   Lid. Give me leave
To wait on you to your horse.
   Char. And me to bring you
To the one half of your journey.
   Giov. Your love puts
Your age to too much trouble.
   Char. I grow young,
When most I serve you.
   Cont. Sir, the duke shall thank you. [*Exeunt.*

SCENE II.

Florence.   *A Room in the Palace.*

Enter ALPHONSO, HIPPOLITO, *and* HIERONIMO.

   Alph. His highness cannot take it ill.
   Hip. However,
We with our duties shall express our care
For the safety of his dukedom.
   Hier And our loves

Enter COZIMO.

To his person.—Here he comes: present it boldly.
       [*They kneel, Alphonso tenders a paper.*

   Coz. What needs this form? We are not grown so proud
As to disdain familiar conference
With such as are to counsel and direct us.
This kind of adoration shew'd not well
In the old Roman emperors, who, forgetting
That they were flesh and blood, would be styled gods:
In us to suffer it, were worse. Pray you, rise.
                                    [*Reads.*
Still the old suit! With too much curiousness
You have too often search'd this wound, which yields
Security and rest, not trouble to me.
For here you grieve, that my firm resolution
Continues me a widower; and that
My want of issue to succeed me in
My government, when I am dead, may breed
Distraction in the state, and make the name
And family of the Medici, now admired,
Contemptible.
   Hip. And with strong reasons, sir.
   Alph. For, were you old, and past hope to beget
The model of yourself, we should be silent.
   Hier. But, being in your height and pride of years,
As you are now, great sir, and having, too,
In your possession the daughter of
The deceased duke of Urbin, and his heir,
Whose guardian you are made; were you but pleased
To think her worthy of you, besides children,
The dukedom she brings with her for a dower
Will yield a large increase of strength and power
To those fair territories which already
Acknowledge you their absolute lord.

Coz. You press us
With solid arguments, we grant; and, though
We stand not bound to yield account to any
Why we do this or that, (the full consent
Of our subjects being included in our will,)
We, out of our free bounties, will deliver
The motives that divert[7] us. You well know
That, three years since, to our much grief, we lost
Our dutchess; such a dutchess, that the world,
In her whole course of life,[8] yields not a lady
That can with imitation deserve
To be her second; in her grave we buried
All thoughts of woman: let this satisfy
For any second marriage. Now, whereas
You·name the heir of Urbin, as a princess
Of great revenues, 'tis confess'd she is so:
But for some causes, private to ourself,
We have disposed her otherwise. Yet despair
              not;
For you, ere long, with joy shall understand,
That in our princely care we have provided
One worthy to succeed us.

Enter SANAZARRO.

Hip. We submit,
And hold the counsels of great Cozimo
Oraculous.
    Coz. My Sanazarro!—Nay,
Forbear all ceremony. You look sprightly, friend,

---

[7] *The motives that* divert *us.*] i. e. *turn us aside* from following
your advice.
[8] ——————————— *that the world,*
    In her whole course of life, *yields not* &c.] This is awkwardly
expressed, a circumstance most unusual with Massinger; but
seems to mean, in her various excellencies and virtues. It is
strangely pointed in Coxeter and Mr. M. Mason.

And promise in your clear aspect some novel
That may delight us.

Sanaz. O sir, I would not be
The harbinger of aught that might distaste you;
And therefore know (for 'twere a sin to torture
Your highness' expectation) your vice-admiral,
By my directions, hath surprised the gallies
Appointed to transport the Asian tribute
Of the great Turk; a richer prize was never
Brought into Florence.

Coz. Still my nightingale,
That with sweet accents[9] dost assure me, that
My spring of happiness comes fast upon me!
Embrace me boldly. I pronounce that wretch
An enemy to brave and thriving action,
That dares believe but in a thought, we are
Too prodigal in our favours to this man,
Whose merits, though with him we should divide
Our dukedom, still continue us his debtor.

Hip. 'Tis far from me.

Alph. We all applaud it.

Coz. Nay, blush not, Sanazarro, we are proud
Of what we build up in thee; nor can our
Election be disparaged, since we have not
Received into our bosom and our grace

---

[9] Coz. *Still my* nightingale,
That with sweet accents &c] This seems to be from Jonson:

"I grant the linnet, lark, and bull-finch sing,
"But best the dear *good angel of the spring*,
"The *nightingale*."

Our old poets give this pleasing office to the nightingale with
great beauty and propriety; thus Sidney:

"The *nightingale*, so soon as *Aprill* bringeth
"Unto her rested sense a perfect waking,
"While late bare earth proud of new clothing springeth,
"Sings out her woes," &c.

The Greek poets, and their echoes, the Romans, usually gave
it to the swallow, and in this too there was propriety.

A glorious lazy drone,[1] grown fat with feeding
On others' toil, but an idustrious bee,
That crops the sweet flowers of our enemies,
And every happy evening returns
Loaden with wax and honey to our hive.

Sanaz. My best endeavours never can discharge
The service I should pay.

Coz. Thou art too modest ;
But we will study how to give, and when,

Enter GIOVANNI *and* CONTARINO.

Before it be demanded.——Giovanni !
My nephew ! let me eye thee better, boy.
In thee, methinks, my sister lives again ;
For her love I will be a father to thee,
For thou art my adopted son.

Giov. Your servant,
And humblest subject.

Coz. Thy hard travel, nephew,
Requires soft rest, and therefore we forbear,
For the present, an account how thou hast spent
Thy absent hours. See, signiors, see, our care,
Without a second bed, provides you of
A hopeful prince. Carry him to his lodgings,
And, for his further honour, Sanazarro,
With the rest, do you attend him.

Giov. All true pleasures
Circle your highness !

Sanaz. As the rising sun,
We do receive you.

Giov. May this never set,
But shine upon you ever !

   [*Exeunt Giovanni, Sanazarro, Hieronimo,*
    Alphonso, and Hippolito.

---

[1] *A* glorious *lazy drone,*] i. e. vain, empty, vaunting: see
Vol. I. p. 142.

Coz. Contarino!

Cont. My gracious lord.

Coz. What entertainment found you
From Carolo de Charomonte?

Cont. Free,
And bountiful. He's ever like himself,
Noble and hospitable.

Coz. But did my nephew
Depart thence willingly?

Cont. He obey'd your summons
As did become him. Yet it was apparent,
But that he durst not cross your will, he would
Have sojourn'd longer there, he ever finding
Variety of sweetest entertainment.
But there was something else; nor can I blame
His youth, though with some trouble he took
     leave
Of such a sweet companion.

Coz. Who was it?

Cont. The daughter, sir, of signior Carolo,
Fair Lidia, a virgin, at all parts,
But in her birth and fortunes, equal to him.
The rarest beauties Italy can make boast of,
Are but mere shadows to her, she the substance
Of all perfection. And what increases
The wonder, sir, her body's matchless form
Is better'd by the pureness of her soul.
Such sweet discourse, such ravishing behaviour,
Such charming language, such enchanting man-
     ners,
With a simplicity that shames all courtship,²
Flow hourly from her, that I do believe
Had Circe or Calypso her sweet graces,
Wandering Ulysses never had remember'd
Penelope, or Ithaca.

---

² *With a simplicity that shames all* courtship,] i. e. all court

Coz. Be not rapt so.

Cont. Your excellence would be so, had you
    seen her.

Coz. Take up, take up.[3]—But did your obser-
    vation
Note any passage of affection
Between her and my nephew?

Cont. How it should
Be otherwise between them, is beyond
My best imagination. Cupid's arrows
Were useless there; for, of necessity,
Their years and dispositions do accord so,
They must wound one another.

Coz. Umph! Thou art
My secretary, Contarino, and more skill'd
In politic designs of state, than in
Thy judgment of a beauty; give me leave,
In this, to doubt it.—Here. Go to my cabinet,
You shall find there letters newly received,
Touching the state of Urbin.

---

breeding. Davenant has profited of these beautiful lines, and
given his interesting Bertha many traits of Lidia:

    " She ne'er saw courts, yet courts could have undone
      " With untaught looks, and an unpractised heart:
    " Her nets the most prepared could never shun,
      " For nature spred them in the scorn of art.

    " She never had in busie cities bin,
      " Ne'er warm'd with hope, nor e'er allay'd with fears;
    " Not seeing punishment, could guess no sin,
      " And sin not seeing, ne'er had use of tears.

    " But here her father's precepts gave her skill,
      " Which with incessant business fill'd the hours;
    " In spring she gather'd blossoms for the still,
      " In autumn berries, and in summer flowers."

[3] *Coz. Take up, take up.*—] i. e. stop, check yourself: This
sense of the word, which is not uncommon, does not occur among
the numerous examples collected by Johnson.

Pray you, with care peruse them : leave the search
Of this to us.
    Cont. I do obey in all things.   [*Exit.*
    Coz. Lidia ! a diamond so long conceal'd,
And never worn in court ! of such sweet feature !
And he on whom I fix my dukedom's hopes
Made captive to it ! Umph ! 'tis somewhat strange.
Our eyes are every where, and we will make
A strict enquiry.—Sanazarro !

Re-enter SANAZARRO.

    Sanaz. Sir.
    Coz. Is my nephew at his rest ?
    Sanaz. I saw him in bed, sir.
    Coz. 'Tis well ; and does the princess Fiorinda,
Nay, do not blush, she is rich Urbin's heir,
Continue constant in her favours to you ?
    Sanaz. Dread sir, she may dispense them as she
        pleases ;
But I look up to her as on a princess
I dare not be ambitious of, and hope
Her prodigal graces shall not render me
Offender to your highness.[3]
    Coz. Not a scruple.
He whom I favour, as I do my friend,
May take all lawful graces that become him :
But touching this hereafter. I have now
(And though perhaps it may appear a trifle)
Serious employment for thee.
    Sanaz. I stand ready
For any act you please.
    Coz. I know it, friend.

---

    [3] Offender *to your highness.*] Mr. M. Mason reads *offending ;*
the word that I have inserted is nearer the old copy, which ex-
hibits, Offended *to your highness.*

Have you ne'er heard of Lidia, the daughter
Of Carolo Charomonte?
    Sanaz. Him I know, sir,
For a noble gentleman, and my worthy friend;
But never heard of her.
    Coz. She is deliver'd,
And feelingly to us by Contarino,
For a masterpiece in nature. I would have you
Ride suddenly thither to behold this wonder,
But not as sent by us; that's our first caution:
The second is, and carefully observe it,
That, though you are a bachelor, and endow'd with
All those perfections that may take a virgin,
On forfeit of our favour do not tempt her:
It may be her fair graces do concern us.
Pretend what business you think fit, to gain
Access unto her father's house, and, there,
Make full discovery of her, and return me
A true relation:—I have some ends in it,
With which we will acquaint you.
    Sanaz. This is, sir,
An easy task.
    Coz. Yet one that must exact
Your secrecy and diligence. Let not
Your stay be long.
    Sanaz. It shall not, sir.
    Coz. Farewell,
And be, as you would keep our favour, careful.
                              [*Exeunt.*

ACT II. SCENE I.

The same.   A Room in Fiorinda's *House.*

Enter FIORINDA *and* CALAMINTA.

Fior. How does this dressing shew?
Calam. 'Tis of itself
Curious and rare; but, borrowing ornament,
As it does from your grace, that deigns to were it,
Incomparable.
   Fior. Thou flatter'st me.
   Calam. I cannot,
Your excellence is above it.
   Fior. Were we less perfect,
Yet, being as we are, an absolute princess,
We of necessity must be chaste, wise, fair,
By our prerogative!—yet all these fail
To move where I would have them. How received
Count Sanazarro the rich scarf I sent him
For his last visit?
   Calam. With much reverence,
I dare not say affection. He express'd
More ceremony in his humble thanks,
Than feeling of the favour; and appear'd
Wilfully ignorant, in my opinion,
Of what it did invite him to.
   Fior. No matter;
He's blind with too much light.* Have you not
     heard
Of any private mistress he's engaged to?
   Calam. Not any; and this does amaze me,
     madam,

---

* *He's blind with too much light.*] Ennobled by Milton—
" dark with excess of light."

That he, a soldier, one that drinks rich wines,
Feeds high, and promises as much as Venus
Could wish to find from Mars, should in his
    manners
Be so averse to women.
  Fior. Troth, I know not;
He's man enough, and, if he has a haunt,
He preys far off, like a subtle fox.
  Calam. And that way
I do suspect him: for I learnt last night,
When the great duke went to rest, attended by
One private follower, he took horse; but whither
He's rid, or to what end, I cannot guess at,
But I will find it out.
  Fior. Do, faithful servant;

      Enter CALANDRINO.

We would not be abused.—Who have we here?
  Calam. How the fool stares!
  Fior. And looks as if he were
Conning his neck-verse.
  Cal. If I now prove perfect
In my A B C of courtship, Calandrino
Is made for ever. I am sent—let me see,
On a *How d'ye*, as they call't.
  Calam. What wouldst thou say?
  Cal. Let me see my notes. These are her lodg-
    ings; well.
  Calam. Art thou an ass?
  Cal. Peace! thou art a court wagtail,
             [*Looking on his instructions.*
To interrupt me.
  Fior. He has given it you.
  Cal. *And then say to the illustrious Fi-o-rin-da—*
I have it. Which is she?
  Calam. Why this; fop-doodle.

Cal. Leave chattering, bull-finch; you would
    put me out,
But 'twill not do.—*Then, after you have made*
Your three obeisances to her, kneel, and kiss
The skirt of her gown.—I am glad it is no worse.
  Calam. And why so, sir?
  Cal. Because I was afraid
That, after the Italian garb, I should
Have kiss'd her backward.
  Calam. This is sport unlook'd for.
  Cal. Are you the princess?
  Fior. Yes, sir.
  Cal. Then stand fair,
For I am choleric; and do not nip
A hopeful blossom. Out again :—*Three low*
Obeisances --
  Fior. I am ready.
  Cal. I come on, then.
  Calam. With much formality.
  Cal. Umph! One, two, three.
                 [*Makes antic curtesies.*
Thus far I am right. Now for the last. [*Kisses the*
    skirt of her gown.]—O, rare!
She is perfumed all over! Sure great women,
Instead of little dogs, are privileged
To carry musk-cats.
  Fior. Now the ceremony
Is pass'd, what is the substance?
  Cal. I'll peruse
My instructions, and then tell you.—*Her skirt*
  kiss'd,
Inform her highness that your lord ——
  Calam. Who's that?
  Cal. Prince Giovanni, who entreats your grace,
That he, with your good favour, may have leave
To present his service to you. I think I have
    nick'd it
For a courtier of the first form.

Fior. To my wonder.

Enter GIOVANNI *and a* Gentleman.

Return unto the prince—but he prevents
My answer. Calaminta, take him off;
And, for the neat delivery of his message,
Give him ten ducats: such rare parts as yours
Are to be cherish'd.

   Cal. We will share: I know
It is the custom of the court, when ten
Are promised, five is fair. Fie! fie! the princess
Shall never know it, so you dispatch me quickly,
And bid me not come to morrow.

   Calam. Very good, sir.
        [Exeunt Calandrino and Calaminta.

   Giov. Pray you, friend,
Inform the duke I am putting into act
What he commanded.

   Gent. I am proud to be employ'd, sir.   *[Exit.*

   Giov. Madam, that, without warrant, I pre-
     sume
To trench upon your privacies, may argue
Rudeness of manners; but the free access
Your princely courtesy vouchsafes to all
That come to pay their services, gives me hope
To find a gracious pardon.

   Fior. If you please, not
To make that an offence in your construction,
Which I receive as a large favour from you,
There needs not this apology.

   Giov. You continue,
As you were ever, the greatest mistress of
Fair entertainment.

   Fior. You are, sir, the master;
And in the country have learnt to outdo
All that in court is practised. But why should we

Talk at such distance? You are welcome, sir.
We have been more familiar, and since
You will impose the province (you should govern)
Of boldness on me, give me leave to say
You are too punctual. Sit, sir, and discourse
As we were used.
   Giov. Your excellence knows so well
How to command, that I can never err
When I obey you.
   Fior. Nay, no more of this.
You shall o'ercome; no more, I pray you, sir.—
And what delights, pray you be liberal
In your relation, hath the country life
Afforded you?
   Giov. All pleasures, gracious madam,
But the happiness to converse with your sweet
     virtues.
I had a grave instructor, and my hours
Design'd to serious studies yielded me
Pleasure with profit, in the knowledge of
What before I was ignorant in; the signior,
Carolo de Charomonte, being skilful
To guide me through the labyrinth of wild pas-
     sions,
That labour'd to imprison my free soul
A slave to vicious sloth.
   Fior. You speak him well.
   Giov. But short of his deserts. Then for the
     time
Of recreation, I was allow'd
(Against the form follow'd by jealous parents
In Italy) full liberty to partake
His daughter's sweet society. She's a virgin
Happy in all endowments which a poet
Could fancy in his mistress; being herself
A school of goodness, where chaste maids may
     learn,

Without the aids of foreign principles,
By the example of her life and pureness,
To be as she is, excellent.   I but give you
A brief epitome of her virtues, which,
Dilated on at large, and to their merit,
Would make an ample story.

    Fior. Your whole age,
So spent with such a father, and a daughter,
Could not be tedious to you.

    Giov. True, great princess:
And now, since you have pleased to grant the
       hearing
Of my time's expense in the country, give me
       leave
To entreat the favour to be made acquainted
What service, or what objects in the court,
Have, in your excellency's acceptance, proved
Most gracious to you.

    Fior. I'll meet your demand,
And make a plain discovery.   The duke's care
For my estate and person holds the first
And choicest place: then, the respect the courtiers
Pay gladly to me, not to be contemn'd.
But that which raised in me the most delight,
(For I am a friend to valour,) was to hear
The noble actions truly reported
Of the brave count Sanazarro.   I profess,
When it hath been, and fervently, deliver'd,
How boldly, in the horror of a fight,
Cover'd with fire and smoke, and, as if nature
Had lent him wings, like lightning he hath fallen
Upon the Turkish gallies, I have heard it
With a kind of pleasure, which hath whisper'd
       to me,
This worthy must be cherish'd.

    Giov. 'Twas a bounty
You never can repent.

Fior. I glory in it.
And when he did return, (but still with conquest)
His armour off, not young Antinous
Appear'd more courtly; all the graces that
Render a man's society dear to ladies,
Like pages waiting on him; and it does
Work strangely on me.
    Giov. To divert your thoughts,
Though they are fix'd upon a noble subject,
I am a suitor to you.
    Fior. You will ask,
I do presume, what I may grant, and then
It must not be denied.
    Giov. It is a favour
For which I hope your excellence will thank me.
    Fior. Nay, without circumstance.
    Giov. That you would please
To take occasion to move the duke,
That you, with his allowance, may command
This matchless virgin, Lidia, (of whom
I cannot speak too much,) to wait upon you.
She's such a one, upon the forfeit of
Your good opinion of me, that will not
Be a blemish to your train.
    Fior. 'Tis rank! he love's her:
But I will fit him with a suit. [*Aside.*]—I pause not,
As if it bred or doubt or scruple in me
To do what you desire, for I'll effect it,
And make use of a fair and fit occasion;
Yet, in return, I ask a boon of you,
And hope to find you, in your grant to me,
As I have been to you.
    Giov. Command me, madam.
    Fior. 'Tis near allied to yours. That you would
      be
A suitor to the duke, not to expose,
After so many trials of his faith,

The noble Sanazarro to all dangers,
As if he were a wall to stand the fury
Of a perpetual battery : but now
To grant him, after his long labours, rest
And liberty to live in court; his arms
And his victorious sword and shield hung up
For monuments.
 Giov. Umph!—I'll embrace, fair princess,

     Enter Cozimo.

The soonest opportunity. The duke!
 Coz. Nay, blush not ; we smile on your privacy,
And come not to disturb you. You are equals,
And, without prejudice to either's honours,
May make a mutual change of love and courtship,
Till you are made one, and with holy rites,
And we give suffrage to it.
 Giov. You are gracious.
 Coz. To ourself in this: but now break off; too
  much
Taken at once of the most curious viands,
Dulls the sharp edge of appetite. We are now
For other sports, in which our pleasure is
That you shall keep us company.
 Fior. We attend you.   [*Exeunt.*

SCENE II.

The Country. *A Hall in* Charomonte's *House.*

Enter Bernardo, Caponi, *and* Petruchio,

 Bern. Is my lord stirring ?
 Cap. No ; he's fast.
 Pet. Let us take, then,

Our morning draught. Such as eat store of beef,
Mutton, and capons, may preserve their healths
With that thin composition call'd small beer,
As, 'tis said, they do in England. But Italians,
That think when they have supp'd upon an olive,
A root, or bunch of raisins, 'tis a feast,
Must kill those crudities rising from cold herbs,
With hot and lusty wines.
    Cap. A happiness
Those tramontanes[5] ne'er tasted.
    Bern. Have they not
Store of wine there?
    Cap. Yes, and drink more in two hours
Than the Dutchmen or the Dane in four and
    twenty.
    Pet. But what is't? French trash, made of
    rotten grapes,
And dregs and lees of Spain, with Welsh me-
    theglin,
A drench to kill a horse! But this pure nectar,
Being proper to our climate, is too fine
To brook the roughness of the sea: the spirit

---

[5] *Those* tramontanes *ne'er tasted.*] i. e. those *strangers*, those
barbarians: so the Italians called, and still call, all who live beyond the Alps, *ultra montes.* In a subsequent speech, the author does not forget to satirize the acknowledged propensity of
his countrymen to drinking: " Your *Dane*, your German, and
your swag-bellied *Hollander*, are nothing to your Englishman."
    If Caponi, as well as Iago, be not, however, too severe upon us,
it must be confessed that our ancestors were apt scholars, and soon
bettered the instructions which they received. Sir Richard
Baker, (as Mr. Gilchrist observes,) treating of the wars in the
Low-Countries about the end of the sixteenth century, says,
" Here it must not be omitted, that the English (who, of all the
dwellers in the northern parts of the world, were hitherto the
least drinkers, and deservedly praised for their sobriety,) in
these Dutch wars learned to be drunkards, and brought the vice
so far to overspread the kingdom, that laws were fain to be
enacted for repressing it." *Chron.* fol. p. 382.

Of this begets in us quick apprehensions,
And active executions; whereas their
Gross feeding makes their understanding like it :
They can fight, and that's their all. [*They drink.*

Enter SANAZARRO *and* Servant.

Sanaz. Security
Dwells about this house, I think ; the gate's wide
    open,
And not a servant stirring. See the horses
Set up, and clothed.
    Serv. I shall, sir.   [*Exit.*
    Sanaz. I'll make bold
To press a little further.
    Bern. Who is this,
Count Sanazarro ?
    Pet. Yes, I know him.   Quickly
Remove the flaggon.
    Sanaz. A good day to you, friends.
Nay, do not conceal your physic; I approve it,
And, if you please, will be a patient with you.
    Pet. My noble lord.   [*Drinks.*
    Sanaz. A health to yours. [*Drinks.*] Well done !
I see you love yourselves, and I commend you ;
'Tis the best wisdom.
    Pet. May it please your honour
To walk a turn in the gallery, I'll acquaint
My lord with your being here.   [*Exit.*
    Sanaz. Tell him I come
For a visit only. 'Tis a handsome pile this. [*Exit.*
    Cap. Why here is a brave fellow, and a right
    one ;
Nor wealth nor greatness makes him proud.
    Bern. There are
Too few of them ; for most of our new courtiers,
(Whose fathers were familiar with the prices

Of oil and corn, with when and where to vent
    them,
And left their heirs rich, from their knowledge
    that way,)
Like gourds shot up in a night, disdain to speak
But to cloth of tissue.

Enter CHAROMONTE *in a nightgown,* PETRUCHIO
following.

Char. Stand you prating, knaves,
When such a guest is under my roof! See all
The rooms perfumed. This is the man that carries
The sway and swing of the court; and I had rather
Preserve him mine with honest offices, than——
But I'll make no comparisons. Bid my daughter
Trim herself up to the height; I know this courtier
Must have a smack at her; and, perhaps, by his
    place,
Expects to wriggle further: if he does,
I shall deceive his hopes; for I'll not taint
My honour for the dukedom. Which way went he?
  Cap. To the round gallery.
  Char. I will entertaim him
As fits his worth and quality, but no further.
                       [Exeunt.

SCENE III.

A Gallery in the same.

Enter SANAZARRO.

Sanaz. I cannot apprehend, yet I have argued
All ways I can imagine, for what reasons
The great duke does employ me hither; and,
What does increase the miracle, I must render

A strict and true account, at my return,
Of Lidia, this lord's daughter, and describe
In what she's excellent, and where defective.
'Tis a hard task : he that will undergo
To make a judgment of a woman's beauty,
And see through all her plasterings and paintings,
Had need of Lynceus' eyes, and with more ease
May look, like him, through nine mud walls, than
      make
A true discovery of her.   But the intents
And secrets of my prince's heart must be
Served, and not search'd into.

          Enter CHAROMONTE.

  Char. Most noble sir,
Excuse my age, subject to ease and sloth,
That with no greater speed I have presented
My service with your welcome.
  Sanaz. 'Tis more fit
That I should ask your pardon, for disturbing
Your rest at this unseasonable hour.
But my occasions carrying me so near
Your hospitable house, my stay being short too,
Your goodness, and the name of friend, which you
Are pleased to grace me with, gave me assurance
A visit would not offend.
  Char. Offend, my lord !
I feel myself much younger for the favour.
How is it with our gracious master?
  Sanaz. He, sir,
Holds still his wonted greatness, and confesses
Himself your debtor, for your love and care
To the prince Giovanni ; and had sent
Particular thanks by me, had his grace known
The quick dispatch of what I was design'd to
Would have licensed me to see you.

Char. I am rich
In his acknowledgment.
 Sanaz. Sir, I have heard
Your happiness in a daughter.
 Char. Sits the wind there ?   [*Aside.*
 Sanaz. Fame gives her out for a rare master-
  piece.
 Char. 'Tis a plain village girl, sir, but obe-
  dient;
That's her best beauty, sir.
 Sanaz. Let my desire
To see her, find a fair construction from you:
I bring no loose thought with me.
 Char. You are that way,
My lord, free from suspicion. Her own manners,
Without an imposition from me,
I hope, will prompt her to it.

   Enter LIDIA *and* PETRONELLA.

         As she is,
She comes to make a tender of that service
Which she stands bound to pay.
 Sanaz. With your fair leave,
I make bold to salute you.
 Lid. Sir, you have it.
 Petron. I am her gentlewoman, will he not
  kiss me too?
This is coarse, i'faith.   [*Aside.*
 Char. How he falls off!
 Lid. My lord, though silence best becomes a
  maid,
And to be curious to know but what
Concerns myself, and with becoming distance,
May argue me of boldness, I must borrow
So much of modesty, as to enquire
Prince Giovanni's health.

Sanaz. He cannot want
What you are pleased to wish him.
Lid. Would 'twere so!
And then there is no blessing that can make
A hopeful and a noble prince complete,
But should fall on him. O! he was our north star,
The light and pleasure of our eyes.
Sanaz. Where am I?
I feel myself another thing! Can charms
Be writ on such pure rubies?[6] her lips melt
As soon as touch'd! Not those smooth gales that
    glide
O'er happy Araby, or rich Sabæa,[7]
Creating in their passage gums and spices,
Can serve for a weak simile to express
The sweetness of her breath. Such a brave stature
Homer bestow'd on Pallas, every limb
Proportion'd to it!
Char. This is strange.—My lord!
Sanaz. I crave your pardon, and yours, match-
    less maid,
For such I must report you.
Petron. There's no notice
Taken all this while of me.   *[Aside.*
Sanaz. And I must add,
If your discourse and reason parallel

---

6   ——— *Can charms*
Be writ on such pure rubies?] This, I believe, alludes to a very
old opinion, that some sorts of gems, (from an inherent sanctity,)
could not be profaned, or applied to the purposes of magic.
The notion took its rise probably from some superstitious ideas
respecting the precious stones employed in the breastplate of
the high-priest of the Jews.
7 *O'er happy* Araby,] So the quarto. Coxeter and Mr. M.
Mason have blundered it into prose; they read, *O'er happy*
Arabia! In *the New way to pay old Debts,* this beautiful simile
occurs again.

The rareness of your more than human form,
You are a wonder.

Char. Pray you, my lord, make trial:
She can speak, I can assure you; and that my
    presence
May not take from her freedom, I will leave you:
For know, my lord, my confidence dares trust
    her
Where, and with whom, she pleases.——If he be
Taken the right way with her, I cannot fancy
A better match; and, for false play, I know
The tricks, and can discern them.—Petronella.

Petron. Yes, my good lord.

Char. I have employment for you.

> [*Exeunt Charomonte and Petronella.*

Lid. What's your will, sir?

Sanaz. Madam, you are so large a theme to
    treat of,
And every grace about you offers to me
Such copiousness of language, that I stand
Doubtful which first to touch at. If I err,
As in my choice I may, let me entreat you,
Before I do offend, to sign my pardon:
Let this, the emblem of your innocence,
Give me assurance.

Lid. My hand join'd to yours,
Without this superstition, confirms it.
Nor need I fear you will dwell long upon me,
The barrenness of the subject yielding nothing
That rhetoric, with all her tropes and figures,
Can amplify. Yet since you are resolved
To prove yourself a courtier in my praise,
As I'm a woman (and you men affirm
Our sex loves to be flatter'd) I'll endure it.

Enter CHAROMONTE *above.*

Now, when you please, begin.
   Sanaz. [*turning from her.*] Such Læda's paps
      were,—
(Down pillows styled by Jove,) and their pure
      whiteness
Shames the swan's down, or snow. No heat of lust
Swells up her azure veins; and yet I feel
That this chaste ice but touch'd fans fire in me.
   Lid. You need not, noble sir, be thus trans-
      ported,
Or trouble your invention to express
Your thought of me: the plainest phrase and
      language
That you can use, will be too high a strain
For such an humble theme.
   Sanaz. If the great duke
Made this his end to try my constant temper,
Though I am vanquish'd, 'tis his fault, not mine:
For I am flesh and blood, and have affections
Like other men. Who can behold the temples,
Or holy altars, but the objects work
Devotion in him? And I may as well
Walk over burning iron with bare feet,
And be unscorch'd, as look upon this beauty
Without desire, and that desire pursued too,
Till it be quench'd with the enjoying those
Delights, which to achieve, danger is nothing,
And loyalty but a word.
   Lid. I ne'er was proud;
Nor can find I am guilty of a thought
Deserving this neglect and strangeness from you:
Nor am I amorous.[8]

   [8] *Nor am I* amorous.] This would be a *strange* declaration
for Lidia to make, when Sanazarro had said nothing to her on

Sanaz. Suppose his greatness
Loves her himself, why makes he choice of me
To be his agent? It is tyranny
To call one pinch'd with hunger to a feast,
And at that instant cruelly deny him
To taste of what he sees. Allegiance
Tempted too far is like the trial of
A good sword on an anvil; as that often
Flies in pieces without service to the owner,
So trust enforced too far proves treachery,
And is too late repented.
    Lid. Pray you, sir,
Or license me to leave you, or deliver
The reasons which invite you to command
My tedious waiting on you.
    Char. As I live,
I know not what to think on't. Is't his pride,
Or his simplicity?
    Sanaz. Whither have my thoughts
Carried me from myself? In this my dulness,
I've lost an opportunity——
                      [*Turns to her; she falls off.*
    Lid. 'Tis true,
I was not bred in court, nor live a star there;
Nor shine in rich embroideries and pearl,
As they, that are the mistresses of great fortunes,
Are every day adorn'd with——

the subject of love; these words, therefore, must be considered
as the begining of a sentence that is left unfinished, and should
be printed thus:
              Nor am I amorous ——— M. MASON.
However "*strange* the declaration" may be, it is actually
made : nor is there the smallest necessity for supposing the sentence to be incomplete. Lidia simply means, I am not apt to
be inflamed at first sight; and the remark is perfectly natural, in her uncertainty respecting the motives of Sanazarro's
conduct.

Sanaz. Will you vouchsafe
Your ear, sweet lady?
  Lid. Yet I may be bold,
For my integrity and fame, to rank
With such as are more glorious. Though I never
Did injury, yet I am sensible
When I'm contemn'd, and scorn'd.
  Sanaz. Will you please to hear me?
  Lid. O the difference of natures! Giovanni,
A prince in expectation, when he lived here,
Stole courtesy from heaven,⁹ and would not to

---

⁹ ―――――――― *Giovanni,*
A prince in expectation, when he lived here,
Stole courtesy from heaven, &c.] This is from Shakspeare,
and the plain meaning of the phrase is, that the affability and
sweetness of Giovanni were of a *heavenly* kind, i. e. more perfect than was usually found among men; resembling that divine
condescension which excludes none from its regard, and therefore immediately derived or *stolen* from heaven, from whence all
good proceeds. In this there is no impropriety: common usage
warrants the application of the term to a variety of actions
which imply nothing of turpitude, but rather the contrary: affections are *stolen*—in a word, to *steal*, here, and in many other
places, means little else than to win by imperceptible progres-
sion, by gentle violence, &c.
  I mention this, because it appears to me that the commentators on our great poet have altogether mistaken him:

  " And then I *stole all courtesy from heaven,*
  " And dress'd myself in such humility,
  " That I did pluck allegiance from men's hearts."
                          Hen. IV. Part I. Act. III. sc. ii

  " This," says Warburton, who is always too refined for his subject, " is an allusion to the story of Prometheus, who stole fire
from thence; and as with *this* he made a man, so with *that* Bo-
lingbroke made a king." If there be any allusion to the story,
(which I will not deny,) it is of the most remote and obscure
kind: the application of it, however, is surely too absurd for serious notice. Steevens supposes the meaning to be,—" I was so
affable, that I engrossed the devotion and reverence of all men
to myself, and thus *defrauded heaven of its worshippers*." Is heaven
worshipped with " affability?" or have politeness and elegance

The meanest servant in my father's house
Have kept such distance.
 Sanaz. Pray you, do not think me
Unworthy of your ear; it was your beauty
That turn'd me statue. I can speak, fair lady.
 Lid. And I can hear. The harshness of your
  courtship
Cannot corrupt my courtesy.
 Sanaz. Will you hear me,
If I speak of love?
 Lid. Provided you be modest;
I were uncivil, else.
 Char. They are come to parley:
I must observe this nearer.   [*He retires.*
 Sanaz. You are a rare one,
And such (but that my haste commands me hence)
I could converse with ever. Will you grace me
With leave to visit you again?
 Lid. So you,
At your return to court, do me the favour
To make a tender of my humble service
To the prince Giovanni.
 Sanaz. Ever touching
Upon that string! [*Aside.*] And will you give me
  hope
Of future happiness?
 Lid. That, as I shall find you:
The fort that's yielded at the first assault
Is hardly worth the taking.

of manners such irresistible charms, that, when found below,
they must of necessity " engross all *devotion*," and exclude the
Deity from our thoughts?—This is not the language, nor are
these the ideas of Shakspeare: and it would well become the
critics to pause before they seriously disgrace him with such impious absurdities.

Re-enter CHAROMONTE *below.*

Char. O, they are at it.

Sanaz. She is a magazine of all perfection,
And 'tis death to part from her, yet I must—
A parting kiss, fair maid.

Lid. That custom grants you.

Char. A homely breakfast does attend your
    lordship,
Such as the place affords.

Sanaz. No ; I have feasted
Already here ; my thanks, and so I leave you :
I will see you again.—Till this unhappy hour
I was never lost, and what to do, or say,
I have not yet determined.   [*Aside, and exit.*

  Char. Gone so abruptly !
'Tis very strange.

    Lid. Under your favour, sir,
His coming hither was to little purpose,
For any thing I heard from him.

    Char. Take heed, Lidia !
I do advise you with a father's love,
And tenderness of your honour ; as I would not
Have you coarse and harsh in giving entertain-
    ment,
So by no means to be credulous : for great men,
Till they have gain'd their ends, are giants in
Their promises, but, those obtain'd, weak pigmies
In their performance. And it is a maxim
Allow'd among them, so they may deceive,
They may swear any thing ; for the queen of
    love,
As they hold constantly, does never punish,

VOL. II.   * K k

But smile, at lovers' perjuries.'—Yet be wise too,
And when you are sued to in a noble way,
Be neither nice nor scrupulous.
    Lid. All you speak, sir,
I hear as oracles ; nor will digress
From your directions.
    Char. So shall you keep
Your fame untainted.
    Lid. As I would my life, sir.   [*Exeunt.*

ACT III. SCENE I.

Florence.   *An ante Room in the Palace.*

Enter SANAZARRO *and* Servant.

Sanaz. Leave the horses with my grooms ; but
    be you careful,
With your best diligence and speed, to find out
The prince, and humbly, in my name, entreat
I may exchange some private conference with
    him
Before the great duke know of my arrival.

———————— *for the queen of love,*
As they hold constantly, does never punish,
But smile, at lovers' perjuries—]
    Ridet hoc. inquam, Venus ipsa.
It would be as well if the queen of love had been a little more
fastidious on this subject. Her facility, I fear, has done much
mischief, as lovers of all ages have availed themselves of it:
but she had it from her father, whose laxity of principle is well
known :
    ———————— *perjuria ridet amantûm*
    Jupiter.

Serv. I haste, my lord.

Sanaz. Here I'll attend his coming :
And see you keep yourself, as much as may be,
Conceal'd from all men else.

Serv. To serve your lordship,
I wish I were invisible.   [*Exit.*

Sanaz. I am driven
Into a desperate strait, and cannot steer
A middle course ; and of the two extremes
Which I must make election of, I know not
Which is more full of horror.   Never servant
Stood more engaged to a magnificent master,
Than I to Cozimo : and all those honours
And glories by his grace conferr'd upon me,
Or by my prosperous services deserved,
If now I should deceive his trust, and make
A shipwreck of my loyalty, are ruin'd.
And, on the other side, if I discover
Lidia's divine perfections, all my hopes
In her are sunk, never to be buoy'd up :
For 'tis impossible, but, as soon as seen,
She must with adoration be sued to.
A hermit at his beads but looking on her,
Or the cold cynic, whom Corinthian Laïs
(Not moved with her lust's blandishments) call'd
        a stone,
At this object would take fire.   Nor is the duke
Such an Hippolytus, but that this Phædra,
But seen, must force him to forsake the groves,
And Dian's huntmanship, proud to serve under
Venus' soft ensigns.   No, there is no way
For me to hope. fruition of my ends,
But to conceal her beauties ;—and how that
May be effected, is as hard a task
As with a veil to cover the sun's beams,
Or comfortable light.   Three years the prince
Lived in her company, and Contarino,

        * K k 2

The secretary, hath possess'd[2] the duke
What a rare piece she is :—but he's my creature,
And may with ease be frighted to deny
What he hath said : and, if my long experience,
With some strong reasons I have thought upon,
Cannot o'er-reach a youth, my practice yields me
But little profit.

Enter GIOVANNI *with the* Servant.

Giov. You are well return'd, sir.
Sanaz. Leave us.—[*Exit Servant.*] When that
     your grace shall know the motives
That forced me to invite you to this trouble,
You will excuse my manners.
Giov. Sir, there needs not
This circumstance between us. You are ever
My noble friend.
Sanaz. You shall have further cause
To assure you of my faith and zeal to serve you.
And, when I have committed to your trust
(Presuming still on your retentive silence)
A secret of no less importance than
My honour, nay, my head, it will confirm
What value you hold with me.
Giov. Pray you, believe, sir,
What you deliver to me shall be lock'd up
In a strong cabinet, of which you yourself
Shall keep the key: for here I pawn my honour,
Which is the best security I can give yet,
It shall not be discover'd.

<hr>

[2] ————— *hath* possess'd *the duke*
What a rare piece she is :] i. e. acquainted, or informed. In
this sense the word perpetually occurs in our old writers. Thus
in *the City Nightcap:* "You, sirrah, we are *possess'd,* were
their pander." Again, in *the City Match:*
    "She is *possess'd*
    "What streams of gold you flow in."

Sanaz. This assurance
Is more than I with modesty could demand
From such a paymaster; but I must be sudden:
And therefore, to the purpose. Can your Excel-
    lence,
In your imagination, conceive
On what design, or whither, the duke's will
Commanded me hence last night?
    Giov. No, I assure you;
And it had been a rudeness to enquire
Of that I was not call'd to.
    Sanaz Grant me hearing,
And I will make you truly understand
It only did concern you.
    Giov. Me, my lord!
    Sanaz. You, in your present state, and future
    fortunes;
For both lie at the stake.
    Giov. You much amaze me.
Pray you, resolve this riddle.
    Sanaz. You know the duke,
If he die issueless, as yet he is,
Determines you his heir.
    Giov. It hath pleased his highness
Oft to profess so much.
    Sanaz. But say, he should
Be won to prove a second wife, on whom
He may beget a son, how, in a moment,
Will all those glorious expectations, which
Render you reverenced and remarkable,
Be in a moment blasted, howe'er you are
His much-loved sister's son!
    Giov. I must bear it
With patience, and in me it is a duty
That I was born with; and 'twere much unfit
For the receiver of a benefit

To offer, for his own ends, to prescribe
Laws to the giver's pleasure.
    Sanaz. Sweetly answer'd,
And like your noble self. This your rare temper
So wins upon me, that I would not live
(If that by honest arts I can prevent it)
To see your hopes made frustrate. And but think
How you shall be transform'd from what you are,
Should this (as heaven avert it!) ever happen.
It must disturb your peace: for whereas now,
Being, as you are, received for the heir apparent,
You are no sooner seen, but wonder'd at;
The signiors making it a business to
Enquire how you have slept; and, as you walk
The streets of Florence, the glad multitude
In throngs press but to see you; and, with joy,
The father, pointing with his finger, tells
His son, This is the prince, the hopeful prince,
That must hereafter rule, and you obey him.—
Great ladies beg your picture, and make love
To that, despairing to enjoy the substance.—
And, but the last night, when 'twas only rumour'd
That you were come to court, as if you had
By sea past hither from another world,
What general shouts and acclamations follow'd!
The bells rang loud, the bonfires blazed, and such
As loved not wine, carousing to your health,
Were drunk, and blush'd not at it. And is this
A happiness to part with?
    Giov. I allow these
As flourishes of fortune, with which princes
Are often sooth'd; but never yet esteem'd them
For real blessings.
    Sanaz. Yet all these were paid
To what you may be, not to what you are;
For if the Great Duke but shew to his servants

A son of his own, you shall, like one obscure,
Pass unregarded.

Giov. I confess, command
Is not to be contemn'd, and if my fate
Appoint me to it, as I may, I'll bear it
With willing shoulders. But, my lord, as yet,
You've told me of a danger coming towards me,
But have not named it.

Sanaz. That is soon deliver'd.
Great Cozimo, your uncle, as I more
Than guess, for 'tis no frivolous circumstance
That does persuade my judgment to believe it,
Purposes to be married.

Giov. Married, sir!
With whom, and on what terms? pray you, instruct
    me.

Sanaz. With the fair Lidia.

Giov. Lidia!

Sanaz. The daughter
Of signior Charomonte.

Giov. Pardon me
Though I appear incredulous; for, on
My knowledge, he ne'er saw her.

Sanaz. That is granted :
But Contarino hath so sung her praises,
And given her out for such a masterpiece,
That he's transported with it, sir :—and love
Steals sometimes through the ear into the heart,
As well as by the eye. The duke no sooner
Heard her described, but I was sent in post
To see her, and return my judgment of her.

Giov. And what's your censure ?

Sanaz. 'Tis a pretty creature.

Giov. She's very fair.

Sanaz. Yes, yes, I have seen worse faces.

Giov. Her limbs are neatly form'd.

Sanaz. She hath a waist
Indeed sized to love's wish.
Giov. A delicate hand too.
Sanaz. Then for a leg and foot—
Giov. And there I leave you,
For I presumed no further.
Sanaz. As she is, sir,
I know she wants no gracious part that may
Allure the duke; and, if he only see her,
She is his own; he will not be denied,
And then you are lost: yet, if you'll second me,
(As you have reason, for it most concerns you,)
I can prevent all yet.
Giov. I would you could,
A noble way.
Sanaz. I will cry down her beauties;
Especially the beauties of her mind,
As much as Contarino hath advanced them;
And this, I hope, will breed forgetfulness,
And kill affection in him : but you must join
With me in my report, if you be question'd.
Giov. I never told a lie yet; and I hold it
In some degree blasphémous³ to dispraise
What's worthy admiration: yet, for once,
I will dispraise a little, and not vary
From your relation.
Sanaz. Be constant in it.

---

³ ——— *and I hold it*
In some degree blasphémous] So the word was usually accented
in Massinger's time, and with strict regard to its Greek deriva-
tion. Thus Sidney :
" *Blasphémous* words the speaker vain do prove."
And Spenser :
" And therein shut up his *blasphémous* tongue."

Enter ALPHONSO.

Alph. My lord, the duke hath seen your man,
and wonders

Enter COZIMO, HIPPOLITO, CONTARINO, *and*
Attendants.

You come not to him. See, if his desire
To have conference with you hath not brought
    him hither
In his own person!
   Coz. They are comely coursers,
And promise swiftness.
   Cont. They are, of my knowledge,
Of the best race in Naples.
   Coz. You are, nephew,
As I hear, an excellent horseman, and we like it:
'Tis a fair grace in a prince. Pray you, make trial
Of their strength and speed; and, if you think
    them fit
For your employment, with a liberal hand
Reward the gentleman that did present them
From the viceroy of Naples.
   Giov. I will use
My best endeavour, sir.
   Coz. Wait on my nephew.
    [*Exeunt Giovanni, Alphonso, Hippolito, and*
       Attendants.
Nay, stay you, Contarino:—be within call;
It may be we shall use you. [*Exit Contarino*]
    You have rode hard, sir,
And we thank you for it: every minute seems
Irksome, and tedious to us, till you have
Made your discovery. Say, friend, have you seen
This phoenix of our age?

Sanaz. I have seen a maid, sir;
But, if that I have judgment, no such wonder[4]
As she was deliver'd to you.
　Coz. This is strange.
　Sanaz. But certain truth. It may be, she was
　　look'd on
With admiration in the country, sir;
But, if compared with many in your court,
She would appear but ordinary.
　Coz. Contarino
Reports her otherwise.
　Sanaz. Such as ne'er saw swans,
May think crows beautiful.
　Coz. How is her behaviour?
　Sanaz. 'Tis like the place she lives in.
　Coz. How her wit,
Discourse, and entertainment?
　Sanaz. Very coarse;
I would not willingly say poor, and rude:
But, had she all the beauties of fair women,
The dullness of her soul would fright me from her.
　Coz. You are curious, sir. I know not what to
　　think on't.—　　　　　　　　　　　[*Aside.*
Contarino!
　　　　　Re-enter CONTARINO.
　Cont. Sir.
　Coz. Where was thy judgment, man,

----

[4] *Sanaz. I have seen a* maid, *sir;*
　But if that I have judgment, no such wonder &c.] It is too
much to say that this simple thought is borrowed; and yet an
expression of Shakspeare might not improbably have hung on
Massinger's mind:
　　　" *Mir.* ——————— *No wonder,* sir;
　　　" But, certainly a *maid.*"　　*Tempest.*
The commentators have amassed a prodigious number of ex-
tracts to illustrate the expression: this from Massinger, however, which appears to me more to the purpose than any of
them, they have, as usual, overlooked.

To extol a virgin Sanazarro tells me
Is nearer to deformity ?
   Sanaz. I saw her,
And curiously perused her; and I wonder
That she, that did appear to me, that know
What beauty is, not worthy the observing,
Should so transport you.
   Cont. Troth, my lord, I thought then——
   Coz. Thought ! Didst thou not affirm it ?
   Cont. I confess, sir,
I did believe so then ; but now, I hear
My lord's opinion to the contrary,
I am of another faith : for 'tis not fit
That I should contradict him. I am dim, sir ;
But he's sharp-sighted.
   Sanaz. This is to my wish.   [*Aside.*
   Coz. We know not what to think of this ; yet
      would not

     Re-enter GIOVANNI, HIPPOLITO, *and*
        ALPHONSO.

Determine rashly of it. [*Aside.*]—How do you like
My nephew's horsemanship?
   Hip. In my judgment, sir,
It is exact and rare.
   Alph. And, to my fancy,
He did present great Alexander mounted
On his Bucephalus,
   Coz. You are right courtiers,
And know it is your duty to cry up
All actions of a prince.
   Sanaz. Do not betray
Yourself, you're safe ; I have done my part.
                 [*Aside to Giovanni.*
   Giov. I thank you ;
Nor will I fail.

Coz. What's your opinion, nephew,
Of the horses?

Giov. Two of them are, in my judgment,
The best I ever back'd; I mean the roan, sir,
And the brown bay: but for the chesnut-colour'd,
Though he be full of metal, hot, and fiery,
He treads weak in his pasterns.

Coz. So: come nearer;
This exercise hath put you into a sweat;
Take this and dry it:[5] and now I command you
To tell me truly what's your censure of
Charomonte's daughter, Lidia.

Giov. I am, sir,
A novice in my judgment of a lady;
But such as 'tis, your grace shall have it freely.
I would not speak ill of her, and am sorry,
If I keep myself a friend to truth, I cannot
Report her as I would, so much I owe
Her reverend father: but I'll give you, sir,
As near as I can, her character in little.
She's of a goodly stature, and her limbs
Not disproportion'd; for her face, it is
Far from deformity; yet they flatter her,
That style it excellent: her manners are
Simple and innocent; but her discourse
And wit deserve my pity, more than praise:
At the best, my lord, she is a handsome picture,
And, that said, all is spoken.

Coz. I believe you;
I ne'er yet found you false.

Giov. Nor ever shall, sir.——

[5] *This exercise hath put you into a sweat:*
Take this and dry it:] This is from Shakspeare; if he had
been suffered to remain in quiet possession of it, the reader
would have little to regret on the score of delicacy:
" ————————— He's fat, and scant of breath:
" Here, Hamlet, *take my napkin, rub thy brow.*"

Forgive me, matchless Lidia ! too much love,
And jealous fear to lose thee, do compel me,
Against my will, my reason, and my knowledge,
To be a poor detractor of that beauty,
Which fluent Ovid, if he lived again,
Would want words to express.   [*Aside.*

   Coz. Pray you, make choice of
The richest of our furniture for these horses,

                 [*To Sanazarro.*

And take my nephew with you; we in this
Will follow his directions.

   Giov. Could I find now
The princess Fiorinda, and persuade her
To be silent in the suit that I moved to her,
All were secure.

   Sanaz. In that, my lord, I'll aid you.

   Coz. We will be private ; leave us.

             [*Exeunt all but Cozimo.*

               All my studies
And serious meditations aim no further
Than this young man's good. He was my sister's
    son,
And she was such a sister, when she lived,
I could not prize too much ; nor can I better
Make known how dear I hold her memory,
Than in my cherishing the only issue
Which she hath left behind her. Who's that ?

         Enter FIORINDA.

   Fior. Sir.

   Coz. My fair charge! you are welcome to us.

   Fior. I have found it, sir.

   Coz. All things go well in Urbin.

   Fior. Your gracious care to me, an orphan, frees
    me
From all suspicion that my jealous fears
Can drive into my fancy.

Coz. The next summer,
In our own person, we will bring you thither,
And seat you in your own.
    Fior. When you think fit, sir.
But, in the mean time, with your highness' pardon,
I am a suitor to you.
    Coz. Name it, madam,
With confidence to obtain it.
    Fior. That you would please
To lay a strict command on Charomonte,
To bring his daughter Lidia to the court:
And pray you, think, sir, that 'tis not my purpose
To employ her as a servant, but to use her
As a most wish'd companion.
    Coz. Ha! your reason?
    Fior. The hopeful prince, your nephew, sir,
      hath given her
To me for such an abstract of perfection
In all that can be wish'd for in a virgin,
As beauty, music, ravishing discourse,
Quickness of apprehension, with choice manners
And learning too, not usual with women,
That I am much ambitious (though I shall
Appear but as a foil to set her off)
To be by her instructed, and supplied
In what I am defective.
    Coz. Did my nephew
Seriously deliver this?
    Fior. I assure your grace,
With zeal and vehemency; and, even when,
With his best words, he strived to set her forth,
(Though the rare subject made him eloquent,)
He would complain, all he could say came short
Of her deservings.
    Coz. Pray you have patience.   *[Walks aside.*
This was strangely carried.—Ha! are we trifled
      with?

Dare they do this? Is Cozimo's fury, that
Of late was terrible, grown contemptible?
Well; we will clear our brows, and undermine
Their secret works, though they have digg'd like
 moles,
And crush them with the tempest of my wrath
When I appear most calm. He is unfit
To command others, that knows not to use it,[8]
And with all rigour: yet my stern looks shall not
Discover my intents; for I will strike
When I begin to frown.——You are the mistress
Of that you did demand.
 Fior. I thank your highness;
But speed in the performance of the grant
Doubles the favour, sir.
 Coz. You shall possess it
Sooner than you expect:——
Only be pleased to be ready when my secretary
Waits on you to take the fresh air. My nephew,
And my bosom friend, so to cheat me! 'tis not
 fair.   [*Aside.*

Re-enter GIOVANNI *and* SANAZARRO.

 Sanaz. Where should this princess be? nor in
 her lodgings,
Nor in the private walks, her own retreat,
Which she so much frequented!
 Giov By my life,
She's with the duke! and I much more than fear
Her forwardness to prefer my suit hath ruin'd
What with such care we built up.
 Coz. Have you furnish'd
Those coursers, as we will'd you?

Sanaz. There's no sign
Of anger in his looks.
Giov. They are complete, sir.
Coz. 'Tis well : to your rest. Soft sleeps wait
    on you, madam.
To morrow, with the rising of the sun,
Be ready to ride with us.—They with more safety
Had trod on fork-tongued adders, than provoked
    me.   [*Aside, and exit.*
  Fior. I come not to be thank'd, sir, for the
    speedy
Performance of my promise touching Lidia :
It is effected.
  Sanaz. We are undone.   [*Aside.*
  Fior. The duke
No sooner heard me with my best of language
Describe her excellencies, as you taught me,
But he confirm'd it.—You look sad, as if
You wish'd it were undone.
  Giov. No, gracious madam,
I am your servant for't.
  Fior. Be you as careful
For what I moved to you.—Count Sanazarro,
Now I perceive you honour me, in vouchsafing
To wear so slight a favour.
  Sanaz. 'Tis a grace
I am unworthy of.
  Fior. You merit more,
In prizing so a trifle. Take this diamond ;
I'll second what I have begun ; for know,
Your valour hath so won upon me, that
'Tis not to be resisted : I have said, sir,
And leave you to interpret it.   [*Exit.*
  Sanaz. This to me
Is wormwood. 'Tis apparent we are taken
In our own noose. What's to be done ?
  Giov. I know not.

And 'tis a punishment justly fallen upon me,
For leaving truth, a constant mistress, that
Ever protects her servants, to become
A slave to lies and falsehood. What excuse
Can we make to the duke, what mercy hope for,
Our packing⁷ being laid open?
   Sanaz. 'Tis not to
Be question'd but his purposed journey is
To see fair Lidia.
   Giov. And to divert him
Impossible.
   Sanaz. There's now no looking backward.
   Giov. And which way to go on with safety, not
To be imagined.
   Sanaz. Give me leave: I have
An embryon in my brain, which, I despair not,
May be brought to form and fashion, provided
You will be open-breasted.
   Giov. 'Tis no time now,
Our dangers being equal, to conceal
A thought from you.
   Sanaz. What power hold you o'er Lidia?
Do you think that, with some hazard of her life,
She would prevent your ruin?
   Giov. I presume so:
If, in the undertaking it, she stray not
From what becomes her innocence; and to that
'Tis far from me to press her: I myself
Will rather suffer.
   Sanaz. 'Tis enough; this night
Write to her by your servant Calandrino,
As I shall give directions; my man

7 *Our* packing *being laid open?*] i. e. our insidious contrivance,
our iniquitous collusion to deceive the duke: so the word is
used by Shakspeare, and others.

Enter CALANDRINO, *fantastically dressed.*

Shall bear him company. See, sir, to my wish
He does appear; but much transform'd from what
He was when he came hither.
    Cal. I confess
I am not very wise, and yet I find
A fool, so he be parcel knave, in court
May flourish and grow rich.
    Giov. Calandrino.
    Cal. Peace!
I am in contemplation.
    Giov. Do not you know me?
    Cal. I tell thee, no; on forfeit of my place,
I must not know myself, much less my father,
But by petition; that petition lined too
With golden birds, that sing to the tune of profit,
Or I am deaf.
    Giov. But you've your sense of feeling.
                    [*Offering to strike him.*
    Sanaz. Nay, pray you, forbear.
    Cal. I have all that's requisite
To the making up of a signior: my spruce ruff,
My hooded cloak, long stocking, and paned hose,
My case of toothpicks, and my silver fork,

----

^{s} *Cal.* *I have all that's requisite*
To the making up of a signior : my spruce ruff,
My hooded cloak, long stocking, and paned hose,
My case of toothpicks, *and my* silver fork,] Calandrino is
very correct in his enumeration of the articles which in his time
made up a complete signior : and which are frequently introduced with evident marks of disapprobation and ridicule by our
old poets. The ruff, cloak, and long stocking, are sufficiently
familiar : *hose* are breeches :
        " Lorenzo, thou dost boast of base renown;
        " Why, I could whip all these, were their *hose* down."
                                The Spanish Tragedy.
Paned hose, are breeches composed of small squares or pannels.

To convey an olive neatly to my mouth ;—
And, what is all in all, my pockets ring
A golden peal. O that the peasants in the country,

In the former edition, I had heedlessly stated *paned* to be
ribbed: which I lament the more, as it has betrayed that unsus-
pecting gentleman, Mr. Weber, into a grievous mistake :

"Oh! my ribs are made of a payn'd hose, and they break."
Ford, vol. ii. p. 468.

To explain this, the editor does me the honour to take my
words literally to himself; adding, out of his own stock, " the
intended pun in the text will be easily understood." It so happens that here is no pun, and, if there were, it would be impossible to understand it. A *rib* made of a *rib* would not be apt
to break; but a rib made of *patch-work* (which is but another
name for *paned work*) might be readily supposed to give way.
In Mr. Weber's next edition he will doubtless follow my example, and correct his meaning:—While he is on this line, *it
will not be much amiss* in him to read *flay*, for *flea*, as the two
words, especially " when taking off skins" is spoken of, are
not altogether synonymous. While I am on this most grave
subject, it may not be amiss to observe that, about this time,
the large slashed breeches of a former reign began to give way
to others of a closer make ; an innovation which the old people
found very inconvenient, and of which they complained with
some degree of justice, as being very ill adapted to the hard
oak chairs and benches on which they usually sat. *Toothpicks*,
the next accompaniment of state, were recently imported from
Italy, as were *forks;* the want of which our ancestors supplied,
as well as they could, with their fingers. Thomas Coryat, (an
itinerant buffoon, with just understanding enough to make himself worth the laughing at,) claims the honour of introducing
the use of forks into this country, which, he says, he learned in
Italy—" where the natives, and also most strangers that are
commorant there, doe alwaies at their meales use a little *forke*,
when they cut their meate, for while with their knife, which they
hold in one hand, they cut the meat out of the dish, they fasten
their *forke*, which they hold in their other hand, upon the same
dish." *Coryat's Crudities,* 1611.
Jonson, who, far more than any of his contemporaries,
" caught the manners living as they rose," lashes the prostitu-
tion of monopolies in his time, by making Meercraft promise
Tailbush and Gilthead to procure them grants for the manufac·

My quondam fellows, but saw me as I am,
How they would admire and worship me!
   Giov. As they shall;
For instantly you must thither.
    Cal. *My grand signior,*
Vouchsafe a beso la manos,[9] *and a cringe*
Of the last edition.
   Giov. You must ride post with letters
This night to Lidia.
    Cal. An it please your grace,
Shall I use my coach, or footcloth mule?
   Sanaz. You widgeon,
You are to make all speed; think not of pomp.
   Giov. Follow for your instructions, sirrah.
    Cal. I have
One suit to you, my good lord.
   Sanaz. What is't?
    Cal. That you would give me
A subtile court-charm, to defend me from
The infectious air of the country.

turing of *toothpicks*, and *forks*. What he says of the former is
too long for my purpose; the latter are thus introduced:
     " *Meer.* Do you hear, sirs?
     " Have I deserved this from you two, for all
     " My pains at court to get you each a patent?
     " *Gilt.* For what?
     " *Meer.* Upon my project of the *forks.*
     " *Gilt.* Forks! what be they?
     " *Meer.* The laudable use of forks
     " Brought into custom here, as they are in Italy,
     " To the sparing of napkins."   *The Devil's an Ass.*
    9 *Cal. My grand signior,*
Vouchsafe a beso las manos, &c.] This is the phrase in which
Calandrino supposes his " quondam fellows" will address him.
I know not whether it be through ignorance or design—but the
modern editors always make their foreign scraps even more
barbarous than the ancient ones. There is no occasion for this.
In Massinger's time these tags of politeness were in every body's
mouth, and better understood than they are at this day.

Giov. What's the reason?

Cal. Why, as this court-air taught me knavish
    wit,
By which I am grown rich, if that again
Should turn me fool and honest, vain hopes
    farewell!
For I must die a beggar.

Sanaz. Go to, sirrah,
You'll be whipt for this.

Giov. Leave fooling, and attend us. [*Exeunt.*[1]

ACT IV. SCENE I.

The Country. *A Hall in* Charomonte's *House.*

Enter CHAROMONTE, *and* LIDIA.

Char. Daughter, I have observed, since the
    prince left us,
(Whose absence I mourn with you,) and the visit
Count Sanazarro gave us, you have nourished
Sad and retired thoughts, and parted with
That freedom and alacrity of spirit
With which you used to cheer me.

Lid. For the count, sir,
All thought of him does with his person die;
But I confess ingenuously, I cannot

---

[1] I have restricted myself to as few remarks as possible on
the beauties of the author, but I cannot forbear observing, on
the present occasion, that the act we have just finished, for language, sentiment, surprising yet natural turns, and general felicity of conduct, is scarcely to be paralleled in any drama with
which I am acquainted.

So soon forget the choice and chaste delights,
The courteous conversation of the prince,
And without stain, I hope, afforded me,
When he made this house a court.
   Char. It is in us
To keep it so without him. Want we know not,
And all we can complain of, heaven be praised
     for't,
Is too much plenty; and we will make use of

    Enter CAPONI, BERNARDO, PETRUCHIO, *and
      other Servants.*

All lawful pleasures.—How now, fellows! when
Shall we have this lusty dance?
   Cap. In the afternoon, sir.
'Tis a device, I wis, of my own making,
And such a one, as shall make your signiorship
    know
I have not been your butler for nothing, but
Have crotchets in my head. We'll trip it tightly,
And make my sad young mistress merry again,
Or I'll forswear the cellar.
   Bern. If we had
Our fellow Calandrino here, to dance
His part, we were perfect.
   Pet. O! he was a rare fellow;
But I fear the court hath spoil'd him.
   Cap. When I was young,
I could have cut a caper on a pinnacle;
But now I am old and wise.—Keep your figure
    fair,
And follow but the sample I shall set you,
The duke himself will send for us, and laugh at
    us;
And that were credit.

Enter CALANDRINO.

Lid. Who have we here?

Cal. I find
What was brawn in the country, in the court
    grows tender.
The bots on these jolting jades! I am bruised to
    jelly.
A coach for my money! and that the courtezans
    know well;
Their riding so, makes them last three years longer
Than such as are hacknied.

Char. Calandrino! 'tis he.

Cal. Now to my postures.—Let my hand have
    the honour
To convey a kiss from my lips to the cover of
Your foot, dear signior.

Char. Fie! you stoop too low, sir.

Cal. The hem of your vestment, lady: your
    glove is for princes;
Nay, I have conn'd my distances.

Lid. 'Tis most courtly.

Cap. Fellow Calandrino!

Cal. Signior de Caponi,
Grand botelier of the mansion.

Bern. How is't, man? [*Claps him on the shoulder.*

Cal. Be not so rustic in your salutations,
Signior Bernardo, master of the accounts.
Signior Petruchio, may you long continue
Your function in the chamber!

Cap. When shall we learn
Such gambols in our villa?

Lid. Sure he's mad.

Char. 'Tis not unlike, for most of such mush-
    rooms are so.
What news at court?

Cal. *Basta!* they are mysteries,
And not to be reveal'd. With your favour, signior;
I am, in private, to confer awhile
With this signora: but I'll pawn my honour,
That neither my terse language, nor my habit,
Howe'er it may convince, nor my new shrugs,
Shall render her enamour'd.

Char. Take your pleasure;
A little of these apish tricks may pass,
Too much is tedious.   [*Exit.*

Cal. The prince, in this paper,
Presents his service.   Nay, it is not courtly
To see the seal broke open; so I leave you.—
Signiors of the villa, I'll descend to be
Familiar with you.

Cap. Have you forgot to dance?

Cal. No, I am better'd.

Pet. Will you join with us?

Cal. As I like the project.
Let me warm my brains first with the richest
            grape,
And then I'm for you.

Cap. We will want no wine. [*Exeunt all but Lidia.*

Lid. That this comes only from the best of
            princes,
With a kind of adoration does command me
To entertain it; and the sweet contents
                        [*Kissing the letter.*
That are inscribed here by his hand must be
Much more than musical to me. All the service
Of my life at no part can deserve this favour.
O what a virgin longing I feel on me
To unrip the seal, and read it! yet, to break
What he hath fastened, rashly, may appear
A saucy rudeness in me.—I must do it,
(Nor can I else learn his commands, or serve
            them,)

But with such reverence, as I would open
Some holy writ, whose grave instructions beat
    down
Rebellious sins, and teach my better part
How to mount upward.—So, [*opens the letter.*] 'tis
    done, and I
With eagle's eyes will curiously peruse it. [*Reads.*

> *Chaste Lidia, the favours are so great*
> *On me by you conferr'd, that to entreat*
> *The least addition to them, in true sense*
> *May argue me of blushless impudence.*
> *But, such are my extremes, if you deny*
> *A further grace, I must unpitied die.*
> *Haste cuts off circumstance. As you're admired*
> *For beauty, the report of it hath fired*
> *The duke my uncle, and, I fear, you'll prove,*
> *Not with a sacred, but unlawful love.*
> *If he see you as you are, my hoped-for light*
> *Is changed into an everlasting night ;*
> *How to prevent it, if your goodness find,*
> *You save two lives, and me you ever bind,*
>   *The honourer of your virtues,* GIOVANNI.

Were I more deaf than adders, these sweet charms
Would through my ears find passage to my soul,
And soon enchant it. To save such a prince,
Who would not perish ? virtue in him must suffer,
And piety be forgotten. The duke's lust,
Though it raged more than Tarquin's, shall not
    reach me.
All quaint inventions of chaste virgins aid me !
My prayers are heard ; I have't. The duke ne'er
    saw me—
Or, if that fail, I am again provided—
But for the servants !—They will take what form
I please to put upon them. Giovanni,

Be safe; thy servant Lidia assures it.
Let mountains of afflictions fall on me,
Their weight is easy, so I set thee free.   [*Exit.*

SCENE II.

Another Room in the same.

Enter COZIMO, GIOVANNI, SANAZARRO, CHARO-
MONTE, *and Attendants.*

Sanaz. Are you not tired with travel, sir?
Coz. No, no;
I am fresh and lusty.
Char. This day shall be ever
A holiday to me, that brings my prince
Under my humble roof.   [*Weeps.*
Giov. See, sir, my good tutor
Sheds tears for joy.
Coz. Dry them up, Charomonte;
And all forbear the room, while we exchange
Some private words together.
Giov. O, my lord,
How grossly have we overshot ourselves!
Sanaz. In what, sir?
Giov. In forgetting to acquaint
My guardian with our purpose: all that Lidia
Can do avails us nothing, if the duke
Find out the truth from him.
Sanaz. 'Tis now past help,
And we must stand the hazard:—hope the best, sir.
    [*Exeunt Giovanni, Sanazarro, and Attendants.*
Char. My loyalty doubted, sir!
Coz. 'Tis more.   Thou hast
Abused our trust, and in a high degree
Committed treason.

Char. Treason! 'Tis a word
My innocence understands not. Were my breast
Transparent, and my thoughts to be discern'd,
Not one spot shall be found to taint the candour
Of my allegiance: and I must be bold
To tell you, sir, (for he that knows no guilt
Can know no fear,) 'tis tyranny to o'ercharge
An honest man; and such, till now, I've lived,
And such, my lord, I'll die.
    Coz. Sir, do not flatter
Yourself with hope, these great and glorious
            words,
Which every guilty wretch, as well as you,
That's arm'd with impudence, can with ease
            deliver,
And with as full a mouth, can work on us:
Nor shall gay flourishes of language clear
What is in fact apparent.
    Char. Fact! what fact?
You, that know only what it is, intsruct me,
For I am ignorant.
    Coz. This, then, sir: We gave up,
On our assurance of your faith and care,
Our nephew Giovanni, nay, our heir
In expectation, to be train'd up by you
As did become a prince.
    Char. And I discharged it:
Is this the treason?
    Coz. Take us with you, sir.[2]
And, in respect we knew his youth was prone
To women, and that, living in our court,
He might make some unworthy choice, before
His weaker judgment was confirm'd, we did

---

[2] *Take us with you, sir.*] i. e. hear us out, understand our
meaning fully, before you form your conclusions: this expression is common to all our old writers; and, indeed, will be frequently found in the succeeding pages of this work.

Remove him from it; constantly presuming,
You, with your best endeavours, rather would
Have quench'd those heats in him, than light a
    torch,
As you have done, to his looseness.
    Char. I! my travail
Is ill-requited, sir; for, by my soul,
I was so curious that way, that I granted
Access to none could tempt him; nor did ever
One syllable, or obscene accent, touch
His ear, that might corrupt him.
    Coz. No! Why, then,
With your allowance, did you give free way
To all familiar privacy between
My nephew and your daughter? Or why did you
(Had you no other ends in't but our service)
Read to them, and together, as they had been
Scholars of one form, grammar, rhetoric,
Philosophy,[3] story, and interpret to them
The close temptations of lascivious poets?
Or wherefore, for we still had spies upon you,
Was she still present, when, by your advice,
He was taught the use of his weapon, horseman-
    ship,
Wrestling, nay, swimming, but to fan in her
A hot desire of him? and then, forsooth,
His exercises ended, cover'd with
A fair pretence of recreation for him,
(When Lidia was instructed in those graces
That add to beauty,) he, brought to admire her,
Must hear her sing, while to her voice her hand
Made ravishing music; and, this applauded,
    dance
A light lavolta with her.[4]

    [3] *Philosophy,* story,] For *story,* the modern editors unneces-
sarily read *history.* The two words were anciently synonymous.
    [4] *A light* lavolta *with her.*] What the dance here alluded to

Char. Have you ended
All you can charge me with?
   Coz. Nor stopt you there,
But they must unattended walk into
The silent groves, and hear the amorous birds
Warbling their wanton notes; here, a sure shade
Of barren sicamores, which the all-seeing sun
Could not pierce through; near that, an arbour
    hung
With spreading eglantine; there, a bubbling
    spring
Watering a bank of hyacinths and lilies;
With all allurements that could move to lust
And could this, Charomonte, (should I grant
They had been equals both in birth and fortune,)
Become your gravity? nay, 'tis clear as air,
That your ambitious hopes to match your daughter
Into our family, gave connivance to it:

is, I cannot tell, nor can I find an explanation of the word in
any dictionary. COXETER and M. MASON.

That's a pity! Dictionaries, generally speaking, are not the
places to look for terms of this kind, which should be sought in
the kindred writings of contemporary authors. *Lavolta,* (literally,
the turn) was a dance originally imported, with many others,
from Italy. It is frequently mentioned by our old writers, with
whom it was a favourite; and is so graphically described by Sir
John Davies, in his *Orchestra,* that all further attempts to explain
it must be superfluous:

   " Yet is there one, the most delightful kind,
    " A lofty jumping, or a leaping round,
   " Where, arm in arm, two dancers are entwin'd,
    " And whirl themselves in strict embracements bound."

Our countrymen, who seem to be lineally descended from
Sisyphus, and who, at the end of every century, usually have
their work to do over again, after proudly importing from Ger-
many the long-exploded trash of their own nurseries, have just
brought back from the same country, and with an equal degree
of exultation, the well-known *lavolta* of their grandfathers,
under the mellifluous name of the *waltz!*

And this, though not in act, in the intent
I call high treason.
   Char. Hear my just defence, sir ;
And, though you are my prince, it will not take
     from
Your greatness, to acknowledge with a blush,
In this my accusation you have been
More sway'd by spleen, and jealous suppositions,
Than certain grounds of reason. You had a father,
(Blest be his memory !) that made frequent proofs
Of my loyalty and faith, and, would I boast
The dangers I have broke through in his service,
I could say more. Nay, you yourself, dread sir,
Whenever I was put unto the test,
Found me true gold, and not adulterate metal ;
And am I doubted now ?
   Coz. This is from the purpose.
   Char. I will come to it, sir : Your grace well
     knew,
Before the prince's happy presence made
My poor house rich, the chiefest blessing which
I gloried in, though now it prove a curse,
Was an only daughter. Nor did you command me,
As a security to your future fears,
To cast her off : which had you done, howe'er
She was the light of my eyes, and comfort of
My feeble age, so far I prized my duty
Above affection, she now had been
A stranger to my care. But she is fair !
Is that her fault, or mine ? Did ever father
Hold beauty in his issue for a blemish ?
Her education and her manners tempt too !
If these offend, they are easily removed :
You may, if you think fit, before my face,
In recompense of all my watchings for you,
With burning corrosives transform her to
An ugly leper ; and, this done, to taint

Her sweetness, prostitute her to a brothel.[5]
This I will rather suffer, sir, and more,
Than live suspected by you.

   Coz. Let not passion
Carry you beyond your reason.

   Char. I am calm, sir;
Yet you must give me leave to grieve I find
My actions misinterpreted. Alas! sir,
Was Lidia's desire to serve the prince
Call'd an offence? or did she practise to
Seduce his youth, because with her best zeal
And fervour she endeavoured to attend him?
'Tis a hard construction. Though she be my
    daughter,
I may thus far speak her: from her infancy
She was ever civil, her behaviour nearer
Simplicity than craft; and malice dares not
Affirm, in one loose gesture, or light language,
She gave a sign she was in thought unchaste.
I'll fetch her to you, sir; and but look on her
With equal eyes, you must in justice grant
That your suspicion wrongs her.

   Coz. It may be;
But I must have stronger assurance of it
Than passionate words: and, not to trifle time,
As we came unexpected to your house,
We will prevent all means that may prepare her
How to answer that, with which we come to charge
    her.
And howsoever it may be received
As a foul breach to hospitable rites,
On thy allegiance and boasted faith,
Nay, forfeit of thy head, we do confine thee

---

[5] *———— prostitute her to a brothel.*] The
quarto reads, to a *loathsome* brothel. The epithet is altogether
idle, and destroys the metre; I have therefore omitted it without scruple, as an interpolation.

Close prisoner to thy chamber, till all doubts
Are clear'd, that do concern us.
 Char. I obey, sir,
And wish your grace had followed my herse
To my sepulchre, my loyalty unsuspected,
Rather than now—but I am silent, sir,
And let that speak my duty.[6]   [*Exit.*
 Coz. If this man
Be false, disguised treachery ne'er put on
A shape so near to truth. Within, there!

Re-enter GIOVANNI *and* SANAZARRO, *ushering in*
 PETRONELLA. CALANDRINO *and others setting*
 forth a Banquet.

 Sanaz. Sir.
 Coz. Bring Lidia forth.
 Giov. She comes, sir, of herself,
To present her service to you.
 Coz. Ha! This personage
Cannot invite affection.
 Sanaz. See you keep state.
 Petron. I warrant you.
 Coz. The manners of her mind
Must be transcendent, if they can defend
Her rougher outside. May we with your liking
Salute you, lady?
 Petron. Let me wipe my mouth, sir,
With my cambric handkerchief, and then have
  at you.
 Coz. Can this be possible?
 Sanaz. Yes, sir; you will find her
Such as I gave her to you.

 [6] This scene is exquisitely written. It must, however, be
confessed, that Charamonte's justification of himself is less complete than might be expected from one who had so good a cause
to defend.

Petron. Will your dukeship
Sit down and eat some sugar-plums? Here's a
        castle
Of march-pane too; and this quince-marmalade
        was
Of my own making; all summ'd up together,
Did cost the setting on: and here is wine too,
As good as e'er was tapp'd. I'll be your taster,
For I know the fashion. [*Drinks all off.*]--Now
        you must do me right, sir;
You shall nor will nor choose.
    Giov. She's very simple.
    Coz. Simple! 'tis worse. Do you drink thus
        often, lady?
    Petron. Still when I am thirsty, and eat when
        I am hungry:
Such junkets come not every day. Once more
        to you,
With a heart and a half, i'faith.
    Coz. Pray you, pause a little;
If I hold your cards,[7] I shall pull down the side;
I am not good at the game.
    Petron. Then I'll drink for you.
    Coz. Nay, pray you stay: I'll find you out a
        pledge
That shall supply my place; what think you of
This complete signior? You are a Juno,
And in such state must feast this Jupiter:
What think you of him?
    Petron. I desire no better.
    Coz. And you will undertake this service for me?
You are good at the sport.
    Cal. Who, I? a piddler, sir.

[7] Coz. *Pray you, pause a little;*
If I hold your cards, &c.] See vol. i. p. 150.

Coz. Nay, you shall sit enthroned, and eat and
drink
As you were a duke.
Cal. If your grace will have me,
I'll eat and drink like an emperor.
Coz. Take your place then :
    [*Calandrino takes the Duke's chair.*
We are amazed.
Giov. This is gross : nor can the imposture
But be discover'd.
Sanaz. The duke is too sharp-sighted,
To be deluded thus.
Cal. Nay, pray you eat fair,
Or divide, and I will choose. Cannot you use
Your fork, as I do? Gape, and I will feed you.
    [*Feeds her.*
Gape wider yet; this is court-like.
Petron. To choke daws with :——
I like it not.
Cal. But you like this?
Petron. Let it come, boy. [*They drink.*
Coz. What a sight is this ! We could be angry
with you.
How much you did belie her when you told us
She was only simple ! this is barbarous rudeness,
Beyond belief.
Giov. I would not speak her, sir,
Worse than she was.
Sanaz. And I, my lord, chose rather
To deliver her better parted[8] than she is,
Than to take from her.

[8] Sanaz. *And I, my lord, chose rather*
To deliver her better parted *than she is*,] i. e. gifted or endowed
with better *parts*, &c. See vol. i p. 40.
 It seems to have been the opinion of Massinger and his fellow
dramatists, that no play could succeed without the admission of

Enter CAPONI, *with his fellow Servants for the dance.*

Cap. Ere I'll lose my dance,
I'll speak to the purpose. I am, sir, no prologue;
But in plain terms must tell you, we are provided
Of a lusty hornpipe.
    Coz. Prithee, let us have it,
For we grow dull.
    Cap. But to make up the medley,
For it is of several colours, we must borrow
Your grace's ghost here.
    Cal. Pray you, sir, depose me;
It will not do else. I am, sir, the engine
                 [*Rises, and resigns his chair.*
By which it moves.
    Petron. I will dance with my duke too;
I will not out.
    Coz. Begin then.—[*They dance.*]—There's more
    in this,
Than yet I have discover'd. Some Œdipus
Resolve this riddle.
    Petron. Did I not foot it roundly.   [*Falls.*
    Coz. As I live, stark drunk! away with her.
    We'll reward you,
       [*Exeunt Servants with Petronella.*
When you have cool'd yourselves in the cellar.

some kind of farcical interlude among the graver scenes. If the dramas of our author be intimately considered, few will be found without some extraneous mummery of this description; and, indeed, nothing but a persuasion of the nature which I have just mentioned could give birth to the poor mockery before us. As a trick, it is so gross and palpable, that the duke could not have been deceived by it for a moment; (to do him justice, he frequently hints his suspicions;) and as a piece of humour, it is so low, and even disagreeable, that I cannot avoid regretting a proper regard for his characters had not prevented the author from adopting it on the present occasion.

Cap. Heaven preserve you!

Coz. We pity Charamonte's wretched fortune
In a daughter, nay, a monster. Good old man!—
The place grows tedious; our remove shall be
With speed: we'll only, in a word or two,
Take leave, and comfort him.

Sanaz. 'Twill rather, sir,
Increase his sorrow, that you know his shame;
Your grace may do it by letter.

Coz. Who sign'd you
A patent to direct us? Wait our coming,
In the garden.

Giov. All will out.

Sanaz. I more than fear it.

[*Exeunt Giovanni and Sanazarro.*

Coz. These are strange chimeras to us: what
    to judge of 't,
Is past our apprehension. One command
Charamonte to attend us. [*Exit an Attendant.*]
                 Can it be
That Contarino could be so besotted,
As to admire this prodigy! or her father
To doat upon it! Or does she personate,[9]
For some ends unknown to us, this rude be-
    haviour,
Which, in the scene presented, would appear
Ridiculous and impossible?—O, you are welcome.

---

9   ——- —— *or does she* personate,
For some ends unknown to us?—this rude behaviour,
Within the scene presented, would appear
Ridiculous and impossible?] So the old copy. Mr. M. Mason
has,

     —— *Or does she personate,*
For some ends unknown to us, this rude behaviour,
Which, in the scene presented, would, &c.
and I have continued it; although the old reading makes very
good sense. To *personate* is used here with great propriety,
for—to play a fictitious character.

Enter CHAROMONTE.

We now acknowledge the much wrong we did you
In our unjust suspicion. We have seen
The wonder, sir, your daughter.
   Char. And have found her
Such as I did report her. What she wanted
In courtship,[1] was, I hope, supplied in civil
And modest entertainment.
   Coz. Pray you, tell us,
And truly, we command you—Did you never
Observe she was given to drink?
   Char. To drink, sir!
   Coz. Yes: nay more, to be drunk?
   Char. I had rather see her buried.
   Coz. Dare you trust your own eyes, if you find
     her now
More than distemper'd?
   Char. I will pull them out, sir,
If your grace can make this good. And if you
     please
To grant me liberty, as she is I'll fetch her,
And in a moment.
   Coz. Look you do, and fail not,
On the peril of your head.
   Char. Drunk!—She disdains it.   [*Exit.*
   Coz. Such contrarieties were never read of.
Charomonte is no fool; nor can I think
His confidence built on sand. We are abused,
'Tis too apparent.

---

[1] ―――――――― *What she wanted
In* courtship,] *Courtship* is used here for that grace and elegance of behaviour which a retired gentleman might suppose to
be taught and practised at court.

Re-enter CHAROMONTE *with* LIDIA.

Lid. I am indisposed, sir;
And that life you once tender'd, much endanger'd
In forcing me from my chamber.
　　Char. Here she is, sir;
Suddenly sick, I grant; but, sure, not drunk:
Speak to my lord the duke.
　　Lid. All is discover'd.　　　　　　　[*Kneels.*
　　Coz. Is this your only daughter?
　　Char. And my heir, sir;
Nor keep I any woman in my² house
(Unless for sordid offices) but one
I do maintain, trimm'd up in her cast habits,
To make her sport: and she, indeed, loves wine,
And will take too much of it; and, perhaps, for
　　mirth,
She was presented to you.
　　Coz. It shall yield
No sport to the contrivers. 'Tis too plain now.
Her presence does confirm what Contarino
Deliver'd of her; nor can sickness dim
The splendour of her beauties: being herself, then,
She must exceed his praise.
　　Lid. Will your grace hear me?
I'm faint, and can say little.
　　Coz. Here are accents
Whose every syllable is musical!
Pray you, let me raise you, and awhile rest here.
False Sanazarro, treacherous Giovanni!
But stand we talking!——

---

² *Nor keep I any woman in my house,*] Coxeter had dropt a
word at the press, and Mr. M. Mason was reduced to guess what
it might be. He failed as usual: luckily the mistake was of no
further consequence than to shew with what pertinacity he per-
sisted in *not* consulting the old copies.

Char. Here's a storm soon raised.

Coz. As thou art our subject, Charomonte, swear
To act what we command.

Char. That is an oath
I long since took.

Coz. Then, by that oath we charge thee,
Without excuse, denial, or delay,
To apprehend, and suddenly, Sanazarro,
And our ingrateful nephew. We have said it.
Do it without reply, or we pronounce thee,
Like them, a traitor to us. See them guarded
In several lodgings, and forbid access
To all, but when we warrant. Is our will
Heard sooner than obey'd?

Char. These are strange turns;
But I must not dispute them.   [*Exit.*

Coz. Be severe in't.—
O my abused lenity! from what height
Is my power fall'n!

Lid. O me most miserable!
That, being innocent, makes others guilty.
Most gracious prince ——

Coz. Pray you rise, and then speak to me.

Lid. My knees shall first be rooted in this earth,
And, Myrrha-like, I'll grow up to a tree,
Dropping perpetual tears of sorrow, which
Harden'd by the rough wind, and turn'd to amber,
Unfortunate virgins like myself shall wear;
Before I'll make petition to your greatness,
But with such reverence, my hands held up thus,
As I would do to heaven. You princes are
As gods on earth to us, and to be sued to
With such humility, as his deputies
May challenge from their vassals.

Coz. Here's that form
Of language I expected; pray you, speak:
What is your suit?

Lid. That you would look upon me
As an humble thing, that millions of degrees
Is placed beneath you : for what am I, dread sir,
Or what can fall in the whole course of my life,
That may be worth your care, much less your
      trouble ?
As the lowly shrub is to the lofty cedar,
Or a molehill to Olympus, if compared,
I am to you, sir. Or, suppose the prince,
(Which cannot find belief in me,) forgetting
The greatness of his birth and hopes, hath thrown
An eye of favour on me, in me punish,
That am the cause, the rashness of his youth.
Shall the queen of the inhabitants of the air,
The eagle, that bears thunder on her wings,
In her angry mood destroy her hopeful young,
For suffering a wren to perch too near them ?
Such is our disproportion.
    Coz. With what fervour
She pleads against herself !
    Lid. For me, poor maid,
I know the prince to be so far above me,
That my wishes cannot reach him. Yet I am
So much his creature, that, to fix him in
Your wonted grace and favour, I'll abjure
His sight for ever, and betake myself
To a religious life, (where in my prayers
I may remember him,) and ne'er see man more,
But my ghostly father. Will you trust me, sir ?
In truth I'll keep my word ; or, if this fail,
A little more of fear what may befall him
Will stop my breath for ever.
    Coz. Had you thus argued   [*Raises her.*
As you were yourself, and brought as advocates
Your health and beauty, to make way for you,
No crime of his could put on such a shape
But I should look with the eyes of mercy on it.

What would I give to see this diamond
In her perfect lustre, as she was before
The clouds of sickness dimm'd it! Yet, take
  comfort;
And, as you would obtain remission for
His treachery to me, cheer your drooping spirits,
And call the blood again into your cheeks,
And then plead for him; and in such a habit
As in your highest hopes you would put on,
If we were to receive you for our bride.
 Lid. I'll do my best, sir.
 Coz. And that best will be
A crown of all felicity to me.   [*Exeunt.*

ACT V. SCENE I.

The same. *An upper Chamber in* Charomonte's
  House.

Enter SANAZARRO.

 Sanaz. 'Tis proved in me: the curse of human
  frailty,
Adding to our afflictions, makes us know
What's good; and yet our violent passions force
 us
To follow what is ill. Reason assured me
It was not safe to shave a lion's skin;
And that to trifle with a sovereign was
To play with lightning: yet imperious beauty,
Treading upon the neck of understanding,
Compell'd me to put off my natural shape
Of loyal duty, to disguise myself
In the adulterate and cobweb-mask

Of disobedient treachery. Where is now
My borrow'd greatness, or the promised lives
Of following courtiers echoing my will?
In a moment vanish'd ! Power that stands not on
Its proper base, which is peculiar only
To absolute princes, falls or rises with
Their frown or favour. The great duke, my master,
(Who almost changed me to his other self,)
No sooner takes his beams of comfort from me,
But I, as one unknown, or unregarded,
Unpitied suffer. Who makes intercession
To his mercy for me, now ? who does remember
The service I have done him ? not a man :
And such as spake no language but my lord
The favourite of Tuscany's grand duke,
Deride my madness.—Ha ! what noise of horses?
                    [*He looks out at the back window.*
A goodly troop ! This back part of my prison
Allows me liberty to see and know them,
Contarino ! yes, 'tis he, and Lodovico :[3]
And the dutchess Fiorinda, Urbin's heir,
A princess I have slighted : yet I wear
Her favours ; and, to teach me what I am,
She whom I scorn'd can only mediate for me.
This way she makes, yet speak to her I dare not ;
And how to make suit to her is a task
Of as much difficulty.—Yes, thou blessed pledge
                    [*Takes off the ring.*
Of her affection, aid me ! This supplies
The want of pen and ink ; and this, of paper.
                    [*Takes a pane of glass.*
It must be so ; and I in my petition
Concise and pithy.

[3]   ——— *Lodovico ;*] i. e. Lodovico Hippolito.

SCENE II.

The Court before Charomonte's *House.*

Enter CONTARINO *leading in* FIORINDA, ALPHONSO, HIPPOLITO, HIERONIMO, *and* CALAMINTA.

Fior. 'Tis a goodly pile, this.
Hier. But better[4] by the owner.
Alph. But most rich
In the great states it covers.
Fior. The duke's pleasure
Commands us hither.
Cont. Which was laid on us
To attend you to it.
Hip. Signior Charomonte,
To see your excellence his guest, will think
Himself most happy.
Fior. Tie my shoe.—[*The pane falls down.*]—
What's that?
A pane thrown from the window, no wind stirring!
Calam. And at your feet too fall'n :—there's
something writ on't.
Cont. Some courtier, belike, would have it
known
He wore a diamond.
Calam. Ha! it is directed
To the princess Fiorinda.

---

4 *But* better *by the owner.*] Mr. M. Mason reads *bettered*, which spoils the climax intended by the author : to complete his emendation, he should have read, in the next line,—*But most* enriched, &c. *States*, in the next line, are statesmen, men of power, &c. a common acceptation of the word.

Fior. We will read it. [*Reads.*

> *He, whom you pleased to favour, is cast down*
> *Past hope of rising, by the great duke's frown,*
> *If, by your gracious means, he cannot have*
> *A pardon;—and that got, he lives your slave.*
> *Of men the most distressed,*
>   SANAZARRO.

Of me the most beloved; and I will save thee,
Or perish with thee. Sure, thy fault must be
Of some prodigious shape, if that my prayers
And humble intercession to the duke

Enter COZIMO *and* CHAROMONTE.

Prevail not with him. Here he comes; delay
Shall not make less my benefit.
    Coz. What we purpose
Shall know no change, and therefore move me
        not:
We were made as properties, and what we shall
Determine of them cannot be call'd rigour,
But noble justice. When they proved disloyal,
They were cruel to themselves. The prince that
        pardons
The first affront offer'd to majesty,
Invites a second, rendering that power
Subjects should tremble at, contemptible.
Ingratitude is a monster, Carolo,
To be strangled in the birth, not to be cherish'd.
Madam, you're happily met with.
    Fior. Sir, I am
An humble suitor to you; and the rather
Am confident of a grant, in that your grace,

When I made choice to be at your devotion,
Vow'd to deny me nothing.

Coz. To this 'minute
We have confirm'd it. What's your boon?

Fior. It is, sir,
That you, in being gracious to your servant,
The ne'er sufficiently praised Sanazarro,
That now under your heavy displeasure suffers,
Would be good unto yourself. His services,
So many, and so great, (your storm of fury
Calm'd by your better judgment,) must inform you
Some little slip, for sure it is no more,
From his loyal duty, with your justice cannot
Make foul his fair deservings. Great sir, therefore,
Look backward on his former worth, and turning
Your eye from his offence, what 'tis I know not,
And, I am confident, you will receive him
Once more into your favour.

Coz. You say well,
You are ignorant in the nature of his fault;
Which when you understand, as we'll instruct you,
Your pity will appear a charity,
It being conferr'd on an unthankful man,
To be repented. He's a traitor, madam,
To you, to us, to gratitude; and in that
All crimes are comprehended.

Fior. If his offence
Aim'd at me only, whatsoe'er it is,
'Tis freely pardon'd.

Coz. This compassion in you
Must make the colour of his guilt more ugly.
The honours we have hourly heap'd upon him,
The titles, the rewards, to the envy of
The old nobility, as the common people,
We now forbear to touch at, and will only
Insist on his gross wrongs to you. You were
      pleased,

Forgetting both yourself and proper greatness,
To favour him, nay, to court him to embrace
A happiness, which, on his knees, with joy
He should have sued for.   Who repined not at
The grace you did him ? yet, in recompense
Of your large bounties, the disloyal wretch
Makes you a stale ; and, what he might be by
       you
Scorn'd and derided, gives himself up wholly
To the service of another.   If you can
Bear this with patience, we must say you have not
The bitterness of spleen, or ireful passions
Familiar to women.   Pause upon it,
And when you seriously have weigh'd his car-
      riage,
Move us again, if your reason will allow it,
His treachery known : and then, if you continue
An advocate for him, we, perhaps, because
We would deny you nothing, may awake
Our sleeping mercy.   Carolo !
    Char. My lord.   *[They talk aside.*
    Fior. To endure a rival that were equal to me,
Cannot but speak my poverty of spirit ;
But an inferior, more : yet true love must not
Know or degrees, or distances.   Lidia may be
As far above me in her form, as she
Is in her birth beneath me ; and what I
In Sanazarro liked, he loves in her.
But, if I free him now, the benefit
Being done so timely, and confirming too
My strength and power, my soul's best faculties
      being
Bent wholly to preserve him, must supply me
With all I am defective in, and bind him
My creature ever.   It must needs be so,
Nor will I give it o'er thus.
    Coz. Does our nephew

Bear his restraint so constantly,⁵ as you
Deliver it to us?
  Char. In my judgment, sir,
He suffers more for his offence to you,
Than in his fear of what can follow it.
For he is so collected, and prepared
To welcome that you shall determine of him,
As if his doubts and fears were equal to him.
And sure he's not acquainted with much guilt,
That more laments the telling one untruth,
Under your pardon still, for 'twas a fault, sir,
Than others, that pretend to conscience, do
Their crying secret sins.
  Coz. No more; this gloss
Defends not the corruption of the text:
Urge it no more.
         [Charomonte and the others talk aside.
  Fior. I once more must make bold, sir,
To trench upon your patience. I have
Consider'd my wrongs duly: yet that cannot
Divert my intercession for a man
Your grace, like me, once favour'd. I am still
A suppliant to you, that you would vouchsafe
The hearing his defence, and that I may,
With your allowance, see and comfort him.
Then, having heard all that he can allege
In his excuse, for being false to you,
Censure him as you please.
  Coz. You will o'ercome;
There's no contending with you. Pray you, enjoy
What you desire, and tell him, he shall have
A speedy trial; in which, we'll forbear
To sit a judge, because our purpose is
To rise up his accuser.

⁵ Coz. *Does our nephew*
Bear his restraint so constantly,] i. e. with such unshaken
patience, such immoveable resolution, &c.

Fior. All increase
Of happiness wait on Cozimo!
                    [*Exeunt Fiorinda and Calaminta.*
    Alph. Was it no more?
    Char. My honour's pawn'd for it.
    Cont. I'll second you.
    Hip. Since it is for the service and the safety
Of the hopeful prince, fall what can fall, I'll run
The desperate hazard.
    Hier. He's no friend to virtue
That does decline it.
                    [*They all come forward and kneel.*
    Coz. Ha! what sue you for?
Shall we be ever troubled? Do not tempt
That anger may consume you.
    Char. Let it, sir:
The loss is less, though innocents we perish,
Than that your sister's son should fall, unheard,
Under your fury. Shall we fear to entreat
That grace for him, that are your faithful servants,
Which you vouchsafe the count, like us a subject?
    Coz. Did not we vow, till sickness had forsook
Thy daughter Lidia, and she appear'd
In her perfect health and beauty to plead for him,
We were deaf to all persuasion?
    Char. And that hope, sir,
Hath wrought a miracle. She is recover'd,
And, if you please to warrant her, will bring
The penitent prince before you.
    Coz. To enjoy
Such happiness, what would we not dispense with?
    Alph. Hip. Hier. We all kneel for the prince.
    Cont. Nor can it stand
With your mercy, that are gracious to strangers,
To be cruel to your own.
    Coz. But art thou certain
I shall behold her at the best?

Char. If ever
She was handsome, as it fits not me to say so,
She is now much better'd.

    Coz. Rise; thou art but dead,
If this prove otherwise. Lidia, appear,
And feast an appetite almost pined to death
With longing expectation to behold
Thy excellencies: thou, as beauty's queen,
Shalt censure the detractors.[6] Let my nephew
Be led in triumph under her command;
We'll have it so; and Sanazarro tremble
To think whom he hath slander'd. We'll retire
Ourselves a little, and prepare to meet
A blessing, which imagination tells us
We are not worthy of: and then come forth,
But with such reverence, as if I were
Myself the priest, the sacrifice my heart,
To offer at the altar of that goodness
That must or kill or save me.   *[Exit.*

    Char. Are not these
Strange gambols in the duke!

    Alph. Great princes have,
Like meaner men, their weakness.

    Hip. And may use it
Without control or check.

    Cont. 'Tis fit they should;
Their privilege were less else, than their subjects'.

    Hier. Let them have their humours; there's
      no crossing them.   *[Exeunt.*

---

[6] ————————— *thou, as beauty's queen,*
Shalt censure *the detractors.*] *Censure,* as I have already observed, is used by our old writers, where we should now use *judge,* and with the same latitude of meaning through its various acceptations.

SCENE III.

A State-room in the same.

Enter FIORINDA, SANAZARRO, *and* CALAMINTA.

Sanaz. And can it be, your bounties should fall
    down
In showers on my ingratitude, or the wrongs
Your greatness should revenge, teach you to pity?
What retribution can I make, what service
Pay to your goodness, that, in some proportion,
May to the world express I would be thankful?
Since my engagements are so great, that all
My best endeavours to appear your creature
Can but proclaim my wants, and what I owe
To your magnificence.
    Fior. All debts are discharged
In this acknowledgment: yet, since you please
I shall impose some terms of satisfaction
For that which you profess yourself obliged for,
They shall be gentle ones, and such as will not,
I hope, afflict you.
    Sanaz. Make me understand,
Great princess, what they are, and my obedience
Shall, with all cheerful willingness, subscribe
To what you shall command.
    Fior. I will bind you to
Make good your promise. First, I then enjoin you
To love a lady, that, a noble way,
Truly affects you; and that you would take
To your protection and care the dukedom
Of Urbin, which no more is mine, but your's.
And that, when you have full possession of
My person as my fortune, you would use me,

Not as a princess, but instruct me in
The duties of an humble wife, for such,
The privilege of my birth no more remember'd,
I will be to you. This consented to,
All injuries forgotten, on your lips
I thus sign your *quietus.*
    Sanaz. I am wretched,
In having but one life to be employ'd
As you please to dispose it. And, believe it,
If it be not already forfeited
To the fury of my prince, as 'tis your gift,
With all the faculties of my soul I'll study,
In what I may, to serve you.
    Fior. I am happy

Enter GIOVANNI *and* LIDIA.

In this assurance. What sweet lady's this?
    Sanaz. 'Tis Lidia, madam, she——
    Fior. I understand you.
Nay, blush not; by my life, she is a rare one!
And, if I were your judge, I would not blame you
To like and love her. But, sir, you are mine now;
And I presume so on your constancy,
That I dare not be jealous.
    Sanaz. All thoughts of her
Are in your goodness buried.
    Lid. Pray you, sir,
Be comforted; your innocence should not know
What 'tis to fear; and if that you but look on
The guards that you have in yourself, you cannot.
The duke's your uncle, sir, and, though a little
Incensed against you, when he sees your sorrow,
He must be reconciled. What rugged Tartar,
Or cannibal, though bath'd in human gore,
But, looking on your sweetness, would forget
* N n 2

His cruel nature, and let fall his weapon,
Though then aim'd at your throat?
   Giov. O Lidia,
Of maids the honour, and your sex's glory!
It is not fear to die, but to lose you,
That brings this fever on me. I will now
Discover to you, that which, till this minute,
I durst not trust the air with. Ere you knew
What power the magic of your beauty had,
I was enchanted by it, liked, and loved it,
My fondness still increasing with my years;
And, flattered by false hopes, I did attend
Some blessed opportunity to move
The duke with his consent to make you mine:
But now, such is my star-cross'd destiny,
When he beholds you as you are, he cannot
Deny himself the happiness to enjoy you.
And I as well in reason may entreat him
To give away his crown, as to part from
A jewel of more value, such you are.
Yet, howsoever, when you are his dutchess,
And I am turn'd into forgotten dust,
Pray you, love my memory:—I should say more,
But I'm cut off.

   Enter COZIMO, CHAROMONTE, CONTARINO,
    HIERONIMO, HIPPOLITO, *and* ALPHONSO.

   Sanaz. The duke! That countenance, once,
When it was clothed in smiles, shew'd like an
      angel's,
But, now 'tis folded up in clouds of fury,
'Tis terrible to look on.
   Lid. Sir.
   Coz. A while
Silence your musical tongue, and let me feats
My eyes with the most ravishing object that

They ever gazed on. There's no miniature
In her fair face, but is a copious theme
Which would, discours'd at large of, make a
      volume.
What clear arch'd brows! what sparkling eyes!
      the lilies
Contending with the roses in her cheeks,
Who shall most set them off. What ruby lips!—
Or unto what can I compare her neck,
But to a rock of crystal? every limb
Proportion'd to love's wish, and in their neatness
Add lustre to the riches of her habit,
Not borrow from it.
    Lid. You are pleased to shew, sir,
The fluency of your language, in advancing
A subject much unworthy.
    Coz. How! unworthy?
By all the vows which lovers offer at
The Cyprian goddess' altars, eloquence
Itself presuming, as you are, to speak you,
Would be struck dumb!—And what have you de-
      served then, [*Giovanni and Sanazarro kneel.*
(Wretches, you kneel too late,) that have endea-
      vour'd
To spout the poison of your black detraction
On this immaculate whiteness? was it malice
To her perfections? or——
    Fior. Your highness promised
A gracious hearing to the count.
    Lid. And prince too;
Do not make void so just a grant.
    Coz. We will not:
Yet, since their accusation must be urged,
And strongly, ere their weak defence have
      hearing,
We seat you here, as judges, to determine

Of your gross wrongs, and ours. [*Seats the Ladies in
    the chairs of state.*] And now, remembering
Whose deputies you are, be neither sway'd
Or with particular spleen, or foolish pity,
For neither can become you.
    Char. There's some hope yet,
Since they have such gentle judges.
    Coz. Rise, and stand forth, then,
And hear, with horror to your guilty souls,
What we will prove against you. Could this
    princess,
Thou enemy to thyself, [*To Sanazarro.*] stoop her
    high flight
Of towering greatness to invite thy lowness
To look up to it, and with nimble wings
Of gratitude couldst thou forbear to meet it?
Were her favours boundless in a noble way,
And warranted by our allowance, yet,
In thy acceptation, there appear'd no sign
Of a modest thankfulness?
    Fior. Pray you forbear
To press that further; 'tis a fault we have
Already heard, and pardon'd.
    Coz. We will then
Pass over it, and briefly touch at that
Which does concern ourself, in which both being
Equal offenders, what we shall speak points
Indifferently at either. How we raised thee,
Forgetful Sanazarro! of our grace,
To a full possession of power and honours,
It being too well known, we'll not remember.
And what thou wert, rash youth, in expectation,
               [*To Giovanni.*
And from which headlong thou hast thrown thyself,
Not Florence, but all Tuscany can witness,
With admiration. To assure thy hopes,

We did keep constant to a widowed bed,
And did deny ourself those lawful pleasures
Our absolute power and height of blood allow'd us ;
Made both, the keys that open'd our heart's secrets,
And what you spake, believed as oracles :
But you, in recompense of this, to him
That gave you all, to whom you owed your being,
With treacherous lies endeavour'd to conceal
This jewel from our knowledge, which ourself
Could only lay just claim to.
    Giov. 'Tis most true, sir.
    Sanaz. We both confess a guilty cause.
    Coz. Look on her.
Is this a beauty fit to be embraced
By any subject's arms? can any tire
Become that forehead, but a diadem?
Or, should we grant your being false to us
Could be excused, your treachery to her,
In seeking to deprive her of that greatness
(Her matchless form consider'd) she was born to,
Must ne'er find pardon. We have spoken, ladies,
Like a rough orator, that brings more truth
Than rhetoric to make good his accusation ;
And now expect your sentence.
               *[The Ladies descend from the state.*⁷
    Lid. In your birth, sir,
You were mark'd out the judge of life and death,
And we, that are your subjects, to attend,
With trembling fear, your doom.
    Fior. We do resign
This chair, as only proper to your self.
    Giov. And, since in justice we are lost, we fly
Unto your saving mercy.   *[All kneeling.*
    Sanaz. Which sets off
A prince, much more than rigour.

    ⁷ *The ladies descend from the* state.] i. e. from the raised plat-
form on which the chairs were placed. See *the Bondman,* p. 16.

Char. And becomes him,
When 'tis express'd to such as fell by weakness,
That being a twin-born brother to affection,
Better than wreaths of conquest.
  Hier. Hip. Cont. Alph. We all speak
Their language, mighty sir.
  Coz. You know our temper,
And therefore with more boldness venture on it:
And, would not our consent to your demands
Deprive us of a happiness hereafter
Ever to be despair'd of, we, perhaps,
Might hearken nearer to you; and could wish
With some qualification, or excuse,
You might make less the mountains of your
    crimes,
And so invite our clemency to feast with you.
But you, that knew with what impatiency
Of grief we parted from the fair Clarinda,
Our dutchess, (let her memory still be sacred!)
And with what imprecations on ourself
We vow'd, not hoping e'er to see her equal,
Ne'er to make trial of a second choice,
If nature framed not one that did excel her,
As this maid's beauty prompts us that she does:—
And yet, with oaths then mix'd with tears, upon
Her monument we swore our eye should never
Again be tempted;—'tis true, and those vows
Are register'd above, something here tells me.—
Carolo, thou heardst us swear.
  Char. And swear so deeply,
That if all women's beauties were in this,
(As she's not to be named with the dead dutchess,)
Nay, all their virtues bound up in one story,
(Of which mine is scarce an epitome,)
If you should take her as a wife, the weight
Of your perjuries would sink you. If I durst,
I had told you this before.

Coz. 'Tis strong truth, Carolo :
And yet, what was necessity in us,
Cannot free them from treason.
　Char. There's your error ;
The prince, in care to have you keep your vows
Made　unto　heaven,　vouchsafed　to　love　my
　　　daughter.[8]
　Lid. He told me so, indeed, sir.
　Fior. And the count
Averr'd as much to me.
　Coz. You all conspire,
To force our mercy from us.
　Char. Which given up,
To aftertimes preserves you unforsworn :
An honour, which will live upon your tomb,
When your greatness is forgotten.
　Coz. Though we know[9]
All this is practice, and that both are false :
Such reverence we will pay to dead Clarinda,
And to our serious oaths, that we are pleased
With our own hand to blind our eyes, and not
Know what we understand. Here, Giovanni,
We pardon thee ; and take from us, in this,
More than our dukedom : love her. As I part

[8] *The prince, in care to have you keep your vows*
　Made unto heaven, vouchsafed to love my daughter.] This attempt to impose upon the great duke is more deplorable than the former. It has falsehood and improbability written on its face : the duke indeed is not deceived by it ; but surely the author shewed a strange want of judgment in this gratuitous degradation of three of his most estimable characters.

[9] *Coz. Though we know*
　All this is practice,] i. e. artifice, or insidious combination. So Shakspeare :

　　"　———— This act persuades me
　　" That this remotion of the duke and her
　　" Is *practice* only." 　　　　　*King Lear.*

With her, all thoughts of women fly fast from us!
Sanazarro, we forgive you: in your service
To this princess, merit it. Yet, let not others
That are in trust and grace, as you have been,
By the example of our lenity,
Presume upon their sovereign's clemency.

Enter CALANDRINO *and* PETRONELLA.

All. Long live great Cozimo!
Cal. Sure the duke is
In the giving vein, they are so loud. Come on,
        spouse;
We have heard all, and we will have our boon too.
Coz. What is it?
Cal. That your grace, in remembrance of
My share in a dance, and that I play'd your part,
When you should have drunk hard, would get
        this signior's grant
To give this damsel to me in the church,
For we are contracted. In it you shall do
Your dukedom pleasure.
Coz. How?
Cal. Why, the whole race
Of such as can act naturally fools parts,
Are quite worn out; and they that do survive,
Do only zany us: and we will bring you,
If we die not without issue, of both sexes
Such chopping mirth-makers, as shall preserve
Perpetual cause of sport, both to your grace
And your posterity; that sad melancholy
Shall ne'er approach you.
Coz. We are pleased in it,
And will pay her portion.—— [*Comes forward.*
                            May the passage prove,
Of what's presented, worthy of your love

And favour, as was aim'd; and we have all
That can in compass of our wishes fall.   [Exeunt.[1]

[1] It is impossible not to be charmed with the manner in which
this play is written. The style is worthy of the most polished
stage. It neither descends to meanness, nor affects a blustering
magnificence, but preserves an easy elevation, and a mild dignity;
and affords an excellent model for the transaction of dramatic
business between persons of high rank and refined education.
As to the subject, it is, in itself, of no great importance : but
this is somewhat compensated by the interest which the principal
characters take in it, and the connexion of love with the views
of state.—The scenes between Giovanni and Lidia present a most
beautiful picture of artless attachment, and of that unreserved
innocence and tender simplicity which Massinger describes in a
manner so eminently happy.

It is to be wished that this were all; for the impression on the
mind of the reader makes him more than usually fearful of any
disturbance of his feelings. But in the drama, as in life itself,
something will ever be amiss. The attractive manner in which
the characters and their concerns are announced is made
to change as the plot advances to its conclusion; and in the
fourth act we are grieved to see them

In pejus ruere, ac retrò sublapsa referri.

The charm of Lidia is dissolved by the substitution of Petronella,—a contrivance which is at once mean and clumsy, and is
conceived in utter defiance of the general character of Cozimo.
The only way of removing this objection was to alter Cozimo
himself, together with the delicacy of the subject. This is done
for the sake of maintaining an unhappy consistency. The duke
is compelled to forego his usual dignity and sagacity. He loses
the very remembrance of his own motives of action, and is
played upon by those who are themselves sunk in our esteem.

The connexion of the plot with an event in the life of Edgar
has been mentioned by the Editor. As to Cozimo, some circumstances seem to point him out as the first grand duke. Pisa
and Sienna are alluded to as recent acquisitions; though Contarino is too complaisant in attributing the conquest to the arms
of his master. There are some personal points which may assist
this conjecture. Cozimo is addressed in a submissive manner,
and seems to be conscious that his resentment is feared by those
around him : and this reminds us of the man who coveted the title
of King, and executed summary justice on a son with his own
hand. However, other circumstances rather allude to a period

not much earlier than the date of this very play; *viz.* some attempt at independance by the Pisans, which Sanazarro might have checked; and some benefit derived to Florence (though not of the kind here mentioned) from the dutchy of Urbino. But why a nephew was called in, when a son was not wanting to either of the Cosmos, or why the state of a childless widower was invented for the great duke, is not so easy to guess: nor is it worth our while.—The dramatist rejects or invents as he pleases; and what he chooses to adopt may be divided between distant ages or countries. The incidents of his arbitrary story are widely dispersed, like the limbs wantonly scattered by Medea; and, if ever to be found, must be searched for in places remote and unexpected :

Dissipat in multis invenienda locis.

END OF VOL. II.